STUDIES IN ILLINOIS CONSTITUTION MAKING
Joseph P. Pisciotte, Editor

CHARTER FOR A NEW AGE

Charter for a New Age:
An Inside View of
the Sixth Illinois
Constitutional Convention

ELMER GERTZ
and
JOSEPH P. PISCIOTTE

Published for the
INSTITUTE OF GOVERNMENT AND PUBLIC AFFAIRS
by the
UNIVERSITY OF ILLINOIS PRESS
Urbana   Chicago   London

*Special appreciation is expressed
to the Field Foundation of Illinois,
whose financial support has made
this series possible.*

LIBRARY OF CONGRESS CATALOGING IN PUBLICATION DATA

Gertz, Elmer, 1906–
Charter for a new age.

(Studies in Illinois Constitution Making)
Includes index.
1. Illinois. Constitutional Convention,
1969-1970. 2. Illinois — Constitutional history.
I. Pisciotte, Joseph P., joint author. II. Title.
III. Series.
KFI1601 1970.A29G47   342.773'0292   80-10837
ISBN 0-252-00820-0

For
SAMUEL W. WITWER,
President of the Sixth Illinois Constitutional Convention,
who persevered, despite many difficulties, and gave
our state a great new charter

Preface

A critical history of a constitutional convention is a solemn undertaking. One should not do it lightly. Such a study must be objective, fair, perceptive, and complete. We hope we have lived up to this expectation. In addition, we wanted our book to be interesting, readable, and memorable in its human aspects. Therefore we sat down from time to time, and casually discussed our respective ideas about the possible contents of the book, the conversations punctuated by irrelevancies, blasphemies, and occasionally obscenities. For future guidance, our words were tape recorded, as befits this electronic age, and then transcribed. This transcript was frequently referred to as we progressed with our task. The finished product would have been as voluminous as a Victorian novel if we had not cut, cut, cut. In the end, a rather sizable book remained — the pages that follow these words. There are accounts therein of individuals, committees, issues, dramas, comedies, tragedies, lightness and darkness, failures and successes.

Our Thanks

We are conscious of the very great debt we owe to many people in writing this book. The credit for much of it belongs largely to these people. We hope that the sum total is nonetheless ours. We accept all blame for whatever merits a hostile reception, and hopefully some praise for what is praiseworthy. Above all, we exonerate our friends from all responsibility.

We are grateful to one person above and beyond all others for the amount and quality of assistance given to us — the one to whom this volume is dedicated. Samuel W. Witwer, who properly figures more prominently in this work than anyone else, devoted countless hours and days to helping us, in personal interviews, in written responses to inquiries, in every possible way. He answered all of our questions and, indeed, anticipated our needs. While not imposing his own views upon us, he has helped us to avoid errors of fact and judgment.

That delightful human being, Elbert Smith, a vice-president of the convention, let us look at his own sparkling pages about the constitutional proceedings that we had shared with him. We have sometimes borrowed his provocative and shrewd assessments of people and events.

Ronald C. Smith, an alert and objective member of the committee on the executive article and the running mate of one of the coauthors in the race for election as delegate to the convention, gathered and arranged the material on his committee that appears in this book. Our role has been to edit and compress his fascinating pages.

Mary Lee Leahy, one of the more dynamic delegates and later a member of Governor Walker's official family, contributed much of the material dealing with the convention committee on general government, particularly the struggle over the section on banking.

Ann Lousin, a member of the research staff at the convention, contributed to us the material on the local government article and many comments scattered throughout our book. She is the coauthor, with delegate Joan Anderson, of a long study of that article which appeared in the *John Marshall Journal of Practice and Procedure*.

Governor Dan Walker, who felt the effects of the new constitution during the four years of his lively administration, was generous enough to grant us a lengthy interview, as did his counsel, William Goldberg. Several pages of this book are derived from the tapes of those interviews, and give important, firsthand insights.

We have not hesitated to borrow extensively from the other volumes that have appeared so far in the series, *Studies in Illinois Constitution Making*, edited by Joe P. Pisciotte and published for the Institute of Government and Public Affairs by the University of Illinois Press. These include *Constitution Making in Illinois, 1818-1970*, by Janet Cornelius; *For the First Hours of Tomorrow — The New Illinois Bill of*

Rights, by Elmer Gertz; *Lobbying at the Illinois Constitutional Convention*, by Ian D. Burman; *To Judge with Justice — History and Politics of Illinois Judicial Reform*, by Rubin G. Cohn; *Ballots for Change — New Suffrage and Amending Articles for Illinois*, by Alan J. Gratch and Virginia H. Ubik; *Politics of the Purse — Revenue and Finance in the Sixth Illinois Constitutional Convention*, by Joyce D. Fishbane and Glenn W. Fisher; *A Fundamental Goal — Education for the People of Illinois*, by Jane Galloway Buresh; and *Roll Call! Patterns of Voting in the Sixth Illinois Constitutional Convention*, by David Kennedy, Jack R. Van Der Slik and Samuel J. Pernacciaro. These studies give insight into the principles and personalities operating at the convention and are integral parts of our story.

Other persons, particularly Jane Carfagno Clark and Linda Knibbs, gave monumental assistance in the preparatory research and writing of this book. Vicki Nethercot, Sandy Marler, Nancy Jackson and Beverly Birzele were typists for us, a not inconsiderable task because of the authors' eccentricities of handwriting and style. Carol Hoaglan willingly responded to our frequent requests to have reproduced countless pages of the manuscript. They somehow always managed to meet our "need it immediately" deadlines. We owe a tremendous debt of gratitude to Jean Baker of the Institute of Government for typing the entire final manuscript and, as always, for cheerfully assisting in the many administrative chores necessary to produce a book of this kind. Anna Merritt, also of the Institute, lent her excellent editing skills to the manuscript to put it into its finished form. She also prepared the very fine index which should contribute markedly to the book's usefulness.

Special thanks go to Jana Howell of the Center for Urban Studies for serving as coordinator for much of the work that was necessary to complete the book. At a time when the authors were separated by distance and numerous other activities, she kept everything moving. Her joy in the enterprise was contagious.

We were assisted greatly by the comments of Dorothy Nadasdy, Glenn Fisher, and Ann Lousin, who were kind enough to read the manuscript at its various stages.

No manuscript would ever be completed without the continuing support of its publisher, and we were extremely fortunate to have the encouragement of Richard Wentworth, director of the University of

Illinois Press, for this book as well as the other volumes in the series. Final production of the book was greatly expedited by the excellent graphics and typesetting performed by Daryl and Janet Standifer of The Graphicshop in Wichita, Kansas.

A very special thanks is due our wives, Mamie Gertz and Anita Pisciotte, for their patience and kindness in the face of our neglect of domestic chores while we were preoccupied with our labors.

Our deep appreciation goes to the Field Foundation of Illinois, particularly Chairman Herman Dunlap Smith, for the Foundation's continued financial support. It was only through their recognition of the need to chronicle the important events of the convention that this book and the entire series has been made possible.

Finally, we must acknowledge that many delegates and staff were good enough to respond to questionnaires we sent them. The recollections we have from all 116 members of the convention and numerous staff are responsible for some of the most interesting pages in this book. They are, indeed, an elite.

Elmer Gertz
Joseph P. Pisciotte

Contents

CHARTER FOR A NEW AGE

I

Overview

In the late 1960s when the movement to write a new constitution for the state of Illinois was beginning to gain momentum, residents of the state were living under a lengthy and detailed constitution that had been written a century earlier for a more agrarian society. In 1870 almost 77 percent of the state's 2.5 million citizens were living on farms or in rural towns, raising their own food and generally providing for their own personal needs. Those individuals not occupied with farming or operating small family businesses were likely to be involved in commerce, manufacturing (especially of farm machinery), or mining.

Geographically, Illinois is located in the center of the nation, midway between the Atlantic and Pacific oceans to the east and west, and almost halfway between the Canadian border to the north and the Mexican border to the south. This elongated state stretches nearly five hundred miles from its northern Illinois-Wisconsin boundary down to its southern tip at Cairo. While Illinois is considered a Midwestern state, a quick glance at a map is enough to show that it begins at a latitude almost as far north as Boston and extends southward to a point as far south as Newport News-Hampton, Virginia. Its people and social institutions reflect this geographical diversity. At the same time, its history and development have been shaped by its geographic location. Trading on the Ohio and Mississippi rivers along the southern boundaries of the state was a prosperous venture during the early 1800s. As railroads spread, they increasingly offered a faster and more convenient method of moving supplies and people across the state to other parts of the country. As transportation by rail became more and more popular, the demand for coal, found so abundantly in its southern counties, soon gave Illinois a deserved reputation as an important mining state. This reputation persisted into the petroleum and gas ages and on into the modern world of electronic and nuclear power.

Delegates to the 1870 constitutional convention reflected the concerns of their times by making provisions for the Illinois General Assembly to pass liberal homestead laws, a free public education system, and protective legislation for miners. A century later, the economic, social, and political interests of Illinois had changed drastically. The state was now recognized as a national leader in industrial, agricultural, and mining production. With its eleven million citizens, it was also the fourth most populous state in the nation.

Illinois' importance in the world of commerce is widely recognized; the state is a principal manufacturer of steel, electrical equipment, chemicals and allied products, nonelectrical machinery, and paper and allied products. Total mining output in 1969 was $661 million, with Illinois mines leading producers in the country of bituminous coal, stone, sand and gravel, petroleum, zinc, and natural gas.

Despite its enormous industrial growth, the state continues to be an agricultural leader. The rich soil found in the prairie lands of Illinois, celebrated in the poems of Carl Sandburg, is a valuable resource enabling farmers of the area to lead the nation in the production of corn and soybeans. A large number of hogs, cattle, and chickens are also raised in the state. With 85 percent of the state's area in farms, Illinois ranked third in the nation in total farm production during the late 1960s.

While ostensibly a successful agricultural-industrial-mining state, the Illinois state government of 1969 was in financial distress. Since Illinois was experiencing no financial difficulties in 1870, the delegates to the Fourth Illinois Constitutional Convention held in that year made few changes in the revenue sections of the 1848 constitution. The 1870 constitution did limit the tax rates for county purposes and restricted local indebtedness. The property tax remained the basic source of state revenue. A hundred years later, however, Illinois was in desperate need of additional income to fund the services increasingly demanded by the public. Indeed, a financial crisis had developed due to the reduction in economic growth and multiplying requests for state aid commitments in areas of welfare, education, conservation, and mental health. As a means of generating additional revenue to support the proliferating governmental programs, and circumventing the 1870 constitution on debt limitation, special districts were created, each with its own taxing powers. By the 1960s, some 6,500 units of local government had been established, more than existed in any other state. Proponents of a constitutional convention call argued that the basic legal structure of the state should be changed to allow for additional administrative and policy-making coodination among local units of government in order to encourage efficient and professional operations. Thus, perhaps as much as anything else, financial difficulties paved the way for a successful convention call vote, especially after the state Supreme Court upheld the flat rate income tax lid.

In addition to the financial situation, Illinois was faced with a population shift that the 1870 constitution could not take into account. By 1969, Chicago was ranked as the second largest city in the United States. Its location at the crossroads of the country's rail and air transportation systems, and its ideal situation on highway and water routes, had contributed to the city's growth. However, both its location and its growth also created problems. In the 1960s the Democrats dominated Chicago politically under the guiding hand of Chicago Mayor Richard J. Daley, often cited as the last of the big city political machine bosses, and praised as the man who made the city work. Although there was a concentration of Democrats in southern Illinois, led by the crafty secretary of state, Paul Powell, the majority of the state's Democrats resided in the Chicago area. The Republican strength in Illinois, while not especially cohesive, was to be found in Chicago suburbs and the 101 counties other than Cook, known collectively as downstate. The typical downstate resident is often suspicious of those from the metropolitan sprawl of Chicago, while the Chicago inhabitant rarely develops much compassion for the needs of those outside the Windy City. These attitudes often prevailed among lawmakers who, rather than passing legislation designed for improving the state's future as a whole, continued to pursue the more limited goals of their Chicago or downstate constituents.

Compounding the Chicago-downstate division, was the dramatic shift in populations elsewhere in the state. Illinois had changed from a basically rural to a basically urban society and was faced with all of the ills we have come to associate with the so-called urban crisis. With a new constitution that would grant broad powers of self-government to cities, towns, and counties by means of home rural provisions, and encourage intergovernmental cooperation, it was hoped that the legislature might be able to concentrate more on general issues of importance to the state as a whole and, at the same time, involve the citizens more intimately with their local government.

Although there had been mild but continuing discontent with the 1870 constitution from the start of the century, the movement for a Sixth Illinois Constitutional Convention began in earnest in Chicago during the forties when a small group of citizens organized the Committee on Constitutional Revision of the Chicago Bar Association. This move was prompted in part by several attempts in Springfield to generate legislative support for a convention call, which had failed.

In 1945 Mrs. Walter Fisher, state president of the League of Women Voters, and Northwestern University Law Professor Walter V. Schaefer, then very active on the Committee on Development of Law of the Chicago Bar Association, along with several others, called on Chicago attorney, Samuel W. Witwer. They asked whether he would accept the chairmanship of a new Bar Association committee, a standing committee to develop a program for constitutional revision. As Witwer recalls it, "in a weak moment," he agreed to do so, being assured by them that the committee would have its work done in a matter of only a few years. Witwer was a graduate of Dickinson College and the Harvard Law School. He came to the Bar of Illinois in 1933 and commenced practicing with the firm of which he became, in time, senior partner. From 1933 until about 1946 he had no active involvement with the Illinois constitution. After 1946, however, he was involved almost continuously. It was his principal civic concern and to it he brought enthusiasm, learning, and increasing acumen.

Early in that period of his developing leadership, he sought to secure the services of people who appeared to have a potential role in politics. Witwer was convinced that a great problem in the past had been that although civic forces had attempted to provide the leadership in constitutional revision, they had failed to recognize it as a difficult political process. He felt that if they were going to succeed this time they would need a close working relationship with and help from political people. Therefore, the committee that Witwer enlisted to serve during the late 1940s included one man who thereafter twice ran for the presidency of the United States, Adlai E. Stevenson; a man who, during the Stevenson campaign, was the national chairman of the Democratic party, Stephen A. Mitchell; a man who became governor of Illinois, Otto Kerner; a man who became solicitor general of the United States, although only for a short time and then went on to the circuit court of appeals, Walter Cummings, Jr.; a man who became a law partner of the most powerful Democratic leader in Cook County at that time and for many years to come, Barnet Hodes; and Schaefer, who was later elected to the Supreme Court of Illinois. Witwer himself had a direct involvement in elective politics, but not with the notable success of some of the other committee members. Thus the committee was a young, able, ambitious, and idealistic group — the spiritual descendants of the early twentieth century progressives in the old Chicago Civic Federation and Citizens' Association of Chicago.

The committee, with its strong potential for political leadership, went to Springfield in 1947 to submit to the legislature a document that Schaefer and Witwer had produced despite great difficulties due to the complete absence of any appreciable literature on Illinois constitutional reform. It was simply a few mimeographed sheets stating why Illinois needed a constitutional convention. Witwer and other Committee members got nowhere. They returned to Chicago, resolved to build a literature of reform. Thus, Hodes wrote on municipal government and home rule, since he was corporation counsel for the city of Chicago at that time. Cummings wrote on the problems of apportionment. Witwer wrote an article for the *University of Chicago Law Review* on the judiciary; this was profoundly influential in the later drafting and adoption of a new judicial article. The committee members addressed basic problems of constitutional law in Illinois, wrote articles, and then induced their friends to have them reprinted. They sent out the reprints by the thousands — to newspaper editors, to civic leaders, influential organizations, in short to people who would mold civic opinion. This was the beginning of an extensive body of literature to which so many people later contributed information, ideas, and printed words.

The intellectual godfather of the movement was a man now largely forgotten. Through his numerous legal writings and his great personal conviction, Kenneth Sears of the University of Chicago law faculty, who had died long before his advocacy bore fruit, continued to exert influence on those interested in constitutional revision. Witwer has never ceased to salute this prophetic man. Sears was extremely concerned about the constitution of the state and felt that Illinois was probably in the worst position constitutionally of any state in the Union. Moreover, he convinced people like Witwer that he was right. This conviction spurred them on and sustained them during many of the later difficult moments.

Further effort was stimulated by the Illinois League of Women Voters, the Chicago Bar Association, the Illinois State Bar Association, and other civic groups; and, after his election as governor, it was spearheaded in 1949 by Stevenson.

Despite the commitment, enthusiasm, and sustained effort, however, the early years produced a series of frustrations. Witwer, who was chairman of the Committee for a Constitutional Convention in 1948 and 1949, went to Springfield; there he testified before committees, took verbal beatings from some legislators, and then failed to get the necessary vote to submit a call for the convening of a convention. The vote was close to the necessary two-thirds mark in the House. The Committee felt it would succeed in the Senate. The infamous West Side Bloc, however, notified Governor Stevenson the night before the key roll call in the House that unless he would agree to kill the Chicago Crime Commission legislative program, the convention call would fail. Their votes were withheld the following day and the call lost by a narrow margin. Then came the counter proposal of Senator Wallace Thompson, the Republican leader, for a so-called Gateway amendment. Similar proposals had been made in the past, but had failed. Their goal was to ease the voting requirements for constitutional amendments by allowing approval by two-thirds of those voting on the amendment itself rather than by a majority of all those voting in the general election. Witwer, Lou Kohn and other "reformers" urged the governor to proceed slowly and suggested that he at least counter with a proposal requiring less than a two-thirds vote on the issue, which might be more easily achieved. Despite personal misgivings, Stevenson felt constrained to support the measure as presented by Thompson, and it passed both houses without difficulty. Thereupon the governor asked Witwer to chair the statewide campaign effort to gain citizen approval. It was an aggressive campaign that was in many ways similar to the later campaign for the call of the Sixth Illinois Constitutional Convention. The result was a significant public response to the necessity of taking a good look at the constitution by the piecemeal amendment method. Perhaps, it was thought, this would work. If not, a tougher try would be attempted later.

Following the adoption of the Gateway amendment in 1950, the campaign committee, known as the Illinois Committee for Constitutional Revision (ICCR), went out of business despite efforts to hold it together. The full committee had consisted of some sixty or seventy civic groups, and collisions were inevitable when differing viewpoints began to emerge over substantive constitutional issues, which could now be presented to the voters under the new Gateway provision. Unfortunately, fifteen years later, after numerous attempts to use Gateway failed to achieve partial revisions, it was clear that the amendment had not helped measurably in advancing the cause of basic constitutional change.

Constitutional revision remained a salient concern with reform-minded groups during the 1950s and 1960s. The move to call the Sixth Illinois Constitutional Convention gained momentum when the first Constitution Study Commission was created by the General Assembly in 1965 at the recommendation of Mrs. Marjorie Pebworth, who became the commission's chairman. Mrs. Pebworth, former president of the League of Women Voters, had been elected to the House of Representatives as a "blue ribbon" candidate in the famous 1964 at-large state election with its blanket-sized ballot. Commission members consisted of six public members appointed by the governor, and twelve legislators.

Following almost two years of study, the commission recommended to the General Assembly in 1967 that the question of a constitution call be placed before the voters in November 1968. The legislature accepted the recommendation. Through the cooperation of concerned citizens and Governor Otto Kerner, the Illinois Committee for Constitutional Convention (ICCC) came into being to develop favorable public opinion throughout the state. By emphasizing the need to write an entirely new constitution rather than concentrating on specific controversial issues, the ICCC was instrumental in obtaining voter approval for the convention from about 60 percent of the 4.7 million individuals voting in the election.

After the first Constitution Study Commission had completed its task and made its recommendation to the legislature, the General Assembly created the second Constitution Study Commission to continue preparations should the call be approved by the citizens. Besides several relevant documents pertaining to the current and previous Illinois constitutions, this commission also presented recommendations for enabling legislation on the subject of a constitutional convention. This legislation, signed by the governor in May 1969, stipulated that the convention convene on December 8, 1969 in Springfield, with two delegates to be selected from each of the fifty-eight state senate districts during a nonpartisan election in the fall. A third Constitution Study Commission was created in October 1969 to provide for the organization of the convention itself and to arrange temporary staff for the convention.

Concern that the convention not develop into a political battle-ground between the Democratic and Republican parties or among various groups within the state was apparent at several stages of the movement towards a Sixth Illinois Constitutional Convention. The staggering defeat of the constitution proposed by the Fifth Illinois Constitutional Convention in 1922 which was rejected by 83 percent of the voters, was due in part to the blatant partisanship of that convention. The 1970 convention delegates, elected in nonpartisan contests, campaigned primarily on platforms calling for a modern and flexible constitution. The judicial selection issue, however, became one of the most political during the delegate races: a system for appointing judges was supported by Republican Governor Richard B. Ogilvie, while Democratic Chicago Mayor Richard J. Daley was strongly in favor of the existing system of partisan elections. Another major issue during the delegate election campaigns was the proposed abolition of the personal property tax, action generally favored by many delegate candidates from both parties. As a whole, the candidates also expressed interest in education and environmental reform.

The pressing need for tax reform in the state indicated that the revenue article would have to receive serious consideration by the convention. Although the 1966 Revenue Amendment, with its provisions for the income tax, was not approved by the voters, it had been widely supported by many political and business interests who were aware that the tax base of state and local governments must be increased.

Numerous other topics were viewed by scholars, politicians, and interested citizens as subjects for major deliberation during the convention: reorganization of the complex system of 6,500 local government units; encouragement of local intergovernmental cooperation; increased local autonomy through home rule powers; creation of a state board of education and review of the role of the state superintendent of public instruction; financial support of the state schools as well as aid to private institutions; review of the governor's powers; election of the governor and lieutenant governor as a team; reduction of the number of state officials elected by the citizens; consideration of the General Assembly's size; creation of single-member legislative districts, or retention of cumulative voting for state representatives; reduction of the voting age to eighteen years; residency requirements for voter registration; revision of the amendatory provisions for changes in the state's constitution; and elimination of the antiquated and outmoded provisions of the 1870 constitution, such as sections on the Illinois Central Railroad and convict labor.

Convention observers were aware of recent failures of the 1966-67 New York convention, because of its obvious political overtones and involvement in church-state issues, and the 1968 Maryland convention, which produced an idealistic document unacceptable to the voters and described as a "magnificent failure." As the Illinois delegates assembled, they were cautioned to write a constitution that, as a package, would both appeal to the citizens and adequately modernize the 1870 constitution. Governor Ogilvie, one of the several keynote speakers during the convention's opening ceremonies, offered this advice to the delegates: "No single party dominates this convention and there is now no heavy footprint of political bossism on this assemblage." Continuing on this theme, Governor Ogilvie told the convention, "The prospects are auspicious for you to write not a Republican or a Democrat or an independent constitution, but an Illinois constitution—a document the people of this state can approve."

The state's constitution was now only a year from being drafted and its new form approved by the people. Between December 8, 1969 and December 15, 1970, when the new document was adopted in a special election, the delegates would approve rules by which the convention would operate, devote long hours to committee meetings, consider committee proposals, and refine through careful debate those articles which would finally be presented as the new Illinois constitution. The history of the Sixth Illinois Constitutional Convention is a story of ultimate success, achieved through years of preparation by reform-minded citizens and study commissions, and nine months of dedicated service by the delegates from all over the state and representatives from numerous interest groups.

CONSTITUTIONAL CHANGES

What did the members of the Sixth Illinois Constitutional Convention accomplish? How does the Illinois Constitution of 1970 differ from the Illinois Constitution of 1870, the one separated from the other by a century of time and even more by the transformation of both the world and the state of Illinois? Differences between the two documents do not, of course, necessarily mean improvements in the latter document. Persons of good faith may well differ in the evaluation of the changes, but changes there were — little ones and big ones, significant ones and lesser ones, verbal and substantive. In fact, by the time they were finished, hardly an article in the basic document was left unchanged despite the desire to alter only that which needed alteration. The delegates had cut four thousand or so obsolete words out of the old constitution — the boundaries article, articles dealing with corporations, warehouses, the Illinois Central Railroad, municipal subscription to railroads or private corporations, canals, convict labor, the World's Columbian Exposition, and snippets and snatches here and there. Their aim was to write a constitution and not a statutory code, as much of the old constitution had been.

These changes are to be found throughout the new document, and below is presented an overview of the substantive changes in the several articles.

Preambles may mean little or much. The delegates interpolated passages to indicate that this indeed is a different world from the old one, having aims undreamed of in the middle of the nineteenth century, such as: "eliminate poverty and inequality; assure legal, social and economic justice; provide opportunity for the fullest development of the individual." They are resounding phrases, reflecting great aims even if they are not operative but simply hortatory, constitutional sermons.

In the Bill of Rights (Article I) substantial changes made were:

a. the equal protection of the laws was added to the due process section;

b. to the searches and seizures section was added the right of the people to be secure against unreasonable invasions of privacy or interceptions of communications by eavesdropping devices or other means;

c. the General Assembly was given the right, not only to abolish the grand jury, but to limit its use;

d. any person accused of a felony and not originally charged by a grand jury was given the right to a prompt preliminary hearing to establish probable cause;

e. it was required that all criminal penalties shall be determined both according to the seriousness of the offense and with the objective of restoring the offender to useful citizenship;

f. the section relating to the right to a legal remedy was strengthened making it mandatory, rather than merely hopeful, or hortatory, and the right of privacy as one expressly protected was added;

g. it was provided that no person shall be imprisoned for failure to pay a fine in a criminal case unless he or she has been afforded adequate time to make payment, in installments if necessary, and has willfully failed to make payment;

h. in connection with the right of eminent domain, the special provision for railroad tracks was eliminated; it was provided that compensation in all cases of public taking be determined by jury;

i. sweeping nondiscrimination provisions were made with respect to employment and the sale or rental of property, in both the private and public sectors, applying them to discrimination on the basis of race, color, creed, national ancestry, sex and physical and mental handicaps unrelated to ability, and making them enforceable without action by the General Assembly;

j. it was provided expressly that the equal protection of the laws shall not be denied or abridged on account of sex;

k. communications that insult or incite hostility to persons or groups by reason of, or by reference to, religious, racial, ethnic, national, or regional affiliation were condemned;

l. subject only to the police power, the individual citizen was given the right to keep and bear arms;

m. to the fundamental principles section was added the cautionary warning that the blessings of liberty cannot endure without the recognition of individual obligations and responsibilities;

n. in a new section, it was emphasized that the enumeration of certain rights was not to be construed as denying or disparaging other rights retained by citizens of the state.

Similarly, in the article relating to powers of the state (Article II), it was pointed out that the enumeration of specified powers and functions was not to be construed as a limitation of powers of state government.

In Article III relating to suffrage and elections, several important changes were made:

a. the General Assembly was given the right to lower the length of residency requirements in election districts and for voting for president and vice-president of the United States;

b. the restoration of voting rights of convicted persons was mandated not later than upon completion of sentence;

c. the provisions for election laws to assure fairness, secrecy, and uniformity were clarified;

d. a State Board of Elections was created with general supervision over the administration of the voter registration and election laws throughout the state;

e. provision was made for a general election date.

Substantial as well as technical changes were made in the legislative article (IV):

a. the electors were given a choice between electing representatives from multi-member districts with cumulative voting or from single member districts (the voters chose multi-member districts);

b. the age requirement of senators was reduced from twenty-five to twenty-one;

c. provision was made for the filling of vacancies by appointment until the next general election;

d. an incumbent, during reapportionment, was permitted to run in any district which contains a part of his old district;

e. probably most important of all, an effective method of reapportionment after each federal census was provided so that the constitutionally mandated requirements of compactness, contiguity and substantially equal population in each district would be assured and there would be no elections at large;

f. annual, rather than biennial, sessions of the General Assembly were required; the provisions with respect to special sessions were expanded so that the legislature itself, as well as the governor, could call such sessions; and the proportion of votes required to authorize closed sessions was increased;

g. a president of the senate was substituted as presiding officer instead of the lieutenant governor;

h. legislative committees and commissions were required to give adequate public notice of meetings and a transcript of legislative debates was required to be made available for public inspection;

i. the requirement that bills be read in full was eliminated, substituting the reading of bills by title only;

j. the power of the governor to veto bills was expanded and reformed — the veto of entire bills and line items of appropriation bills was continued, the power to reduce appropriations by the "reduction veto" was given, and the "amendatory veto" power was given;

k. the legislature was required to provide for uniform effective dates for legislation, and provisions were incorporated to encourage the General Assembly to conclude its regular business by July 1 of each annual session;

l. the provisions with respect to special laws were clarified;

m. the power of the House of Representatives to conduct investigations to determine if cause exists for impeachment was established;

n. the number of days during which either house of the General Assembly can adjourn without consent of the other house was increased.

Many changes in Article V relating to the executive were made:

a. the election of all elected executive officers, beginning in 1978, was required in the even-numbered years in which the President of the United States is not elected, so that there would be concentration on such state officials alone, and the treasurer was permitted to succeed himself;

b. the required age of the governor and lieutenant governor was lowered to twenty-five years and the same age requirement was made for other elected constitutional officers, and the residence requirement was reduced from five to three years;

c. the governor and lieutenant governor were required to run as a team in the general election, so that they would both belong to the same party, and the General Assembly was given the authority to provide for the joint nomination for the two offices;

d. the canvassing function for election returns for the executive offices was transferred from the General Assembly to the secretary of state;

e. the provisions with reference to gubernatorial succession were modified;

f. a procedure by which the governor might rearrange the administrative responsibilities of agencies responsible to him was set forth, giving either house of the General Assembly the power of rejection if existing statutes would be affected;

g. the governor was given the power to grant reprieves, commutation and pardons on such terms as he thinks proper;

h. the governor was given the power to prescribe the duties and powers of the lieutenant governor;

i. the office of comptroller was created, with the powers and duties heretofore provided for the auditor of public accounts;

j. the treasurer was required to safeguard all state funds and securities and to make disbursements upon order of the comptroller;

k. all executive officers were required to provide the governor with information relating to their offices;

l. all officers of the executive branch may be required to give bond.

Substantial changes were set forth for the judiciary in Article VI:

a. the basic rules for jurisdiction of the Supreme Court were given;

b. the distinction between circuit judges and associate judges was eliminated, and the General Assembly was given the power to change the number of circuit judges allocated to Chicago and suburban Cook County, to dispense with the election of a circuit judge in each county, and to divide circuits for the purpose of electing judges;

c. magistrates were replaced by associate judges in the Circuit Court, serving for four years, subject to the rules of the Supreme Court, rather than regulation by the General Assembly, and they were required to be licensed and resident attorneys;

d. original jurisdiction concerning legislative redistricting and the disability of the governor was taken from the Circuit Court in those cases in which the Supreme Court has original and exclusive jurisdiction;

e. at the December 15, 1970 referendum, the electors were given the choice of either elective or appointive judges, and they chose to continue elective judges;

f. the Supreme Court was granted the power to determine standards of ethics for all judges, and judges were forbidden to hold other positions of profit;

g. counties were given the right to pay circuit judges a supplemental salary;

h. a Judicial Inquiry Board, consisting of lawyers, judges, and nonlawyers, was created to receive, investigate, or initiate complaints against judges, and the Illinois Courts Commission was required to hear complaints filed by the Judicial Inquiry Board, with power to discipline or remove judges for misconduct or inability to perform their duties;

i. the power of the Supreme Court to reassign judges was clarified to give greater flexibility and efficiency;

j. Supreme and Appellate Court clerks were made appointive, rather than elective as in the past;

k. it was made possible for two or more counties to elect and have a combined state's attorney, rather than the inflexible requirement of a state's attorney for each county.

Basic changes were made in the local government article (VII), centering around the creation of home rule:

a. numerous clarifying and simplifying provisions were added with respect to counties and other units of government;

b. only the election of a sheriff, county clerk, and treasurer was made mandatory for each county; other county officers may be appointed or elected as provided by law; any county office may be created or eliminated by referendum; a county may elect a chief executive officer; the sheriff and treasurer may succeed themselves in office;

c. provisions were made for the formation, elimination, or consolidations of townships;

d. the most important provision in this article and one of the most far-reaching of the entire constitution dealt with home rule for counties and municipalities — automatically for municipalities of more than 25,000 population and to counties having an elected chief executive officer; other municipalities were given the right to become home rule units by referendum; municipalities and counties were to have the right to cease having home rule powers by referendum; home rule units are given broad general power to regulate for the protection of public health, safety, morals, and welfare, to license for regulatory powers, to tax, and to incur debt, provided they could not license for revenue or impose income taxes or the like, or punish felons; power to tax could be denied or limited for home rule units by the General Assembly, which may also require the holding of referenda for the incurring of debt; home rule powers generally were to be construed liberally; several other provisions that were highly pertinent for the exercise of home rule powers;

e. municipalities and counties not exercising home rule powers have only certain specified powers and those granted by law;

f. school districts and other units of local government, other than counties and municipalities, have only certain specified powers and those granted by law; and officials of these units of local government may not be appointed by the judiciary;

g. fee officers were eliminated;

h. governments on all levels were permitted to cooperate in working out common problems and to contract with other governments and private parties to share services; and

i. provision was made for the initiative and referendum as to those matters requiring the approval of the electors.

An entirely new finance article (VIII) was incorporated into the constitution, providing:

a. the basic objective of public money being spent only for public purposes as provided by law and that financial records were to be maintained and open for public inspection;

b. the governor is to prepare and send to the General Assembly an annual budget, showing all projected receipts and disbursements for all state offices, and such budget shall be balanced, no money being authorized for expenditures unless it is expected to be received from all sources;

c. the creation of the office of auditor general, elected by three-fifths vote of each house, for a term of ten years, to audit the funds of the state and to report both to the General Assembly and the governor;

d. the General Assembly is mandated to pass laws prescribing the manner in which local governments are to account and report the use of public funds.

The revenue article (IX), too, has new features:

a. it affirms the exclusive power of the General Assembly to raise revenue by law;

b. it gives the General Assembly the power to classify nonproperty taxes and to grant exceptions, deductions, allowances, and credits;

c. it prohibits a graduated income tax and establishes a ratio between such taxes for individuals and for corporations and permits tie-ins with federal income tax laws;

d. it constitutionalizes the classification of real property taxes in Cook County, subject to law;

e. it provides for the abolition of *ad valorem* personal property taxes on or before January 1, 1979, and the concurrent replacement thereof by other taxes;

f. it permits the grant of homestead exemption and rent credits by law;

g. it permits the General Assembly to equalize taxes in overlapping taxing districts;

h. it provides for safeguards in connection with tax sales on real estate;

i. it sets forth certain restrictions on the state debt.

The education article (X), brief in size, has some new features:

a. it sets forth higher educational goals than in the previous constitution and places the primary financial responsibility upon the state;

b. it creates a State Board of Education and gives it the power to appoint a chief state educational officer (instead of the previously elected officials).

There is an entirely new and far-reaching environment article (XI), providing:

a. the duty of the state and each person to maintain a healthful environment;
b. the right of each person to enforce this right to a healthful environment through legal proceedings.

The militia article (XII) is new in only one respect: it eliminates discrimination against women and eliminates the age requirement.

The general provisions article is filled with new sections:

a. it requires candidates for and holders of public office to disclose significant financial interests;
b. it permits anyone to sue the state, except as otherwise provided by the General Assembly;
c. it protects the pension and retirement rights of governmental employees;
d. it permits the granting of corporate charters only by general laws, and not by special legislation;
e. it declares public transportation to be an essential public purpose and permits the use of public funds for such purpose;
f. it permits branch banking when authorized by law passed by an extraordinary majority of the members of the House and Senate.

The constitutional revision article (XIV) is considerably more liberal than in the 1870 constitution:

a. it provides for the automatic submission to the people of a vote for a constitutional convention at least once every twenty years;
b. it lowers the required vote in the General Assembly for the calling of a convention from two-thirds to three-fifths in each house;
c. it relaxes somewhat the popular vote for the convening of a convention or the ratification of constitutional revisions or amendments;
d. it establishes a limited procedure whereby the people may petition to amend and actually amend structural and procedural subjects in the legislative article;

e. it specifies how the General Assembly may ratify a proposed amendment to the federal constitutional convention.

Propositions to abolish the death penalty and to lower the voting age to eighteen were defeated by the voters at the same time that they approved the new constitution generally, and retained multi-member districts by cumulative voting and the election of judges.

Thus, generally for the better, the new constitution has incorporated many notable changes in the basic charter of the state. But this new charter did not just happen. We have already mentioned the efforts of many citizens in the decades of the 1930s to the 1950s. Now it is appropriate to go back to 1965 and begin at the beginning of the final product, the first of three constitutional study commissions approved by the legislature on August 17, 1965. From there we will go full circle, through the personalities, problems, and work that would result in the new constitution for the state of Illinois.

II

Prelude to Action

Before a new constitution for the state of Illinois could become a reality, four elections would have to be held — the call for the convention, a primary and general election of delegates, and a referendum for adoption of the convention's work-product. In this chapter we discuss the individuals, groups, and strategies involved in launching the revision process through a successful campaign call for a convention. We also discuss briefly the ballot position controversy which temporarily stalled progress toward a convention, as well as the two elections held for the selection of the convention's 116 delegates. The focus in this volume is on the convention itself; a full and more detailed study of the campaigns and elections surrounding the convention can be found in another volume in this series, JoAnna M. Watson's *Electing a Constitution: The Illinois Citizen and the 1970 Constitution.*

THE CONVENTION CALL CAMPAIGN

Once the initiating resolution had weathered the criticisms and legislative obstacles of the General Assembly, the convention call received enthusiastic and widespread organizational and editorial support. Such early public involvement was only the beginning of similar responses that were to be crucial factors in the Illinois success story.

Almost immediately after the end of the 1967 legislative session, an informal group of civic activists gathered to lay the groundwork for the upcoming referendum campaign. This group was spearheaded by members of the League of Women Voters and Chicago Bar Association, long-time agitators for constitutional revision. Throughout the summer of 1967 this informal committee met weekly to solicit names of potential members for a statewide citizens committee.

The weekly meetings culminated in a public meeting on October 25, 1967, at the Chicago Bar Association to which were invited representatives of all significant civic, business, and professional groups in the state. Approximately eighty people attended. The speaker's table reflected the spirit of cooperation between civic and political adherents. Past campaigns had shown that such cooperation was essential if a constitutional venture of this sort was to succeed.

At this meeting the Citizen's Constitutional Information Service (CCIS) was reinstated and a steering committee was elected by those in attendance. The CCIS was an adjunct to the ICCR; it served as an educational rather than promotional organization, and tax exempt contributions could be made to it. Legal, civic, and educational organizations dominated the steering committee membership. Missing at this early stage of the campaign organization was the support of the State Chamber of Commerce and the Illinois Agricultural Association; also missing was opposition which developed later against a constitutional convention.

The Search for a Chairman

The major task of the steering committee was to approach the governor with a "pre-tested" list of possible chairmen for the state campaign committee. All individuals considered for the chairmanship were to be screened for their willingness to serve before the governor became publicly involved in the selection process. This approach was the result of a lesson drawn from the aborted revenue campaign of 1966 in which repeated attempts by the governor to appoint unwilling citizens as chairmen had given the entire venture a poor image. The steering committee's standards for selection of a chairman were concise and straightforward. First, there would be cochairmen — a business leader from Cook County and a farm leader from downstate. Second, whether or not retired, the cochairmen should be sufficiently free from their regular commitments to be able to devote virtually full time to the campaign effort. The third criterion, which went unheeded, was that one of the chairmen should be a woman. The committee also included other requirements for the Chicago-based chairman: He should be an outstanding civic leader, not identified with the regular organization of either party.

A list of thirteen possible chairmen was sent to the governor's office in early November. Two months later the appointments of Kingman Douglass and William Kuhfuss, representing Chicago and downstate respectively, were announced by the governor. Neither had been on the initial list submitted by the citizen's committee although Kuhfuss had been discussed by the committee. Douglass, the outcome of a search by Witwer among his Commercial Club friends, proved an ideal choice. As an investment banker and member of the inner civic elite, he was in a position to assume the heavy financial role a division of labor was later to place upon him. Kuhfuss, president of the Illinois Agricultural Association, and the governor's choice, possessed the means, through local farm bureaus, to disseminate information downstate. Although Douglass and Kuhfuss were not household names, they nevertheless had the potential to fill the roles they would be asked to perform in the coming months.

Although the major responsibility of the steering committee had been facilitation of chairmen selection (it is doubtful that the governor would have acted without prompting by a citizens group), they had two other important functions. One was to obtain tax exempt status for campaign donations, and the other to set up a headquarters from which the campaign would operate. The headquarters' office was opened in February 1968, under the temporary directorship of Mrs. Peggy Norton and with money remaining from the accounts of the old ICCR.

The first formal meeting of the ICCC was called for March 15, 1968, by the newly appointed cochairmen. In attendance were Governor Kerner and a core group of members invited by Kerner to serve on the Board of Directors. The steering committee also assumed positions on the ICCC Board of Directors and passed their responsibility for campaign organization to the permanent officers.

The actual campaign for the convention call was formally launched at a luncheon at the governor's mansion in Springfield on April 16, 1968. Invited were some one hundred business, labor, professional, agricultural, civic and state political leaders. The purpose was promotional, and special attention was given to press and photographic releases. The luncheon theme — Why My Group Favors Con Con — was carried out by supportive remarks from the various groups in attendance. Douglass and Kuhfuss, in a report on campaign and publicity plans, reiterated what they believed to be the major campaign hurdles — "Our biggest campaign problems are voter apathy and the fact that we must compete for public attention in a presidential election year."[1]

Ballot Problems

Past failures in Illinois in obtaining approval of constitutional propositions were due in part to the extraordinary majorities required by the constitution for adoption of amendments or convention calls. Consequently, frequent attempts had been made to develop a ballot that would be more congenial to the approval of amendments. Ever since 1950 — when Gateway had been passed — state statutes had required a separate blue ballot for constitutional propositions: each ballot carried a notice to the effect that failure to vote the ballot is the equivalent of a negative vote and that each ballot must be returned to the election judge upon leaving the voting booth whether it has been used or not. In the past, defeat of constitutional amendments had generally been the result of nonparticipation by large numbers of voters, presumably indifferent or apathetic to the constitutional question. However, after 1950 when the blue color of the ballot triggered an awareness of the type of electoral issue with which voters were to deal the rate of nonvoting on constitutional issues dropped by one-half. Constitutional reform campaigners have emphasized this aspect of the ballot and have attempted to promote an association between the blue ballot and "good government." Nevertheless, fears persisted in the 1968 campaign as predictions were made for a large November election turnout. The three-way presidential race was stirring considerable interest nationwide, and it was felt this would bring a significant number of typically constitutional nonvoters into the electoral arena. Concern among these voters for state issues or offices would not be very high. The potential for nonparticipation on the constitutional convention call was increased.

[1]ICCC press release, Chicago, April 12, 1968.

State Representative Harold Katz (D-Glencoe), in an attempt to offset the adverse vote of the nonvoter, proposed a "party-circle" form of ballot. With such a ballot the constitutional convention question would be placed on the regular ballot and be automatically voted upon whenever an individual cast a straight party vote. Since the ballots would carry the stated or endorsed position of each party and since both political parties were believed to be for the call of the convention, the automatic vote formula seemed a suitable guarantee for approving the convention call.

The Katz proposal received early support from the *Chicago Sun-Times*, but the opponents, who were of two types, were to carry the day. One group believed the party-circle plan would enhance chances for success of the convention call, and since they opposed the entire idea of an unlimited constitutional convention they opposed the plan. The other group of opponents led by Witwer and Chicago attorney Louis Ancel, were actually strong and active supporters of the call. They believed, however, that such a move on the part of the legislature to amend the statutes at this late date indicated serious doubt about passage of Con Con altogether. Witwer explained: "If we had come along in the eleventh hour, having gotten the favorable vote on the joint resolution for Con Con, and if we then basically changed the rules of the game, it would have looked bad. It was my view that this would cause irritation on the part of many voters and afford a ready argument for our opponents; all we would have succeeded in doing would have been to give the opposition a ready-made case for defeating the call. Also, I believed the Katz proposal should have been defeated because I considered it a rather dubious way to do constitutional amending. I still do not want the process to be made so easy that it becomes almost a decision of the political bosses of the two parties as to whether or not we are going to change the constitution."[2]

Almost as soon as the party-circle plan was laid to rest a second challenge to careful voter consideration of the convention call was presented. A number of county officials sought legislative authorization to place the constitutional question on the voting machines rather than on the separate blue paper ballot. Lake County officials claimed they could save the county $60,000 in election expenses. Con

[2]Taped interview with Samuel Witwer, fall 1968.

Con proponents, however, estimated a loss of hundreds of thousands of blue ballot votes if the legislation were to pass. The bills for machine voting were subsequently tabled in legislative committee, but in the week before the election Cook County Clerk, Edward Barrett, nevertheless placed the convention call ballot on approximately 3,000 voting machines within his jurisdiction. Following a heated encounter and under threat of mandamus by Louis Ancel and Samuel Witwer, Barrett withdrew the Con Con question from the machines and offered it to the voters on a separate blue sheet of paper, as in all other counties. The action, however well intentioned, was clearly illegal (Attorney General Opinion, August 1966). Furthermore, considering the need for as much support as possible from heavily populated, pro-amendment Cook County, this incident had major electoral significance.

A Statewide Effort

In the summer of 1968, after almost a year of organizational activity, the citizen committee began to implement what was to be the basic strategy for a successful campaign — strong support by both political parties, unremitting support by the mass media, and support by civic, business, professional, agricultural, and labor organizations. There was also an attempt on the part of convention proponents to avoid issues as much as possible. Widespread support by the parties, media, and interest groups required an "issueless" campaign, for beyond the supporters' basic agreement to have a convention "take a look at an outmoded document," lay broad ideological and practical cleavages.

In addition to a statewide citizens committee which would provide centralized leadership, a successful day at the polls would also require a finance committee, local campaign committees, a campaign theme, adequate literature, and a campaign timetable.

Financing the Campaign. In the space of five months, the finance committee raised over $235,000, of which $210,000 came from business and civic leaders. Generally, financial appeals were directed to known contributors of civic "causes"; for example, one of the principal sources for potential donors was the Chicago Symphony list. Few attempts were made to solicit donations of the five and ten dollar variety since the returns were believed to be disproportionate to the time and effort spent on such solicitations. However, contact for small contributions was made through several other channels. Adlai Stevenson III, a known supporter of Illinois constitutional reform, added an item for Con Con contributions to one of his newsletters. Similarly, Governor Otto Kerner, who by this time had resigned as governor to accept an appointment to the U.S. Circuit Court of Appeals, was approached for his cooperation in writing to a number of his friends. Approximately $3,500 was added to ICCC finances as a result of about eighty such letters written by Kerner. In addition, the Chicago Bar Association distributed letters signed by prominent member lawyers to solicit support through financial contributions.

No organizations contributed to the ICCC fund with the exception of $5,000 contributions from the Cook County Republican and Democratic committees. Instead, endorsing groups and local citizen committees expended their resources internally in an attempt to educate their own members to conduct their own campaigns.

The Local Campaigns. Citizens committees were formed in cities in twenty-one counties throughout the state to demonstrate evidence of a groundswell of support for constitutional revision and to motivate grassroots support for the convention referendum. The objective was never completely obtained since constitutional reform was not a single or local issue for which mass support could be generated. However, statewide organizations with local affiliates, e.g., the League of Women Voters and the Illinois Congress of Parents and Teachers, were instrumental in establishing support groups. Grassroots support was primarily organizational, and the groups involved were mostly business, civic, or professionally oriented. Those local committees that were formed did help promote the call campaign and disseminate information about the convention; nonetheless their importance was somewhat dissipated by the decision not to open downstate campaign offices as had been common in previous blue ballot amendment campaigns. "We wished to avoid diversionary tactics,"[3] explained Cochairman Douglass.

The ICCC expended few financial resources directly on local citizens committees but did hire two field workers — William Sommerschield and John Alexander — to assist the local organizations. Both were to become convention delegates.

[3]Taped interview, fall 1968.

The local campaign committees established speakers' bureaus, distributed materials, purchased newspaper advertising, sponsored parades or booths at county fairs, and sought editorial support for the convention referendum.

Ultimately, the impact of the local Con Con committees on the referendum was impossible to determine. It was not clear whether a successful vote in a county was because, or in spite of the presence of a local campaign committee.

The Campaign Theme. Strategists knew from past blue ballot campaigns and from survey research, that the blue ballot symbolized government improvement and reform. But they also knew that those who would normally vote "no" on blue ballot issues would do so principally because they believed constitutional revision "raises taxes." Thus, while the question of constitutional revision had a positive connotation for many voters, tax issues clearly had to be avoided during the course of the campaign. The main theme, then, for the campaign had to emphasize the need to modernize or update the one-hundred-year-old Illinois constitution, the need for a document that could govern in the space age. The efforts of the ICCC had to insure massive Con Con awareness among the voters whose principal reason for going to the polls in November was to select a President of the United States. From these numbers, approximately 65 to 70 percent of the registered electorate, the convention question had to poll a positive majority.

The simple slogan "Vote the Blue Ballot" was frequently used by the ICCC. Its effectiveness was due to the fact that many voters relate the blue ballot to good government, while others, once they were made aware of the issues, would vote affirmatively after a simple instruction to vote on the question.

In fact, a survey of voter intentions in September showed that among informed voters on the constitutional issue, 62 percent would vote yes, 10 percent would vote no, 27.3 percent were undecided. The percentage of "yes" voters had doubled since a previous poll, while undecided voters were reduced by half. As voters became aware of Con Con, they moved most often into the "yes" rather than the "no" ranks.

Getting Out the Word. The ICCC began extensive print media advertising approximately four weeks before the election; radio advertising began two weeks later; and use of television time was concentrated almost entirely in the last few days. In fact, television advertising was limited by available resources and beamed primarily to major population centers throughout the state. The ICCC did not avail itself of public service time since this could have conferred upon the opposition an opportunity to secure equal time — a lesson learned from the abortive Maryland constitutional convention experience. Dissemination of information also included distribution of roughly 3.5 million grocery shopping bags marked "Vote Yes on the Blue Ballot" through the outlets of a major grocery chain in Illinois a week prior to the election; and 1.8 million blue ballot reminders were distributed among Illinois school children to be taken home the day before the election. Those reminders were not intended to direct parental voting but to make them aware of the issue and to vote.

The Counter Campaign

The call for the convention was not without opposition. Principal opponents were the AFL-CIO (with its one million members), and ad hoc associations such as the Committee to Oppose Con Con in Illinois, headquartered in Quincy, and a Save Our State committee (S.O.S.) of Winnetka (formerly the Save Our Suburbs and Save Our Schools committees). There was no apparent coordination of activity among these opposition groups. In fact, their reasons for opposing the convention call were inconsistent. On the one hand, labor's stress was upon a "soak the poor" theme which warned of control in the convention by business interests, especially in rewriting revenue provisions. Ad hoc groups warned of impending socialism. Still others emphasized what they perceived to be an impractical approach to the task at hand. Thus, Troy Kost, of the Township Officials of Illinois, said, "Dreamers and do-gooders are behind the Con Con. . . . Those who will serve in the convention will not be the objective people because these people will be unable to spend long periods of time from their jobs to do this work."[4]

Convention opponents were united in their attempt to counter the arguments that the constitution was old and needed revision. They argued, for example, that the 1870 Illinois Constitution was one

[4]Troy Kost of the Township Officials of Illinois in *Telegraph*, Alton, April 30, 1968.

hundred years *younger* than the U.S. Constitution, and that a constitution was a sacred document not to be tampered with. State AFL-CIO President Ruben Soderstrom proclaimed, "There are some things you don't change — the Lord's Prayer, the Sermon on the Mount, the Ten Commandments, and the Illinois Constitution."[5]

Despite this barrage of opposing arguments, a simple overall opposition campaign theme — "Don't be Conned Into Con Con" — and an estimated $50,000 spent by labor to defeat the convention call, the total effect of the opposition upon the November vote was minimal. Not only were the arguments inconsistent, but the largest group, labor, was split with the United Auto Workers and a handful of smaller unions even endorsing the constitutional convention.

The Final Weeks

Less than a month before the convention call campaign was over, Governor Samuel Shapiro, who had succeeded Kerner, declared a Blue Ballot Week. The principal function of the week was a bipartisan dinner in Chicago, sponsored by the Chicago Bar and the ICCC. Ward and township committeemen of both parties were invited to attend in an effort to solicit their active support on the constitutional issue. Also present were both gubernatorial candidates and Cook County committee party leaders, Republican Edmund Kucharski and Democrat Richard J. Daley. Undoubtedly, the major efforts of the parties would be focused on election of candidates to national and state office, but precinct workers did distribute over two million sample blue ballots in Cook County and a quarter million downstate.

The ICCC wrote to the 102 county clerks to remind them of the blue ballot voting procedures, i.e., that the Election Code called for individuals to vote the blue ballot first and deposit it in the ballot box before being permitted to enter the voting machine; also that the blue ballot has to be placed on top of all other paper ballots as they are handed to the voters.

The November 1968 call for a convention was considered by a substantial number of voters — 4,700,000 — and approved by a vote of 2,900,000 to 1,100,000. The convention thus received slightly over 60 percent of the vote, well over the needed majority of those voting in the

[5]*Rockford Register - Republic,* May 4, 1968.

election. However, several events and obstacles remained before the convention would convene on December 8, 1969.

SELECTING THE DELEGATES

The Seventy-fifth General Assembly created the Second Constitutional Study Commission which recommended to the legislature and Governor Ogilvie the enabling act under which the delegates were to be elected and the convention organized. The act called for a primary and general election, both to be conducted on a nonpartisan basis. The nonpartisan provision faced judicial challenge under the constitutional language that delegate elections must be "conducted in the same manner" as the partisan elections for state senators. However, the Illinois Supreme Court in *Livingston v. Ogilvie* (43 Ill. 2nd 9) rejected the argument and held that "in the same manner" meant only that delegates must be elected by the people in free and equal elections, by ballot.

Ballot Controversy

Over five hundred candidates filed the necessary petitions to seek election to the state's sixth constitutional convention. One hundred and sixteen were to be selected; two each from the state's fifty-eight senatorial districts. The placement of their names on the ballot, however, resulted in an unexpected and bitter controversy. The names were to appear on the ballot without party label, but both parties had a high interest in the election outcome; each wanted to make certain that the other did not receive any special advantage. Moreover, although research on the subject is not at all clear, popular wisdom has it that a top position on the ballot brings with it an electoral advantage, not exactly a tribute to voter selectivity.

Democrats generally favored a system that would allow Democratic Secretary of State Paul Powell to list candidates in the order in which they filed their nominating petitions. Powell would thus be able to determine who filed first, a determination which was not always obvious. The Republicans favored a lottery system in which the names of the candidates would be coded on slips of paper, placed in a hat, and then drawn by either Governor Ogilvie or someone designated by him as his representative. The Democrats opposed this plan because the secretary of state's office is the official election agency of the state, and because according to the constitution, the delegates had to be elected "in the same manner"as members of the Illinois Senate. Two other methods were considered — alphabetical listing and rotation — but without serious chance of adoption since they were opposed by Powell.

The Democratic position initially prevailed, and on Monday, July 7, 1969, some one hundred people were in a line in front of the secretary of state's office in Springfield waiting for the doors to open at 8:00 a.m. Some had conducted nightlong vigils to insure the top position on their district's ballot. Heated arguments and brief scuffles developed when Don Ed, head of the index division of the office of secretary of state, attempted to enter the office with petitions that had been mailed, rather than delivered by a candidate. Police were summoned, and Ed explained that those petitions that had been received in the mail would be processed before those delivered in person. The procedure was defined as a longstanding practice in the legislature; thus incumbents and persons favored by the secretary of state would receive the top position on the ballot.

Rejecting the notion that tradition should take precedent, two Chicago candidates, Bernard Weisberg and Mary Lee Leahy, both independents, filed suit against Powell. Weisberg, in the U.S. District Court in Chicago, claimed that Powell's actions were unconstitutional, arbitrary, and discriminatory. He also accused Powell of notifying regular party organizations, both Democratic and Republican, that preferential treatment would be given candidates other than those delivering petitions in person. He asked the court to issue a preliminary and permanent injunction restraining Powell from certifying the order of placement until ballot position could be determined in some manner other than that traditionally used.

In a second suit, filed in Sangamon County Circuit Court, Mrs. Leahy charged that "unless the court intervenes to insure fair elections, public confidence in the constitutional convention will be undermined and the success of the convention will be jeopardized."[6]

On July 15, U.S. District Judge Joseph Perry issued a temporary order restraining Powell from assigning positions or certifying ballots. Meanwhile, Sangamon County Circuit Judge William Chamberlain ruled that Mrs. Leahy had failed to show the need for an immediate

[6]*Champaign-Urbana News Gazette*, July 9, 1969.

injunction against Powell, and consequently dismissed her suit. Mrs. Leahy charged that Judge Chamberlain should have disqualified himself on the basis of his close prior relationship with Powell.

In Chicago, Judge Perry refused to issue a permanent injunction restraining Powell from certifying the ballot position or the candidates for nomination. On August 9, however, the U.S. Court of Appeals for the Seventh Circuit reversed Perry's ruling and ordered Powell to discard a "discriminatory" listing of candidates. The court also set up the procedure for determining the ballot positions — petitions filed in person would remain in the order in which they were accepted, and mailed petitions would be inserted among the delivered petitions on a random basis determined by a lottery.

Powell initially refused to accept the court ruling, stating, "My position is that I don't intend to hold a lottery. I am going to continue to hold elections as has been done for the last fifty years. The federal court has no business in this at all."[7] The state electoral board delayed certifying the ballot for the election until attorneys for the secretary of state's office had time to petition the court to vacate its ruling. The court refused the petition, holding that ". . . nothing in the Illinois Constitution, laws or public policy supports the action of the Secretary of State against which our order was directed."

After nearly a month of public controversy, the state electoral board agreed on August 12 to comply with the court order and to certify the ballot. A lottery would be held for the primary ballot positions. Positions for the general election ballot would be in the order of the primary vote received — the greatest vote-getter would be number one, with the others to follow in descending order.

Delegate Elections

The primary election was held on September 23, 1969, and the general election on November 18, 1969. While the people showed temporary interest in the convention during the initial call referendum, and the campaigns in many districts were intense and hard fought, voter interest fell sharply on the actual election of delegates. The voting in the primary and general elections marked a low in recorded electoral history in Illinois. The primary voter turnout averaged only 18

[7]*Champaign-Urbana Courier*, July 23, 1969.

percent; the general election average turnout was up somewhat, but only for an average of 27 percent.

The low voter turnout could be attributed in part to the absence of party labels from the ballot. At the same time, however, the nonpartisan elections did have an impact on many individuals who might not otherwise have sought — and won — delegate seats. The two major parties were involved in the elections to some extent; the Chicago Democratic organization elected candidates and downstate Democratic and Republican hopefuls vigorously sought their party's endorsement. But because of their nonpartisan nature, the elections contributed to a diversity among the delegates, and resulted in a group of delegates that perhaps more closely resembled a cross-section of the Illinois population. There were to be sure party regulars, but as discussed in later chapters, among the survivors of the two elections were individuals who would contribute markedly to the convention and its outcome.

III

The First Days

The Sixth Illinois Constitutional Convention was scheduled to convene December 8, 1969, scarcely two months after the Third Constitution Study Commission had held its first meeting. The enabling legislation for the commission was signed into law by Governor Ogilvie on July 23, 1969, but due to delays by the legislature in making its appointments, the commission was not organized until October 9. A great deal of work had to be accomplished in the intervening two months if the convention groundwork was to be prepared adequately. The Second Study Commission had made a major contribution by preparing the research and background materials for the delegates, but the preparations necessary for getting the day-to-day work of the convention under way — the staffing, the rules, etc. — were charged to the third commission. The manner in which the latter body completed its tasks, and presented them to the convention, would determine how expeditiously — or abortively —the 116 individual delegates would begin to function as a group.

This chapter tells the story of the crucial first days as the delegates went about laying the groundwork for the months to follow. They formed interpersonal relationships, tried their debating skills, eliminated some but took on other fears, and began to realize the enormity of the task they faced. They did this in large part through the delegate orientation, the election of officers, and the adoption of rules under which the convention would operate.

WELCOMING THE DELEGATES

To expedite their efforts, the members of the Third Constitution Study Commission formed into three subgroups — subcommittees on convention rules, convention staffing, and delegate orientation. The staff and members of the Second Constitution Study Commission strongly favored an orientation session for the novice constitution writers. Similar efforts in other states had been investigated and the consensus was that it was an excellent forum for the delegates to become acquainted and to begin the organizational phase of the convention; this organizational phase, in turn, might determine how expeditiously the basic work would proceed. One hundred and sixteen rather diverse individuals —black, white, even one Filipino, many ethnic and economic groups, men, women, Republicans, Democrats, independents, Chicagoans, suburbanites, downstaters — would be coming together, most of them total strangers, and all bringing with them separate and ofttimes conflicting values, goals, and backgrounds. Orientation sessions might place them on a common footing and start the deliberation in a more relaxed atmosphere.

Primary responsibility for putting together the delegate orientation session rested with Alice Ihrig, long active in the League of Women Voters, and Professor Samuel K. Gove, of the University of Illinois; both were commission members. The program began on the evening of Friday, December 5, 1969, with registration and a brief session in the chambers of the House of Representatives in Springfield where the convention would formally convene three days later. As the delegates took their seats, they perhaps did not realize they were meeting the very people who would be their seat-mates for the duration of the convention. Seats were assigned alphabetically at this first session as well as all those that followed. The arrangement was impersonally fair. It did not have the partisanship quality of a political body, for the delegates had been elected without party labels and parties were not to play a role at this convention.

Opening remarks to this initial gathering of the convention delegates were made by Senator Robert Coulson, cochairman of the Third Constitution Study Commission. He introduced William Alderfer, the state historian, who put the Sixth Illinois Constitutional Convention into historical perspective. How would this new constitution fare?

Would it actually produce a superior product, one suited for the industrial age? Alfred E. Driscoll, former governor of New Jersey and a strong advocate of state constitutional reform, addressed the delegates next. He drew on his own experience as governor when New Jersey had successfully rewritten its basic document some twenty years previously. State constitutional experts often point to the New Jersey experience as one of the better examples in modern times. Most such efforts have failed. Driscoll urged the delegates not to lose sight of their purpose and the nature of a state constitution. He warned against the temptation to write legislation into the constitution. He stressed that the document should be as brief and lucid as possible. His sage remarks were well received. He would be the first of several out-of-state people the delegates would invite to the convention to share their thoughts and experiences.

The League of Women Voters, ever-present at the convention and helpful throughout its nine-month duration, provided a brief and convivial reception following the speeches; thereafter the delegates dispersed throughout the city to begin what was to become a regular institution in the months to come — informal, small group sessions where a good deal of the business of constitution making would take place, alliances and friendships formed, the measure of many members taken.

The program for the following day consisted largely of administrative matters and a review of some of the services and assistance the delegates could expect. Senator Robert McCarthy, cochairman of the commission, presided. Representative Robert Day, commission member and chairman of the subcommittee on Site and Selection, brought the members up to date on the logistics surrounding opening day ceremonies. The director of the Illinois State Library, Alphonse F. Tressa, extended his full cooperation, as he outlined the facilities that would be available. He would be setting up a special library unit containing convention related materials and would assign staff members specifically to it. The delegates were urged to use this material, just as Congressmen use the facilities of the Library of Congress. Representative John Conolly, chairman of the Illinois Legislative Council, discussed the services of the council and also offered its assistance to the delegates, as did Representative Bernard McDevitt, chairman of the Legislative Reference Bureau. The bureau would become the primary drafting agency for member proposals, and the council's chief contribution would be the preparation and publication of a weekly summary of convention developments. Perhaps the person getting the greatest attention was the representative from the state auditor's office, who explained the delegates' remuneration and the procedure they would have to follow to begin receiving pay and allowances. For some it meant considerable amounts. For all it was more than pin money. The delegates were told that they had a total budget of $2,977,980 to complete their task. The legislative enabling act provided that each member of the convention, except the president and vice-president (note the singularity of vice-president and the absence of secretary), would receive $625 per month for a period not to exceed eight months. The limitation of time for compensation was intended, at least in part, to prevent a repetition of the 1920-1922 constitutional debacle. The president was to receive $1,500 per month and the vice-president $1,200 per month for a period not to exceed nine months in each instance. The extra month in the case of those two top officials was a recognition that they might have chores to perform after mere members of the convention were freed from their duties.

In addition to the monthly salary, each member was also to be paid $75 for each day he was in attendance at the convention or its committees, not to exceed one hundred days. Here again, there was clear evidence that the legislature was determined that the members of the convention would not dally. Their compensation was not lordly, in most instances less than their normal earnings, and often delegates served at financial sacrifice; but the legislature took no chance that anyone would prolong the deliberations because of the attraction of added compensation.

Each member was also given a mileage allowance for the required travel to and from convention sites at the rate of fifteen cents per mile, a gross postage allotment of $120, and expenses at the same rate as that established by the General Assembly for members of interim commissions and committees of the legislature. Certain elected public officials, such as legislators, would serve as members of the convention, but they would receive only travel, postage and expense allowances, and no salary or other compensations.

Thus, if the convention completed its work in the prescribed time, its members would be compensated adequately, or at least modestly; if not, they would have to serve unrewarded for their extra labors.

After a luncheon at the St. Nicholas Hotel, John Brooks from the staff of the Maryland constitutional convention, Robert C. Pebworth of the commission, and Louis Ancel, also of the commission, spoke to the delegation, Brooks reviewed the Maryland experience, underscoring his feeling that the submission of the proposed constitution as a total package was a significant factor in its defeat in Maryland, despite the high quality of that package. Pebworth, widower of the highly regarded state representative who had done so much to bring about the constitutional convention, stressed the important role the media would have to play during the convention and after its adjournment in selling the document to the voters. Ancel had served as chairman of the commission's subcommittee on rules. He formally presented the draft of suggested rules that his committee put together. He stressed that the rules were only suggestions, but that they could expedite the organizational phase of the convention if they were used as a point of departure for adopting the permanent rules. Ancel's draft would become the point of discussion throughout the orientation session and did in fact serve as the basis for the rules ultimately drafted by the convention.

At a dinner that evening the brief program was made up largely of remarks of Kingman Douglass, Jr. and William Kuhfuss. They had served as cochairmen of the 1968 convention call campaign. Their main contribution to the program was an offer of support in a campaign for adoption of the new constitution, when it was finally completed. Of course, they would watch the proceedings of the convention and hope for a document that the business and agricultural interests they represented could accept and campaign for wholeheartedly.

The final remarks of the orientation program were made Sunday afternoon by George Braden. Braden, on leave from General Electric's legal department, had been a veteran of constitution writing in several states, and had coauthored with Professor Rubin G. Cohn the volume that was to become the "bible" of the convention, *The Illinois Constitution: An Annotated and Comparative Analysis.* His topic was the mechanics of drafting the constitution. He hammered away at such matters as writing for the long view, rather than the passing moment; brevity and simplicity; intent and judicial review; exclusion of legislation; and the role of skilled draftsmen and a style and drafting committee. Braden, who later was to be retained as special counsel on drafting matters for the convention, also cautioned the delegates not to attempt to write what was ideally the best constitution, but rather the best constitution that could be accepted by the voters. Perfection, he indicated, was a recipe for disaster. Since the delegates were less than angels, they would be wise to settle for less than a divine charter.

The remainder of the orientation program was taken up with nonsubstantive matters. Mayor Nelson Howarth of Springfield hosted a reception on behalf of the city for the delegates at the Old State Capitol. It was mostly a social event used by the press photographers to get some local color into their stories of the delegates. It was also the first time the delegates would be together in the beautifully restored building, and James Hickey, Lincoln curator for the State Historical Library, related to them the many historical events that took place there, including Lincoln's "house divided" speech. The delegates did not know that this building would later become the center of their activities, although some were already studying the advantages of such a convention site.

The session ended that evening with a reception at the state's executive mansion, hosted by Governor and Mrs. Ogilvie. It was a most pleasant affair, one of relaxed harmony. It served as a proper ending for the orientation session — a further chance for the delegates to become acquainted and make the transition from private citizen to public delegate — as well as the perfect launching point for the next day's formal start of official convention business. The reception and the orientation served also as the setting for questions, discussions, strategies, and decisions concerning the president and other leaders of the convention. Suddenly, all realized that they were essential parts of a historic process. Their efforts and decisions would determine the future of the state of Illinois.

CHOOSING A PRESIDENT

Throughout the period when candidates for election as delegates of the constitutional convention were under consideration, one name attracted special attention. Delegates were to be chosen, at least nominally, on a nonpartisan basis, but both parties did, in fact, express preference for

particular candidates for their ranks. But most Republicans, Democrats, and independents alike seemed to share the feeling that Samuel
W. Witwer would become the president of the convention when it
assembled in Springfield. For once, political considerations were
shunted aside in the desire to give outstanding leadership to the
convention. For twenty years Witwer had led the effort to revise the
old constitution. No one else had so prolonged and dedicated a record
in this endeavor; certainly no one else who was running for election as a
delegate could claim such perseverance. Also contending for the
presidency was a young man named Peter Tomei — brilliant, able,
forceful, almost as if sensing he was not long for this world. There were
others in various parts of the state who were eager to be selected, but to
the press and to the public generally, it seemed preordained that
Witwer would be selected as president when the delegates assembled.
In the election for delegates in his district, he obtained more votes than
any candidate in the entire state. True, it was only a few hundred more
votes than the number obtained by Richard Daley, the mayor's oldest
son and namesake, but it was enough to indicate the special quality of
his candidacy.

Samuel W. Witwer was not the sort of person to wear his ambitions
on his sleeve. He was hemmed in by an almost excessive sense of
propriety. Surveying the situation after the 1968 referendum assured
the holding of a convention, he could properly feel that he was the man
for the position. He was the only one who could say that he had worked
continuously for constitutional reform on a bipartisan basis. He did not
too overtly campaign for the presidency before his election as a
delegate. However, he did let key persons know that he was deeply
interested. He talked with Governor Ogilvie on the matter a number of
times throughout the year 1969. While the governor did not expressly
promise his support, he made it clear to Witwer that he was well
qualified and the logical choice. Top men on the Chicago newspapers
talked with him about the presidency, and he certainly did not
discourage them from suggesting that he should be the choice to head
the convention. He avoided expressing himself on substantive issues,
so as not to chill his supporters. In a sense, this was the sort of subdued
campaigning that Thomas Dewey (incorrectly in this case) thought
would win him the presidency of the United States in 1948. There is
always the temptation to avoid unnecessary controversy that may
interfere with one's ambitions.

Not everyone encouraged Witwer. Young Tomei was fair or brash enough to tell Witwer of his shortcomings, as Tomei saw them and he talked with a few newspaper people in the same manner. There were rumors, too, of downstate efforts to turn the tide. Republicans like Elbert Smith, John Parkhurst, and David Davis, distinguished legislators and men of great intelligence and savvy, were talked of in some circles. An uninhibited Democrat from the middle of the state, John Knuppel, beat the drums in his own behalf. He wrote to the delegates telling why he should be selected, but got nowhere. He was never a serious contender against Witwer, nor were any of the others.

The issue had not yet been resolved definitely when Witwer and the other delegates assembled in Springfield on December 5, 1969 for the orientation session. Throughout the evening Witwer met with a number of members, some in delegations, who wanted to assess him before casting their votes. Some urged him to come out openly, even blatantly, for election; but he held back, not out of diffidence, but an inbuilt sense of timing. He conferred with Elbert Smith and others. Smith gave him much encouragement, but did not close the door to his own candidacy, should circumstances warrant it.

That night, too, Witwer learned from the Cook County Democratic leader at the convention, Thomas Lyons, that Lyons would like to be selected as temporary president of the convention, and he would then support Witwer as permanent president. At that time, Witwer had no objection to such an arrangement if it would not result in a delay in the election of a permanent president. He had already learned that Dwight Friedrich, who could best be described as one of the gray eminences from downstate, David Davis, and perhaps others, were plotting for such postponement in order to take away some of the projected powers of the president or perhaps elect a person of their own choosing. It was at this point that Elmer Gertz, meeting Witwer for perhaps the first time, cautioned him against acceding to any arrangement which would give anyone else the temporary presidency. Gertz felt that this was only a ploy to get rid of Witwer. He, however, professed to be unworried.

At the orientation session, Louis Ancel explained the proposed rules of the convention in a way that justified a strong president with authority to appoint the committees and their chairmen. This caused considerable thought among the delegates on the subject of who would be able to wield such authority and in a manner that would enhance the chances of success at the convention. Some were skeptical that any convention could succeed in producing a salable product. All agreed there would be no chance of success unless the leadership were thoughtfully selected and with a broad base of support. This seemed to point to Witwer's low-key approach. In a shriller voice, John Knuppel continued to push his own candidacy, in marked contrast with Witwer's subdued, yet persistent, efforts.

Witwer felt more confident that he would be the ultimate choice when Mayor Daley telephoned him to say that he would have the support of the Daley organization. All the mayor wanted in return was complete fairness in the appointment of committees and their chairmen and in the management of the convention. He did not seek specific commitments of any kind, and Witwer gave none to him or others.

Thomas Lyons continued to press for the post of temporary president. Among several new arguments, he told Witwer that if he were not named it might look like a completely Republican affair. By now Witwer saw the dangers Gertz had spoken of and told Lyons and others that he definitely sought the temporary as well as the permanent presidency. He knew that from the beginning the presiding officer would have to be firm in order to prevent tampering with the rules and maneuvering for partisan purposes. Lyons still persisted in his personal ambition, despite Witwer's reassuring and unyielding arguments.

Some time before midnight of December 7, a delegation of independents and good government people, including Joan Anderson, Wayne Whalen, and Bernard Weisberg, asked to see Witwer. They were fearful that Witwer was "dealing" with the Daley organization. He learned, too, that some of the women delegates, led by Betty Howard, were so alarmed over this prospect that they were actually looking for a new candidate. The delegation sought to persuade Witwer that it was dangerous to deal with politicians and former officeholders, and that he ought to be as nearly nonpolitical and pristine pure as possible. Witwer reassured the group as to his good intentions, and they subsequently supported him for the presidency.

By 11:00 a.m. on December 8, Witwer learned that he would be the choice for both temporary and permanent president. Evidently Mayor

Daley, upon his arrival in Springfield, had told Lyons he ought to yield. When Witwer saw the mayor that morning, he was greeted very warmly and given every encouragement. Witwer could not help feeling that his firmness and fairness were winning the prize for him. He could not then know the pains he would experience in the actual performance of his duties.

The rules for electing the president were included in the enabling legislation that provided for the order of business at the convention. The governor was to call the first meeting to order and to perform various ceremonial tasks. Among these was the delivery of a speech and the installation of delegates, each to have his individual moment of glory with the aid of Secretary of State Paul Powell, the chief justice of the supreme court, Robert Underwood, and an official photographer. The governor was to proceed with the nominations for temporary president. First he recognized Delegate John Alexander, who moved to limit the number and length of nominating and secondary speeches. This was gladly accepted by the delegates and immediately honored in the breach by Joseph Meek, who placed Witwer in nomination with a very flavorful, if not florid, speech which ran much beyond the prescribed limits.

Betty Ann Keegan, a Democrat from Rockford who was later to demonstrate high qualities of leadership and character, seconded Witwer's nomination. William Fay, who later became chairman of the Judiciary Committee, and Joseph Tecson, who became chairman of the Executive Committee, made other seconding speeches for Witwer.

Three others were placed in nomination — David Davis and two Chicago blacks, Thomas Hunter and Leonard Foster. Hunter withdrew his name from consideration, declaring it "a great honor to one approaching the evening of his life."[1] Witwer received 88 votes, Davis 15, and Foster 10. Three members did not vote — Witwer himself, Father Lawlor, and Joseph Sharpe, who, moments previously, had suffered a mild heart attack. Finally, Witwer's election as temporary president was made unanimous on motion of Leonard Foster. The governor then handed the gavel over to Witwer, wishing him and the members of the convention the very best. What was to follow in the next nine months included much of the best and some of the worst of

[1]*Record of Proceedings, Sixth Illinois Constitutional Convention,* Vol. II, p. 12.

mankind, all characteristic of a free and open deliberative body in the heart of America.

As the newly elected temporary president of the convention walked down to the rostrum, David Davis, one of the defeated candidates, stepped forward and warmly congratulated Witwer. Applause came from the entire room. It seemed warm and friendly. In any case, Witwer needed to cherish it for there were to be many moments when there would be heat rather than warmth, unfriendliness rather than friendliness. He knew that such was the price he had to pay in an assembly of strong-willed persons, at least some of whom regarded themselves as superior to him and to their other new colleagues.

As Witwer went up the steps to the rostrum, he was greeted by Chief Justice Underwood and by a succession of four governors of the state — Stratton, Kerner, Shapiro, and Ogilvie. Only the most renowned, the late Adlai Stevenson, was missing. Witwer had worked closely with these governors and, particularly, with Stevenson in 1948, 1949, and 1950 as they strove to update the basic charter of the state. It was a moment for memory and pride.

In accepting his election as temporary president, Witwer spoke briefly and advised the delegates he would address them more fully a bit later. He expressed the hope that the applauding delegates would think as well of him in May as they apparently did in December.

Shortly thereafter, a younger delegate, Charles Shuman, son and namesake of the longtime leader of the state's agricultural community, asked to be recognized. Dwight Friedrich, who had the same purpose in mind, had yielded to him. Shuman wished to alter the order of business as set forth in the Enabling Act under which the delegates were assembled and business had been conducted thus far. He moved that the body next consider the number of vice-presidents the convention would have; the Enabling Act provided for only one. Witwer responded that pursuant to the Enabling Act, he would move immediately to the election of the permanent president. Shuman appealed the chair's ruling and lost on a voice vote. It is significant that thereafter, despite whatever opposition there was to him, Witwer's rulings were sustained on appeal in all instances but one. This firmness prevented the sort of chaos that might have resulted if the delegates, rather than the president, had been in the saddle in the general conduct of business. Witwer reflected the role of the delgates; he believed in majority rule. But he had self-respect, too, sometimes to the point of giving offense to those who chose not to like him.

Friedrich, who would contrive to plague the president and others who differed with him, asked the presiding officer if he would proceed with the election of other officers after the election of the permanent president. Davis, more courteous in manner but just as persistent as Friedrich, made the same inquiry. Witwer replied, almost orotundly: "It is the intention of the chair. . .to follow strictly the order of business prescribed in the Enabling Act unless this body as a deliberative body votes to changes that order of business. I have been appealed, the appeal has lost, and at this point the order of business before us is the election of a permanent president of this convention. I would now like to turn to that and receive nominations."[2]

Witwer was now careful to recognize first those who he knew would nominate him. He had struggled too long and too hard to be thwarted. Moreover, he knew that others also felt he had earned the honor.

Joseph Meek, who was often to play a ceremonial role thereafter, was recognized by Witwer. He declared that he wanted to "repeat my nomination from an hour ago of a gentleman named Samuel Witwer as permanent chairman of this convention so that we might get along with the business at hand."[3] Fortunately he did not repeat his overlong speech of the previous hour.

Odas Nicholson, a black woman lawyer from Chicago and a member in good standing of the Daley contingent, gave a gracious seconding speech, significant in that it showed that the Daley forces were honoring the mayor's commitment to Witwer. Miss Nicholson would often be heard from during the course of the convention —articulate, intelligent, eloquent, sometimes querulous, and generally effective. She and her faction would not always be so kindly disposed towards Witwer, especially when he offended the Cook County Democrats by his support of judicial merit selection.

Charles Shuman, the downstate farmer delegate, a Republican who had unsuccessfully appealed Witwer's ruling on the order of business, now arose to second Witwer's nomination. It was a gracious act, wholly characteristic of a publicly low-keyed man whose inner vehemence was often suppressed.

[2]Ibid., p. 13.
[3]Ibid., p. 13.

Paul Mathias, a quiet, gracious delegate from central Illinois, now moved to close the nominations. Witwer, feeling it inappropriate that he preside at this juncture, turned the gavel over to young Frank Cicero, the other delegate from his district. Cicero was one of the small band of independents destined to play a major role at the convention. Thomas Miller, a Republican from a Chicago suburb, seconded Mathias's motion to close nominations, which carried readily. Cicero directed a roll call for the election of the permanent president. The call was interrupted briefly when Dwight Friedrich sought to explain his vote and was ruled out of order by Cicero, who firmly repressed all efforts at deviation from the business at hand.

The vote was 107 for Witwer, with the remaining nine not voting. Modestly, Witwer himself had again refrained from voting. Joseph Sharpe was still absent because of his illness. Those who failed to vote for Witwer were an assorted lot: Father Lawlor and his district colleague, Louis Marolda, who almost invariably went along with him during the course of the convention; Wendell Durr, a downstate Democrat; Frank Stemberk, a Chicago Democrat; Samuel Martin and Charles Young, two downstate Republicans; and Maxine Wymore, a Republican who soon became a personal ally of Friedrich. It was at least mildly surprising that Stemberk, Wymore, and Young, who had voted for Witwer as temporary president, did not vote for him as permanent president. Marolda and Martin had been part of the small contingent that had voted for Davis for temporary president. And Davis had been a part of the even smaller group that had cast its vote for Foster.

After the roll call, the persistent Friedrich was permitted to explain his vote. He said that those who had their ears to the ground knew what was going to happen. The Witwer election had been arranged in what he implied was an unholy alliance with the Cook County Democrats, "Only a crumb would be fed to downstate." He further argued that "these same votes [sic] who can do this can also cause this convention and every committee of it to be dominated by Cook County. These same votes [sic] who have put together this arrangement can also decide every issue in this convention, including the recommendations to the people, every one of them."[4] He begged the cabal not to abuse

---

[4]Ibid., p. 15.

the power which they obviously had. He then went on to damn the United States Supreme Court which, he said, had spawned "our present dilemma . . . the one man-one vote decision. . . . If the [Court] had had to stand for election, we would probably still have law and order and state sovereignty which we don't have."

For the first of many times during the convention, Elmer Gertz rose to defend not only Witwer but also the openness and equality of the delegates. He said that this, and presumably no sinister forces, would prevail throughout the deliberations of the convention. Gertz declared:

> Those of us who looked eagerly to the election of Samuel Witwer as temporary and permanent president of this convention did so, not necessarily because we love Sam Witwer, but because we thought and think now that he is going to be the kind of presiding officer that Senator Friedrich says we want. We are 116 delegates. Each of us is equal in debate and in casting our votes. I don't think anyone has to have any fear that there is going to be a conspiracy or cabal. We are going to be a deliberative body, and each of us will do whatever we can to achieve success at this convention, even if it may mean at times overruling the chair. We welcome Sam Witwer and we know at the end of this convention we will feel about him as we do now.[5]

Frank Cicero now proclaimed Samuel W. Witwer president of the Sixth Illinois Constitutional Convention. The newly elected president spoke warmly but briefly. He would ask unanimous consent to make more formal and full remarks the next day. He appealed to the delegates for their help, their patience, their advice, and he thanked them for their vote. One could readily sense his joy and determination on this culminating moment that was in fact only a beginning of the larger task of the convention.

Witwer the Man

It is difficult to draw a portrait of Witwer in either broad or limited terms. He does not lend himself to glib generalization or hyperbole. Thus, many delegates assumed that he was a blue blood, a scion of upper-crust parents, nurtured in comfort. True, he went to good schools — Dickinson College and Harvard Law School — and he dresses with conservative tastefulness and is soft-spoken and well-

[5]Ibid., p. 15

mannered. But his parentage was working class, and he was born in Pueblo, Colorado, not in the Eastern establishment. He had to earn his way up. If he had achieved a comfortable level of living, with a fine home in affluent Kenilworth, it was not through inheritance, but by elevating himself through hard and persistent, not to say dogged work. He was a Republican, but not because of upper-class prejudices. There is little of the standpatter in him. He had readily accepted some of the supposedly liberal ideas of social welfare without ceasing to be acceptable to his conservative clients and associates. He arrived at his nonradical political philosophy by a process of thought, rather than through his purse.

These things alone would not have differentiated him from other non-New Deal delegates at the convention. To many colleagues he presented the image of a stuffed shirt, albeit in the words of George Braden, "a nice stuffed shirt." He seemed unable to unbend. He appeared to them stiff and formal, as if ordinary human contacts were distressing. Such, in fact, was far from the case. He was sensitive, sometimes too sensitive. He could be deeply hurt and troubled by slights and offensiveness, more so by ingratitude and disloyalty. By the same token, he was highly touched by thoughtfulness, expressions of esteem, evidence of loyalty. While he did not wear his heart on his sleeve, an observant person would have no difficulty in knowing when he was offended and when he was pleased, although he might say nothing in either case. He was often thin-skinned. The abuse that he sometimes received from the more raucous partisan delegates hurt him deeply, but he was almost equally upset by the lack of personal support on the part of the independents, who he felt owed much to him. He had given them greater representation in the leadership roles of the convention than their small numbers merited, but they were sometimes more unkind than those who owed little to him. He could not accept this, philosophically, as a fact of life. While it was not his wont to say anything publicly, deep down he resented the attitude of many such delegates.

To understand Witwer's role in the writing of the constitution, it is essential that one understand one central point: the writing of an excellent and acceptable constitution was the very most important thing to this man at this time; all else paled in comparison. Thus, he was committed to his responsibilities and, as a consequence, to an extraordinary work schedule that excluded almost everything else; while he was a Republican, he was not a Republican first, but rather a constitutional reformer; and, although he knew as much as anyone at the convention about the many issues under discussion, he carefully selected the ones that needed to be discussed fully.

Witwer's sense of responsibility was frequently misunderstood. At times, he seemed too serious. He could not appeal with a quip or loosen his reins with mock humor. All was seriousness. The team had to be controlled tightly. He was not flexible — although he was innovative — and he could not relax. This seriousness and inability to relax also extended to his relationship with individual delegates, but here it must be pointed out that he made a conscious decision early in the convention that he would not become a buddy of the delegates. He felt that familiarity outside the convention hall breeds contempt, and that if he went out in convivial activities with the delegates night after night, his leadership would not hold up and that he would be too tired to carry on his arduous tasks. He felt that it was better to succeed in the end than to be the popular toast of the crowd. He preferred instead to be around the convention hall tending to business, knowing that was how effective results would be achieved. He made the correct decision. For the most part he maintained his serious posture which sustained the strength of his leadership with those delegates who might otherwise not have respected his role and position.

As for his politics, there is little question that Witwer was a Republican. For the duration of the convention, however, partisan considerations were put on the back burner. Republicans at the convention, such as Charles Shuman and William Sommerschield, felt that as a Republican who had been favored in the past with the nomination of his party for the United States Senate, he ought to give leadership to the party at the convention through a regular caucus and other means. They declared that he was the only one who could give such leadership; no one else would have the necessary position and authority to do so. They claimed that this hiatus in leadership gave the Daley Democrats a dangerous advantage, although there were more Republicans than Democrats at the convention. Witwer insisted that, without destroying his party credentials, he had to be above partisan politics if he was to succeed in his historic task. He felt that if he took part in a party caucus, he would polarize the convention and lose his authority with the delegates where it was most necessary.

At the same time leaders of the Daley organization, like Lyons, Elward, and McCracken, sometimes ragged him unmercifully and undeservedly. Indeed, if they had been given real justification by reason of partisanship on his part, it would have made a shambles of the convention. Most of the issues were not really partisan. They pertained to the basic government of the state regardless of partisan politics. Witwer saw this and would not be diverted by the partisans of either camp, nor by the clamorous independents.

On some of the basic issues Witwer tried to exert behind-the-scenes leadership, more often than not succeeding, although he was seldom given credit for this. Now and then he spoke up on what he regarded as moral issues, such as opposition to capital punishment, support of fair employment and housing practices, opposing the sanctioning of guns. At such times he showed genuine fervor and determination. He did not hesitate to lobby for such just causes. He took part in the debate on judicial selection, but he was not willing to wreck the convention on this rock. He exerted influence on the revenue article, particularly with respect to real estate and personal property taxes. He was willing to constitutionalize real estate classification for the Cook County Democrats because he knew how both necessary and expedient it was. He played a role in the reapportionment question and in the amending process. He felt that if the right sort of amending article were achieved, the entire convention effort would be worthwhile despite other defects in the product. Above all, he was the principal and tireless battler for speeding up the work of the convention, sometimes standing alone and, in the end, having his way in this vital respect.

THE VICE PRESIDENTS AND CONVENTION SECRETARY

Several weeks before the convention convened, Witwer, in anticipation of his becoming the president, had decided that there would have to be more than one vice-president, although the Enabling Act provided for only one. He reasoned that if he, a Republican, became president the single vice-president would have to be a Democart and, like himself, would come from Cook County. This would create an imbalance in leadership that would be resented downstate and could readily imperil the work of the convention.

Thus, about a week before the delegates first met, Joseph Meek telephoned Witwer with the happy inspiration that Thomas Lyons, a Democrat from Chicago, and Elbert Smith, a Republican from Decatur, be chosen as vice-presidents. Both were men of reputation, experience, and ability, and would generally be acceptable to the political organizations, the delegates, and the public. Witwer expressed interest in the idea.

Shortly afterwards the suggestion was made that there be a third vice-president. Witwer's first thought was that there ought to be a woman from downstate, someone like Betty Ann Keegan, a Democrat from Rockford, whom everyone admired and liked. It soon became apparent that many, if not most, delegates preferred that the third vice-president be one of the younger delegates. John Alexander, a Republican from Virden, who had been an intern of Senator W. Russell Arrington, the Republican leader in the Senate, aspired to the position and did some electioneering. Alexander came to Witwer's room at the State House Inn where many of the delegates resided during the opening days of the convention, and urged Witwer to support him. This Witwer declined to do, saying that while he would not oppose Alexander, he would not involve himself in the contest. Witwer said that it would be inappropriate for him to campaign, however discreetly, for any vice-president.

Soon after his election as vice-president, Alexander suggested to Witwer that he thought it a good idea that he, Alexander, become a sort of ambassador-at-large to the young people of the state. He said he would visit the college campuses and bring tidings of good will from the convention. Witwer strongly dissented, telling Alexander that it was his duty to attend the convention as a delegate and vice-president, and not to absent himself. The relations between the two men were never good. Witwer turned over the gavel to Alexander now and then, although he preferred having Lyons or Smith in the chair during the times that he was not himself presiding. Witwer did not often absent himself from the convention, but sometimes his duties called for him to be out of the convention hall. At other times, he felt it would be an act of courtesy to let one of the vice-presidents preside. Smith presided with grace, humor, and judiciousness. He was very popular with the delegates and the public in this role. Certainly, he had a lighter touch than Witwer, who took his duties so seriously that he could not often relax. Lyons presided fairly and competently, but without Smith's pixie qualities. Alexander presided adequately, but did not participate actively in much of the work of the convention.

While it is clear that there was scarcely concealed resentment between Witwer and Alexander, it is not known if this resentment had an influence on Alexander's decision to oppose the adoption of the new constitution. The convention, as we shall see, gave opportunities for service and advancement to many delegates, young and old, but for whatever reason, Alexander was unable to take advantage of this opportunity.

With Lyons and Smith, Witwer's relations were generally cordial, despite their political differences and diverse personalities. Witwer felt he was dealing with men of essential good faith. It was not often that differences flared openly, except on divisive issues such as judicial selection.

The choice of a secretary for the convention was relatively simple. It was felt that women and blacks were underrepresented and that the Cook County Democratic organization had not received its fair share of official positions. The president and two of the vice-presidents were Republicans. Witwer was from outside Chicago while both Smith and Alexander were downstaters. It was only natural that someone from the Daley organization in Chicago be selected for the one remaining slot, and Odas Nicholson was selected as that person. Miss Nicholson was attractive, articulate, and determined. In the prescribed circumstance, she was as good a secretary as the delegates could have selected, whether black or white, male or female. She worked hard, did her job well, and made her presence known throughout the deliberations. From time to time, other duties were assigned to her, and she fulfilled those responsiblities as well. Occasionally, in the heat of the bitter controversy over judicial selection, she could be sharp-tongued and curt, but generally she conducted herself with grace. She was respected by all.

RULES OF THE GAME

When the Constitutional Study Commission sat down to draw up rules for the convention, it was faced by a dual challenge — to devise rules that would facilitate the creation of a functional and salable document, while at the same time allowing each delegate a sense of participation great enough to ensure identification with both the process and the result. Added to that was the necessity of presenting these rules in a way that would make even the more controversial among them palatable to all delegates. Commission members realized that a lengthy and divisive rules fight could delay the convention and rouse animosities which would plague the entire proceedings.

One of the principal goals was to break away from the procedures typical of the Illinois legislature — not just to provide a more deliberative, creative atmosphere, but also to avoid giving unfair advantage to those delegates skilled in manipulating parliamentary procedure. The commission drew from many sources: the rules and proceedings of past Illinois conventions as well as conventions held in other states over the past twenty years, a draft prepared by the Chicago Bar Association, the legislative experience of commission members, and material from students of the constitutional process throughout the country.

As the rules developed, it became apparent that some would be critical to the style and success of the convention. It was thought essential, for instance, that the convention presidency be a strong position, with power to appoint committee members and to select the officers of those committees. Furthermore, to encourage in-depth study of one subject area and avoid scheduling conflicts, the commission agreed to recommend that each member be appointed to only one substantive committee. As a counter-balance — to minimize resistance to this limitation — the commission recommended creation of a committee of the whole to discuss proposals brought up from the substantive committees; in this way every member would have the opportunity to discuss each substantive area in a relatively informal setting with unlimited debate and to propose amendments to committee proposals.

Early discussions revealed that some of the more sophisticated delegates were well aware of the implications of these key rules. Seventeen such delegates met in Springfield at the end of November to discuss the rules, structures, and procedures to be adopted by the convention. They questioned the wisdom of limiting delegates to one substantive committee arguing that it would tend to produce isolation and narrowness. They suggested membership on two committees, with an average of twenty-one members per committee — a size though unwieldy by the commission. While the majority seemed satisfied with the concept of a strong president, some suggested the system used in the Illinois Senate at that time — a Committee on Committees to handle appointments, subject to approval of the convention. There was also substantial support for allowing committee members to choose their own officers, even at the cost of some efficiency.

When Louis Ancel, chairman of the subcommittee on rules, presented the commission's "suggested draft" of rules to the delegates at the orientation session on December 6, it was obvious he was prepared to counter these objections before they were raised. Analogizing the convention to an orchestra, he said the commission had asked itself "how each delegate could play his part most effectively and still produce a harmonized composition." He explained that the commission members felt this purpose would best be accomplished by assigning each member to only one subject-matter committee while utilizing a committee of the whole for general debate. He noted the success of such a procedure in other conventions and stressed the importance of limiting each member to a manageable workload. With no overlap in committee membership, there would be no problem in securing attendance of the full membership without conflicts.

As to the president, Ancel went on, there must be a conductor who keeps the musicians working together toward a common goal. Stressing the differences between the convention and the legislature — its size, its nonpartisan nature, the severe time limit — he explained that the commission believed the delegates would select a fair, tactful, energetic, and knowledgeable president and that the convention would be best served by centralizing power in this individual. Such, he said, had been the experience in all recent successful conventions and the power had never been abused. Allowing the president to pick committees and committee officers tended to reduce polarization and conflict, especially in the early stages of the convention; it also freed the delegates early to turn to their main task. That power, Ancel noted, was balanced to some extent by the requirement that these appointments be subject to approval by the delegates as a body.

Other points of potential conflict were touched upon briefly. There had been no provision, for instance, for detailed financial disclosure by the delegates because of doubts as to its constitutional validity. The conflict of interest issue was also dealt with less thoroughly, since it was not considered as great a problem in the drafting of a constitution as in the creation of legislation; in the latter circumstance it might have a more immediate and special impact upon various interest groups. There was no provision for direct submission of proposals by the public, although private individuals would be able to present their suggestions to their delegates, appear before committees, and present petitions. No schedule for completion of the convention's work had been included, not because it was unnecessary, but because it was thought that dates could more appropriately be worked out by the president as the work progressed. The commission's recommendation that final action be taken by an ordinary majority of the members elected and serving was, according to Ancel, with one exception, the invariable practice of recent constitutional conventions. Requiring any greater majority, he stated, would bias the convention in advance toward the status quo.

During the afternoon of December 8, newly-elected convention president Witwer appointed a temporary rules committee with himself as chairman, James Kemp as vice-chairman and members Robert Canfield, David Davis, Paul Elward, Anne Evans, John Karns, Thomas McCracken, John Parkhurst, Elbert Smith, Bernard Weisberg. The committee was fairly united on the proposal it returned to the convention on December 16. Moreover, that proposal differed only slightly from the "suggested draft" produced by the Constitutional Study Commission. The number of vice-presidents had been raised from two to three; there had been a slight adjustment in proposed committee membership and, in addition, a public information committee had been added to the group of procedural committees; it was also suggested that each member proposal be required to appear on the relevant committee's agenda at least once; motions to reconsider had been made somewhat more available; a deadline for submission of member proposals had been inserted; and the right to explain one's vote had been added to the rule on recognition during roll call. The only close vote on what might be considered a critical rule was the six-to-five decision to give the president power to appoint committee members. Weisberg had moved to establish a nominating committee;

his proposal failed only when Witwer, already convention president, broke the tie in favor of granting himself this power.

During the convention itself the most striking feature on the debate on rules was the extent to which the delegates lingered and stalled on those matters the study commission had considered least important, and skimmed over those thought most important. The concept of a powerful presidency carried without discussion after Paul Elward, who had earlier expressed hostility to this idea, rose to withdraw his objections and compliment Witwer on the manner in which he had conducted himself throughout the temporary rules committee hearings and his fairness in assigning membership to that committee. The rule limiting each delegate to membership on only one substantive committee likewise passed without discussion. Final passage of the proposed constitution by a simple majority also passed without discussion. The many variations and adaptations on Robert's *Rules of Order,* which made the convention a different species from the legislature and allowed unlimited debate in the committee of the whole, were discussed only briefly and with little heat.

Yet, consideration of the rules — which began December 16 — was not ended until January 22, occupies some two hundred pages of the transcript, and eventually revealed the beginnings of rifts which often seemed like chasms by the end of the convention. If the important rules slipped by unnoticed, how did the convention expend so much time and energy in this area? The answer at first seems obvious: they must have been discussing unimportant rules. But, of course, what is "unimportant" is a matter of opinion; debate over seemingly insignificant rules in fact often revealed significant philosophical differences.

The first rule to provoke significant debate was Rule 15, dealing with the procedural committees. George Lewis proposed a fourth procedural committee to serve as liaison with the three principal branches of government. He argued that such liaison was just as crucial as public relations or information, but freely admitted that he had a special interest in finding an outlet for constituent suggestions — a place to which he could refer those suggestions considered inappropriate for inclusion in a constitution without simply telling the folks back home their ideas were not usable. Joseph Meek echoed Lewis and added that the committee could serve a screening function for proposals that might otherwise endlessly clog the business of the convention. Peter Tomei and Parkhurst countered that the convention structure was already capable of screening irrelevant proposals, and Frank Cicero called the proposal a threat to the right of the substantive committees to decide for themselves what was proper for inclusion and what was legislative detail. There was further discussion reflecting a concern that the convention keep itself isolated from the other branches of government; the delegates clearly thought, especially early in the convention, that theirs was a special mission best unsullied by too much contact with the politics-as-usual world of the legislature. Lewis's motion failed.

The proposed Rule 21 touched off a flurry of concern over what constituted adequate notice of committee meetings. The maverick Father Francis Lawlor, a political novice and one of the earliest members to express from the floor his fear of being steamrolled by the efficient Cook County organization, pushed for specific mailed notices of each meeting. His concern was shared by Lewis Wilson of Moline, who proposed similar changes. Both motions were ultimately defeated and the rules committee proposal, which depended primarily on posting notices, passed. However, the fear of Cook County had manifested itself in the rules discussion. When Rule 48, proposing a February deadline for member proposals, came up, Lawlor voiced the fear in his speech: "I think, considering the vast body of material that we are attempting to cover in a state constitution, that there should be some sufficient time allowed where you may have the opportunity to look into the findings of other committees — their proposals — to examine them and to convince yourself whether or not you might want to add something to that or let it stand as is. I think all of you are going to be amazed at the efficiency of the Cook County machine."[6]

A proposal for extending the deadline to March 15 was nevertheless defeated after Parkhurst and Elward argued that the delegates must have a deadline to push them to begin working over the Christmas holidays. Tomei also called for an early deadline, urging the delegates to resist the impulse to push through ego-oriented proposals and turn their efforts instead toward the teamwork required to fuel the committees and keep them running smoothly. The rule was ultimately adopted but only after the deadline had been extended to a compromise date, March 3.

[6]Ibid., p. 96.

Discussion of Rules 31 and 45, concerning motions to reconsider in the convention and in the committee of the whole, produced one of the few restrictions on debate added on the floor of the convention. The committee had recommended a rule allowing any member to move for reconsideration, but the words "who voted on the prevailing side" were inserted to qualify "member" in Rule 45 and assumed by implication to carry back to Rule 31. The only other noteworthy restriction on debate added on the floor was Elmer Gertz's amendment to Rule 58, limiting individual speeches in convention sessions to ten minutes instead of fifteen. Later Gertz said that he thought it would have been even better to have limited debate to five minutes so as to school the delegates in economy of phrasing.

By contrast, Rule 53, allowing the convention to limit debate by majority vote, was modified on Bernard Weisberg's motion to provide "that any member who shall not have had an opportunity to speak on the pending matter prior to the completion of debate which has been limited in accordance with this rule shall be entitled, upon request, notwithstanding such limit, to speak for not more than five minutes."[7] It was clear throughout the rules discussion that even those concerned with keeping the convention on schedule feared a stifling of debate more than they feared delay.

Whatever discussion the rules governing structure and conduct of the convention provoked, was insignificant compared to the controversy touched off by the rules governing expulsion from the convention, conduct of lobbyists, and financial disclosure by the members themselves. These rules, which, as it turned out, had little significance after passage, were the hang-up which delayed final passage of rules until January 22.

Rules 60 and what was initially numbered 61, dealt with the convention's right to police its own membership and punish or expel members engaging in disrespectful or contemptuous behavior. Discussion was heated between those who hesitated to interfere with anyone's right to vote, especially on a long-term basis (among them Peter Tomei and Arthur Lennon), and those who repeatedly assured the convention they had the highest confidence in the quality of the delegates, yet resisted giving up the convention's right to police itself

[7]Ibid., p. 98.

(including Frank Cicero, Leonard Foster, and David Davis). The issue was resolved by deleting Rule 61, providing for expulsion, and all references to expulsion in Rule 60. The idea was apparently to leave *Robert's Rules* on expulsion although the question never arose during the life of the convention.

With the deletion of the original Rule 61, what had been Rule 62 dealing with registration of lobbyists, moved into the spotlight and became the new number 61. The temporary rules committee had originally recommended a simple statement that persons subject to the Constitutional Convention Lobbyists Registration Act passed by the legislature must comply with the provisions of that act. When the rule was brought up for discussion on January 7, however, it had been rewritten by the permanent rules committee and contained additional requirements not included in the legislative act — among them a requirement that those affected must file copies of their reports with the secretary of the convention as well as the secretary of state, and that they report to the secretary of the convention all expenditures over $200 on behalf of delegates allowed by the Registration Act. This new section, which exempted purchase of tickets to certain campaign events such as golf days and dinners, and expenditures toward special purpose days to honor or promote candidacies, was highly unlikely to have any relevance at all to the convention, as became apparent rather early in the debate on this rule. Nevertheless, there was an outcry against what some delegates, who had apparently not read the Registration Act, saw as a condonation of bribery. Robert Canfield of Rockford objected to "saying that a lobbyist can hand out up to $200 to any individual."[8] Elward expressed concern that the rule, as submitted, did not extend coverage to groups unless there was direct contact with a member; he cautioned that large groups could form under meaningless titles and attempt to sway public opinion without ever contacting a single delegate. His arguments, however, were lost in the outburst of indignation at any rule which seemingly required private citizens to register before contacting their delegates. Dwight Friedrich received applause for saying, "I think when we start putting the clamps on people and discouraging them from speaking out on the business of self-government, we are going in the wrong direction."[9]

[8]Ibid., pp. 144-145.
[9]Ibid., p. 145.

Weisberg also expressed concern that the rule was too broad and might mean that a group "as a condition of lawfully engaging in public discussion would have to register with the secretary of state."[10] Lester Buford drew an ovation by rising to call for an end to haranguing so that the body could "get on with the business of the convention."[11] Shortly after his speech, the convention did pass the rule as originally proposed, providing simply for compliance with the Lobbyists Registration Act. If Buford had hoped that termination of the argument over lobbyist registration would mean a quick progression to the main business of the convention, he was sadly mistaken. Buford, who was tempermentally allergic to battling over trifles, would have similar experiences throughout the convention.

On January 8 the convention turned to Rule 62, which had appeared in the original committee draft as a simple requirement that a member who had "a personal or private interest" in any proposal should so disclose. When introduced on the floor, this rule had been amended by the permanent rules committee on a vote of nine to three (with one abstention), to provide for a rather detailed disclosure of solely economic interest. Davis, the vice-chairman of the rules committee, introduced the proposal but declined to speak on its behalf; instead, he yielded the floor to Elward, whose name became synonomous with the proposal for detailed disclosure. Elward argued that the convention must take action in regard to disclosure if it expected to be able to deal with that problem in regard to the three regular branches of government within the constitution itself.

Discussion of the Elward proposal was interrupted by William Fay's motion to substitute for the rules committee language, the language of the original proposal by the temporary rules committee, calling simply for disclosure of personal or private business interests in pending matters. David Connor suggested adding to the Fay language, so that the rule would read, "Any member who had a significant personal or private interest, economic or otherwise, shall disclose that fact to the convention." His wording was accepted by Fay and this version became known as the Fay/Connor proposal. The Fay/Connor substitution passed on a roll call vote, 62 for, 49 against, 1 voting present. Elward immediately attempted to introduce what he called

[10]Ibid., p. 151.
[11]Ibid., p. 152.

Rule 62A, which was simply the text of his version of Rule 62. The chair ruled this out of order.

When the convention reconvened on January 13, Witwer explained his position on the status of Rule 62. He ruled that the body had voted to substitute the Fay/Connor language for the Elward language, but had never voted on whether to adopt what was then the main motion, that is, the Fay/Connor language. This ruling provoked anger and confusion, but Witwer stuck to it. Netsch attempted at this point to combine the two proposals, but her motion was ruled out of order. Parkhurst appealed Witwer's ruling on the appropriateness of the Netsch amendment, but the body sustained Witwer. When it came to a vote, the Fay/Connor proposal was defeated 54-58.

When it looked as though the Elward/Fay/Connor language might pass, Friedrich moved to add language barring any member from accepting compensation for services as a member of the convention if that member was also being paid for services as an employee or officer of the state or any subdivision thereof or any municipal or tax-supported institution. The proposal apparently had the desired effect; though a motion to re-refer the entire discussion of disclosure to the rules committee had failed repeatedly in the earlier parts of the debate, a like motion immediately passed.

When the rules committee came back with its next report on Rule 62 on January 22, two important changes had been made. Although the language was still basically that of the Elward proposal, the number of reports had been cut down from bimonthly to once and the requirement to file a list of persons and entities [which need be described only by type of activity in which they engage] to whom the member has furnished compensated services valued at more than $1,000 during the twelve-month period prior to the filing of the statement, had been eliminated. This language had been considered especially objectionable with respect to lawyers and their clients because of the traditional secrecy of the lawyer-client relationship.

By common consent, the word "statement" was substituted for the word "disclosure" throughout this version on motion of Stanley Johnson, who said: "I would hate for us in the constitution to provide for full disclosure of the economic or financial interests and then in later years have someone come back to see what this Convention adopted for itself under the banner of disclosure and come to the conclusion that that was what we had in mind."[12] Meek called the proposal "tyranny of the majority" and Friedrich termed it an insult to the members. Nevertheless, it passed with minor changes and became the rule of the convention. Delegates were to ignore it; it was virtually never to be mentioned again; yet it had occupied a major part of the convention's debate for three days while the main business of the convention stood in abeyance.

One of the Democratic leaders confided to Gertz that he had gone along with Elward only because Elward was so attached to his idea. He personally thought them unimportant. How many were similarly motivated, one could not know with any certainty.

[12]Ibid., p. 259.

IV

The President Takes Charge

When the Sixth Illinois Constitutional Convention convened on December 8, 1969, it was indeed a body *de novo*. It was required to begin its deliberations immediately, but a good deal remained to be done before the convention could be fully operable. Fortunately the constitution study commissions had done preparatory work unequaled for any other state convention. Nonetheless following his election, the president had little time to reflect on his victory; he had to set about the difficult and important tasks of appointing committee members and a convention staff as well as establishing an acceptable work schedule. The manner and speed with which he accomplished this would have a profound impact on the success of the convention and its work product.

THE COMMITTEE CONTROVERSY

When Witwer delivered his inaugural address on the second day of the convention, he laid down, in his always meticulous fashion, his blueprint for leadership as convention president. The address contained numerous points which were to become prophetic as key elements for a successful convention. Perhaps none was as profound, however, as Witwer's proposed framework for the appointment of members to the committees and to the important positions of committee chairmen. The president stated, "I shall strive for appointment of balanced and representative committees which will be free from domination by any interest group, faction or party.""[1] He was committed to a committee process that would be as open as possible, and he was determined not to "load" any committee to attain a preconceived result. Similarly, he was not inclined to appoint anyone as chairman who had a prior special interest in the work of that committee or who would be a "special pleader" for a particular cause. His address was a pledge to the selection of persons who would be representative in terms of partisan identification, geographical distribution, race, age, and sex. While Witwer was correct in anticipating the importance of the committee appointments, even he could not have anticipated the difficulty of the task, nor the long-term impact it would have on the workings of the convention and on the interpersonal relationships between him and the delegates.

The final number and subject matter of the convention's committees largely followed the recommendation of the Constitution Study Commission, which in turn had drawn on the experience of recent conventions in other states (primarily Maryland) and the 1920 Illinois Constitutional Convention. The Illinois delegates settled on nine substantive and three procedural committees through which to conduct their business. By convention rule, the makeup of the committees was as follows:

Substantive Standing Committees	*Members*
Committee on Bill of Rights	15
Committee on the Legislature	11
Committee on the Executive	11
Committee on the Judiciary	11
Committee on Revenue and Finance	18
Committee on Suffrage and Constitutional Amendment	9
Committee on Local Government	15
Committee on Education	11
Committee on General Government	11
	112

Procedural Standing Committees	
Committee on Rules and Credentials	11
Committee on Style, Drafting and Submission	11
Committee on Public Information	8
	30

[1]*Record of Proceedings, Sixth Illinois Constitutional Convention,* Vol. II, p. 32.

In addition to the criterion of balance that Witwer imposed upon himself, the rules of the convention contained additional requirements that further complicated Witwer's already cumbersome task. Each committee was to have a chairman and vice-chairman (except the committee on rules and credentials on which the president was required to serve as chairman); each member, except the president and three vice-presidents, was to be appointed to only one substantive standing committee; and the committee on style, drafting and submission was to be composed of at least one member from each substantive standing committee. The president was an ex efficio member of all procedural committees. Each of the vice-presidents was a nonvoting ex officio member of those substantive standing committees to which he was assigned by the president. This was for the purpose of achieving a kind of overall, loosely structured supervision. It was not intended to tie the hands of the leadership of the committee members and leadership.

The three vice-presidents were voting members of the three procedural standing committees. Vice-President Smith was assigned the Bill of Rights Committee, and to the committees on local government and general government. Witwer assigned Vice-President Lyons to the Revenue and Finance Committee, Executive Committee, and the Committee on the Legislature. Vice-President Alexander was given assignment to the Suffrage and Constitutional Amendment Committee, the Education Committee, and the Judiciary Committee. As it turned out, the vice-presidents held these supervisory duties lightly, possibly more lightly than they should have.

Witwer, then, had 160 appointments to make — 112 members to the nine substantive committees, 30 members to the three procedural committees (the rules actually placed no limit on the member appointments to the Style, Drafting and Submission Committee or the Public Information Committee), 17 committee chairmen and vice-chairmen, and nine vice-presidential appointments ex officio to the procedural committees. Each of the appointments was to be made by the president "after consultation with the vice-presidents," and all required majority approval of the members of the convention.

The ultimate responsibility, however, rested solely with the president; this had been a significant factor in the Constitution Study Commission's decision to recommend a strong executive. This presidential responsibility was challenged by several delegates who sought to have the appointments made by a committee on committees. Although ultimately unsuccessful, the effort generated strong initial support. It was led by Dwight Friedrich of Centralia and aided by Paul Elward of Chicago, both men of exigent personality. The proposal received considerable attention during the week-long recess while the Temporary Rules Committee was in session. When the committee recessed for the weekend, the outcome of the vote was uncertain. At that time it appeared that the Cook County Democrats would support the concept of a Committee on Committees; however, early proponent Elward underwent a change of heart, probably goaded by his fellow members of the Democratic organization, and he withheld his support when the committee reconvened on Monday morning. Even so, newly-elected President Witwer, who had appointed himself chairman of the Temporary Rules Committee, had to cast the dramatic tie-breaking vote to enable the committee to recommend 6 to 5 that the president be given sole right of appointment of committee members and chairmen. With that vote, the battle was won and there was little chance of reversal on the floor of the convention.

Delegate Elward set the tone when he rose at the initial presentation of the proposed rules on December 16, 1969 to explain his reversal "so that no one may be taken by surprise." He continued:

> . . . after consultation with a great many delegates from all parts of this state and all different groups and after reflecting further on the wisdom of the action of the Rules Committee and the debate that took place there last week on this subject, I do not — I repeat, I do not — intend to pursue the matter of a Committee on Committees on the floor of this house; and I intend to cast my vote in favor of giving the president the power to appoint not only chairmen and vice-chairmen but members of the committee as well.
>
> I am persuaded to this point of view, Mr. President and my fellow delegates, by a number of factors, not the least of which is the manner in which the Chair has conducted itself throughout lengthy Rules Committee hearings as well as the fairness in assigning membership on the Rules Committee to the different groups and sections which exist in the Convention of necessity.[2]

[2]Ibid., p. 50.

Elward's remarks were received with considerable applause from the delegates and were graciously accepted by Witwer who reaffirmed his intention to be as impartial as possible in making the appointments. Seldom thereafter was Elward as judicious and generous in his appraisal of the president. Witwer did exercise his stated goal of balance in making the Temporary Rules Committee apointments, and he did show considerable objectivity in presiding over the ofttimes strained meetings while the proposed rules were debated, but it was unlikely that this alone altered the position of the veteran and sometimes contentious Elward on so crucial an issue. It was also possible that those who were appointed from Chicago underscored, for Elward, Witwer's pledge to be fair with the Chicago Democratic organization, and that their chances of fair treatment were better with one strong executive than with a committee made up largely of downstate delegates (because they had the numbers and, therefore, the votes) who would be tempted to curb the power of their Chicago counterparts.

The significance of this early procedural battle should not be taken lightly, for it was one of the first of a series of "turning points" in the convention. For one thing, it served to crystallize the question of a strong executive to lead the convention. For another, it is clear that a different result should have had considerable consequences, possibly requiring weeks to complete the selections; then too, the mood and atmosphere of the convention might have altered from one of openness and independence to one of political partisan dealing. It is not an overstatement to say that had the concept of a committee on committees prevailed, the same type of delays and polarizations could have developed that ultimately led to the debacle of the 1920-22 Illinois Constitutional Convention. Undoubtedly, many who came to the convention from the legislature or other positions of political power were reluctant to give up accustomed power without at least a test of strength. The president's position, however, survived that test, and with the adoption of the total rules the concept of a strong executive with the power to lead became a reality. There would be countless battles over procedure and substance, as would be expected in a deliberative body of this nature, but aside from a weak attempt to censure the president for his open confrontation with Friedrich over the latter's assertion that Rubin Cohn was acting as a lobbyist and not as a staff member, and some restlessness over the Gardner nonspeech, there was no further effort to undercut the president's authority. He might, at times, be treated rudely or disdainfully, but his powers remained undiminished.

Once his authority to make the committee appointments was established, Witwer preceded with the arduous task of putting all the appointment pieces together. He had asked the delegates to give him an informal indication of their first, second, and third committee preferences, not as a firm guide for appointment, but to indicate where their interests lay. Witwer may well have had in mind the recent defeat of other proposed state constitutions where delegate preference at the convention was the basis for committee assignments. In Maryland, for instance, upwards of 70 percent of the convention members received their first choice, with the remainder receiving their second choice. Delegate David Linn brought this to the attention of the Illinois delegates and suggested that Witwer's intention of relying on other criteria as well was a good omen, since Maryland's product was defeated at the polls.

Even if it had been Witwer's desire to make appointments to the committees based on delegate preference, the uneven distribution of the requests would not have allowed him to do so. The first, second, and third choice breakdown was as follows:

Committee	First	Second	Third	Fourth
Local Government	25	25	12	62
Revenue and Finance	28	8	13	41
Judiciary	15	17	16	48
Legislative	12	17	15	44
Executive	4	10	7	26
Bill of Rights	6	6	7	19
General Government	6	7	12	25
Education	5	7	9	21
Suffrage and Amendments	1	3	5	8

Fifty-three, or nearly half, of the 112 delegates to be appointed to the nine substantive committees had a first preference for the thirty-three positions on either the Local Government Committee or the Revenue and Finance Committee. That alone meant twenty members would not receive their first choice. Eighty expressed a first preference for only four of the committees — Local Government, Revenue and Finance, Judiciary, and Legislative. The remaining five committees —Executive, Bill of Rights, General Government, Education, and Suffrage and Amendments — drew only twenty-two delegates as a first preference. Just one delegate, Peter Tomei, wanted the evidently unpopular Committee on Suffrage and Amendments as his first choice; only eight listed it as any preference at all, one short of the required nine to be appointed to that committee. While not requested to do so by the president, several delegates took the opportunity to make their bid for a particular procedural committee or for a much coveted committee chairmanship.

A review of the preference does not reveal any significant pattern when party or geographical distribution is considered; in other words, there was no evident attempt to spread preferences among politically or geographically identified groups. In general, the delegates were operating more from the standpoint of their own interests and backgrounds, and possibly from statements they had made during their campaigns. Taxes, home rule, judicial selection, and the legislature were the most visible issues during the campaign. However, state aid to private and parochial schools received considerable campaign attention.

While Witwer was not attempting to turn the convention into one in which party would be the controlling factor, he did correctly recognize the need for partisan balance on the committees. It was necessary to insure adequate representation for Cook County without allowing members from that area to dominate the committee structure. Downstate Democrats, jealous of Cook County's rule of the party and seeming rule of the state, had to be appeased, and, of course, the substantial Republican contingent, though not a cohesive bloc, could not be overlooked as a significant part of the convention's makeup. Appeasing the independents, while just as necessary, often turned out to be as useful as it was demanding, since they took on something of a "wild card" status in the dealing of committee assignments. The independents were not only independent of the parties, but often independent of each other.

However, since the delegates were elected on a nonpartisan basis, the simple determination of their party preference proved difficult in many instances. The convention had been convened for little more than a week when Witwer first started dealing with these matters, which imposed some limitation on attempts to judge its precise party composition. Moreover, Witwer had not yet had a chance to meet or talk with many of the delegates. As an alternative, he had to rely on the convention's early and limited voting record, the biographies published in the secretary of state's convention handbook, and, at times, simple gossip to determine individual delegate party preference. At this point, Witwer classified the delegates (excluding the president and vice-presidents) as thirty-two Cook County Democrats, thirteen downstate Democrats, forty-nine Republicans, and thirteen independents. He had difficulty, initially, in classifying five delegates — two (Foster and Anderson) because they did not seem to fit into even the loosely defined groups being used for identification, and three (C. Parker, Green, and Kenney) because he had no reliable information upon which to categorize them. Four of the five eventually were correctly identified as Republicans; Foster remained in a category all his own, although nominally a Democrat.

The three vice-presidents played markedly different consultant roles in making the selections. Witwer met with Lyons in Chicago on a number of occasions, talked frequently with Smith by telephone, and had at least one lengthy meeting with him in Chicago. The president spoke with Alexander several times over the telephone, but the vice-president was unable to journey to Chicago because of the need to tend the family business in Virden. In any case, the conversations between them were less than satisfactory, due in no small part to different interpretations of the term "consultation." Lyons and Smith recognized that the ultimate decision rested with Witwer; Alexander felt that consultation afforded him the right of certain unilateral selections. Lyons did not attempt overtly to veto any of Witwer's selections; some disagreement did arise over Lyons' strong feeling that some delegates Witwer described as "Democrats" could not qualify as such. Lyons argued that independent Democrats and Democrats from downstate were not to count in determining the proportionate representation that Witwer sought. This was particularly argued over with regard to the chairmanship appointments, with Witwer holding fast to the position that Messrs. Gertz, Karns, and Lewis were to be viewed as Democratic allotments. Witwer finally yielded to the extent that he characterized Gertz as an independent. During the first week of the recess, Witwer concentrated on the chairmanships. In subsequent weeks, he applied the same criteria to the total makeup of the committees.

Chairmanships

As soon as he had begun the task of appointing the chairmen and vice-chairmen, Witwer began to see the difficulty he faced. He received numerous letters and telephone calls from delegates who felt they were qualified for the leadership positions and demonstrated no reluctance to ask for the jobs. Witwer had promised to complete the appointments prior to the reconvening of the convention on January 6, 1970. His effort was further complicated and delayed by "pressure" from outside the convention. There were some who felt that they, too, had a right to participate in the selection process.

In an article appearing in the *Chicago Tribune* on December 21, 1969, it became evident that this influential newspaper was expecting Maurice W. Scott of Springfield, executive vice-president of the Illinois Taxpayers Federation, to be named chairman of the Committee on Revenue and Finance. The *Tribune*, Scott, and his many supporters would be disappointed. Witwer knew Scott to be an excellent man with a vast knowledge of taxation and one who would be a strong member of this committee. But to appoint him chairman was sharply counter to Witwer's intent not to place in the chairmanships persons who held hard and fast positions on the issues for which they were to provide leadership. Similarly, Lyons and the Chicago Democratic organization proposed McCracken as chairman of the coveted Revenue and Finance Committee. McCracken was as unacceptable as Scott. McCracken, while recognized by the president as a first-rate tax lawyer, was almost a full-time counsel to "Parky" Cullerton, county assessor of Cook County and a powerhouse in the regular Democratic organization.

During their December 23 and 24 meetings, Witwer and Lyons hammered out the percentage of chairmanships, vice-chairmanships, and members that would constitute a proportionate share of appointments for the Democrats. Rather than quibble over the precise percentage between 36-40 percent, Witwer felt it more important at the outset to reassure the Democrats, who were unquestionably in a minority, that they were receiving fair play, even if the "portion" of a chairmanship had to be resolved in favor of the Democrats. Lyons did not propose any black members as chairmen, nor did he initially propose any downstate Democrats for the leadership positions. In fact, he proposed downstate chairmen only after Witwer insisted that they had to be afforded proportionate representation in the appointments as part of the total number allowed the Democrats. Lyons, for his own part, insisted that Witwer could not claim any chairmanships awarded to Dawn Clark Netsch, Wayne Whalen, Frank Cicero, Peter Tomei, or Elmer Gertz, as being in the Democratic column, for these were independents who had defeated Cook County Democratic organization candidates in the elections.

While all of this relatively public activity was going on, there was also a good deal of behind-the-scenes action. Witwer consulted not only Richard Lockhart, who had an unusual knowledge of political and public personalities and fine judgment as well, he also worked with old and knowledgeable friends whom he liked and trusted, men like Louis Ancel and Alan Jacobs.

On December 28, Witwer telephoned all of the proposed chairmen and invited them to come to Chicago for a press conference on Tuesday, December 30. He also telephoned some of the vice-chairmen, such as James Kemp and Charles Coleman, Chicago blacks, who were members of the Democratic organization. At the time they did not object to those appointments. Witwer was unable to reach Robert Canfield of Rockford, reported to be skiing in New England. Nor could he reach Mrs. Netsch, who was in Jamaica. She had called earlier to express great displeasure at Witwer's failure to name her as chairman of one of his committees. She then cabled him to insist upon a chairmanship. Witwer recognized her outstanding ability, but he found her to be unacceptable to the Democratic organization and to many Republicans as well. In the circumstances, she had to regard herself as fortunate in being made vice-chairman of such a major committee as Revenue and Finance. It did not, in the least, daunt her willingness to express herself vigorously at all times and, as we shall see, she became a driving force in the convention.

On December 29, at about 2 p.m., Witwer received a telephone call from James Kemp, stating that he and three other black delegates, all organization Democrats, desired to call upon him to discuss their disappointment at his failure to name one or more of them as a chairman of one of his committees. Witwer declared that the problem was basically an internal one within the Democratic Party. He advised them to discuss the matter with Lyons. Kemp replied that this had been done, but nothing had come of it. Witwer thereupon told Kemp that he and his associates should come to Witwer's office and that he would invite Lyons to be there also. Kemp, Patch, Hunter and Coleman, the members of the black delegation, arrived at Witwer's office almost immediately. They forthrightly expressed their irritation, if not anger. They said at a meeting of a black caucus, of which more would be heard, it had been agreed that there had to be at least one black chairman. They had told Lyons of this some days previously. Witwer assured them that he had not heard of this nor had Lyons suggested to him the appointment of a black as one of the allotted Democratic chairmen. Since Lyons had not yet arrived at this point, Witwer telephoned him again, and Lyons said he would come to the office at once. This he did, accompanied by Elward. The two, Lyons and Elward, conferred with the blacks for almost an hour, while Witwer attended to other business. At about 4 p.m., Witwer was told that the group was stalemated. They wanted Witwer to drop one of the independents or a Republican in order to make way for at least one black chairman. Witwer said that he would not be put in the middle. They would have to resolve their own differences, perhaps by dropping David Stahl as chairman of the Committee on Public Information and giving a place instead to a black. Witwer made it clear that he would make a public announcement of his appointments on the following day. Lyons told him to call if he had a change of mind, apparently feeling that Witwer, confronted with a black and white issue, would yield out of expediency. But Witwer remained firm. Lyons spent the entire evening at his ward headquarters expecting Witwer's call of concession. Witwer felt secure in his decision because no one could properly charge him with prejudice. He had been on the Board of the Chicago Urban League for years, and his race relations record had been consistently good.

The next morning, at 10 a.m., the announced press conference took place at the State of Illinois Building in Chicago. Just before its start, Lyons again asked Witwer if he had changed his mind about a black appointment. Witwer remained firm. Kemp and Coleman were there and were introduced and photographed with the other chairmen and vice-chairmen. Witwer felt the press conference went well, except that Frank Maier, a reporter for the *Chicago Daily News*, complained that his newspaper had been scooped by a rival newspaper, *Chicago Today*, in the revelation of the names. Witwer could only guess about who was to blame for the unwarranted "leak." He was sure it was not his press agency. He surmised it was one of the ten informed delegates who probably had a penchant for giving "scoops" if he could personally gain in the process.

In general, Witwer was pleased by what seemed to be the general reaction to the committee leadership announcement. But the next day he received a telephone call from Louis Ancel, one of his close associates in the earlier discussion on appointments. Ancel was deeply concerned about a call he had received from Carl Wiegman, chief editorial writer of the *Chicago Tribune*. Wiegman stated that the *Tribune* could not understand what had possessed Witwer in making some of the appointments, particularly those of Elmer Gertz, John Karns, and Joseph Tecson. Ancel thought it urgent that Witwer call Wiegman and discuss the matter with him. After all, the good will of the *Tribune* might be essential at some future time. Witwer called and suggested a meeting, while making it clear that he regarded his appointees as good men and women. Wiegman suggested that Clayton Kirkpatrick, editor of the *Tribune* might sit in on such a meeting. This in itself indicated the importance the *Tribune* attached to the matter. At 2 p.m. that day, Witwer was scheduled to meet with Wiegman and Kirkpatrick in the latter's office. When he arrived, he found that not only Wiegman and Kirkpatrick were present, but George Tagge, long-time political editor for the paper, and John Elmer, the *Tribune's* convention correspondent, as well.

Witwer did not particularly care to discuss the reasons for his appointment in the presence of Tagge and Elmer. The former had been persistently an opponent of constitutional revision over a period of more than twenty years, and had been hostile to Witwer during that time. Witwer made it clear that he was not going to apologize for his appointments, although he would be glad to explain his reasons for making them. If the *Tribune* had any questions, he would try to answer them. It quickly became apparent that Tagge and Elmer were chiefly opposed to the appointment of Elmer Gertz as chairman of the Bill of Rights Committee. Apparently Gertz had been too liberal for the

Tribune in years past (although they often had consulted with him when he was a leader in the housing movement and when he had represented Nathan Leopold in the effort to get him out of prison). Besides, Gertz had written a book in which he was critical of the *Tribune*. Actually, Gertz had not only written an unpublished book, but a long and widely circulated pamphlet called *The People vs. The Chicago Tribune*, as well as other writings critical of the *Tribune* in the era of Colonel McCormick. Witwer opined that Gertz was essentially a classicist in civil rights and liberties and would make a good chairman. George Tagge responded that it was laughable to refer to Gertz as a civil liberties classicist.

Tagge then attacked Karns, indicating that Karns had no knowledge of revenue. He asked on what conceivable grounds Karns could be named as a chairman of so important a committee. Witwer said that, frankly, he wanted the chairmanship to go to a Democrat to balance the appointments of Republicans, and Karns was the best of those available. Tagge insisted that Maurice Scott would have been much better — that Scott would think of saving the taxpayers money while Karns would not. Witwer explained patiently why he had not named Scott, despite the high regard in which he held Scott.

Tagge then asked if they might go on record so that he could write his column on the matter the following Saturday. Witwer refused to permit this. Tagge tried to assure Witwer that he was simply trying to be helpful. Witwer responded that it would be the first time in twenty years that Tagge had ever made any effort to be helpful to him in campaigning for constitutional reform.

The objection to Tecson was not pressed. Apparently the *Tribune* people were satisfied that Tecson, a Republican leader, would at least be neutral on the issue of an elected state attorney general.

Witwer felt that despite the remaining differences, the conversation was essentially friendly, notwithstanding the apparent disappointment and opposition of Tagge. However, he was annoyed and somewhat dismayed at the *Tribune's* attitude and became more determined not to let the *Tribune* or anyone else deter him. Even when some of his aides suggested that perhaps he ought to yield on the Gertz appointment, Witwer remained adamant.

On January 3, 1970, the *Tribune*, as expected, published a double-column lead editorial slamming the appointments of Gertz, Karns, and George Lewis. Gertz, in particular, was castigated as a noisy, ineffectual busybody, who would mess up the bill of rights. Ironically, *Chicago Today*, another *Tribune* paper, commended Witwer's appointments, particularly those of Gertz, Tomei, and McCracken. Thus, Gertz was both damned and praised by the same media institution, speaking with two voices.

During the course of the convention, the *Tribune* constantly hammered away at the Bill of Rights Committee. Indeed, this turned out to be the most controversial convention committee; at its head was Elmer Gertz, by no means a shrinking chairman. Gertz, for his part, made it a policy to be equally friendly and fair to all of the newspapers, including the *Tribune*. He was always available to the press but did not seek their attention by being constantly near the press table as did some of the delegates.

Toward the end of the convention, strange to say, the *Tribune* had a change of heart with respect to Gertz. When the Union League Club of Chicago gave a dinner in honor of the delegates, Clayton Kirkpatrick, editor of the *Tribune*, and Carl Wiegman, chief editorial writer, came up to Gertz, and publicly said that they owed him an apology, that he was "a great delegate." In later years, the *Tribune* published front page articles in which Gertz was quoted in a friendly manner and editorials in which he was praised. In other ways, too, the *Tribune* showed that the past was forgiven, if not forgotten. This pleased Witwer as much as it did Gertz for they had remained loyal to one another.

Memberships

Meanwhile, during early January 1970, Witwer had to work assiduously on the membership of the committees now that the chairmen and vice-chairmen had been chosen. Again, he had the faithful assistance of Richard Lockhart and Louis Ancel, not too scarred by the experience with the *Tribune* and the black leadership. Of course, Witwer continued to confer with Lyons, who seemed determined to load the Revenue and Finance Committee, Local Government Committee, Judiciary Committee, and Education Committee, with organization Democrats. He seemed less concerned about the other committees. Witwer would not permit any stacking of the decks, and his first considerations were for balance not loyalty. Witwer wanted the committee results to derive from good-faith deliberations and nonpartisanship.

Witwer worked tirelessly through Friday, Saturday, and Sunday. He had lengthy telephone conversations with Elbert Smith and John Alexander, the former easy to deal with, the latter more trying. Alexander complained that he had not been sufficiently consulted and that his views had not won acceptance. He believed that the rules gave him the right to more input in committee selections than Witwer was ready to concede. Thus, it was becoming increasingly difficult for the two men, the older and more experienced man and the younger and more demanding person. It was too early to say whether this was simply the usual problem of misunderstandings between old and young.

Specifically, Alexander wanted Witwer to switch some of the committee appointments, apparently to achieve some of the objectives Alexander had in mind. For instance, he wanted an independent, such as Father Lawlor, to be transferred from the Bill of Rights Committee to the Executive Committee where he could influence the decision on elective or appointive state officials; he also wanted Witwer to remove a person of unknown views on the issue of lowering the voting age and to replace her by an advocate of eighteen-year-old suffrage. Witwer made few changes as a result of the young man's importunities since he felt they were attempts to stack the committees. Alexander, in turn, seemed bitter and resentful and threatened to — but never did — take the floor to appeal some of the selections.

On December 27, Witwer finalized the chairmanship and vice-chairmanship appointments as follows:

Committee	Chairman	Vice-Chairman
Bill of Rights	Elmer Gertz Chicago	James H. Kemp Chicago
Legislative	George J. Lewis Quincy	Lucy Reum Oak Park
Executive	Joseph A. Tecson Riverside	Charles A. Coleman Chicago
Judiciary	William L. Fay Jacksonville	Harold M. Nudelman Chicago
Revenue and Finance	John M. Karns, Jr. Belleville	Dawn C. Netsch Chicago

Committee	Chairman	Vice-Chairman
Suffrage and Constitutional Amendment	Peter A. Tomei Chicago	Charles W. Shuman Sullivan
Local Government	John C. Parkhurst Peoria	Philip J. Carey Chicago
Education	Paul E. Mathias Bloomington	Anne H. Evans DesPlaines
General Government	Thomas J. McCracken River Forest	Robert R. Canfield Rockford
Rules and Credentials	Samuel W. Witwer Kenilworth	David Davis Bloomington
Style and Drafting	Wayne W. Whalen Hanover	Lewis D. Wilson Moline
Public Information	David E. Stahl Chicago	David Kenney Carbondale

Four of the chairmanships were assigned to the Democrats — legislative, revenue and finance, general government, and public information. Lewis and Karns were from downstate; McCracken was from Cook County outside Chicago, and Stahl, the deputy mayor of Chicago, was from the city. The Republicans would hold the leadership of five committees — executive, judiciary, local government, education, and rules and credentials. None were from the city of Chicago; Witwer and Tecson were from suburban Cook County; Fay, Parkhurst, and Mathias represented downstate Illinois. Of the three "major" committee chairmanships — local government, revenue and finance, and judiciary — all were held by downstate delegates (two Republicans and one Democrat). In terms of chairmanships in proportion to their numbers, the independent group of delegates did quite well, receiving two substantive committees (bill of rights and suffrage and constitutional amendment), and one procedural committee (style and drafting). Gertz and Tomei represented Chicago districts; Whalen a district in northwestern Illinois. No women or black delegates were appointed as chairman of a committee.

Witwer, however, did appoint two blacks and three women delegates as vice-chairmen. Kemp and Coleman were both Chicago Democrats. Netsch, the only independent delegate to receive a vice-chairmanship, was also from the city, and Republicans Reum and

Evans were from suburban Cook County. Besides Kemp and Coleman, the Democrats received two other vice-chairmanships — Carey on Local Government and Nudelman on Judiciary. Both were from Chicago. Republicans were appointed to seven of the assistant leadership positions, including all three of the second positions on the procedural committees. None was from the city of Chicago. Shuman, Canfield, Davis, Wilson, and Kenney were all elected from downstate districts.

While it may not have been Witwer's intention at the time, over-representation by independents can perhaps be viewed as compensation for one of their number not being included in the makeup of the conventionwide leadership. The Republicans held the presidency and two vice-presidencies; the Democrats one vice-presidency and the secretary of the convention. Perhaps the rationale for "shorting" the Democrats the one committee position given to the independents was the satisfaction received from the committees to which their representatives were appointed. They held either a chairmanship or vice-chairmanship of every committee, and held leadership positions on those committees that were considered vital to the Cook County organization, i.e., Judiciary, Local Government, and Revenue and Finance.

Consequently, Witwer did achieve his goal of balance where party identification was involved. With the shift of one leadership position from the independent group to the Democrats, he would have accomplished virtual proportionate representation. Witwer hoped to establish a feeling of fairness and a sense of balance where committee assignments were concerned and felt that he had done so. Thus, except for important housekeeping details, he was now ready to proceed with the business of the convention.

THE CONVENTION STAFF

In addition to apportioning delegates to the various committees and choosing chairmen for each of them, President Witwer also had the responsibility of selecting an executive director of the convention, who would be able to work with him and at the same time direct a large and multi-purpose staff. For this post he appointed Dr. Joe P. Pisciotte, coauthor of this volume, who had served with the constitution study commissions in 1968-69.

No constitutional convention in the history of the state had had a larger and more varied staff than the Sixth Illinois Constitutional Convention. The last such gathering, in 1920-22, had had only a handful of employees; that may have been one of its fatal flaws.

At the top level, under Pisciotte and Witwer, was an executive assistant, John C. Brooks, who had held a significant post at the recent Maryland Constitutional Convention; James T. Otis, a part-time general counsel to the convention; a consultant, Richard Lockhart, who, as we have seen, was constantly of use to President Witwer; a parliamentarian, Richard Murphy, who had trying moments, indeed, as he attempted to untie knots at a sometimes obstreperous and technical convention; a highly competent administrative assistant, Dorothy A. Nadasdy; another able administrative assistant, Richard J. Carlson; four secretaries to this top administrative echelon (Beverly A. Criglar, Yvonne L. Ahrens, Judy Cleary and Celia B. Fitzsimmons), another secretary, Josephine Geroske, for the office of the vice-presidents, and Marilyn Clarke, secretary to the secretary of the convention.

And there was a public information office, with James T. Bradley and Caroline A. Gherardini as its information officers, in addition to the Public Information Committee of the convention delegates, headed by David E. Stahl, as chairman, and David Kenney, as vice-chairman. Edna M. Lutes, and Maribeth Gaule assisted in the office.

A visitors' center was also maintained, with Larry H. Scott and Patricia J. Williams as codirectors. There was, of course, a constant stream of visitors to the convention and they required direction, assistance and entertainment.

In addition, there were a number of less visible, but no less important staff people. The chief clerk of the convention, Gerald L. Sbarboro, had a staff of five, including his chief assistant, James Snopko.

The convention had a library service of two, a research pool of eight coordinated by Richard J. Carlson, an accounting office of three, a secretarial pool of six coordinated by Betty B. Bradley, a convention chambers operational staff of thirteen, consisting of a sergeant at arms and head doorkeeper (Ivan I. Petefish), four other doorkeepers, and eight page-messengers. And there were photostat machine operators, and other receptionists-typists.

Surely none could complain of inadequacy in numbers, whatever may have been thought about quality or congeniality. It took genuine management skills and much money to keep this vast staff on an efficient and productive level, generally behind the scenes and without regard to the more vocal and publicly displayed efforts of the 116 delegates. More than forty rooms were devoted to space for the various activities, in addition to the rooms occupied by the committees.

Witwer first became acquainted with Pisciotte during the period that both served on the Constitution Study Commission in 1968-69. Pisciotte was then a member of the staff, and Professor Samuel Gove was chairman. Witwer and Pisciotte developed a close relationship on the highly important subcommittee preparing proposed rules for the convention, chaired by Louis Ancel. Witwer agreed with the manner in which Pisciotte sought to structure the rules to create an open convention, with full debate by all delegates, including those holding minority viewpoints. These rules were an important element, Witwer thought, in the ultimate success of the convention.

Witwer also felt that he and Pisciotte thought alike as to the manner in which the convention should function. Witwer publicly led the convention and he was truly in general charge of what went on, but he did delegate the day-by-day administration to Pisciotte and his staff. Witwer had learned a lesson from the way in which Chairman Vernon Eney ran the Maryland convention. Eney was a brilliant man, totally dedicated and tireless, but he was unwilling to share responsibility with this staff; he simply could not delegate work. Witwer recognized that his duties as president were manifold, and that he could not attend to all of them by himself. He simply had to rely upon those who were closer to the details to assist him. The essence of leadership, as he saw it, was close cooperation between the president and his staff, particularly Pisciotte. Their offices were adjacent to each other. Witwer kept Pisciotte fully informed and Pisciotte, in turn, kept him fully informed as to all major developments, including the hiring of all important staff people. They became truly devoted and loyal. There was personal warmth and trust in their relationship. While Witwer was not on terms of intimacy with each staff member, he did know most of them, and he defended them on those occasions when delegates attacked them. He never lost his faith in them and they in him, and this, too, contributed to the success of the convention.

Witwer and Pisciotte were delighted with their first assistant, Dorothy Nadasdy, whom they regarded as outstanding in every respect. She was easy to deal with, devoted, loyal, dedicated. She could assume leadership, and was innovative. They felt that the convention's work would have suffered without her. She was largely responsible for putting together the all-important payroll and accounting procedures; she tended to the massive printing demands; and assumed general supervision of much of the administrative staff. She, more than anyone, worked closely with Witwer and Pisciotte on the daily responsibilities of moving the business of the Convention.

The parliamentarian, Richard Murphy, was perhaps the unsung hero of the convention. He had to be around all of the time because one could never be sure when a problem would arise. The presiding officer, whether Witwer or one of the vice-presidents, could leave at intervals; but Murphy had to be there. Delegates could doze or be inattentive; Murphy not only had to be awake, he had to be alert. He had to guide the presiding officer on controverted and complex parliamentary points, making decisions quickly, by instinct at moments. He could not court popularity and often faced abuse and undeserved insult. One young delegate in particular fancied himself a parliamentary authority and lectured Murphy on his rulings, sometimes punctuating the lecture with profanity. Murphy wanted to quit several times. His wife, also an able parliamentarian, worried about him. He survived the convention, knowing it was an experience that truly challenged his years of training and professional activity. Few others could have met the challenge.

Each committee at the convention, substantive and sometimes procedural, other than the ad hoc special and limited purpose committees, had its own offices, facilities, and staff — a counsel, sometimes a consultant, sometimes a special counsel, an administrative assistant or two, a secretary or two, sometimes a page, and whatever other special help might be required in emergencies. The counsel were, in most instances, men of the highest eminence in academic circles, in other instances bright young attorneys who were clearly on the way up the professional ladder. Dallin H. Oaks, staff counsel of the Bill of Rights Committee, Glenn W. Fisher of Revenue and Finance, Jack F. Isakoff of the Executive Committee, Rubin G. Cohn of the

Judiciary Committee, and George Braden of the Committee on Style, Drafting and Submission would have been regarded as stars in any constitutional gathering; the other counsel were all able, conscientious, and bright. The administrative assistants were of varying quality and usefulness.

Next only to the quality of the delegates, the success of the constitutional convention depends upon its staff, particularly in the higher echelons.

Although they were not formally staff members, there were several persons who stood out for their services before, during, and after the convention, and who greatly influenced the success of the convention. Particularly noteworthy among these were Louis Ancel, Alan Jacobs of Bozell & Jacobs, and Roger Henn of the Union League Club of Chicago.

Louis Ancel had worked for decades to secure improvements in the constitution. While his major concern had been in the field of municipal law and the article relating to local government, he had a broad interest in the total constitution and the importance of bringing it up to date to serve the needs of modern times. His work was continuous, but he preferred working behind the scenes. Witwer viewed Ancel as one of the unsung heroes of Illinois constitutional history and felt that not enough was known about his work nor enough credit given him for his many contributions. Thus, he had actively supported numerous blue ballot campaigns. He had served with notable distinction on the two preparatory Constitutional Revision Commissions and his work in drafting the rules, with the assistance of Pisciotte, was of enormous importance to the convention and helped get it started on the right footing. Throughout the convention Witwer consulted with Ancel regularly. There was scarcely a week that the two did not talk by telephone more than once. Witwer turned to him as an advisor on numerous occasions when he felt that the "heat was on," and Witwer always found him steadfast in his loyal support. The work that he did in the referendum campaign to attempt to interest Mayor Daley, particularly in the home rule benefits of the new constitution, was of critical importance. Later he was deeply involved in the preparation of the Gertz case against the legislative initiative attempt and supported it at every level.

As early as 1948, Alan Jacobs had begun with his uncle Nathan

Jacobs to work for Illinois constitutional reform. The public relations firm known as Bozell and Jacobs then began a series of representations of the Illinois Committee for Constitutional Revision in one blue ballot campaign after another. For the most part, their services represented a high degree of public commitment and sacrifice. Alan Jacobs had a particularly sensitive concern for the improvement of government at the local and state level and assisted Witwer in his preparation to serve as president of the convention. It had been Witwer's hope to secure his public relations services to guide the convention, and Jacobs was prepared to do so. However, when the Public Relations Committee met in Springfield, they decided not to use the Jacobs agency. This was in large measure due to a charge by Paul Elward and others that Witwer was bringing Jacobs in for his own personal benefit, and that there was even the possibility of some sort of "loading" of the expense rolls to give benefits to the agency. Witwer felt this was highly unfair, Jacobs withdrew, and Witwer was only sporadically able to involve him in the work of the convention. His agency was engaged by the Douglass-Kufuss organization in the adoption referendum and proved to be of enormous support.

Richard Lockhart, a quiet, loyal, and intelligent man, had assisted Witwer on blue ballot campaigns since 1954, from the time he came out of the university. He is a man of unique insights into political affairs and techniques. He has taken great interest in the personalities in the General Assembly and in state and local offices. Witwer sought Lockhart out to assist him immediately upon his election as a delegate when he first thought he had prospects of becoming president of the convention. Later he made Lockhart his part-time special assistant. Lockhart was of special importance to Witwer for the background information he found on issues and people. This was particularly helpful to Witwer during the early days of the convention when the president was endeavoring to appoint the various chairmen and committee members.

Roger Henn and others on the staff of the Union League Club of Chicago were extremely supportive of the convention from start to finish. The Club provided a grant of $10,000 for initial convention preparatory research. Henn coordinated meetings during the convention to express appreciation for the delegates' efforts, and at the close of the convention the Club sponsored the major dinner honoring the delegates. There were other organizations which were especially helpful and encouraging. For example, Caterpillar Tractor of Peoria held a reception and day-long meeting with the delegates, and had cast a special convention medallion. Illinois Bell gave a contribution to produce a movie which told the convention story and was used throughout the state in the public relations campaign.

THE WORK SCHEDULE

Perhaps the most burdensome aspect of Witwer's job as president was the feeling he expressed from the start that the greatest danger to the constitutional convention would be the failure to keep the work moving, to hold all the necessary "readings," and to complete the job within the nine-month period for which funds had been voted by the legislature. Early in the convention he realized that there were delegates of legislative and political experience who viewed the convention as a session of the Illinois General Assembly. These delegates — and they were from both parties — felt that decisions should be allowed to be delayed, thereby giving leverage in the closing period. If this were to occur, Witwer feared that in the scramble to adjourn, bargains would be made and provisions would be adopted without adequate deliberation. Thus, from the time the convention argued the rules and continuously thereafter, Witwer felt it necessary "to *press — press — press*," as he phrased it. This was a recurrent theme in his dealings with the committee chairmen, with the delegates in session, and in almost daily conversations with the executive director and his staff. At first the pressure had to do with logistics, the ability to build staff, to secure space, and to provide the facilities needed by the delegates in order to do their work. Witwer felt the pressure keenly when it became evident that the convention would have to yield its quarters in the State Capitol to the House of Representatives for a special session on April 1, 1970. It was then suggested by some delegates that the convention would work only as the House of Representatives permitted it to, a course totally unacceptable to Witwer.

The battle to get the use of the historic Old State Capitol is in itself a lengthy story. Witwer was turned down several times, and only by the strategy of appearing to take the convention to Champaign or elsewhere was he able to build sufficient interest among Springfield citizens to secure consent for the use of the Old State Capitol. Even then, many of the delegates were more attuned to the political atmosphere of the present capitol, unconcerned about the delays which would have been experienced had the convention stayed there, to say nothing of the demanding effects.

Strangely enough, within a week after the convention moved to the Old State Capitol, there developed a growing appreciation by the delegates that Witwer had done the right thing. Thereafter, seldom did anyone criticize the move. It gave the delegates a sense of mission, serving in such a historic setting. The convention did far better work, and the delegates came to a recognition that they were indeed doing the people's business and making history. Indeed, the move to the Old State Capitol was one of several major turning points of the convention.

The work schedule followed was based on a proposal made by Peter Tomei, who had discussed it with Witwer before presenting it to the committee chairmen and to the convention. There were several revisions of that schedule and battles over specific aspects, such as whether to work on particular dates and, if so, for how long. Thus, when the convention was facing the Easter recess, Witwer was very much concerned that the convention had not shown the capacity to resolve, even at first reading, any of the substantive questions. It was for that reason that he urged Peter Tomei to move ahead with the report of his committee. Earlier, Joseph Tecson had suggested some sort of a trial debate on a question such as separate submission. He had encountered so much difficulty and provoked such technical dispute over the rules that he withdrew and was very reluctant to be a "guinea pig" this time. So, when Tomei was prepared to go forward, Witwer rejoiced, only to be shocked to find that Wayne Whalen and a few others were maneuvering to override his wishes. The reason given by Whalen was that he feared the convention could not agree on standards of revision. While the argument had some appeal, Witwer was unwilling to accept the proposition that the delegates were facing a do-nothing convention. He felt that Whalen was wrong in taking this stand without consultation and pursuing it until the final minute, when he realized that he could not win the vote. Over the weekend preceding the ballot on that issue, Witwer worked hard, and, happily, was able to secure the assistance of Lyons and the Democratic bloc. When this became known to Whalen, he withdrew his motion.

It will always be viewed as a minor miracle that, having delayed so long in completing its work on second reading, the convention was able to recess in mid-August and come back prepared to make short shrift of third reading and to vote adjournment sine die. There were a number of reasons for this. First of all, having debated the issues on first and second reading so fully, most delegates realized that just about everything had been said that could be said and that an extensive third reading debate would be a waste of time. Secondly, the fact that the convention was running out of money, that its staff members were going back to their universities and colleges, and that even the space in the Old State Capitol would soon have to be released, all had salutory effects in bringing the convention to what proved to be a rather sudden windup. Of course, the emergence of a winning coalition on August 28, 1970, provided the "muscle" needed to bring the convention to such a conclusion. Had the coalition not held together, the convention would not have been able to wind up its affairs without a lengthy recess and a great deal of turmoil and uncertainty would have followed. Had the convention found it necessary to return to the General Assembly for further appropriations, it would certainly have encountered great difficulty, and the legislative attacks on the delegates would have been severe and of long duration. Witwer feared the state might experience a repetition of the 1920-22 fiasco. He definitely was worried over the possibility that the coalition would not hold together and that his ability to deal further with the Democratic bloc would be totally destroyed if he showed any partiality until the strength of the coalition was demonstrated. Rubin Cohn, in his monograph, *To Judge with Justice*, accurately depicts the dilemma Witwer faced in dealing with the coalition before coming out openly in its support.

V

Delegates and the Deliberative Process

A group portrait of the delegates against a background of the convention activities makes an interesting picture to contemplate. As in the case of any picture by an individual artist, the final product will depend on the vision of that artist although some aspects will stand out no matter who takes the brush in hand. The following pages are an attempt to draw a portrait in words of the delegates and their convention work. The first part is a general picture of the group as a whole; this is followed by descriptions of some of the loosely formed, and variously perceived subgroups that existed throughout the convention period or appeared and then disappeared from time to time. A portrait of the different leadership groups is also presented. Finally, there are sketches of delegate interaction within the committee structure along with more detailed delineations of voting patterns which show more clearly the relationship of individuals in the group to the work being done.

A GROUP PORTRAIT

As a group, the delegates were conscientious in the performance of their duties and in attendance at sessions of the convention and its committees. Moreover, they had a strong sense of history. Each sensed that he or she was an integral part of a great historical event; this was especially true after the convention moved to the Old State Capitol Building in the very shadow of the memory of Abraham Lincoln.

90

True, a few tried to do as little as possible and some struggled to reduce the number and length of committee meetings; but when it came to the crunch, as in the last days of the convention, they were ready to serve seven days a week, with long hours and no financial compensation. They were ambitious, both for themselves and for the convention. Some seemed driven. Even the less industrious delegates put in more effort than many legislators usually do. There were relatively few politicians of the old style who were there for what was in it for them personally, and even they were touched, at times, by a sort of penumbral glow from the more dedicated delegates. All were interested in good government. Their goal was a good basic charter, one that would be acceptable to the citizens of this state, and one that could be written within the allotted time and budget allowed.

They were not, however, interested in change simply for the sake of change. They often loved the solemn old document that they were revising. They wanted to cling to it if they could. Changes, whether in language or in substance, had to be necessary. All of this meant that they had to be studious and hardworking. They had to pore over many pages. They could take nothing for granted.

Almost without exception, the delegates were articulate and communicative. How they loved to talk! In the beginning and in the end, and at all times in between, there was the word; nay, many words — wise and thoughtful often enough, occasionally foolish, redundant frequently. Only a few were almost invariably silent as if intimidated by the talkers.

Everybody picked on President Witwer. After he announced his appointments there developed a cult of antipathy for Witwer. The harder he tried, and the more he achieved, the more some demeaned him. It was fashionable to denigrate his motives, his methods, his manner. Of course, there were some who had the utmost faith in his integrity, intelligence, and aims. Some of that faith must have abided in the secret places of the hearts of all delegates, but it was not always popular to express it, whether you were a Republican, a Democrat, or an independent. Some who had most reason to be grateful to Witwer were least loyal. That is the tendency of democracies — to demean and to destroy their leaders. Witwer weathered the clamor, some would say, with a kind of grandeur.

Groups within the Group

No single faction controlled the convention. There were blocs of votes that were generally predictable. The regular Democrats from Chicago were the most cohesive, except for the defections of the black delegates on various provisions of the bill of rights. The liberal independent Democrats — mostly from Chicago — tended to vote as a bloc, but this was seldom by prearrangement. The so-called "mountaineers" — the delegates from the southernmost districts in Illinois — voted together, although David Kenney, a faculty member at Southern Illinois University, seemed to be more a member of the midstate moderate Republican bloc. It seemed a fact of the convention's life that, aside from the regular Democrats from Chicago who had a kind of team spirit, each delegate went his own way. Delegates who might have risen to positions of political leadership and thereby control votes, ultimately did not seem able to control more than their own vote.

Members of the Cook County regular Democratic organization, which included at least two delegates from the suburbs, privately protested that they were free agents. "I don't take orders from anyone down here," one delegate told Ron Smith. Another told him that there were no caucuses. Privately they made derogatory remarks about the ostensible floor leader for the regular Democrats, Paul Elward. Elward, a fairly massive man with a penchant for sarcasm, at times abrasive, always ready to pick apart a parliamentary point and generally to raise hell on any given issue, was known by the rank and file regular Democrats as "The Jolly Green Giant." He was regarded as Mayor Daley's spokesman, although Elward himself was quick to deny that he took orders or advice from the mayor. No doubt Elward, by virtue of his many years as a state representative and member of the 49th Ward regular Democratic organization, knew what the stakes were on almost every issue, and did not need coaching. He was rarely denied support from the other regular Democrats, in spite of their cloakroom disdain for him. A private man, and a hardworking student of state government revision, he was not "one of the boys." Nonetheless, on only one occasion, did a regular Democrat openly break with him: one day, to the delight of many, the respected Thomas McCracken arose and fired at Elward, "Anyone who says that, doesn't know what he is talking about."

There were all sorts of pressures. Several of the independents, for instances, were under frequent verbal assault. It even took the form of elbowing in the elevator, taking a cigarette out of a delegate's mouth and throwing it away, and a variety of other such tactics. The late Peter Tomei tired of his seatmate, Martin Tuchow, hassling him about joining the regular Democrats. Tomei had been a regular Democratic precinct captain until he decided to run for election to the constitutional convention. The regular Democrats refused to endorse him, and instead endorsed two serving legislators, Elward and Senator Esther Saperstein. Tomei proceeded to overwhelm all other contenders in his district, and Elward barely scraped by Saperstein in the general election. Whether Saperstein was deliberately trimmed is one of the minor secrets of history.

The Illinois legislature, in passing enabling legislation to hold the convention, was influenced by Peter Tomei's jeremiad, "How Not to Hold a Constitutional Convention: A Study of the Illinois 1920 Constitutional Convention," published in the *Chicago Bar Journal*. He urged that the convention not be partisan — or at least that the convention delegates be elected on a nonpartisan ballot — and that the convention be limited in duration. Partisan politics and an unlimited time schedule had doomed the 1920 convention.

The legislature provided that salaries were to be paid out over an eight-month period, and that additional compensation of $75 a day be paid, limited to $7,500. The delegates lived with a hundred-day working schedule throughout the convention, and when most delegates had received their last paycheck, most of the work was completed and there was a genuine desire to finish the convention's business. In the end, the expense money ran out and the delegates found themselves working for nothing. Yet, because they had been so diligent in moving through the bulk of the work, there was a great sense of commitment to furnish the people of the state of Illinois with an honorable document worthy of ratification. They labored under a bright star. If they drafted a decent, progressive document, they would be well regarded by history. If they failed, some future Peter Tomei would write articles on their failure. They were success oriented. By the end of the convention they had been sufficiently heralded as the bright hope of Illinois. For most of them, it was unthinkable that they would turn against the product of the convention.

Most of the delegates were good people — reasonably honest, reasonably bright, and reasonable in every sense. But a handful of delegates had a deleterious effect upon the proceedings. They were almost wholly negative influences. Although few in number, they had to be reckoned with because they could obstruct, hamper, thwart, mislead. Some were bad influences simply because they talked too much, out of ignorance, vanity, or enlarged vocal chords. They took up the time of the delegates, delayed action, made decisions difficult, prolonged the convention. True, the rules provided limitations on the length of speeches, but no rules could limit the number of speeches, motions, amendments, the whole gamut of parliamentary procedures. After all, this was a deliberative body, and delay and frustration seems to be a hallmark of the democratic process. Some, however, were worse than well-meaning time consumers. They were malicious, devious, technical — determined to throw monkey wrenches into the machinery. They had such amazing skill at times that one wished their ability were properly directed. A few wanted the convention to fail. Even before it began, they were sure that its product would not be good. They were going to work towards its defeat. Zealots and ideologues caused much of the difficulty. They were so sure of their own good faith that they distrusted all others. Fortunately these persons were in the minority. In the end they did not prevail because of the good sense, good fortune, and determination of the overwhelming majority of the delegates. They brushed aside all who stood in their way, and in this they were aided by a presiding officer who was determined that the convention would succeed.

Elbert Smith Looks at His Colleagues

Each delegate, of course, had his own view of his fellow delegates. It is impractical, of course, to consider all of the diversity of viewpoint, least of all the idiosyncrasies coming out of a special or limited vision. One delegate in particular, however, was in a unique position to appraise his colleagues because of his own long-time participation in state politics and his shrewdness of vision. Elbert Smith, one of the vice-presidents, often thought about those with whom he was enjoying the fellowship of this convention. He did not have the president's responsibility and could be more relaxed; by nature he was humorous and popular. What follows is largely a free rendering of what Elbert Smith observed.

The acquaintanceship among the delegates was not as thin, Smith believed, as is often the case when so large a body gathers for the first time. A number of the delegates had been together previously and known to each other through a variety of common activities, public, civic, fraternal, business, and religious. Two delegates in particular, Joseph Meek and Samuel Witwer, were known to all Republicans because they had successively, although unsuccessfully, opposed Paul H. Douglas in the 1954 and 1960 campaigns for the United States Senate. Somewhat less known were Edward Jenison, who had served in the United States House of Representatives, and Smith himself, who had served as state auditor of public accounts and as a state senator. Perhaps a dozen others had served in the Illinois legislature, some at the same time. They included David Davis, Thomas Lyons, Dwight Friedrich, James Strunck, Robert Canfield, and Samuel Martin in the Senate; and John Leon, Victor Arrigo, Paul Elward, Louis Bottino, and John Parkhurst in the House. The latter, known to virtually all as "Parky," had been considered one of the leading legislators, as had Walter Reum, husband of delegate Lucy Reum, whose top lieutenant he would become.

At least five delegates had been members of the Constitutional Study Commission of 1965 and 1967, whose efforts had led to the call for the convention. Some, like Meek and Maurice Scott, had been lobbyists in Springfield; others had held appointive positions in the executive branch of state government, thus becoming familiar names and personages in some quarters. Others were recognized, at least by name, because of the notorious, if not notable, activities in which they had participated: Elmer Gertz because of his notorious cases, such as the freeing of Nathan Leopold, setting aside the Jack Ruby death sentence, and the defense of *Tropic of Cancer*; Albert Raby because of his close association with Dr. Martin Luther King, Jr. in the civil rights movement; Father Francis X. Lawlor, because of the block clubs he had organized in order to stem massive black intrusions into white neighborhoods.

Some were known because of their descent from citizens of prominence — David Davis whose grandfather was a Supreme Court justice, a United States senator, and a member of the 1847 Illinois Constitutional Convention; Richard Daley's father was, of course, Mayor Daley of Chicago; Franklin Dove's grandfather was an appellate court judge and also a member of the 1920 Illinois Constitutional Convention; Charles Shuman's father was the president of the American Farm Bureau Federation; James Thompson's father served as president pro tempore of the Illinois State Senate; and Henry Green's grandfather served in the 1920 Illinois Constitutional Convention. Would they become more than sons of their fathers, or grandsons of their grandfathers? They would have heavy burdens to overcome in their reflected glory.

The League of Women Voters afforded a broad umbrella of association. Some of the delegates were league personalities. They shone in its light and rose under its aegis. These included Republicans and Democrats, all of considerable independence because of the aura of civic good that the league reflects. Independence in politics was one tie that united a group of the delegates, although partisan politics held even more together.

The lawyers, educators, farmers, bankers, merchants, and businessmen among the delegates had their professional and trade associations, conventions, meetings, committees, and contacts of various kinds. They would tend to become kindred spirits when not divided by special or other more personal concerns.

Vice-President Smith felt that the indoctrination meetings prior to the convention had a profound effect upon the delegates. "Suspicions were high," he commented. "If one delegate asked another the time of day, he could expect that before receiving an answer in a low voice, the other delegate might make a quick inspection to see who might be listening and to see if the one who asked really did not have a watch."

This was not mere whimsy, the sort of humor that distinguished Smith, as when he told the convention later that the Bill of Rights Committee had wished its chairman, Elmer Gertz, a speedy recovery from an illness by a "vote of 8 to 5."

Smith wondered what it was the delegates had to fear. Perhaps those who nursed a profound hope that the structure of Illinois government could be improved were afraid that there were others who would band together to stifle genuine efforts at reform. Smith himself felt that such fears were not without foundation. In his warmly human fashion, he reassured them that the Establishment — whether in business and commerce, in religion, or in the professions and politics — becomes nervous at the prospect of change. Members of the establishment recognize, more than do the reformers, that not all change brings about improvement. Some reforms are regressive, even disastrous. These people preferred growth, natural accretions, gradual improvements. Changes that developed out of such a process could be understood and embraced.

He felt that on the political level there was indeed cause for suspicion about an opponents' proposals. The independents, siding with the Democrats by virtue of not wanting to be regarded as Republicans, had seen their hopes and projects scuttled time after time by the all-powerful Daley Democrats. The League of Women Voters, mostly Republicans simply because they were not Democrats, had to overcome not only Democratic opposition, but the obstructions of downstate Republicans who could be called Bourbon and Tory in their politico-social viewpoints.

Downstaters of all persuasions were suspicious of Chicagoans, who were looked upon as partisans of Lucifer. The suburbanite played both sides of the street without recognizing any inconsistency. A Democrat from Wilmette or Highland Park feared the Chicago Democrats as much as he scorned Republicans of all forms and habits. Smith phrased it this way: "A downstate Republican just can't pass the physical even to be a journeyman independent." None of them, he thought, was able to gain the affection of the Egyptians, the Illinoisans from the southernmost end of the state, an area often called "Little Egypt" because of city names like Cairo. He described the Egyptians as "cohesive and fiercely loyal." If you speak ill of one in Chester on the Mississippi, you can expect retaliation from a fellow from Metropolis on the Ohio, or one from Mt. Carmel on the Wabash. They are perhaps the most fearless of all Illinoisans. That may be why there are so few of them. They go to the Hambletonian (championship harness race) at DuQuoin as a Muslim goes to Mecca. They revere Southern Illinois University as an Italian reveres Rome.

Within this large mass of delegates and among the various subgroups, blocs, and factions, certain individuals stood out. These were the leaders. A few were in actual leadership positions, chosen by their colleagues to guide them through the convention process; others were turned to from time to time in unofficial ways because of their particular knowledge, experience or temperment. Their significance to the convention is incontrovertible.

The Convention Elite

Who were the leaders of the convention, and what qualities contributed
to their leadership. Asked for top level and secondary level convention
leaders, representatives from among the delegates, convention staff,
the press, and elsewhere came up with two lists of persons, one
containing thirteen names, the other six. The first consisted of:

Samuel W. Witwer, president of the convention

Thomas G. Lyons, a vice-president of the convention

Elbert S. Smith, a vice-president of the convention

Philip J. Carey, vice-chairman of the Local Government Committee

Elmer Gertz, chairman of the Bill of Rights Committee

John M. Karns, chairman of the Revenue and Finance Committee

Thomas J. McCracken, chairman of the General Government
Committee

Dawn Clark Netsch, vice-chairman of the Revenue and Finance
Committee

John C. Parkhurst, chairman of the Local Government Committee

Lucy Reum, vice-chairman of the Legislative Committee

Peter A. Tomei, chairman of the Suffrage and Constitutional
Amendment Committee

Wayne W. Whalen, chairman of the Style, Drafting and Submission
Committee

Betty Ann Keegan, member of the Local Government Committee

Obviously officers of the convention were given a special opportunity
to show leadership. In fact, all but one on the first list, Betty Keegan,
were in leadership positions. Thus, the president and two of the
vice-presidents readily won places on the first team. However, John
Alexander, the third vice-president, did not place on either the first or
second team. He was not truly a leader. It should be added that
Alexander may have been unduly criticized at times; because he was
young and inexperienced, perhaps he should not have been expected
to have the polish of the older members. In any case, he was an
example of opportunities missed. Odas Nicholson, the secretary of the
convention, was on the second list. Leading an important committee of
the convention was another way of achieving a leadership role. Thus,
the chairman of the Bill of Rights Committee (Gertz), the chairman
and vice-chairman of the Revenue and Finance Committee (Karns
and Netsch), the chairman and vice-chairman of the Local Government

Committee (Parkhurst and Carey), the chairman of the Suffrage and Constitutional Amendment Committee (Tomei), and the chairman of the Style, Drafting and Submission Committee (Whalen) were all on the top level list. Other committee chairmen and vice-chairmen were not, although some of them, but by no means all, were on the so-called second team. Whalen was the only chairman or vice-chairman of a nonsubstantive committee to be named; but it was clear that his committee had greater responsibility and opportunities than any other procedural committee.

It should be noted that three women (Mrs. Netsch, Mrs. Keegan, and Mrs. Reum) were among the top leaders, and other women were in the next echelon of leadership. Clearly, men largely dominated the convention, although the women were by no means silent and often played significant roles on single issues and in the general progress of the convention. All except Mrs. Keegan were lawyers. At least five of the first list (Carey, Karns, Lyons, Parkhurst, and Smith) had previously held public office. All, except Whalen, had been active in public affairs.

There were four Republicans (Witwer, Smith, Parkhurst, and Reum) among the thirteen top leaders, five Democrats (Lyons, McCracken, Karns, Carey, and Keegan), and four independents (Gertz, Tomei, Whalen, and Netsch). The independents were also nominally Democrats, making the group top-heavy with Democrats. Mrs. Keegan could also be called an independent, although with impeccable party credentials. For the most part, it was not really a partisan group. Most of the leaders could be characterized as good-government proponents rather than rigidly partisan.

Five of the thirteen (Karns, Smith, Parkhurst, Whalen, and Keegan) were from downstate, although Whalen, elected from downstate, practiced law in Chicago. The remainder were from Cook County, with only Witwer, McCracken, and Reum being from the suburbs.

What sort of human being were they, what kinds of personalities did they have, what were their characteristics? About Witwer we have already said a great deal. His portrait has already been drawn. Smith was articulate, humorous, low-key, and skilled in compromise. Lyons seemed older than his actual years; he was shrewd, articulate, fast on his feet, ambitious, sometimes aloof, a politician's politician. Karns was convivial, low-keyed in leadership, displaying deference and legal understanding. Carey was the prototype of the reasonable organization man, with a kind personality that was inoffensive even when he was pushing his goals. McCracken was blunt and honest in his partisanship, extremely well informed in his areas of competence, sometimes brilliant, always shrewd. Parkhurst was experienced in political maneuvering, in love with life, entertaining and convivial, sometimes devious in arriving at his purposes. Mrs. Netsch was complex, hard-working, unyielding, tough, informed, and bright. Tomei, too, was intense, driven, bright, highly organized, articulate, and ambitious. Whalen was manipulative, even devious at times, often distant, intelligent, with great skill in draftsmanship. Mrs. Keegan was warm, feminine, friendly, courageous, high principled, not unyielding. Gertz, probably the best known of the delegates nationally but not locally, was articulate, hard-working, informed and willing to reason with those who differed with him. He was as close to the partisans as to his own independent group, sometimes more so. Lucy Reum, like Dawn Netsch, was vice-chairman of a committee rather than chairman. Her influence was perhaps felt more in the convention than in her committee as she proved capable of winning support from the delegates regardless of political affiliations. She, along with Mrs. Keegan, was an architect of the final compromise that made the convention a success.

It is easy to see why this group of persons assumed leadership. They were first among equals. They were listened to even by their opponents. They were respected, whether they were liked or not. They gave a rich and enriching tone to the convention. It would have been a far different body without them.

Several others could be placed on a second level of leadership at the convention. Opinions differed as to some of them who might have been included among the topmost leadership. The six in the second level also contained some well known names:

David Davis, a lawyer from Bloomington, a conservative Republican, a former state senator, chairman of the Rules Commmittee

William Fay, a Jacksonville lawyer, a Republican, chairman of the Judiciary Committee

James Kemp, a black trade unionist, a part of the Daley organization, a member of the Illinois Fair Employment Practices Commission, vice-chairman of the Bill of Rights Committee

Paul Mathias, a Republican from Bloomington, a lawyer, chairman of the Education Committee

Odas Nicholson, a highly articulate and intelligent black woman lawyer from Chicago, a member of the Daley organization, secretary of the convention

Joseph Tecson, a Republican from Cook County, a party leader, a lawyer, chairman of the Executive Committee.

Thus far, we again have members of the official family of the convention — the secretary, four committee chairmen, a vice-chairman, persons active politically and in public life, one woman and five men, three from Cook County and three from downstate, two Democrats, and four Republicans.

Others could readily be added to this second rung of leadership: Maurice Scott, Bernard Weisberg, Mary Lee Leahy, Jeffrey R. Ladd, David E. Connor, Paul Elward, Frank Cicero, and Richard M. Daley (the last largely because of his father). Some would add to or subtract from this list. At any rate, there were people who played substantial roles in what some would regard as a star-studded body. As diverse and experienced persons as John Parkhurst and Thomas McCracken, the one a Republican and the other a Democrat, said that more than half of the delegates, possibly as many as 80 percent, were superior to the persons who generally sit in legislative bodies. Perhaps this was because there was a single task to perform that "good" people were willing to give a finite amount of time to a "good" goal.

And there was a group of delegates who established reputations at the convention and created personal auras for reasons not necessarily connected with achievement, but nonetheless adding to the atmosphere of the convention. This group included Joseph T. Meek, J.L. Buford, Victor A. Arrigo, Dwight P. Friedrich, Leonard N. Foster, Charles A. Coleman, Edward H. Jenison, John L. Knuppel, Father Francis X. Lawlor, and George J. Lewis. Some would add others to this list as well. Indeed, every delegate was a personality in his or her own way. The delegates would always thereafter carry memories and impressions of their variegated group. It was certainly not a dull group, and the proceedings seldom lacked color.

THE DELIBERATIVE PROCESS

The full-group, subgroup, and individual portraits described above were all set against a background of convention activities that were aimed at the development of a revised charter for the state of Illinois. Much of the deliberation that resulted in the final document took place in committees; how these functioned are, therefore, of some import. Basic to their work, was a series of other documents.

First of all, there was the 1870 Illinois Constitution as well as the earlier constitutions of the state; there was the federal constitution, and there were the constitutions of the various other states. These were the raw materials from which committee members and delegates generally were to work. Some participants were tempermentally committed to reaffirming exactly what was in the 1870 constitution. Some were willing to consider substantial advances and certain changes of verbiage. None wanted to retreat from it totally.

To assist in deliberations, there was the Braden and Cohn commentary on the 1870 constitution, the studies put out by the Constitution Research Group, the Model State Constitution, and other similar treatises.

The Committee Process

Many committee members had come to the convention with pet ideas of their own or thoughts that had been implanted in them by concerned citizens and pressure groups. The machinery for considering these things was both simple and logical, and it worked exceedingly well. At the outset all members were free to introduce so-called member proposals; these were cleared through the Legislative Reference Bureau so that, at least superficially, they would be phrased properly. They were then individually assigned by the convention president to the appropriate committee.

After a considerable period of time, March 3 was set as a deadline for the filing of member proposals. This was briefly extended, and then the time for filing such proposals was at an end. Of course, this did not create a hardship. Every committee member could suggest amendments and new proposals during the subsequent deliberations of his own committee. In addition, every delegate to the convention could suggest amendments and substitutions from the floor of the convention during the course of debate. This was not a closed convention; indeed, all of the deliberations were open, with the press and public admitted at all times. Nor was there a closed committee setup. Committees valued discussion, differences of opinion, the unexpected.

All committees of the convention had many meetings at which witnesses were heard and often interrogated. There were extended debates. The committees had the assistance of counsel and others. Ultimately, each committee came up with its proposals based upon the majority vote of the committee. This was supported by a majority report; there were minority reports as well.

The convention resolved itself into the Committee of the Whole for consideration of the proposals of the committees. There was unlimited debate, unlimited right to amend and substitute, and votes were taken on every amendment, every substitution, and what was left. There was approval on first reading, and what was approved was sent to the Committee on Style and Drafting for language changes, but presumably not for changes in substance. The Committee on Style and Drafting reported back in writing to the convention for second reading consideration. Again, there was unlimited debate and the right to amend and substitute; votes were taken, and once again approval was sought by the Committee of the Whole after which the proposal returned to the Committee on Style and Drafting.

Finally, the proposals came back for final vote before the convention in formal fashion in plenary session. At this stage, there could be no substantive amendments or substitutions without suspension of the rules; this required approval by a majority of the delegates elected. Nonetheless, some changes were proposed following suspension of the rules, and some changes were in fact made; others were beaten back. In the end, the proposals evolved into the form in which they were submitted to the voters as a proposed constitution; there were also certain so-called separate submissions.

This process, briefly and categorically described, shows at once the potential for achieving a wise result. The built-in safeguards, the public attention focused upon the deliberations, the desire of each delegate to express himself fully and frankly, the general atmosphere that is part of a constitutional convention, all contributed to a result in which virtually every delegate took pride. On final reading, for example, the bill of rights was approved with only one negative vote and a few abstentions. This indicates, despite all the interim differences, a true consensus. It was achieved only through sweat, dedication, and perhaps even inspiration. This is a story of the achievement and how it was brought about by the 116 delegates who were more than the usual representative body.

Hundreds of member proposals were introduced at the convention, covering a multiplicity of subjects. Almost every delegate had his own pet project, major or minor. But when one sifted what was on the minds of most delegates, there were a few subjects that preoccupied them above all else. There were the big issues over which blood would be spilled and voices raised. Genuine feelings were involved. First of all, there was concern for the revenue structure of the state, a desire to make certain that all taxes would be limited and controlled, in particular that income taxes and personal property taxes be curbed, and, in some instances, eliminated. Chicago delegates, more than downstaters, wanted the extra-legal classification of real property to be preserved and constitutionalized as the only practical and fair means of assessment in a community desperate for funds to carry on its activities. There was also the continuing problem of school funding and administration. Everyone wanted to educate the young, even to provide higher education for them; but where were the funds to come from? Should not the state bear all or a major part of the burden? If so, how was the state to get the money? And how were the schools to be administered to prevent waste and to secure efficient management? There was great concern, too, about the environment, uncomplicated at the time by fear of an economic recession. Some thought that this was the most important matter before the convention. The atmosphere was being polluted, the rivers and streams were being contaminated, great health hazards were being created; something drastic had to be done. Many others were deeply concerned about the system of justice. Was it not being corrupted in the same way that the atmosphere was being ruined? Delegates differed as to methods. The organization Democrats and many downstate Republicans wanted the judicial elective system to be preserved; strengthened perhaps, but certainly preserved. Many others wanted a system of appointive judges in order to get politics out of the court. At times it seemed as if this issue divided the delegates more than any other. There was another group, mostly downstate Republicans but including some Democrats and independents, who felt that multi-member legislative districts with cumulative voting were wrong, unfair, a threat to good government. They felt the convention had to substitute single member districts for the old system. Chicagoans felt very deeply that the root cause of many of their difficulties was their subservience to the General Assembly; that they had to run to Springfield when they had serious problems; that Springfield was not interested and, furthermore, did not understand. The solution was home rule for Chicago and possibly other municipalities and counties, particularly Cook County. Many feared that this would turn Chicago over to the wolves, who would tax, tyrannize, and misgovern. But none could be unconcerned about this problem. In this area, as in a few others, it was felt that if Chicago could not have its way, it would defeat any constitution that was produced. Now and then other issues came to the fore, but these were the big issues, these were the matters that concerned virtually all of the delegates because they concerned their constituents — those who had sent them to the convention and those to whom they would have to answer.

As Ann Lousin, a perceptive staff member, observed, there could be endless speculation on the role of the standing substantive committees at the convention. Were they the true decision makers of the convention? Did the delegates rely upon the committees' suggestions to a great extent? Or were the real decisions made on the floor instead of committees? These were imponderables, which can never be completely answered. However, the raw data yield a significant fact, as Ms. Lousin has shown. If one counts the preamble as a section of the constitution, there are 136 sections of the document. Of these, only seven were proposed on the floor of the convention.

To put it another way, about 95 percent of the sections were drafted originally by either the majority or a minority of a committee. In fact, Articles IV, V, VI, VII, X, XI, XII, and XIV contain no section which did not first appear in some form in a committee report. To anyone who has observed legislative bodies, this reliance upon committee decisions must appear a remarkable achievement. It is clear that President Witwer's appointments to committees were so carefully balanced that on virtually all substantive issues, as well as minor ones, the convention did not adopt an idea which had not first been researched, discussed, and adopted by at least three members of a substantive committee.

Another point of speculation raised by Ms. Lousin and others is whether the 1970 constitution is largely a new product or essentially a revision of the old constitution. While one may argue over whether a "substantially revised" section is really a complete rewrite of the 1870 provision, the official explanation of each provision of the proposed document provides an illuminating guide to the views of the delegates themselves, at least those who participated in the process of drafting it. This explanation was prepared pursuant to the enabling act creating the mechanisms for the convention; it was written by a committee of the delegates toward the end of the convention. The convention adopted the explanation, subject to revision by the convention officers. Thus, few delegates actually reviewed it in toto. But the official explanation probably reflects, as well as any document, the delegates' view on whether a given section was essentially "new" or a "revision" of an 1870 provision. In fact, the enabling act specifically mandated the convention to state how the proposed section changed prior law.

Using the official explanation as a guide, only 34 of the 136 sections are truly "new." Of the 103 "carry-over" sections, the spectrum runs from those identical to the old sections (largely in the bill of rights) to those which are designated "minor rephrasings" of the ancestor provisions, to "slight revisions" and on to those called "substantial changes" from the 1870 constitution. Obviously, some of the greatly revised provisions contain subsections with entirely new matter, such as the addition of a judicial inquiry board to Article VI, sec. 15, judicial discipline. Nonetheless, it is intriguing that, by the delegates' own standard, exactly 75 percent of the sections had substantive roots in the old constitution. In fact, Articles IV, VI, and XII contain only revisions of the old constitution. In contrast, all of Article VIII, (finance), all of Article XI, (environment), and great parts of Articles VII, IX, and XIV are entirely new provisions.

What does this indicate? We are indebted to Ms. Lousin for the following and, we think, logical answer: the delegates were reluctant to tamper with many time-honored provisions, such as the guarantees of individual liberty in the bill of rights and the recently-revised judicial article. However, where modern technology had suggested problems and solutions unheard of in 1870 — such as environmental pollution and the need for comprehensive state finance — the delegates were willing to create entirely new concepts. The 1970 constitution, then, is cut of both old cloth and new, sewn together with different writing styles that sometimes conflict, even jar, but which as a total document is substantively quite coherent and balanced.

Among the 580 member proposals that were referred to committee, the largest number - 92 - went to the Legislative Committee, and the smallest - 32 - went to the Executive Committee. Other committees varied considerably in the number of member proposals referred to them:

Bill of Rights	80
General Government	77
Revenue and Finance	77
Judiciary	75
Suffrage and Constitutional Amendment	56
Local Government	54
Education	37

Only the president of the convention, who assigned proposals to the committees, and two other delegates — David Davis and Edward Jenison — failed to file member proposals. Witwer, however, felt he had inspired several proposals, some of them quite important. He believed quite firmly that he had to maintain a free and open position so that he would not be charged with partisanship in a supposedly nonpolitical convention. This did not, however, prevent Witwer from talking informally to delegates or even, on occasion, appearing before committees. When he visited the Suffrage and Constitutional Amendment Committee, Chairman Tomei invited him to address the nine members of his committee. In the course of his remarks, Witwer made suggestions not unlike those which eventually came out of Tomei's committee. After all, not long previously he had written an article on the subject for the *Chicago Bar Record*. He proposed periodic submission to the voters of a call for a constitutional convention and the retention of separate ballots for all constitutional proposals. When the committee submitted its report, incorporating in one form or other Witwer's suggestions, Frank Cicero, elected to the convention from Witwer's own district, proposed changes which Witwer regarded as unwise. In this instance he did not hesitate to speak out. Witwer's activities in connection with the judiciary were more pronounced, he thought, than appeared on the surface. He spent hours in quiet talk with delegates who might be influential in the result and he strengthened the hand of Judiciary Committee Chairman William Fay as much as he could without trying to dominate him. When he spoke on the floor in favor of appointive judges, he was criticized by some for being too vigorous in his advocacy. He felt that he was at least partly responsible for the favorable result on first reading. He thought that perhaps five or six delegates changed their minds as a result. In the same way, his voice was heard on and off the floor, on the rentention of cumulative voting for state representatives. He appeared before the Revenue Committee on several occasions and spoke largely off-the-cuff on the personal property tax and on the classification of real estate for tax purposes.

There were other areas in which Witwer was not content to sit back. Whenever he thought a particular result would be harmful or helpful on the ultimate purpose of producing a document that would win voter approval, he did not hesitate to use his influence. He knew that the constitution could not be approved if Mayor Daley fought it, and, to the distress of many Republicans, he tried to appease the mayor in those relatively few areas where the document was most vulnerable.

Deliberations Turn to Votes

During the months of deliberations at the convention, both in plenary session and in Committee of the Whole, the delegates, in common with other similar parliamentary bodies, employed several types of votes —roll call votes, division votes, and voice votes. Most votes were taken by either a voice expression or a show of hands; toward the end of the convention division votes by standing were frequently used to save precious convention time, which was rapidly slipping away. Two hundred and seventy-one time-consuming roll call votes were taken, not only on the final passage of provisions as required by Rule 50 of the convention rules, but also on many other occasions when at least ten of the delegates wanted to "make a record." Sometimes the record was made on what would normally be regarded as trivial grounds, as when the Daley stalwarts resisted the Gertz motion for adjournment on the final working day before the ceremonial closing.

Individual delegates, the press, and constituents, of course, were keenly interested in individual delegate voting behavior. It was the single most important indication of how a particular delegate was performing at the convention. Delegates had campaigned on particular issues and their recorded votes were an indication of their willingness to make good on a particular promise. The excuse of "campaign oratory" would not do. The statewide press frequently reported how the convention as a whole voted on a measure, and local newspapers, especially small rural weeklies, reported the roll call vote of the delegates from their particular area. The delegates were not concerned solely with the impact their vote would have on an issue and ultimately on the campaign for ratification, they were also concerned with the future. Many of them harbored ambitions for future elective office, some scarcely concealed. They were continually aware that their record at the convention might have a positive or negative effect on their ability to obtain such elective office.

While the delegates were elected on a formally nonpartisan basis, there was continual mutual interest in voting behavior among the delegates who shared a common partisan affiliation or common support from a particular interest group. It was not long before the delegates began looking for voting keys from delegates who held leadership positions among the various identifiable groups in the convention. Several delegates, largely as a result of interest among the delegates, attempted to do some general and certainly unscientific analysis of the roll call voting behavior.

Vice-President John Alexander, for example, who held a degree in political science, analyzed seven pivotal issues that were voted on in the course of first reading of the bill of rights. For each favorable vote on them, he gave one point. The perfect liberal would, therefore, have seven points; the fewer points you had, the less liberal you were. Not unexpectedly, Paul Elward, one of the Daley leaders, was the first to criticize the "study," calling it a "silly waste of time and not an accurate reflection of anybody's political philosophy." But, according to Alexander's test, he had voted liberal only once. Another Daley leader, convention Vice-President Thomas G. Lyons, who also had voted liberal only once, commented, "I don't think my liberal record is going to be tarnished by this survey." The eloquent hardliner, Thomas Kelleghan, rated zero on the Alexander test. Jeffrey Ladd, who considered himself a "conservative responsible Republican," was disturbed to find himself in the upper levels of liberalism with a six. "The study is very unscientific," he said. Did this lead him ultimately to cast the one vote against the bill of rights on final reading? Elmer Gertz was one who commented favorably on the Alexander study. He found it "basically sound," and observed, "It's the most interesting document to come out of the convention so far." It was not often that he would have such praise for Alexander.

According to Alexander, you were a liberal if you voted *for* (1) the elimination of the alleged federally unconstitutional clause in the freedom of speech section, (2) abolition of capital punishment, and (3) extending the rights of collective bargaining to public employees; and if you voted *against* (1) deletion of the provision requiring a prompt preliminary hearing for persons charged with felonies, (2) including the unborn in the due process section, (3) an amendment to the antidiscrimination section intended to protect property owners' rights, and (4) the right to bear arms section.

A majority of the convention favored the liberal position on three of the issues and opposed four. While the figures or the ratings had no real impact on the convention, they were regarded with a good deal of interest, and it may be useful to make a few general comments about them. Republicans and Democrats as a whole were 3.1 in the rating, just below the middle; independents as a whole were near the top with 6.3; suburban delegates were somewhat more liberal than Chicago delegates, 4 to 3.3; while downstaters were 3.1. The women averaged 5.3, while the men averaged 3.1; overall the convention delegates rated about neutral, 3.4.

Peoria delegate David Connor was the next to play the voting analysis game. He took advantage of the computer facilities at his bank to show how each delegate compared in voting with every other delegate on first, second, and third readings. There was no attempt by Connor to use the computer to describe individual delegates or groups of delegates as liberal, conservative, radical or reactionary. The raw data provided the basis for some interesting comparisons and observations. The delegates who comprised the Chicago Democratic organization group turned immediately to see how they compared with the voting scale of the mayor's son, Richard M. Daley, on those measures most sought after or opposed by the Chicago organization. There were several surprises, at least on the surface; for instance delegate Al Raby, civil rights activist, and President Witwer had the greatest degree of similarity in voting patterns at one stage of the proceedings.

A third analysis of delegate voting patterns — this one by Thomas Kelleghan — was prominently displayed in the corridors. He had his own means of determining who was revolutionary, which meant those who voted in opposition to his notion of sound principles.

A detailed and systematic study of delegate roll call behavior was done after the convention was adjourned and is presented in a book in this series entitled *Roll Call! Patterns of Voting in the Sixth Illinois Constitutional Convention,* by David Kenney and his associates. They studied 221 of the 271 roll call votes in an attempt to describe and interpret the voting behavior of the convention members. They point out that roll call voting is only one set of measurable and explainable behavior patterns, and that there are numerous other aspects of delegate behavior that do not fall within the scope of roll call analysis. Participants or observers of the convention or of any deliberative body, for that matter, will be quick to point out that the final roll call vote does not reflect compromises, activity, or motivations that preceded the actual vote. This was certainly true in a deliberative body such as the Illinois Constitutional Convention, which comprised 116 non-partisan elected delegates, who came from diverse districts and backgrounds and who were operating from multivariate points of view and motivations. Such roll calls do not describe or reflect the leadership of the total convention or the leadership of subgroups within the convention, nor do they reveal the countless and constantly changing individual relationships among the delegates. But as Kenney and his colleagues correctly point out, roll call voting can indicate similarities and differences among the convention members; it is also "hard data," and therefore the only "quantifiable" measure of delegate behavior.

In their analysis of the 221 convention roll call votes Kenney and his group found that 173 fit into 13 clusters of highly related roll calls:

1. Daley orthodoxy
2. Status quo vs. change
3. Democrats vs. Republicans
4. Jacksonian viewpoint
5. Cosmopolitan vs. local interests
6. Delegate interest disclosure
7. Fundamentalist vs. modernist
8. General vs. particular interests
9. Urban financial needs
10. Human rights and liberty vs. property rights and authority

11. State tax power
12. Partisan privilege
13. The conciliators

Based on the clusters and the scale scores developed by Kenney and his colleagues, — and charted in their book — they made several general statements and observations. First, they concluded that the roll call voting behavior at the Sixth Illinois Constitutional Convention was highly structured, and that the best explanation for the voting behavior was party affiliation. The partisan identities were substantially related to regional distinctions. Chicago elected almost all Democrats; the Cook County suburbs were represented almost totally by Republicans; and only downstate was there any real partisan mixture. The correlations of region with dimension scores are not as sharp as those of party, but follow the same outline. The authors concluded that the personal characteristics of the convention members provide partial and secondary explanations for the roll call voting behavior. It could not be determined whether or not the age, religious affiliation, race, sex and income of convention members were systematically related to their voting on the various issues. Generally speaking, only weak relationships between these variables and the voting scales developed, except among particular subgroups of members. It is not surprising, however, that some relationship would be found between several of the demographic variables that constituted the delegates and their respective voting behavior; this is particularly true in view of the makeup of the convention and in view of President Witwer's continual admonishment to the convention leadership concerning balance among the several groups of the convention.

Regardless of how the analyses of the various votes were made — and may still be made in the future — what mattered to the individual delegates as they lived through the daily deliberative process, was the ultimate successful outcome of their convention. To understand fully how that success was in fact achieved one must look at the wide variety of committees that met over and over again to reach agreement on specific issues as well as at the numerous events and special tasks that required time and attention.

VI

Special Committees and Special Events

Rules 14 and 15 of the convention provided for nine substantive and three procedural committees. These were permanent committees existing for the duration of the convention. However, Rule 16 anticipated the need by the convention, or more specifically by the president, for temporary or ad hoc committees to be created for a particular and temporary purpose. These were to play a key role not only in conducting the business of the convention, but in the shifting relationships between the president and the delegates as well. During the course of the convention, there were specific events that also had an impact on the interpersonal relationships between the delegates, which in turn had an indirect effect on the deliberations and ultimately on the new document. Several of the more prominent events — moving to the Old State Capitol and hearings throughout the state — are discussed in this chapter.

SELECT COMMITTEES

President Witwer put Rule 16 to good use and during the course of the convention created nine select committees. They were the committees on: the convention's budget, the convention journals, chaplaincy, Section 13, statutory transition, convention housing, move to the Old State Capitol, closing day ceremonies, and the president's address to the people. These select committees were in addition to those of a ceremonial and necessarily brief nature, such as those appointed to escort visiting dignitaries to the rostrum. The nine select committees were of a procedural or quasi-substantive nature and served a variety of purposes, only one of which was to carry out the specific activity for which it was nominally created. An underlying and equally important function of the committees was to assist President Witwer in giving additional responsibilities to those delegates who felt they might not be used to their full capacities in their appointments to the standing committees. Witwer occasionally used an appointment to a procedural standing committee to offset some unhappiness in the substantive standing committees; however, because of the limited number of delegates appointed to these procedural committees, there were still those who felt they had not been given their due share of responsibility in the convention.

The first select committee appointed by President Witwer was announced on January 8, moments before the day's adjournment, with the very simple statement: "The chair has an announcement to make concerning a new select committee appointed by the Chair pursuant to the rules. We are going to need a committee on the constitution's [sic] budget. This is a very important matter, and the chair is asking the following people to serve on that special committee: Mr. Miller will be chairman, Mr. Arrigo, vice-chairman, Mr. S. Johnson, Mr. Cooper, Mrs. Willer, Mr. Connor, and Mr. Ozinga."[1] Thomas Miller was given the chairmanship by the president largely because of his unhappiness over not being appointed either as a chairman or to the substantive committee of his choice. The president also attempted to keep some of his "open and balanced" guidelines in making the appointments to the budget committee. Even though it continued in existence throughout the whole time of the convention, the committee never really functioned as an ongoing body. The occasional budget reports it made were put together largely by the convention staff and reviewed by Chairman Miller with the executive director before they were presented to the delegates.

The select committee on the convention journals had a very limited function, but it too persisted throughout the convention. On January 27, after the convention had been in session almost a month, it received the first copies of the daily journals. David Davis asked the chair for

[1]*Record of Proceedings, Sixth Illinois Constitutional Convention*, Vol. 11, p. 178.

twenty-four hours to look at the journals before attempting convention approval, and President Witwer at this point asked the approval of the convention to appoint a select committee on the journals. There were no objections and Witwer proceeded to appoint Ted Borek as chairman of the committee on the journals, and designated delegates, Dove, Foster, Pughsley, and Ladd to serve on the committee. The journal committee was not created without some controversy. Delegate David Stahl, immediately after the announcement of the appointments, asked to be recognized and pointed out that according to Rule 10 the convention secretary "shall cause to be kept and furnish to each member a printed journal of the proceedings of the convention for the previous day."[2] Stahl then asked whether or not a committee had just been formed to review the work of the secretary, and suggested that the secretary could at least be an ex officio officer of the newly created committee. Witwer replied that it was understood that Miss Nicholson would have the assistance of the committee and would indeed be expected to attend as an ex officio member.

Stahl's inquiry stemmed, in part, from the concern about the duties of the secretary since they had been added on to the rules when the position of secretary was created to achieve a necessary balance among the leadership of the convention. Stahl was from the city of Chicago and a member of the Chicago Democratic organization, as was Secretary Nicholson. No conflicts arose and the select committee on the journals functioned largely as a one-man operation. Ted Borek took his role as chairman of that committee quite seriously, and it was he who assumed the responsibility for going over the journals each day and offering the motion to the convention for their approval.

Perhaps the least functional and least controversial committee, and one that had only limited visibility throughout the convention, was created by the president on January 22, when Witwer told the delegates: "I would like to appoint an ad hoc committee on the chaplaincy so that this committee may assist our staff in securing the services of ministers and chaplains and rabbis for every session as proposed yesterday by Father Lawlor. The committee will consist of Mrs. Wymore, as chairman, Mr. Sharpe, Father Lawlor, Mr. Scott, and Mr. Garrison."[3] The appointment of two of the committee

[2]Ibid., p. 272.
[3]Ibid., p. 263.

members was logical, as Reverend Sharpe and Father Lawlor were the two clergy members of the convention. Maurice Scott was to be appointed to several ad hoc committees. President Witwer felt that since Scott was a permanent resident in Springfield and had long-time familiarity with the city, he would be helpful to any committee to which he was appointed.

Section 13 of the enabling act, under which the convention was created and operating, charged the convention with the task of determining the mechanics of keeping the voters informed about its work, about the manner and form of voting, the manner and form of tabulating votes, the date of the referendum, and other related matters. President Witwer did not feel that this function belonged precisely to any of the procedural committees for he anticipated that it would require a good deal of work. Accordingly, he created what was to be known as the Section 13 committee. In announcing creation of the committee, he stated:

> Now this committee is not intended to take on the job of determining in what manner we shall present our work product in relationship to the question of package or seriatim, or a combination thereof. That, as we understand, was the subject of an announcement the other day following action of the rules committee. But we do need this. There is a lot of work involved and we have to start now. So I have asked Miss Nicholson — so that I might have close liaison with the officer group — to serve as chairman. I have asked Mr. Jenison to serve as vice-chairman, and Messrs. Coleman, Dunn, Dvorak, Stanley Johnson, Mrs. Pappas, Charles Shuman, Ron Smith, and Jim Thompson to serve on that committee with the officers, the vice-presidents, and the chairman of the public information committee and the chairman of the committee on style and drafting is also ex officio.[4]

Witwer asked Miss Nicholson to convene her committee as soon as possible and also gave her the authority to create subcommittee assignments. The Section 13 committee was not a function to be taken lightly, and delegate Nicholson devoted a good deal of time to its leadership, in addition to her duties as secretary of the convention and serving with the Judiciary Committee. She worked throughout the duration of the convention on putting together the necessary materials

[4]Ibid., p. 867.

to be presented to the public and was required to continue working after the adjournment sine die of the convention.

The next select committee created by President Witwer also stemmed from necessary but unanticipated activity, that is, the impact of a newly proposed constitution on existing statutes of the state. More specifically, what would be immediately necessary for effective statutory transition? As President Witwer said: "We have learned from study of problems which developed in other states which had constitutional conventions that in some states, at least, they found that it was necessary before the convention adjourned sine die to study the extent to which statutory law might be dislocated in consequence of provisions of the changed constitution. And sometimes this became quite a problem, and because of the late start on it, it became very difficult to get it done without delaying the sine die adjournment."[5]

So the chair, after consultation with the three vice-presidents, appointed a special committee on statutory transition headed by eminent lawyers of the convention. Arthur Lennon was named chairman, Frank Dove, cochairman, and Robert Butler, William Lennon, David Linn, Michael Madigan, James Parker, Louis Perona, and Martin Tuchow were named as members. Lewis Wilson was asked to act ex officio since he was vice-chairman of the style and drafting committee. They would have the job of studying the problem and advising the convention.

A week later President Witwer appointed a special committee on convention housing to deal with the very practical problem of what would happen to the living facilities of delegates and the convention's facilities if the convention found that it could not adjourn sine die by August 8. President Witwer declared:

> The committee will be charged with making recommendations to cover (a) a suitable chamber in which to hold plenary sessions of the convention; (b) suitable office space for officers, committees, and staff; and (c) suitable housing accomodations [sic] for delegates and staff who are nonresidents of Springfield and vicinity. The committee is to make its recommendations to the president as soon as possible, but in no event later than August 1.

The membership of the committee will be as follows: Albert A. Raby,

---

[5]Ibid., III, p. 2277.

chairman; Virginia Macdonald, cochairman; James S. Brannen, J.L. Buford, Henry Carter Hendren, Jr., Frank Orlando, Edwin F. Peterson, Gloria S. Pughsley, and Maurice W. Scott.[6]

On July 21 Raby reported to the convention. He had met with William Alderfer, the state historian, to find a way to allow the convention to remain in the building throughout August and at the same time allow Alderfer and the State Historical Library to begin orderly movement into its new facility. Raby's report, while not conclusive, contained a suggestion that the delegates bring sleeping bags to Springfield if necessary; concern over housing then spilled over into the more basic concern over the date of adjournment. The committee of regular chairmen had met with the president and vice-presidents, and Revenue Committee Chairman John Karns presented to the delegates a suggested schedule that called for adjourment on August 29. The date for adjournment of the convention was dictated not only out of a concern for housing and facilities, but also out of the pending depletion of the convention's appropriated funds. Thomas Miller, as chairman of the special committee on budget, also made a report on July 21; throughout this time Miller had been working closely with the president and the staff to make certain that the funds were properly used and that the convention did not overspend. On July 21 the convention did adopt, by a vote of 92 to 5, the report of Karns calling for an August 29 adjournment, and President Witwer expressed his appreciation to Karns, Raby, and Miller for their work on these very important procedural items.

In anticipation of the end of the convention and its adjournment sine die, President Witwer, on August 11, appointed his special committee on closing day ceremonies. He asked Jeffrey Ladd and Clifford Kelley to serve as cochairmen and he asked Betty Howard, Father Lawlor, Buford, Wenum, Miller, and Yordy to serve as committee members. The committee was charged with the duty of recommending to the convention a program of speakers, special guests to be invited, guest attendance in the chamber, the manner of signing the document, and such other logistical and ceremonial arrangements that would be necessary to assure an appropriate and efficient closing day session. The cochairmen were directed by Witwer to report back to

[6]Ibid., IV, p. 2650.

the convention as soon as possible, but in no event later than August 24. The committee, however, because of what turned out to be an enormous task and because of the limited staff available at this point, did not make its first report until August 31. At that time Kelley reported to the full convention that the tentative date for the closing ceremonies was set for Thursday, September 3 at 12 noon in the Old State Capitol. He reviewed such details as the number of people (400) that would be admitted to the hall for the ceremony and the breakdown of the number of persons that would be invited by each delegate. Closed circuit television would be installed to accommodate an overflow of those who would be visiting the convention ceremony, but who would not be able to be admitted to the main chamber. Kelley also reviewed the dignitaries that would be invited to the ceremony and those that would be invited to speak. Among those invited to attend would be the mayor of Chicago and the governor of the state, as well as the two U.S. senators, twenty-four congressmen, all of the members of the General Assembly, the state central committeemen of both parties, the leaders of various organizations, and the news media. He set forth the tentative agenda for the day, which in large part would be the normal order of business of the convention. He asked that there be agreement on limiting speeches and debate during the closing ceremonies. The committee hoped to limit the ceremony to three hours and asked that only those delegates who were invited to do so previously take part in the actual ceremony. In continuing with the theme of the convention, the committee would strive for balance of geographical, party, and racial distribution.

The second report was made to the convention on September 1 by Ladd. He reviewed the progress of acceptances from the 417 people in the dignitary classification who had been invited to the ceremony. He reported that Betty Howard was chairing a subcommittee on the printing and development of the souvenir program and he took a good deal of pleasure in reporting that delegate Kelley had managed to arrange for Mahalia Jackson to sing at the ceremony, and that such items as parking, security, car control passes, the clergy, were being attended to. The Illinois Historical Society was making arrangements for the use of Lincoln's desk for the actual signing of the new document, and the society would also donate an appropriate pen for the signing. The Illinois League of Women Voters would donate 500 souvenir pens for the delegates and their guests of the day.

Kelley and Ladd, on behalf of the committee, made their reports in the spirit of cooperation and at the same time with a sense of urgency as only two days remained before the scheduled date for the closing ceremony. But, as perhaps could have been expected in a body made up of such diverse and controversial individuals, even such a seemingly simple matter as a report on closing day ceremonies could not pass without a good deal of debate. What turned out to be a somewhat significant controversy will be discussed later in this volume in Chapter XVIII. Also discussed in that chapter is the committee on the president's address to the people.

THE MOVE TO THE OLD STATE CAPITOL

One of the most difficult procedural tasks faced by the convention was finding a suitable permanent home. Article XIV of the Constitution of 1870 stipulated that the General Assembly would, in the enabling legislation, designate the place of the convention meeting. The Second Constitution Study Commission, in making its recommendation, and the General Assembly, in adopting the legislation, considered several factors. Although most state constitutions did not specify where a convention was to be held, a great majority had been convened in state capitals, usually in the chamber of the larger legislative body. Illinois had historically followed that practice. After the 1818 Statehood Convention at Kaskaskia, the 1847, 1862, 1869, and 1920 conventions had all been held in Springfield in the House chambers. Of those states which had recently convened constitutional conventions, New York, Kentucky, Maryland, Michigan, Pennsylvania, Connecticut, Rhode Island, and Hawaii, had met in their respective capitals. New York, Kentucky, and Michigan were constitutionally required to do so. The others did so by choice.

The use of a college campus was initiated in 1947 when New Jersey selected Rutgers University at New Brunswick as the site for its convention. It was felt that the campus provided a central location in the state and retreat from the statehouse and from the political implications associated with it. Alaska followed the New Jersey precedent and in 1950 convened its delegates at a distance from the capital, at the University of Alaska at Fairbanks. The Hawaii

Statehood Convention of 1950 was held in Honolulu, but the actual meetings of the convention were conducted in the national guard armory rather than at the statehouse. Similarly, the Michigan convention of 1961 was held in the capital city, but away from the capitol building. The Ohio legislature in 1911 directed the 1912 convention to meet in the hall of the House of Representatives in Columbus, but with the authority to adjourn to any place within the state for meetings. More recently, the Arkansas Constitutional Revision Study Commission recommended that a convention be held in the House of Representatives chambers, and the Hawaii convention in session in 1968 was required to be convened in the same manner as the 1950 Statehood Convention.

The selection of the statehouse in Springfield as the convention site presented several advantages, particularly with regard to the logistical problems, the ebb and flow of initiating and continuing the operation of a constitutional convention. Physically, the chambers of the House of Representatives offered a ready-made hall for the deliberations and voting of the 116 delegates in plenary session. Committee rooms were available, and facilities existed within Springfield for housing and feeding the delegates and others temporarily in the city for the convention. Of equal importance was the presence of staff and clerical personnel familiar with the legislative process who could assist in the work of the convention. Newspaper, radio, and television staffs were there, and much of the library material needed by the delegates and research people was already located in one of several Springfield libraries. Further, many of the state officials who might be needed for information and testimony would be in close proximity to the House. Overlaying these logistical considerations was the somewhat nebulous factor that Springfield, as the state's capital, is the focal point of state government activity. It contains the symbols upon which the people generally rely for their awareness of state government and serves as a basis of popular support and consensus. However, as pointed out by Peter A. Tomei in his article, "How Not to Hold a Constitutional Convention," a convention held in the statehouse would not be without its shortcomings. The 1920 convention, he pointed out, took on an atmosphere of a super-legislature, and this tended to make it unduly responsive to numerous appeals by special interest groups. In addition, the convention was required to recess whenever the General

Assembly went into session. In the 1943 Missouri convention there was a feeling among some delegates that convening in the capital provided an opportunity for state officials to have undesirable power and influence in the convention process.

A college campus had several advantages. The National Municipal League had recommended that the New Jersey and Alaska experience be considered by planners of conventions, partially because an atmosphere of scholarly detachment may have a favorable impact upon both the delegates and the people. The major campuses in Illinois contained some facilities for housing and feeding the delegates; rooms suitable for hearings, committee meetings and plenary sessions; and the library in some instances would parallel the Springfield collections. The staffing problem could be partly alleviated by the availability of university staff on the temporary or part-time basis often required by a convention. The several campuses throughout Illinois would give the legislators several alternative locations that would make the convention geographically accessible and acceptable to many areas of the state.

Offsetting the advantages of an academic location would be the necessity of modifying the campus facilities to handle the operations of a deliberative and policymaking assembly, possible conflict with the university schedule in the use of facilities, transportation problems (depending upon which campus would be designated), and the nonavailability of persons who have the needed expertise on the day-to-day operations of state government under the existing constitution. Many of the towns in which the colleges and universities are located would not be able to handle the substantial influx of additional people requiring housing and other services. Added to these disadvantages would be the difficulty involved in selecting the college or university from among the many throughout the state. Rivalries might create problems, rather than solve them.

The city of Chicago presented a third alternative to either the statehouse in Springfield or a college campus. Chicago is the population center of the state and this would enhance public awareness of and interest in the convention. Located within the city would be numerous convention facilities, several of the state's major universities and libraries, and several law schools. The city's business eatablishments could easily handle the auxiliary services required by delegates;

communications facilities are already in existence, and Chicago, with its many public buildings, is the state's "second seat of government."

Perhaps the major criticism of the selection of Chicago as a convention site would be the negative response it would create on the part of those residing in downstate Illinois. That part of the state has always been suspicious of the big city. There would be the charge that a convention convened in Chicago would favor the Chicago political interest in the era of the powerful Daley organization. Chicago would offer numerous business and social distractions to the delegates that would not necessarily be present in a more sylvan setting.

The General Assembly, then, had several alternatives from which to select the site for the convention. These were:

The statehouse in Springfield

A Springfield location away from the statehouse, such as the restored Old State Capitol

A college or university campus located in downstate Illinois

A college or university campus located in Chicago

A location in Chicago other than a college or university campus, e.g., one of the convention facilities

A city other than Springfield or Chicago, such as Peoria, Rockford, etc.

Among the many factors legislators had to weigh in making their selection were:

Accessibility from all points throughout the state (travel time and availability of transportation)

Convention logistics (library, staff, meeting rooms, housing, communications facilities, printing, internal transportation, etc.)

Convention atmosphere

Impact on the public

Influence on interest groups

Conflict with schedules of other institutions

Overall cost

Following the recommendation of the Constitution Study Commission, the General Assembly held that the convention was to convene in the hall of the House of Representatives of the General Assembly in the capitol building in the city of Springfield, and that all further proceedings of the convention were to be held at such places and in such manner as might be determined by the convention. In so doing, the legislature set the stage for an internal convention conflict. What ultimately resulted was perhaps the most important logistical decision of the convention.

After the opening of the convention on December 8, the delegates settled into the House chamber and rapidly adjusted to their new quarters. Even more quickly, they grew to like not only the plush, official chairs of the chamber, the public address system, the electronic voting machines, the spacious gallery, the adjacent meeting rooms, press, cafeteria, auxiliary services, among other things, but also the "heady" feeling of occupying the "seat of power" in the state of Illinois. Complacency was short-lived, as the convention's tenure in the chambers was to become complicated by two factors: the roof over the House chambers and the House galleries was scheduled for extensive remodeling, and the Illinois General Assembly was scheduled to return to Springfield in April 1970 for a three-month legislative session. Spokesmen for the secretary of state's office, which was in charge of the renovation, indicated the planned renovation would not force the convention to move elsewhere. The return of the General Assembly presented a bigger problem. Could the 116 delegates coexist with the 177 state representatives, using the same desks, chairs, telephones, lockers, files, voting machines, meeting rooms, and the rest of the legislative paraphernalia?

Differing points of view began to emerge after President Witwer publicly stated on January 9 that the convention might have to leave Springfield because of the anticipated legislative session. Witwer and Executive Director Pisciotte felt quite strongly that the business of the convention could not be conducted on an alternating basis with the General Assembly. Neither particularly wanted to leave Springfield, but in the absence of adequate facilities in the capital city, Chicago had to be considered again. The University of Illinois was no longer a possibility, since the date had passed beyond which the university could commit the space.

There was immediate reaction in the Springfield community to the convention being moved elsewhere. Not surprisingly, the public officials and business community began to move to insure that the convention — and the corresponding prestige and dollars — would stay in Springfield. The general manager of the now defunct Leland

Motor Hotel offered to make available the public facilities of the hotel to the convention on a cost-free basis. Mayor Nelson Howarth publicly urged Witwer to keep the convention in the state's capital, assuring Witwer that: "Springfield can and will make available for the convention adequate conference, assembly, and housing facilities. Springfield's central location, its availability for all wire and press services, its established political and social research facilities, statewide attraction as the people's capital and scene of so many historical events, make it the ideal location for deliberations by the Illinois Constitutional Convention."

Alternative sites in Springfield were investigated, including buildings at the state fairgrounds, the state armory, and the hall of flags in the state's Centennial Building. However, momentum began to build for moving the convention to what should have been accepted as the natural home for the delegates from the outset: the Old State Capitol, then in the final stages of renovation for use as a tourist attraction and the future home of the Illinois State Historical Library. Witwer had always been favorably disposed toward the Old State Capitol because of its historical significance — Lincoln had served there while in the Illinois legislature; he delivered his famous "House Divided" speech there; and the 1870 constitution was written there. Others recognized the importance of such a setting for drafting a new constitution and argued accordingly. Jim Winning, a Springfield attorney, made the suggestion in December 1968 when he was contemplating running for delegate. In January 1970, the executive board of the Springfield Central Area Development Association passed and sent to Governor Ogilvie a resolution that he consider allowing use of the Old State Capitol for the convention. Denny Kelley, SCADA executive director, Owen Anderson, executive manager of the Springfield Association of Commerce and Industry, and Mayor Howarth met with Witwer to lend their support. Earl W. Henderson, Springfield civic leader and architect of the capitol renovation, favored the move, as did other leaders in the downtown business community.

The proposed move was not without opposition. There was a normal bureaucratic resistance among state government agencies that would be affected by the move or lack of move on the part of the agencies. Following the occupancy of the Old State Capitol under-

ground facilities by the State Historical Library, a series of moves was
to take place in a rather complex shift and reassignment of space in
several state buildings. That would all have to be held up for at least six
months until the convention vacated the Old State Capitol. William
Alderfer, head of the Historical Library, had to have mixed feelings.
He readily recognized the historical value of having yet another
landmark event take place in the already famous building, but he had
worked for some time to have the underground facilities made
available for the Historical Library. To see his plans delayed and to see
someone else as the occupant of the structure was an unsettling
experience.

The people in charge of the Old State Capitol — the Department of
Conservation and the Capital Tour Guides — reacted in shock at the
possibility of damage to the various artifacts which might result from
giving a large number of people constant access to the renovated
building. It did not seem to occur to them that, in any event, people
would be trampling on the precious floors, once the building was open
for its present purpose.

The press was quick to join the debate. The *Waukegan News-Sun*
editorialized against the move, urging that the delegates stay in the
House chamber at least until the legislature returned in April and that,
after April, a schedule be worked out whereby the convention would
meet some of the days of the week and the House would meet the other
days. The *News-Sun* position derived from a similar suggestion made
by two members of the House — Paul Elward and Victor Arrigo
—who were also delegates to the convention. Elward maintained that
the potential conflict between the dual use of the House was more
imagined than real. He believed most of the convention work for the
first five or six months — through May or June — would be done in
committees. "By the time they get ready to vote on the committee
reports and recommendations late next spring, the House should be
out of session," he said.

The *Illinois State Journal* took the opposite position, calling the Old
State Capitol a ready-made solution to the convention's space
problem. Their editorial underscored the historical and logistical
advantages of the building and ended with the statement that, "In such
a setting, Illinois could draw from its illustrious past in forging a
brighter future."

In early January (during the Christmas break) Witwer instructed Pisciotte to investigate thoroughly the use of the Old State Capitol and stated that he wanted that to become the permanent home of the Sixth Illinois Constitutional Convention. Pisciotte's inquiry served not only to bring to the surface the resistance to such a move, but also underscored the changes needed before the delegates could move in. The House chamber had just been furnished at great cost with original and copied artifacts from the Lincoln period. Safe removal and storage of the items had to be insured, as did the protection of the expensive carpeting that had just been laid. Security, lighting, air conditioning, a sound system, parking, telephones, etc. would also require attention. In addition, furniture would have to be manufactured and space provided for the delegates. Finally, there was the overriding matter of solving all these as well as other problems not only within the budget limitations of the convention but also before the Illinois General Assembly returned to Springfield on April 1. Pisciotte spent many hours in the chamber working out possible arrangements to seat the 116 delegates in the hall and assuring himself that the room could hold the convention, before he reported back to Witwer that it could be done. Then in a meeting with William S. Hanley, assistant to Governor Ogilvie, Pisciotte discussed the details of a possible move. Hanley recommended to Ogilvie that the convention be allowed to convene in the Old State Capitol but suggested a series of conditions that the convention would have to meet.

Following a meeting on January 14 between Witwer and Ogilvie, the governor issued a press statement offering the restored Old State Capitol for use by the convention: "We have studied the project for the past ten days and I am convinced that the Old State Capitol can meet the major needs of the Convention for chambers and for office space. The use of this historic setting will not only keep the convention in the capital city but also lend a very desirable aura to the proceedings of the Convention." The offer had the approval of the state historian, William Alderfer, and the Department of Conservation.

President Witwer, obviously overjoyed and excited about having obtained the offer from Ogilvie, took the news straight into the afternoon session of the convention. After recounting the many events of great historical significance that had taken place in the Old State Capitol, Witwer stated, with great emotion and some pride: "And so you can sense the historic significance of this building. It was in the same chambers that the Constitutional Convention of 1869 held its sessions and drafted the constitution which we are now reviewing. It will now be in the same chambers that we shall draft the Constitution of 1970 which will give this state a great constitution for many years to come."[7]

Ted Borek rose immediately and as he was often to do, moved acceptance by the convention of Governor Ogilvie's offer of the restored building. William L. Fay of Jacksonville and the 49th District, which included the city of Springfield, seconded the acceptance motion, but requested that Maurice Scott from Springfield join him in the motion. Scott then asked permission to "third" the motion and added his support for acceptance of the offer and to keep the convention in Springfield where it belonged. Borek withdrew his motion in deference to Scott. John Knuppel spoke to the motion, pointing out that he had lived for more than two decades within a stone's throw of New Salem, where Lincoln "came as a young man and lived and loved and matured into manhood." Knuppel, too, urged the convention to adopt the resolution of acceptance and added that the use of the building would have a great impact on the ability of the delegates to carry the new constitution to the people of the state for adoption.

The motion prevailed with applause, but, as was often the case in the early days of the convention, there was some grumbling among the delegates and observers. There were those who did not want to leave the spacious quarters of the current capitol and go into what were erroneously assumed to be inadequate facilities. At least two delegates were upset at the thought of attempting to shuttle between the two capitols, as were several members of the press corps who would be covering both the convention and the legislative session. Some displeasure was also expressed over the surprise announcement by Witwer; more specifically, some were irritated that they had not been consulted in advance.

In fact, Witwer did engage in a great deal of consulting, discussion, and exchange with a variety of individuals and groups, both within and without the convention. Executive Director Pisciotte investigated all

---

[7]Ibid., II, p. 224.

possibilities and worked closely with the governor's office, but the decision to move the convention to the capitol was indicative of Witwer's approach to the presidency of the convention. Like President Truman, he believed that "the buck stops here." He took most seriously his role under the rules of the convention and felt that the day-to-day responsibility of moving the business of the convention to its final objective was clearly his. That included decisions on procedural and administrative matters, as well as substantive and political aspects of the convention. In his inaugural address to the convention, Witwer had said, "I am going to be dependent on your help, your counsel, your patience, and your good will." In the decision-making process on the move to the Old State Capitol, he had abided by the first two and hoped to be granted the other two.

The Convention Moves

On February 26 Witwer appointed what, up to that point, was one of the more important committees, one that dealt with one of the more unanticipated procedural functions of the convention. He created an ad hoc committee for the arrangements for moving into the House chambers of the Old State Capitol. The convention staff was progressing quite well in putting together the detailed and complicated logistics of literally creating a legislative chamber in the Old State Capitol but the move was not yet fully accepted and approved by the delegates. To get the delegates involved in the move and to promote an opening ceremony in the new facility that would increase cohesion among the delegates and boost the progress of the convention, Witwer created the committee with his statement: "I would like to appoint at this time a committee to work with the chair and the staff for suitable observance of the day that we move into the old Capitol Building. We view this, as do a great many people, as a rather historic day, since it will represent the fourth convention to be held in that room. I am going to ask that we have on that committee David Connor as chairman, Mrs. Leahy, Mr. Sommerschield, Mr. Foster, and Mr. Carey."[8] But before the president could finish his statement, Mr. Connor rose to indicate that he did not wish to serve as chairman nor to serve on the committee. Mr. Witwer made no attempt to urge him to do so and

[8]Ibid., p. 373.

immediately appointed Philip Carey to serve instead as chairman. Carey and the committee worked with the staff in arranging an opening day ceremony in the Old State Capitol. It was to be one of the more memorable days of the convention.

The convention moved to the Old State Capitol on March 20, 1970; in the two preceding months space remained a problem for the delegates as well as the staff. While the House chamber itself was spacious, space for the rapidly growing staff was insufficient. When the convention convened in December 1969, it had had no staff and no space. One small office behind the House chamber was loaned to Witwer by Representative Art Telscer. That office, some one hundred feet square, became the office not only for President Witwer but also for the newly appointed executive director. There the two began to put together the administrative structure of the convention. By mid-January, when the staff had increased to thirty-six, Pisciotte had rented approximately 3,000 square feet of space in a private office building across from the capitol for the staff and officers of the convention as well as several of the substantive committees. This space was vacated in March when the move was made to the Old State Capitol and other locations in downtown Springfield.

THE CONVENTION AND THE ILLINOIS CITIZEN

Early in its deliberations the convention's Public Information Committee began discussing the feasibility of holding committee hearings throughout the state and open to the public. The idea of moving the convention away from its seat in Springfield and into closer physical proximity with the people was apparently unique in American constitutional experience; it was a concept that raised at once the possibility of delay and confusion, and of valuable public input. It was also coupled with the public relations image of listening to the people. On January 7 President Witwer announced the appointment of a subcommittee to deal with the question of out-of-Springfield hearings. David Stahl was made chairman of this subcommittee, and Joseph Tecson, John Parkhurst, and John Karns were named as members. They were among the convention's most respected and resourceful delegates.

On January 13 Stahl moved the adoption of the subcommittee's report, which recommended a week of public hearings in various locations around the state. The concentration of meetings in the Chicago area was striking, and Stahl commented that it was deliberate:

> The feeling of the subcommittee was that as Springfield is roughly in the geographical center of the state of Illinois, many people who would be interested in testifying or coming to or participating in the affairs of this Convention would have the opportunity throughout the state to do this in Springfield.
>
> However, there are over seven million people in the Chicago metropolitan area and we felt that this once, at least, some special effort should be made to give them the opportunity to present their views directly to the Convention.[9]

To this end, one day of meetings was scheduled in the suburban ring around Chicago and two days within the city itself. Meetings were also to be held simultaneously in Rockford, Peoria, and Marion. The committee sitting at each location would include a member of each substantive committee.

While some delegates were concerned that their areas had been overlooked in the selection of sites, support for the proposal was wide spread. Only Joseph Meek spoke against it, and he urged simply that the Revenue and Finance Committee members be allowed not to participate with other committees and be left free to make their own decisions on the value of participation. Meek quickly withdrew his resolution when it became apparent there was no general support for it and persistence on his part would merely delay the proceedings. Father Lawlor, who had expressed opposition to the idea of leaving the seat of the convention even before the subcommittee was formed, did not speak on Stahl's motion. Parkhurst rose to speak warmly in favor of the proposal as a new and worthwhile experiment in constitution-making, calling it Witwer's "brainchild" and praising it as a service to the people of the state and a significant step in ensuring public acceptance of the convention's product. The motion to take the hearings to the road passed easily on a voice vote.

Response to the initial meetings was good enough to encourage the delegates to set aside yet another day for public hearings in some downstate areas thought to have been neglected on the first swing

[9]Ibid., p. 196.

through the state. Hearings were scheduled in Champaign, East St. Louis, Alton, Effingham, Olney, Quincy, and Rock Island-Moline. In all, committees were in session 201 hours on the road before about 7,300 citizens in actual attendance. Testimony was heard from 1,270 individuals during the 25 separate hearings between February 9 and March 6. Press coverage was good, sometimes surprisingly so, and the delegates were pleased.

In substance, much of what the delegates heard was duplicative, not only of testimony heard before the substantive committees in Springfield, but of considerations raised by the members themselves. Taxes were a frequent topic, as were electoral reform, pollution, abortion, gun control, and state aid to private schools. Citizens appeared to argue pro and con on lowering the voting age, eliminating townships and other units of local government, and shortening the ballot to lessen the number of elective positions. There were entreaties to provide for home rule for local governmental units, eliminate the constitutional ban on lotteries, authorize the General Assembly to classify real estate, and open up the closed primary system in Illinois. Suggestions on restructuring the legislature ranged from proposals for a unicameral system to a detailed paper on establishing single-member house districts with overlapping senate districts. One of the most unusual suggestions came from Peoria, where a former mayor testified in favor of merging Illinois with one or more other states in an attempt to solve such common problems as pollution.

While it is unlikely that the delegates heard anything on the road they could not have heard in Springfield, the road shows were generally considered a success. From an external perspective, they were successful in generating the image of an open convention determined to gather ideas from the people who would have to approve and live with the convention's product. From an internal perspective, the hearings had exposed delegates from various geographical and philosophical extremes to the thoughts of constituents at the other extremes. Henry Green of Urbana, a lifelong resident of Champaign County, where he knew his neighbors and the election judges, was shocked by the concern for electoral reform and the intense support for making registration and voting more accessible in the cities. Interviewed after sitting on the panel hearing testimony in Chicago, he summed up the experience by saying: "One comment stands out in my mind. A witness said 'They can sure find us with the tax bill, but there's no effort like that to make us part of the electorate.' " Clifford Downen, another downstater, commented that what he had heard convinced him that no delegate was going to get everything he wanted in Springfield: "There's going to have to be a lot of compromising. Both sides are going to have to bend a little to get a constitution that will please a majority of the people."

Thus the road shows made real to the delegates what each of them had been telling the others all along — there really was a body of people out there with widely divergent views, and pleasing enough of them to pass a constitution was not going to be simple.

VII

Lobbyists, Interests, and Media

In the accomplishment of its task, the Sixth Illinois Constitutional Convention was dependent upon two groups who were not popularly elected members of the convention nor on its payroll — lobbyists and the media. In this chapter we review the nature of their involvement and discuss the several functions they performed. Their significant and indispensible contribution was in providing the essential two-way flow of information between the delegates and the public. Lobbyists and the media regularly perform this function for state legislative bodies, and in this general way, the convention and the Illinois General Assembly were similar. There was differences, however, in the manner in which the lobbyists and media related to the convention, and the specific purposes which each served in the convention's success.

LOBBYISTS AND INTERESTS

In anticipation of the convening of the constitutional convention, the Illinois General Assembly, on June 20, 1969, adopted the Constitutional Convention Lobbyists Registration Act, known as Public Act 76-1847. It was reasonably comprehensive. It spelled out definitions of persons required to register under the act and those not required to do so. It defined the resources that could be stipulated as "expenditure" for promoting or opposing inclusions of provisions in a new constitution; it defined such terms as "compensation," "reasonable and bona fide expenditure," and other related terms. The act provided that persons obligated to register under the law must do so with the Illinois secretary of state and outlined procedures for such registration. Appropriately, the act declared that nothing in it could be construed to infringe upon the right of citizens to petition convention delegates or any other public official, as guaranteed in the constitutions of the United States and the state of Illinois. There were reasonably stiff penalties for violating the law.

The delegates incorporated the act into Rule 57 of the constitutional convention, which simply stated that persons subject to the act must comply with its provisions. It was adopted with no debate; in fact, it was passed with very little attention.

The lobbying activity carried out in the constitutional convention was, in many respects, different from that in the Illinois General Assembly, and the extent of that activity never approached what takes place at any given time during General Assembly deliberations. Ian D. Burman, in his contribution to this Con Con series, *Lobbying at the Illinois Constitutional Convention*, concludes that the Sixth Illinois Constitutional Convention was, in the last analysis, an opportunity unused by many interests in Illinois state government and politics. That is not to say that there were not individuals present at the constitutional convention who had registered under the Lobbyists Registration Act, or who attempted to influence, either positively or negatively, the drafting of a new constitutional document. Burman divides the functions of interest groups at the convention into two categories: those performed at the convention; and those performed in the campaigns to call the convention and to gain approval of the convention's product. Functions relating to the convention were grouped, somewhat technically, into five activities: (1) cheerleader, (2) sounding board, (3) technical information, (4) interest representation, and (5) interest aggregation.

The first function, cheerleading, involved giving moral support to the delegates and reassuring them that someone cared. Those preparing for the convention had expected lobbyists to converge on the convention in hordes, bothering delegates and interfering with their deliberations. But their apprehensions were not fully realized, for many lobbyists normally operating in a legislative setting failed to devote more than minor portions of their time to the convention. Such a "noninterest" posture on the part of many private interest groups throughout the state caused many of the delegates to wonder occasionally if, in fact, their efforts were known to the people of the state and if, in fact, anyone cared. There were, however, many groups that recognized the importance of the convention and the long-term impact it would have on the future of the state. Giving consistent and virtually full-time attention to the convention were such groups as the League of Women Voters, the Illinois State Chamber of Commerce, the Welfare Council of Metropolitan Chicago, the Illinois Agricultural Association, and the Illinois Municipal League. The presence of such groups, on a continual basis, certainly was not crucial to the constitution-making process, but it did assist delegates at those stages of the convention when doubts arose about the efficiency of their efforts. It also served to enhance the relationship of those groups with the delegates when crucial decisions were being made on a rapid fire basis late in the convention. In short, a positive, if limited, reciprocal relationship did develop.

The press of time and the many demands on the delegates, together with a seeming disinterest on the part of some elements of the public, often made it difficult for the delegates to keep in touch with their districts or "the voters back home." Many of the delegates attempted to use the interest group representatives as "sounding boards," to determine how their individual proposals and those put forth by the convention as a whole were being received, not only by their districts, but by the state as a whole. Of course, they did not rely on such representatives as their sole channel of communication with the public, but for many it was a significant source of information.

Interest groups provided technical information on many issues in the convention and responded to numerous requests from individual delegates, but they did not fulfill the informational function to the same extent as in the legislature. One reason may have been that the convention was dealing with a more limited, if basic, scope of topics and issues, and the convention's research staff was of a far greater capacity than is that of the legislature. The preparatory work conducted by the Constitutional Study Commission on most of the topics with which the delegates dealt was rather substantial and there had been developed prior to the convention a good body of literature on most of the provisions of the Illinois constitution. With such an impressive array of background material, a qualified convention staff, the limited need for detailed technical information (such as that required in a legislative body) and, certainly, the ample and varied knowledge of the delegates themselves, the need for interest groups to supply information was of secondary and limited importance.

While testimony from representatives of interest groups and interested individuals did not serve an informational function, it did serve as a vital public relations device for the convention, since it provided an opportunity not only to receive but to impart information. It also served as a vital point of contact with the state citizenry, an important ingredient that was to enhance the chances of adoption of the convention's work product at a later date.

Another function carried out by interest groups identified by Burman — but again not to the same extent as in the General Assembly — was interest aggregation or, as it is ofttimes referred to in the General Assembly, "the agreed bill process," that is, the development of a compromise between opposing interests before submission of the measure. Historical accounts of the General Assembly tell of numerous instances in which interest groups put together such compromises and presented them to the General Assembly. At the convention, by contrast, almost all major compromises were worked out by the delegates, either in committee or on the floor, with very little input from lobbyists. That is not to say that nondelegates did not have a significant voice in the final decisions to the convention, but in all cases the delegates themselves controlled the decisions, and it was never left to others to work out the compromises. Suggestions, information, and positions were sought from those representing various interests, but the final working out of the conflicts was done by one or more of the delegates, depending upon the issue involved.

By the time the convention was in full swing in May 1970, fifty-six organizations had registered as convention lobbyists. But even at that point, and for the remainder of the convention, the registration or nonregistration of individuals operating on behalf of interest groups never became a point of concern by the president or the delegates. While the convention was lightly lobbied, at least in terms of those who registered and in comparison to the General Assembly, those who did recognize the convention as a significant policymaking body stood out in that they were quite active and gave the convention great attention.

The above mentioned Illinois League of Women Voters, the Illinois Chamber of Commerce, the Illinois Agricultural Association, the Welfare Council of Metropolitan Chicago, and the Illinois Municipal League had full-time representatives at practically all of the committee meetings and convention sessions. The Chicago Bar Association also gave considerable attention to the convention, but did not have representatives present at all times. Several statewide organizations with broad interests, which were expected to give heavy attention to the convention — such as the state AFL-CIO, the Illinois Retail Merchants Association, the Illinois Congress of Parents and Teachers, Taxpayers Federation of Illinois, the Illinois Manufacturers Association, the Illinois Education Association, and various civil rights organizations — did little beyond presenting viewpoints before committees and contacting delegates in an almost off-hand fashion, nothing sustained or continuous. There were other, smaller, single-purpose groups which made their views known, but without active participation.

In addition to the very active and the not so active groups, there were also those whose attendance ebbed and flowed as tides turned for or against a particular issue or interest. Such groups included the Illinois Bankers Association, the Illinois Coroners Association, the Township Officials of Illinois, womens rights groups, state and local employee pensioners groups, groups promoting rights for the handicapped, and sportsmen's groups concerned about guns and conservation. On any given day a committee or the entire convention could be flooded with large numbers of members from any of these groups, seeking to make known to the delegates that the group was not only interested in the particular issue, but that they represented numbers which could be translated into votes on referendum day.

Lobbying at the convention, then, involved primarily a few large associations in nearly constant attendance, with a handful of smaller interest groups coming in force to Springfield only as issues of particular concern to them were debated in committee or on the floor. The activities of the latter were manifested mostly through testimony before committees or through mail to delegates. On some issues there was a flood of mail, as when pensioners became concerned about their rights.

For his study, Burman relied on interviews with several of the delegates after the adjournment of the convention and concluded that two overriding reasons accounted for the comparatively light lobbying activity.

First, there was the feeling among lobbyists, either real or imagined, that the delegates would be less receptive to pressure tactics than were their legislative counterparts. That feeling stemmed in part from the assumption that the nonpartisan election had produced a special type of delegate who would behave differently than the regular lobbyists of Springfield had become used to. There was an uneasiness among the lobbyists since they felt, rightly or wrongly, that the delegates would be "do gooders," who would be more concerned with broad constitutional principles in an idealistic manner rather than specific group interests, and that the "rules of the game" would be different because the delegates would not have the pressure of seeking reelection. In addition, it was felt that most of them lacked hardnosed political experience. That is to say, the delegates would not understand the role that lobbyists had come to play in the policymaking process in the General Assembly.

This perception was incorrect, and while the delegates certainly did not need to seek reelection as delegates, they were constantly concerned about the acceptance of their product, and many of them had ambitions in elective politics beyond that of a constitutional convention delegate. While many of the delegates may have arrived at the convention scene with little or no experience in the ways of government and politics, for the most part, they were quick to learn the ways of real-world politics. The lobbyists were incorrect in their assumption that the delegates would somehow be hostile. The difference between the two types of policymakers in their receptivity of lobbyists was less than it appeared. Furthermore, the delegates grew more receptive toward interest groups as the convention progressed, as the uneasiness or fear of the unknown lessened and, particularly, as the delegates became more and more aware of the need for public support for the proposed constitution. Toward the end, when the hours of attendance became long, those lobbyists who were in Springfield frequently became an integral part of the process and close working relationships developed between many of them and the delegates.

The second major factor was the feeling among lobbying groups, again real or imagined, that the issues before the constitutional convention were of a broad long-term nature and would not have a profound immediate impact on their particular interests, that their interests would best be served by continued attention in the legislature. Many of the groups normally operating in the state political scene held a regular myopic view and could not perceive the long-term impact the convention would have on virtually all of the groups and interests in the state. They failed to recognize the convention as an alternate avenue for obtaining the relief sought by them.

Some simply failed to recognize that the rules of the game were different, the leadership was different, the pressures were different. Delegates elected under a nonpartisan label were less likely to be directly answerable to the immediate goals of the political parties. A good example of the difference involved nondiscrimination in housing. Elmer Gertz, chairman of the Bill of Rights Committee, commented, "It couldn't be put through the legislature. But we were able to put it into the constitution. I don't think we could have achieved it in years if we had to depend upon the legislature alone." Those interest groups which recognized the functions of the constitutional convention came away with something. The IAA obtained its sought-after special treatment in the assessment of agricultural land at no greater rate than residential land; the pension groups got a constitutional guarantee of their pension rights; the township officials obtained a constitutional stipulation against consolidating or dissolving townships without a popular referendum. The list of other lobbying successes is rather long. Civil rights advocates placed fair housing and employment provisions in the constitution; women's rights groups obtained equal protection under the law for women even though Illinois would long delay acceptance of ERA in the federal constitution; lobbyists for the physically and mentally handicapped won a clause again discrimination in property and employment; the Illinois Municipal League came away with one of the most unrestricted home rule provisions in any state; environmentalists received a separate article granting individuals the right to sue to maintain a healthful environment; small bankers retained a degree of restriction against branch banking; the Chamber of Commerce gained a fixed ratio between personal and corporate income tax; young people between the ages of eighteen and twenty-one got the question of the eighteen-year-old vote placed before the voters;

and the highly controversial issues of elected versus appointed judges and single member versus cumulative voting with multi-member districts had their day as separately submitted propositions. Two of the more visible lobbying groups, however, went away emptyhanded. The Coroner's Association, despite a hard fight, lost constitutional recognition for the office of county coroner and the sportsmen's interests, which also lobbied virgorously, failed to achieve a conservation article. But, alas, the gun lobby obtained constitutional recognition of the individual citizen's right to bear arms.

Many groups in Illinois, then, can be said to have seriously misjudged the opportunities presented at the convention. Their initial impressions of delegates were erroneous and distorted. It was such superficial impressions that, for the most part, discouraged many lobbyists from playing their natural role in the deliberative processes of the Sixth Illinois Constitutional Convention. It was not until after the adjournment of the convention and the adoption of the new Illinois Constitution that many of the groups became aware of its impact and sought to obtain legislation that would mitigate the impact of constitutional provisions viewed as detrimental to their interests.

In addition to these misconceptions, Burman sets forth a number of other, less important reasons for the comparatively, light lobbying: 1) delegates acting as "inside lobbyists" at the convention; 2) difficulty on the part of some lobbyists in determining the convention's scheduling, which in turn may have discouraged some from paying attention to the convention; 3) competition for lobbyists' attention from a legislative session held on occasion concurrently with the convention; and 4) a feeling that prevailed throughout Springfield that the convention would not be able to complete its business successfully or that if it did its product would be rejected by the voters, thus making it unnecessary for lobby groups to pay attention to the activities taking place in the Old State Capitol. To cite one example, as powerful and astute a lawyer as Don Reuben, counsel for the *Chicago Tribune*, told Gertz that he was paying no attention to the convention because its proposed constitution would be defeated.

Many delegates came to the convention with close ties to a particular interest group and, whether intended or not, served as an inside lobby for that group. For example, Paul Mathias had been a prominent member of the IAA staff for years and was instrumental in assisting the

IAA in obtaining its sought-after assessment provisions in the constitution. Maurice Scott continued as executive secretary of the Taxpayers Federation, while serving in the convention; Joseph Meek had retired as the head of the Retail Merchants Association before becoming a delegate, but continued to be recognized as a part of that association by everyone who participated in or viewed the convention's activities. Both Peter Tomei and Samuel Witwer had been chairmen of the Chicago Bar Association's committee on constitutional revision, and James Kemp and William Lennon came to the convention as recognized leaders among union officials. As a civil rights advocate, there was Albert Raby, who had been cochairman with Dr. Martin Luther King, Jr. of the Chicago Freedom Movement and a member of the board of Operation Breadbasket. On the other side stood Catholic priest Francis X. Lawlor, an organizer of the Association Block Clubs in Chicago. Louis Bottino aided educational interests, since he had been president of the Northeastern Division of the Illinois Education Association. David Connor was recognized as one of the chief spokesmen for branch banking by virtue of his position as a Peoria bank president. Mary Lee Leahy was champion of environmental rights. Odas Nicholson fought for women's rights. Henry I. Green aided the cause of state and local government workers' pension rights. Frank Cicero promoted the eighteen-year-old vote. Elmer Gertz and Bernard Weisberg, like Raby, were vitally interested in civil rights, generally. The Farm Bureau had numerous delegates operating on its behalf largely because the bureau was one group that had endorsed and given support to such delegates in their campaigns for election to the convention. Among these were Charles Shuman, James Parker, and Joseph Meek, to name only a few.

Those who wished to deal with the convention were faced with procedures that were different from those used by the legislature. Whereas the General Assembly focused on member-sponsored bills, which followed a continual identification through the committee and floor debates, the convention used a combination of member proposals and committee proposals, with member proposals becoming committee proposals after being assigned to a committee.

The convention refused to rubber stamp committee reports, and it was not uncommon for an item emanating from a committee to be sharply amended or for a minority report to be substituted for a majority report. Those attempting to obtain a favorable vote or prevent something from happening might feel a sense of victory in committee, only to find that their efforts had been to little avail and that they had to start from scratch when the issue reached the floor of the convention. Because of the absence of the political party structure in the convention, lobbyists could not depend upon a "caucus position" to give permanence to their particular positions. The convention operated with several loosely identified groups and with a president providing leadership but not the type that allowed him to deliver specific votes on particular issues. He was one among many, influential and an important one to be sure, but limited in power.

Convention lobbying was more easygoing, more subtle than that which takes place in the halls of the General Assembly. In essence, it was soft sell. Those who recognized this were the more successful in their efforts. Such a combination of firm but gentle and persistent pressure was best carried out by the League of Women Voters, the IAA, the Metropolitan Welfare Association, and the Illinois Municipal League. In contrast, there were those who took the "hard sell" approach, such as the Coroner's Association, the Illinois Bankers Association, and the Coalition of Associations interested in the rights for handicapped. They aggressively went after votes among the delegates, but their efforts were often dysfunctional, as many of the delegates reacted negatively. For example, Walter Oblinger of the Illinois Coroner's Association, in a last ditch effort to save the coroners offices, got the County Officers Association — a loose confederation which existed mostly on paper — to pass a resolution stating that if one county office were left out of the constitution all member organizations would oppose the new constitution. The delegates, who were continually concerned about positive group endorsements of their efforts, thought that the resolution was a premature commitment on the part of the groups involved to oppose a document not yet written. This did not rest well with them and it was an important factor in the failure of the coroners to overcome the substantial opposition to retaining their constitutional status.

The Illinois Bankers Association carried out its hard sell tactics for perhaps the longest time in the convention. While the bankers drew very negative reactions from those opposed to their position, they also achieved some successes. They were able to eliminate the constitutional requirement that any change in the banking provisions be put to a referendum and obtained some wording for change in the legislature that could be favorable to their particular interests. In fact, in the General Assembly sitting in 1977, a branch banking provision was passed that allowed branch banks to be developed within twenty five miles of the parent organization.

Success was also achieved by the Coalition of Associations interested in achieving a bill of rights provision for the physically and mentally handicapped. In the end, the delegates gave the handicapped almost everything they asked for, but it was only after some heated controversy and some show of force and threats. It was successful in part because Elmer Gertz and his cohorts induced Delegate Richard Daley to become a sponsor of the provision. And, in the end, it became difficult for delegates to vote against the provision when, on third reading, the convention chamber was packed with handicapped persons in wheelchairs and on crutches.

THE MEDIA

The media, in all its modern forms, were well represented at the convention, and while not official lobbyists or participants, were quite influential in the work product and success of the convention.

Some forty individuals made up the regular media corps covering all or part of the convention proceedings. Seven represented the Associated Press and United Press International wire services. Three newspaper chains — Chamberlain-Loftus, Copley, and Lindsay-Schaub — assigned reporters, as did the Capitol Information Service, The *Bloomington Pantagraph*, *Illinois State Journal*, *Illinois State Register*, *Peoria Journal-Star*, *Rockford Morning Star*, *St. Louis Globe Democrat*, and the *St. Louis Post-Dispatch*. Five Chicago dailies were represented: the *Daily News*, the *Defender* (the black newspaper), *Sun-Times*, *Chicago Today*, and the ancient and powerful *Tribune*. Reporters from seven radio and television stations (WBBM, WCIA, WCVS, WGN, WICS, WMAY, WTAX) were present, mostly for major events. Only one television station, WCIA from Champaign, established the convention as a full-time beat, thus eliminating the need for its reporter Tony Abel to divide his time between the convention and the Illinois General Assembly. Others appeared on the scene irregularly. But wherever one went, the media representatives were present, not only in the substantial press rooms provided for them, but in all places where delegates and staff and those purported to be "in the know" congregated, committee rooms, corridors, hotels and motels, and above all, in the bars. Of course, the press was not content to rely simply upon the convention's information bureau headed by Jim Bradley and Caroline Gherardini, or the public information committee chaired by the knowledgeable David Stahl, who had his schooling in Chicago's city hall. Nevertheless, the media did not lack for material or facilities with which to report the convention activities. Press releases, daily summaries, weekly wrap-ups, radio feeds, and news conferences were regularly provided. The convention staff also arranged the Old State Capitol facilities to allow the media convenient and efficient space in which to work. Permanent space in the office complex was assigned to those regularly covering the convention, telephones were installed, and the delegates floor debate was piped into the media area to preclude the need to be constantly on the convention floor. On the floor, special elevated work areas were built to accommodate the press; space was provided in the balcony for the television cameras.

As was true among the delegates, the media who covered the convention had their leaders and memorable characters. Chick McCuen wandered between Chicago and Springfield and always managed to make his presence felt among the delegates, even by those who did not know that he simply represented NBC and its Chicago outlet, WMAQ. He sent hearts fluttering, glasses clinking, and tongues wagging. The Chicago newspaper correspondents were varied and effective. There was marked contrast between the cold John Elmer and the warmly feminine Edith Herman, both of the *Tribune*. The young John Camper was totally different from his cynical and perceptive *Daily News* stablemate, Ed Gilbreth. Others created special images — among them, Charles Wheeler III, Tony Abel, Coleman Mobley, Alan Crane, Steve Schickel, Caryl Carstens. They were everywhere, with microphones, cameras, notebooks, but they were most effective when they depended only upon their abilities to pry out information. They were quick to create a mini-crisis, as when the Bill of Rights Committee barred the press from its inquisition on administrative assistant Lawrence Miller, or when it withheld the several Dallin Oaks memoranda from prying eyes. Frequently they played up personalities. Frequently they gave different accounts of the proceedings, but by and large, they were fair, factual, helpful, and in many respects as institutionalized in the convention proceedings as were the delegates and staff.

In anticipation of the significant role the media would play in the convention's success, the Third Constitution Study Commission sponsored an orientation session for the press. The three-day conference, organized by the University of Illinois Institute of Government and Public Affairs and the College of Communications, was attended by some fifty representatives of newspapers, wire services, radio, and television who would be involved in covering the convention. The commission had learned from recent conventions in other states not only the importance of the media, but some difficulties that could be anticipated. In other states, the convention-press relationship was not always a positive one, and did little to enhance the chances of success. Illinois, on the other hand, brought the media into the process at an early date.

At the press orientation, both procedural and substantive topics were discussed. Briefings were held on the major issues the delegates would be debating, and the media was given the first public look at the convention rules drafted by the commission and to be presented to the delegates at their orientation. The underlying theme, however, throughout the media conference was the basic difference between a session of the Illinois General Assembly and the constitutional convention. One was partisan, the other non-partisan; one a continuing body, the other sitting only once for a specific time period. The legislature makes laws for specific and immediate needs, the convention would be charged with adopting a broader policy that would establish the long-term framework of the relationship of Illinois government to its citizens. The rules, the participants, the daily output, and the environment would not be the same for the two policy-making bodies. The differences would in turn require new approaches by the media in its coverage of the convention, its deliberations, its participants, and its daily and total work products. For example, the media could not expect that even the most minor substantive issues would be resolved early in the convention. At the outset attention would be focused on procedural and logistical activities necessary to get a new deliberative body underway. These would not make for good daily copy.

In spite of the press orientation and the attempts by the convention president and staff to keep the media fully informed, there was a period early in the proceedings when the media was not positive toward the convention. Some of the media regulars in Springfield were privately predicting a convention failure. They were perhaps reflecting the atmosphere of the convention itself, which in the initial weeks was not at a positive peak. The rules were being debated, budget and facilities were uncertain, and the staff had not yet been fully hired or stabilized. The delegates had simply not yet gotten into the substance of their task. Their restlessness carried over to the media.

Once the convention settled into its routine, and substantive issues began to emerge from the procedures, the attitudes changed. The functional interdependence of delegates and media also began to emerge. The delegates needed the reporters to keep their constituents informed, and the reporters needed the delegates in action to produce stories to report. It was in this atmosphere that the several roles of the media developed.

First, they provided the basic mechanisms for the two-way flow of information between the convention and the public. The absence of good news coverage would have increased the uncertainties that surrounded the delegates. Anticipating public response to their decisions was difficult at best; the citizen feedback generated by the stories filed by correspondents became indispensible as the weeks of the convention wore on.

Second, the media served as a conduit of information within the convention itself. As an organization, the convention was complex and large enough to have internal communications problems. There were 116 delegates, and dozens of staff members, all divided into nine substantive and three procedural committees. Committee meetings, held at all hours, were interspersed with the plenary sessions and committee of the whole meetings. Countless formal and informal gatherings were constantly being convened, in the meeting rooms, in the hallway, over lunch, or in the president's office. The media often helped communicate to delegates and staff what other delegates and staff were doing. They often did this through conversations, but mostly through their reported stories. Frequently the convention participants watched the ten o'clock news or read the morning paper to find out what others had done. The media was an integral part of the conventions communication system.

Third, the media served a selling function on behalf of the delegates' final work product. Through their regular reporting, mostly of a positive nature, the public developed an awareness of the convention and the openness by which it operated. But equally important, many of the regular press corps became advocates of the proposed document during the adoption campaign. Doubtless they were influential on endorsement decisions. Several appeared as experts on programs discussing the substance of the new constitution.

One television reporter, Tony Abel, consulted with other state constitutional conventions on the role of the media in the Illinois success story. Of course one does not know whether that success was because of or in spite of the media, but it is difficult to imagine successful proceedings without them. They performed vital formal and informal communications functions, and in so doing, were as much a part of the process as the elected delegates and paid staff.

VIII

Controversy from Within and Without

During the course of the convention, two major incidents disrupted the work of the delegates and perhaps even threatened the success of their efforts. One involved the seating of a delegate.

THE GIERACH CHALLENGE

The 1870 Illinois Constitution contained a few basic provisions that applied to future constitutional conventions. One of these read: "Before proceeding the members shall take an oath to support the constitution of the United States, and of the State of Illinois, and to faithfully discharge their duties as members of the convention."[1] Another stated: "The qualification of members shall be the same as that of members of the Senate."[2]

Moreover, the qualifications for members of the Senate are also prescribed in the same constitution which the members had recently taken an oath to uphold. Included among the constitutional qualifications is the following language: "No person shall be a Senator . . . who shall not have been . . . for two years next preceding his election a resident within the territory forming the district from which he is elected."[3]

James Gierach, a twenty-five year old lawyer, had grown up in the

[1]Article XIV, section 1, *Constitution of the State of Illinois,* adopted May 13, 1870.
[2]Ibid.
[3]Article III, section 3, *Constitution of the State of Illinois,* adopted May 13, 1870.

Sixth District, but upon his marriage a year or so earlier, had moved into another district where he appeared to have established residence; indeed, by his voting registration, he declared this residence a matter of public record. The move was supposed to facilitate his attendance at law school.

In 1969, after an absence of about one year, he returned to the Sixth District, again took up residence and engaged in the practice of law with his father. He testified later before the convention committee that he had always intended to maintain his residence in the district.

A few months later he stood for election as a delegate from the Sixth District and received the second highest vote in this highly contested election. At about the time of the election, a child was born to the young couple. They could well ask what the events that followed could augur for all of them.

Based upon a claimed failure to meet the residence requirement, the Gierach election was challenged and protested twice in court, principally by one of the numerous candidates who had been defeated in the Sixth District election and who, in fact, had finished seventeenth in a field of eighteen candidates. Obviously, he did not think he could be seated in place of Gierach. One can only speculate as to his motives. He may have proceeded out of rectitude or rancor or something in between. At any rate, there was a challenge. The courts and other forums where the protests had been lodged dismissed the challenge for lack of standing and jurisdiction; they admonished the convention, once it had been organized, to be the sole judge of its own membership, and suggested that the convention have exclusive jurisdiction over the matter. The Supreme Court of Illinois upheld the lower court rulings. Gierach had not yet taken his oath of office.

The day the convention opened, James Gierach appeared and took the oath of office with the other 115 delegates. Almost immediately formal objections were filed by the unsuccessful litigant in the courts to contest his right to a seat at the convention.

Sustaining the objection would have created a vacancy; a different delegate would not have been seated. The convention did not have before it a contest between two candidates to determine which had won the election. The matter pending was simply a question of whether or not Gierach met the requirement of being a resident of the Sixth District for two years preceding his election. Thus, if Gierach were out, no one would be substituted for him, and the district would go underrepresented.

An ad hoc committee was appointed by President Witwer to consider the problem. It was headed by Thomas Hunter, a lawyer and a black, loyal to the Democratic organization. The committee heard testimony, examined exhibits, and received and reviewed briefs; meanwhile a growing segment of the convention was becoming sentimentally attached to Gierach, the youngest of the delegates. Many found it increasingly tempting to vote to retain him. Hunter confided to a friend that he felt delay was the best arbiter, and there was delay aplenty.

Yet, there was a substantial body of opinion among the delegates that the success of the convention would be impaired if the convention acted, by majority vote, to ignore facts that were becoming increasingly evident to them. Vice-President Smith and others suggested that if the assembled delegates were willing to violate openly the 1870 constitution, could adherence be expected to a 1970 constitution drafted by these same delegates? Smith felt that the basic integrity of the convention body was being tested. He was especially sensitive to such an issue, because he had succeeded a corrupt auditor of public accounts in office and had the duty of giving credibility to a besmirched position. He had learned the utility of honesty.

Furthermore, as Smith phrased it: "In the realm of law a constitution is superior to a statute, an ordinance, a rule, regulation or executive order. Legislative bodies, executive officers and courts are all expected to revere and respect a constitution. Undeviating adherence is commanded to the plain language of a constitution. The provisions of a constitution may be changed or repealed but only by action of the people."

Then, too, there was the question, also posed by Smith: "Should the convention show itself to be a body of softies — bleeding hearts — drawing aside from rectitude and plain duty? Each delegate has taken an oath to faithfully discharge his duties as a member of the convention and to support the constitution of the United States and the State of Illinois. Would not a knowing, willful omission to perform a duty — a deliberative violation of the clear language of the Illinois constitution — be flat out corruption?"[4]

---

[4]Taken from the personal writings of Elbert Smith.

Could a rational legal basis be found to support a vote to reject the challenge to Mr. Gierach's claim to membership in the convention? The briefs submitted on his behalf did not provide much help. Although well prepared by able lawyers, the main precedent for a supporting argument was a single case in Maryland. There, the state's highest court had held that Theodore McKeldin, whose nonresidence in Baltimore was occasioned by reason of his service as governor — the Maryland constitution required the governor to be a resident of Annapolis during his term of office — need not be a resident of the city of Baltimore in order to vote there.

The discussion that ensued showed the delegates to be of three minds. Some felt that Gierach's declaration of voting residence in the Ninth District within the two-year period resolved the question against him on a legal basis, and that to hold otherwise would call the convention's integrity and the concept of residency into question. Among these purists were Chicago independents Albert Raby, Mary Lee Leahy, and Bernard Weisberg, and Republican Stanley Johnson of DeKalb. Others rose to praise Gierach and call upon their fellow delegates to spare the young man's reputation and political future by exercising mercy in casting their votes. Yet a third group insisted that friendship could be reconciled with law, contending that, for various reasons, Gierach's apparent violation of the requirements for seating was, in fact, not a violation at all.

Among this third group was Maurice Scott, who argued that the Rules Committee had been Gierach's jury and that jury's acquittal should stand. Thomas Lyons added that intention was the critical factor in residency, and that Gierach's intention to maintain his residency in the Sixth District was manifested in several ways — among them his storing personal belongings within the district and applying for a driver's license from his parent's address. Wendell Durr pointed out that one of Gierach's residency statements — either the one for voting in the Ninth District or the one for running in the Sixth District — had to be incorrect, and that a "superjury" of 14,000 voters had opted to believe the statement of candidacy.

Thomas Kelleghan elaborated on the body of case law, attempting to define residency, and argued that intent was paramount; Gierach's intent to maintain his Sixth District residence was, Kelleghan thought, established beyond doubt by his own testimony. Arthur Lennon argued that the convention had no power to judge a delegate's residence. His contention was that there was a legal difference between being eligible to run and being qualified to serve, and that the question of residence went only to a candidate's eligibility to run. Since the convention's charge was only to rule on the qualification of its members, Lennon went on, Gierach's eligibility to run was not before the body. Eligibility, he argued, citing a 1953 attorney general's opinion, could properly be tested only in a separate suit at law.

"The Gierach challenge just would not go away," Elbert Smith later said. "The bona fide, card-carrying scholars performed diligent research. Other delegates went about, like a well-digger witching for water, hoping for a clue to a valid reason to support Gierach." Elmer Gertz, who in the end supported Gierach, reasoned that if he could urge the commutation of a death sentence for a murderer, he could refrain from wrecking the career of a young lawyer, however technically improper his decision might be. Thomas McCracken later thanked Gertz for his compassion with tears in his eyes. Gertz had to confess to himself that had the vote on Gierach come at the outset of the convention, he might have voted against him on legal grounds. Whatever the cause for delay, Gertz felt that at that relatively late point in the convention deliberations it would have been singularly unfortunate to act harshly, if with a punctilious regard for the law. Mercy can revise the law at times, as Portia remarked so eloquently in a different context. This, then, was a case where the letter of the law truly killeth.

After extensive discussion and public hearings in both Springfield and Chicago, the Committee on Rules and Credentials voted eight to five with two abstentions to recommend to the convention "that the objection to the status of Mr. Gierach . . . be dismissed as being without merit . . . ."[5] On April 8, 1970, delegate Thomas Lyons moved adoption of the committee report.

When the vote was called, the recommendation to dismiss the challenge passed seventy-one to thirty-six, with four voting pass and two answering present. The Chicago organization vote helped, but there were independents and downstaters behind the young delegate as well. Among those voting for seating were Dove, Durr, Gertz,

[5]*Record of Proceedings, Sixth Illinois Constitutional Convention,* Vol. II, p. 606.

Knuppel, Netsch, Scott, Tomei, Willer, Martin; Ozinga, Gierach's fellow delegate from the Sixth District, passed his vote. Votes not to seat were cast by Connor, Foster, Johnson, Leahy, Parkhurst, Elbert Smith, Charles Shuman, Weisberg, and President Witwer, among others.

Gierach rose to thank the body for its support, quipping that he doubted any other person had ever been elected to the same office for the same term so many times, "twice by the electorate, five times by three different branches of our court system including state and federal, and two subcommittees, and once by the Committee of the Whole."

Gierach's record at the convention was that of a Daley loyalist, with nothing either to distinguish or mar it. Since then he has played an honorable role as lawyer and citizen.

In less than six weeks following the happy resolution to the Gierach challenge, the convention was again embroiled in a controversy. This potentially devastating incident became known as the Gardner Imbroglio.

THE GARDNER IMBROGLIO

On the morning of Wednesday, May 13, 1970, the *Illinois State Journal* of Springfield reported that John W. Gardner, head of the Urban Coalition and secretary of the Department of Health, Education, and Welfare in the Lyndon Johnson administration, would deliver "a major policy address" that morning at the Illinois Constitutional Convention. The *Journal* said Gardner's speech was "expected to center on events of the past two weeks." The *Peoria Journal-Star* of the same morning said: "He [Gardner] was invited to address Con-Con on the subject of urban problems by Convention President Samuel W. Witwer some weeks ago. It was reported yesterday, however, his speech will also touch on the national events of the past several weeks, including the movement of troops into Cambodia and the disorders on college campuses."[6]

Unbeknownst to the editors of the *Journal* and *Journal-Star*, convention President Witwer had withdrawn the invitation to Gardner

[6]*Peoria Journal-Star,* May 13, 1970.

at about the time their papers were going to press. Controversy about that decision was to provoke debate within a matter of hours not only in Illinois but also, surprisingly enough, throughout the nation.

In explaining Gardner's absence to the delegates Wednesday morning, and in a press conference later that day, Witwer said he had cancelled the talk solely on his own initiative after seeing the text of the remarks Gardner planned to deliver. Press accounts said Witwer's tone was angry and his voice often rose[7] as he called the proposed speech a "foreign policy broadside condemnatory of the President of the United States"[8] and expressed fear that the speech would "fragment the convention," turn it into "a battleground over Cambodia," and cause the delegates to become "embroiled in extraneous issues."[9]

Gardner had accepted an invitation extended several months earlier by Witwer to address the convention on urban problems and possible solutions, considered vital and controversial in drafting a new constitution. Witwer said it was only the evening before that he had learned of a "total and complete" shift of emphasis from constitutional urban reform to issues of national policy,[10] a shift so substantial that the speech as Gardner intended to deliver it made only "the most oblique reference to constitutional reform."[11] Witwer's intense concern for averting partisan debate and emotional controversy at the convention had been well established by May 1970. Not surprisingly then, he asked Gardner, over the telephone, to return to his original topic, one "germane to the purposes of the convention" and offered to provide a hall in Springfield for Gardner to present his foreign policy address if he would first keep his commitment to speak on urban affairs.[12] When Gardner refused, the invitation to speak was withdrawn, and Gardner, who had stopped over in Chicago after a trip to the West Coast, returned to Washington where he hurriedly released portions of the speech at a well-attended press conference. The text decried "the growing crisis of confidence in our leadership" brought on by the Nixon administration's move into Cambodia and argued that the

[7]*St. Louis Post-Dispatch,* May 14, 1970.
[8]*Chicago Sun-Times,* May 14, 1970.
[9]*Chicago Sun-Times,* May 14, 1970.
[10]*Chicago Sun-Times,* May 14, 1970.
[11]*Chicago Sun-Times,* May 14, 1970.
[12]*Chicago Sun-Times,* May 14, 1970.

United States could not be peacekeeper in the Asian world. It warned of possible national disintegration if moderate Americans did not counteract the proponents of violence and said any possible geopolitical advantages in the war must be seen as pitifully small by contrast with the erosion of spirit the country had experienced.

Gardner subsequently contended that his remarks were germane to constitution making, since they called for a revitalization of political institutions. He claimed, however, that his hosts had been told in advance about the broad area to be covered by the speech, that they had voiced no objection, and that he had withdrawn when left with the option of "making an impromptu set of remarks on state constitutional reform,"[13] a statement which Witwer correctly denounced as untrue.[14] According to Gardner, convention staff director Richard Carlson had assured him "it would be perfectly all right for me to talk about general things and the state of the nation."[15] He suggested that Witwer had underestimated the resilience of the convention delegates and that the withdrawal of the invitation, if intended to silence dissent on the war, was "not a very effective attempt."[16] Throughout his Washington press conference, Gardner consulted frequently with Lloyd Beck, a representative who had conducted the actual telephone negotiations with the convention people Tuesday night. "He [Witwer] said he didn't think it would be appropriate to have these sentiments expressed — particularly about the President," Gardner said. "At another time he mentioned there were 40 'hard-core' Democrats in the group, followers of Mayor Daley, and that he could not answer for their behavior." Both Gardner and Beck indicated their impression that Witwer meant the Democratic delegates might interrupt the speech on grounds they were supportive of the Vietnam war.[17] Gardner said that Witwer's original invitation to him to speak had suggested he "throw down the gauntlet" — a remark he interpreted to call for a challenging, issue-related talk.[18]

Reaction in Illinois and throughout the country was swift and severe. Though the majority of the delegates applauded Witwer's

[13]*Washington Post*, May 14, 1970.
[14]*Chicago Sun-Times*, May 14, 1970.
[15]*Chicago Sun-Times*, May 14, 1970.
[16]*Washington Post*, May 14, 1970.
[17]*Chicago Sun-Times*, May 14, 1970.
[18]*Chicago Daily News*, May 14, 1970.

announcement and one delegate offered to introduce a resolution of support, a few reacted angrily. Delegate Albert Raby termed the decision "crude censorship" and claimed that many delegates were deeply disturbed. He said Witwer's withdrawal of the invitation without consulting the convention illustrated the "very arrogance of power and isolation of leadership to which Mr. Gardner was going to speak,"[19] and argued that the prepared remarks were relevant to the work of the convention. Robert Bockiewicz of the Lindsay-Schaub News Service reported that a committee chairman was "outraged" by Witwer's decision, yet conceded that only fifteen delegates thought the speech should have been allowed.[20]

Illinois Lieutenant Governor Paul Simon, who had himself earlier addressed the delegates on constitutional reform, criticized Witwer for refusing to adhere to the principles of free speech and telephoned Gardner to express his own regret about the cancellation. Convention Vice-President Elbert Smith, one of the most liberal delegates on the basis of his voting record, expressed "great approval" of Witwer's decision and said "the convention ought not be a forum for national affairs."[21] Elmer Gertz, chairman of the Bill of Rights Committee, assured Witwer of his support, although he was in agreement with Gardner's views on the war in Asia. Gertz felt the convention ought to stick to convention problems, and not intrude into foreign policy.

On Thursday, May 14, Richard M. Daley, a Chicago delegate and son of Chicago Mayor Richard J. Daley, initiated a move to place the text of Gardner's speech in the convention record. While Mayor Daley had been openly critical of Witwer's actions, his son assured Witwer that the Democratic delegation would not support any resolution to censor him. Gardner's remarks in Washington had suggested that the Chicago Democrats were integral to the decision to cancel his speech. Witwer denied this and contended that his remarks about Chicago Democrats had been distorted; he had not, he said, intended to indicate Illinois Democrats were "hawklike" on the war, but only meant to make clear to Gardner that there were strong adherents to both political parties at the convention and that any speech which aggravated differences between those parties could generate controversy

[19]*St. Louis Post-Dispatch,* May 15, 1970.
[20]*Champaign-Urbana Courier,* May, 15, 1970.
[21]*Decatur Herald,* May 14, 1970.

which would ultimately destroy the work of the convention. Witwer concurred in Daley's motion to place Gardner's speech in the record and the motion passed 66-22. There was angry objection by a few delegates, including Mary A. Pappas, a suburban Republican, who called the speech "immaterial and irrelevant to the goals of the convention."[22]

Meanwhile, in Chicago, Mayor Daley was angrily denouncing the rumor that his son had been involved in the decision to revoke Gardner's invitation. "My son is at the convention speaking for himself," he said, "but your rumor was very ill-founded, because if he had any of the blood that ran through his grandfather or his father, you wouldn't find a Daley stopping anyone from talking. You would find him out on the street championing the right of anyone to speak." The mayor went on to say that one of the country's problems was the unwillingness of some people to listen enough and said he had read Gardner's books and felt Gardner accurately described the problems facing the nation, especially the cities.[23]

Whether Witwer's decision to cancel Gardner's speech was right or wrong, there is no question that the ramifications were tremendous. What might in Illinois have been but one more diatribe against the war, overnight became a national cause celebre. The *New York Times* of May 15 said: "The nation slides toward isolation in irrationality when politicians at a convention called to draft a state's basic law can suppress as irrelevant a carefully reasoned appeal to halt the disintegration of American society. This is precisely what happened when John W. Gardner was barred from telling the Illinois Constitutional Convention that America is being torn apart by the growing tendency to tolerate violence at home and abroad."

David Brinkley, of NBC News, introduced a film excerpt of Gardner's Washington press conference with these remarks:

> John Gardner, former secretary of Health, Education and Welfare and now head of the Urban Coalition, was invited to Springfield, Illinois, to make a speech to the Illinois Constitutional Convention.
>
> He went to Springfield, carrying mimeographed copies of the speech he was to make. But when they read an advance copy of his speech, the invitation was cancelled.

[22]*Chicago Tribune,* May 15, 1970.
[23]*Chicago Sun-Times,* May 15, 1970.

They said he could make another speech, but not that one. So he returned to Washington and didn't make any. Instead, he called a news conference and read some of what he would have said in Springfield had they allowed him to speak.

Newsweek, in its May 25 issue, described Gardner as so outspoken on the war "that he was denied a forum in Illinois last week and had to release the text in Washington."

Probably the most widely disseminated piece was *Fortune's* June 9 editorial, published simultaneously as an advertisement in the *New York Times*, which described the United States as a "divided, frustrated, and anxiety-ridden country" and went on to say:

> A measure of the present crisis was the last-minute refusal of the Illinois Constitutional Convention to let John W. Gardner make a long-scheduled speech. Gardner, a Republican who had served a Democratic President as Secretary of Health, Education, and Welfare, is one of the most patiently reasonable figures in public life. The Illinois convention, stirred up by its own passionate argument over Cambodia, feared the effect of Gardner's warning that "the nation disintegrates." By refusing to listen, the convention, which is not composed of excitable students or nervous guardsmen, demonstrated that the nation was indeed disintegrating.

Back in Illinois, the reaction of the smaller papers was uniformly supportive of Witwer. This language from an editorial in the *Aurora Beacon-News* is typical:

> The Convention has plenty of work and problems of its own without wasting its valuable time and becoming involved with national and international issues. Nor should it ever become a forum for partisan political speech-making.
>
> Gardner was guilty of exceedingly poor judgment if not outright rudeness by attempting to use a purely state body as a platform from which to attack those in Washington with whom he disagrees.

Among the larger papers, the conservative *Chicago Tribune* and its sister paper, *Chicago Today*, also supported Witwer's right to deny Gardner a forum at the convention, though the *Tribune* described the actual decision to cancel as "a tactical error." The *St. Louis Globe-Democrat* praised Witwer and suggested that Gardner procure a soapbox and stand on street corners. However, the two Field papers in

Chicago, throughout the convention strong in their support of Witwer and the convention's work, and thorough in their coverage of the deliberations, were highly critical of the decision. The *Sun-Times* on May 15 suggested that it abridged freedom of speech and dissent and said that, even though Gardner had apparently "stretched his invitation out of shape," he should have been allowed to speak as a matter of fundamental principle. The *Daily News* on May 16 conceded that convention officials were justified in "hitting the ceiling" when they saw the text of Gardner's speech, but nevertheless decried the decision to cancel. "That decision," read the editorial, "smacks of panic, generated by the overcautious mood that has afflicted the convention from the beginning."

Response from the public was immediate. Witwer received dozens of letters and telegrams, many of which termed his decision "stupid" or "repressive." One writer suggested that he pause to read the First Amendment to the United States Constitution before proceeding further with the redraft of the Illinois document. This initial flurry preceded Witwer's public response, which took the form of a letter to the editors of major newspapers and magazines criticizing his decision. After publication of that response, which explained the terms under which Gardner had been invited and pointed out that convention officials had offered to help Gardner find access to another forum in Springfield for his policy address, critical letters dwindled rapidly and favorable comments increased. One writer offered Witwer, for his amusement and consolation, the following quotation from a commencement address delivered by Gardner some time before the incident in Springfield: "The reformers couldn't have been less interested in the basic adaptability of a society that posed tough and complex tasks of institutional redesign, that bored them to death. They preferred the joys of combat, of adversary relationships, or villain hunting."[24]

Upon Witwer's personal insistence, his response eventually ran in the *New York Times, Fortune, Newsweek,* and both Field papers, though none of the papers or magazines involved retracted their initial adverse comments. In private correspondence, the publishers of *Fortune* admitted they had been in error to imply there had been

[24]Letter to S. Witwer dated May 20, 1970.

discussion of Cambodia on the floor of the convention, but contended that their editorial was based on "the concern of the delegates and their strong discussions on the Cambodian question as well as the circumstances of the Gardner speech" outside the official record of the convention. Witwer replied that the delegates never engaged in strong discussion on the Cambodian question, either formally or informally. According to Witwer, the delegates did not fear Gardner's comments, but only resented his attempt to use the convention as a forum for delivering a foreign policy statement in contradiction to the terms of his invitation. In fact, Witwer's suspicions that Gardner had planned to use the convention as a forum for his foreign policy speech were confirmed a year later at an impromptu Chicago airport press conference.

Edward Gilbreth, who covered the convention for the *Chicago Daily News*, commented in a follow-up article that Witwer's own disappointment at not hearing Gardner's original speech on constitutional reform and the urban crisis was lost in the larger controversy over the withdrawal of the invitation to speak on Cambodia.[25] As Gilbreth noted, it was Witwer's enormous respect for Gardner's knowledge in urban affairs that initiated what ultimately became one of Witwer's worst moments at the convention.

To get back to the beginning, the letter which began the saga was dated January 28, 1970. In it Witwer commented that he had closely observed several of Gardner's recent speeches on urban problems and saw them as "provocative challenges to those of us involved in the fight for institutional reform to the solution of our urban crisis. I would deeply appreciate your throwing down this gauntlet before the Illinois Constitutional Convention."

Many weeks followed before any further contact was had with Gardner. Then in mid-March the convention was visited by William G. Colman, retired executive director of the Advisory Commission on Intergovernmental Relations. Colman, a consultant to the Local Government and Revenue and Finance committees at the convention, revealed that he had also been serving as consultant and speech writer to Gardner and the Urban Coalition. When he learned of the apparently dormant invitation, he agreed to encourage Gardner to

[25]*Chicago Daily News*, May 18, 1970.

accept. Almost immediately thereafter, the convention received word
of Gardner's acceptance of the invitation. When May 13 was selected
as the date for the speech, convention staffers entered into conversations
with Colman, who said he had been asked by Gardner to prepare some
suggested remarks. These conversations, which centered on the
progress of the Local Government and Revenue and Finance
committees, continued for some weeks. Colman said that while he did
not expect Gardner to use his suggestions verbatim, he anticipated the
incorporation of substantial amounts of the recommended material.

On the morning of Monday, May 11, convention Public Information
Officer James Bradley received a call from Harold Levy of Gardner's
staff asking if Gardner could deviate from his original printed remarks
to make "a major policy statement." Bradley's account of the
conversation is that he was told the changes would incorporate
references to the events of the two preceding weeks, but that he
believed this new material would be tied in to the urban crisis. Richard
Carlson, convention administrative assistant, then took the phone and,
according to his account, agreed it would be "all right to broaden the
speech if you keep it within the context of the convention." Neither of
these assistants notified Witwer or other convention officers of their
conversation with Gardner's staff.

When advance copies of the speech Gardner actually intended to
give arrived the evening of Tuesday, May 12, the staffers involved
immediately realized they had a problem on their hands. Brooks called
Colman, who was attending a meeting in Maryland. When apprised of
the changes, Colman expressed distress and agreed to contact
Gardner's aides in hopes of persuading him to expand his remarks to
include a discussion of constitutional revision. This avenue of
approach met with no success.

At the same time, Bradley delivered a copy of the speech to David E.
Stahl, the convention's Public Information Committee chairman.
Stahl reportedly exclaimed, "Oh, my God! He can't say that."[26] Stahl,
a Chicago Democrat, joined Witwer, Bradley, Pisciotte, Carlson, and
Charles Dunn in Witwer's office, where unsuccessful attempts to
reach Gardner occupied the next four hours. The gathering in
Witwer's office disbanded and Witwer returned to his apartment,

[26]*Chicago Daily News*, May 14, 1979.

from where he finally reached Lloyd Beck in Washington. Beck, in turn, called Gardner at a motel near O'Hare Airport.

Witwer commented to the press the following day that he had spoken with Beck, imploring him to persuade Gardner to return to his original topic and to deliver the attack on Nixon from a hotel in Springfield. According to Witwer, Beck stated that Gardner did not want to deliver the foreign policy speech if it might hurt the convention and that the decision to cancel Gardner's appearance was a mutual one.[27] Beck characterized the exchange as friendly, "with neither anger nor apology in the tone of either man."[28]

There were postscripts to the week's controversy. Dwight Friedrich, a conservative Republican delegate from Centralia, made contact through U.S. Senator Ralph Tyler Smith (R. Ill.) with aides to President Nixon suggesting the possibility of inserting a response to Gardner's attack in the convention minutes. This request was politely declined.

Gardner's comments continued to suggest that Witwer had asked him at the last minute to deviate from his anticipated text,[29] and Witwer doggedly pursued each reference to the incident in an attempt to dissipate rumors of repressiveness and closemindedness at the convention. The final, and perhaps most cutting irony, came in the biographical statement on Gardner published in the 1971 Yearbook to the Encyclopedia Britannica which stated that:

> When Illinois Constitutional Convention officials told the former Health, Education, and Welfare Secretary John W. Gardner he could not give a speech he had written at their invitation — because of its contents — he flew back to Washington and gave it to the press. The noise over his "muzzling" only increased the attention paid his thesis that there was "a growing crisis of confidence" in our leadership. It also demonstrated Gardner's skill at identifying problems that touched inner cords of Americans of all classes and political stripes and for mobilizing remedial action in Washington.

Had the convention censured Witwer, it is likely that he would have resigned, possibly creating irreducible turmoil. If there is a lesson in this whole sad business, it is that a constitutional convention must stick

[27]*Chicago Tribune*, May 14, 1970.
[28]*Chicago Daily News*, May 14, 1970.
[29]*Chicago Sun-Times*, May 13, 1970.

to its prescribed work and not permit itself to be diverted by issues and personalities not really relevant to that work. It is also not enough to be right in a logical sense; one must be psychologically right as well.

While the Gierach and Gardner affairs were being considered by the convention, the basic work of the committees went on. We turn now to those committees, roughly in the order set forth in the state constitution but not necessarily following the historical chronology of each story.

IX

An Outstanding Bill of Rights

Dallin H. Oaks, legal counsel to the Bill of Rights Committee, perhaps correctly assessed the development of the Illinois Bill of Rights when he stated: "Whether by design or by inadvertence President Samuel W. Witwer's appointments to the Bill of Rights Committee assembled what was easily the most remarkable group of delegates at the constitutional convention." He further observed: "The Bill of Rights Committee gave distinguished service to the people of Illinois. Though one may disagree with some provisions in the finished product, the Bill of Rights is an admirable document worthy of study and emulation."[1]

There had been no great demand for a changed Bill of Rights during the long process of educating the electorate of the state to the need for constitutional revision, either during the many campaigns waged by the delegates, or when the people of Illinois were being asked to vote on a call for a constitutional convention. People were generally pleased, as well they might be, with what the state had. In some quarters there was a fear that any change would be for the worse, rather than for the better; that there was the danger of going backward, rather than forward.

THE CHAIRMAN

Elmer Gertz unexpectedly found himself chairman of the Bill of

---

[1] Elmer Gertz, *For the First Hours of Tomorrow* (Urbana: Institute of Government and Public Affairs, University of Illinois, 1972), pp. xi-xii.

Rights Committee. At an early age, Gertz had learned that many people, young and old, educated and uneducated, white and black, are frequently subjected to outrageous breaches of their constitutional rights. He became a lawyer rather than an architect or journalist, to which he aspired in almost equal degrees, because he wanted to make certain that fundamental rights would be preserved for all people and that he would have a share in that great task. The same feeling prompted him to become a founder of the first multi-racial literary society at the University of Chicago and, later, to participate in efforts at creating a community dedicated to civil rights. His law practice, his writings, his public and private activities, have been a crusade against infringements of constitutional rights. It was that dedication and his commitment to a strong Bill of Rights which compelled him to run for election as a delegate to the Sixth Illinois Constitutional Convention.

The *Chicago Tribune* protested editorially against the appointment of Gertz as chairman of the Bill of Rights Committee; in addition to insulting him personally, it said: "The Illinois Constitution now contains a perfectly good Bill of Rights. Many eminent citizens have urged that it be left as it is and labor leaders have warned that they will fight any changes. If the Bill of Rights Committee turns its hearings into a hunting ground for ideological freaks and peddlers of utopian schemes, the whole convention is likely to be discredited in the eyes of the voters."[2]

Notwithstanding the *Tribune's* criticism, there were those who thought that Gertz was highly suitable for the chairmanship because of his long association with the struggle for individual rights, his independent attitude, and his maturity of thought. Not the least of his supporters was Samuel Witwer; after making the controversial and challenged appointment, he never waivered in his support of Gertz nor in his feeling that the appointment was not only the correct choice, but perhaps one of his best appointments during the convention.

COMMITTE MEMBERS

In appointing members to the Bill of Rights Committee, Witwer had in mind the concept of committee balance — political, ideological,

[2]*Chicago Tribune,* December 31, 1969.

geographical, racial — and was not aware of the powder keg of individuals that he had collectively put together. Gertz, on the other hand, frequently thought Witwer had wanted to surround the controversial chairman with such a variety of strong-willed persons who disapproved of him that he would be incapable of carving the Bill of Rights in his own image.

When asked to designate their choices for committee assignment, only four of the fifteen persons ultimately chosen — Arrigo, Lawlor, Weisberg, and Gertz — had named the Bill of Rights Committee as their first choice. Only two other delegates — Nicholson and Jaskula — had said that their prime choice was the Bill of Rights Committee, but they had been given other assignments. One delegate, Kelleghan, had said that the Bill of Rights Committee was his second choice and another, Raby, had named it his third. Thus the committee consisted largely of men and one woman who had not asked to be on it — Kemp as Vice-Chairman, Dvorak, Fennoy, Foster, Hutmacher, Arthur Lennon, Macdonald, Pechous, and Wilson, these nine in addition to those six who had requested appointment. Eleven other delegates would have been glad to serve on the Bill of Rights Committee, with varying degrees of enthusiasm, but in keeping with his concept of committee balance, Witwer assigned them to other substantive committees.

In the end, there were seven Catholics, six Protestants, and two Jews on the committee; four blacks and eleven whites; only one woman and fourteen men; seven from Chicago, five from the suburbs, and only three downstaters; six Republicans, five Democrats (including the unpredictable Leonard Foster), three independent Democrats, and one special kind of independent (Father Lawlor); ten lawyers, one priest, one housewife, one politician, and one teacher; of the lawyers, six had been or were presently connected with governmental agencies, chiefly in prosecution, and two, including the chairman, were known for defense work, while one, Kelleghan, was sometimes on one side and sometimes on the other.

There is another, more realistic way of profiling the committee. Three (Gertz, Raby, and Weisberg) were the most liberal of the group; four (Kemp, Foster, Wilson, and Mrs. Macdonald) were a swing group, going from liberal to moderate and sometimes conservative; four (Arrigo, Dvorak, Fennoy, and Pechous) were moderates capable, like the others, of going in unexpected directions; and the remaining four (Hutmacher, Lennon, Kelleghan, and Father Lawlor) were almost invariably conservative. The most liberal bloc were Chicagoans, independent, two Jewish and one black. The swing group was equally divided between blacks and whites, Democrats and Republicans; two were from Chicago, one from a suburb, and one from downstate; it included the one woman on the committee. The moderates consisted of three Democrats and one Republican; two suburbanites, one downstater, and two Chicagoans; one black, three whites; two Catholic, two Protestant. The conservatives were Republicans, except for the independent Lawlor; one downstater, two suburbanites, and one Chicagoan; all four were Catholics. Ethnically, there were Irish, Scotch-Irish, English, Italian, Bohemian, German, Jewish, and black members.

Above and beyond all else, they were personalities: diverse, strong, willful, inquisitive, suspicious, amiable, acrimonious. This colorful committee and its work are described in more detail in *For the First Hours of Tomorrow*, a book by the chairman of the committee and co-author of this volume. We have relied heavily on this earlier volume for what follows in this chapter.

A few words here about some of the committee members will have to suffice.

Bernard Weisberg, as general counsel in Illinois for the A.C.L.U., was a long-time battler for constitutional rights. A graduate with honors from the University of Chicago and its law school, a graduate student in sociology and education, an accomplished musician, he brought his many cultural and intellectual gifts to the committee. He had waged a brilliant campaign for election as a delegate and had challenged the secretary of state, the legendary Paul Powell, in a famous lawsuit concerning electoral practices. Some later confessed that there were conservatives who at the beginning thought Weisberg and Gertz the most dangerous persons at the convention.

Lewis D. Wilson was an unflappable lawyer and businessman from Moline. He was the retired general counsel and vice-president of John Deere and Company, the largest private employer in the state, a one-time director and vice-president of the Illinois State Chamber of Commerce, a long-time trustee of the Illinois Taxpayers Federation, on the Board of Governors of the United Republican Fund of Illinois, and an active participant in the Goldwater presidential campaign; he had all of the respectable credentials and was, at the same time, a man of substance and charm.

Mrs. Virginia Macdonald was a Texan by birth, a devoted Episcopalian, and long active in the leadership of the Republican party. It was assumed by the more conservative delegates that she would, naturally, help to contain Gertz, Raby, and Weisberg. They were astounded to find that she was governed by principles rather than politics. She was a confidante of the promising young organization Democrats, Richard M. Daley, son of the mayor, and his associate, Michael Madigan. She grew to cherish her unasked for association with the Bill of Rights Committee and was one of its great defenders.

James H. Kemp, vice-chairman of the committee, was very strong-willed, articulate, and unfathomable. Gertz felt that the two men ought to be close, since Kemp had been a member of the Illinois Fair Employment Practices Commission from its outset, and Gertz had been one of those most responsible for the passage of the law creating the commission. Furthermore, Gertz had served without compensation as special counsel for the commission in connection with the famous Motorola case, which established the validity of the agency. Gertz went to great lengths to placate and humor him at all times, but learned not to depend too heavily on his bright, unpredictable vice-chairman.

There were amazing differences between two of the most highly cultured members of the committee — Victor A. Arrigo and Leonard N. Foster, as far apart as planets traveling in distinct and distant orbits. Arrigo was soldier, prosecutor, and legislator (he and Paul Elward were the only two members of the General Assembly elected as delegates). Next to his love for things Italian and artistic, he cherished the legislature and was quick to lecture on the virtues of that body.

Foster, a black, was the committee member least impressed by Arrigo. For that matter, Foster was not very patient or admiring of anybody. He had singular gifts, evidenced by degrees in psychology, sociology, music and law. In turmoil much of the time, he was one of the most eager members of the committee. Nobody could ignore him; many nursed wounds inflected by his sharp tongue. He and Arrigo gave color to the deliberations of the committee and to the entire convention.

Arthur T. Lennon was a very shrewd and sometimes cunning

attorney. He was conservative on most issues and ingenious in expressing reasons for every position he took, pro and con. A classic example of his skill came to light during discussion on the due process section of the Bill of Rights. His insertion of the words "including the unborn" led to a memorable struggle, as the phrase seemed to make it constitutionally impossible to legalize abortion.

On another front, purporting to be in favor of nondiscrimination, Lennon proposed an extension of the provision for nondiscrimination in employment and property that would have made it unlikely for the section to receive a majority vote on the floor of the convention. His substitution called for nondiscrimination in every area, including country clubs. Lennon took his work seriously. He produced witnesses, he participated in the debates, and fielded all over the lot, and to cope with him, his opponents had to be equally resourceful and perceptive.

Father Francis X. Lawlor was at once the simplest and most complex member of the committee. Whenever anyone wanted to indicate the range of personality and viewpoint on the Bill of Rights Committee, he would say that the membership went from Father Lawlor to Raby. In neither instance was this really a fair simile. Neither person was completely like the public impression of him. Gertz tried to make Lawlor feel that he was being treated properly. He took walks with Lawlor and invariably would ask, "Father, have I been fair to you today?" And always the priest would say, "Yes, Elmer, you have been fair." On one walk Lawlor remarked that he had the reputation of being a racist, but that he really was not one. He said he was deeply concerned about the people in his community, that they were losing their homes and businesses and schools and churches, and that he did not know how to cope with the situation. He thought the block groups could help.

Thomas C. Kelleghan had read deeply in political science, philosophy, history, and the law. He was a natural conservative, distrustful of the new, which he was inclined to look upon as radical and revolutionary. He had much of the prosecutor in his makeup, and could make witnesses feel they were on trial. He cherished old institutions like capital punishment. He was less inclined than some to concede the good faith of opponents. Kelleghan could be charming on occasion, especially when near his lovely wife and children, or when the day's business was at an end and all were relaxing together. Normally, however, he was a fighter, breathing fire and brimstone, and he made the meetings volcanic.

In sharp contrast to Kelleghan was Albert A. Raby, an enigmatic character. Those who really had only a slight knowledge of him thought he would be a loud character, a rabble rouser; they were surprised, if not shocked, by his quiet demeanor and moderation. A profound believer in nonviolence — Dr. Martin Luther King, Jr., was his ideal — he was at the same time a fighter for the rights of all people. He often went by instinct, rather than research. A layman in the midst of lawyers, this was a gift to be valued. Weisberg and Gertz found his collaboration indispensable. Sometimes the three stood alone.

Finally, it should be mentioned that while he professed to hold no dogmatic beliefs, Albert Raby exerted a basically religious influence on the committee. Virginia Macdonald, who sat next to him, was one of his greatest admirers, benefiting from the depth of his compassion and intelligence.

The legal counsel for the committee was Professor Dallin H. Oaks of the University of Chicago Law School, where he had been presiding, firmly and fairly, over disciplinary proceedings involving student sit-ins. He had also been assigned by the Department of Justice in Washington to work on the problem of the exclusionary rule which prohibited use of evidence obtained in violation of a person's constitutional rights, made necesary by the *Miranda* decision and other pronouncements of the Warren Court. He was far more conservative than the chairman of the committee. Gertz developed admiration for him despite all differences.

Oaks analyzed every proposal that came before the committee, sometimes off-the-cuff at committee meetings, but more often in memoranda — his "L.A.R.A.M.s" that became so famous in the convention and which stood for Legal and Research Advisor's Memoranda. Ultimately there were fifty such memoranda comprising a total of 660 pages. At least one memorandum was devoted to both the pro and the con argument on everything suggested for the committee's consideration. Even the less conscientious members of the committee tried to read them, if they read nothing else, and would discuss them with Oaks and among themselves.

Numerous stories circulated about the committee, most of them dealing with some of the more bizzare aspects of this sometimes bitterly divided, highly personal, brilliant, and committed groups of persons. Frank Cicero said that more people visited the Bill of Rights Committee than Lincoln's tomb. It was appropriate that there be this concern over basic issues. Fighting words had given birth to the earliest Bill of Rights, and vigilance was still required to preserve those hard won rights of free men.

The extensive press coverage of the Bill of Rights Committee deliberations might be faulted for overstating what was garish and extreme, and underplaying the valid and conscientious work of almost every member of the committee. The shrewd and sometimes cynical Edward S. Gilbreth of the *Chicago Daily News* was quite right when he said that no committee at the convention had been as "beleaguered" as the Bill of Rights Committee; for the reason that it "faces the most emotionally charged questions that will come before the convention." He listed some of these issues, including: "how to phrase guarantees of basic liberties in a climate of public opinion increasingly auspicious of the right to dissent." He said that Gertz, as chairman, had "tried to reject any attempts to stifle debate on the committee." He observed, with his usual perspicacity: "A few other chairmen, mindful of the disproportionate attention focused on Gertz's committee, hope to get proposals 'eased out' of their committees with a minimum of dissent. This move, if successful, could result in a number of bland committee reports."[3]

THE COMMITTEE GOES TO THE CONVENTION

By late spring, Witwer began urging the Bill of Rights Committee to file its full report, or at least a substantial segment of it, without delay. Many on the committee were annoyed, even outraged, by the pressure being put on them. They were notorious for the long hours they devoted to their work. The chairman was often described as a Simon Legree in his cracking of the whip.

At last they neared the finishing point, and the chairman became as eager as the president of the convention to file a report. Formal notices of a deadline were sent out. A final meeting was held. Still a few,

[3]Edward S. Gilbreth, "5-day week being urged for Con Con," *Chicago Daily News,* April 4-5, 1970.

notably Foster, felt that more time was required. After the "final" meeting, Gertz became adamant and declared that the report would be filed, despite anyone.

An order of presentation was agreed upon. They would first present those sections on which there was unanimous agreement; then the more contested ones would be presented, starting with those sections that were unchanged. Gertz saw no harm and much good in such a special order of presentation. At first, President Witwer disagreed, but when he realized how strongly the committee felt and that trouble might ensue, he yielded. In the end, this approach took much less time than had committee members plunged into acrimonious discussion of highly controversial sections — for example, the rights of the unborn. As it was, the less divisive sections were gotten out of the way with little trouble.

Committee counsel Dallin Oaks drafted the majority report, but he had the benefit of the thinking of everyone on the committee. No one could reasonably claim he had been slighted. The report pointed out that the committee had given almost twenty weeks of intensive consideration to its assigned task. The committee had received eighty-one member proposals from President Witwer, many combining a variety of subjects and some confined to a single or just a few ideas. The report listed all of these proposals, and told of the more than 250 witnesses the committee had heard, most of whom were not delegates. These witnesses ranged from true experts to zealots, some supporting, some opposing, the various proposals. The report listed the vast amount of written material received and considered, and indicated that the committee had dealt with a large number of controversial issues. Notwithstanding the dangerous areas into which they ventured, committee members passed some issues — nine sections indeed — by unanimous vote. They recommended the retention unchanged of twelve of the original twenty sections of the article. True, they urged amendment of the preamble and of eight sections, and added seven new sections. In some instances, the vote was very close and sometimes changed between the first and the second vote, permitted under the special rules of the committee. The committee could truthfully say, as suggested by Arthur Lennon: "In all cases the issues were squarely faced, vigorously debated, and firmly decided."

It was now up to the convention to dispose of what they had proposed.

There was discussion — sometimes acrimonious — concerning the manner, as well as the order, in which various sections of the preamble and bill of rights were to be presented. It was agreed that Gertz would lead off the discussion, giving an overall account of the article and the work connected with it; furthermore, he would be up front in the convention hall, prepared to field the discussion and answer questions not handled by other members of the committee.

It was the chairman's feeling and almost all of the committee members agreed, that each member ought to make one or more presentations. There were enough sections for all. The question was how and to whom they should be distributed. Some were natural choices; some refused to present any sections; and some were so well qualified that the problem was one of limitation.

As Edward S. Gilbreth phrased it in the *Chicago Daily News* at the beginning of June 1970, battle lines were being formed at the convention as the long-awaited bill of rights report was about to come up for consideration on first reading. The committee, Gilbreth said, had "wrestled" with the "hottest issues." Now the convention as a whole would face the day of judgment on such basic matters as abortion, gun control, the death penalty, free speech, rights of privacy, search and seizure, and eminent domain, not to mention such other explosive matters as nondiscrimination, preliminary hearings for those accused of felonies, a new preamble — the inventory of fireworks was almost inexhaustible. There were twenty-seven proposed sections, the preamble, and ten majority reports. How long would it take the convention to battle its way through the agenda? The optimists, according to Gilbreth's soundings, were saying two weeks; the pessimists, a month. And the convention could not really spare that time. President Witwer was constantly reminding the delegates they were a month behind schedule. There were rumors of deals between downstate delegates and Cook County Democrats, between this group and that, on various proposals, but even deals could not stop oratory under the generous rules of the convention.

On May 22, 1970, the report of the Bill of Rights Committee was formally presented to the convention. One week later, with the convention acting as a committee of the whole, five sections with no changes from the 1870 constitution were approved; no section on which any delegate raised a question or suggested the consideration of amendments was voted on. The first reading debate on the Bill of Rights continued for seven more days, interspersed with some of the more lively debate to occur at the convention.

Although Chairman Gertz stressed the ultimate degree of committee agreement despite the large number of controversial issues, ten minority reports were in fact filed by the committee. Five of them won in whole or in part — those who disagreed with the phrase "including the unborn," the eminent domain section, certain aspects of the preliminary hearing, public employees, and fines. Six of them lost in whole or in part — those who disagreed with the preamble, truth in libel, certain aspects of the preliminary hearing, individual dignity, right to arms, and bail. All things considered, this record was by no means a bad one. But it became clear that neither in the committee sessions nor on the floor of the convention, whether on first, second, or final reading, was anything a foregone conclusion so far as the Bill of Rights and the members of that committee were concerned.

While the first-reading debate was still going on in the convention committee of the whole, the *Chicago Sun-Times* published one of its numerous editorials on the work of the committee. It said, in part:

> We have found occasion for both criticism and praise, because the Bill of Rights contains sensitive, controversial, even volatile, matter. Still to be debated, for instance, is an unfortunate freeing up of the right to keep and bear arms. Our stand there is well known. We favor more control, not less.
>
> Nonetheless, we think it proper that the committee which constructed the proposed Bill of Rights be credited for a difficult job well done.

The editorial told of the dedicated spirit in which the committee had worked and concluded: "We commend the Bill of Rights Committee, a disparate group of individuals, for doing as well as it has with this basic task."[4]

The Due Process Clause

On the day the convention took up the due process clause, Father Lawlor offered the invocation, significant in view of the day's business. The grim priest preached on the sacredness of life. "Help us," he

[4]Editorial, "A Document in Democracy," *Chicago Sun-Times,* June 7, 1970.

implored, "to respect this right to life which You gave to all others."
He gave, in brief compass and in the guise of a prayer, the arguments
against destroying "those in need, the poor, the blind, the lame, the
lepers" and, by implication, although he did not directly say so, the
human fetus.

It was Arthur Lennon's task to defend the use of the words
"including the unborn" in the due process and equal protection
section, the phrase that many feared would prevent the legalizing of
abortions. This was before the decisions of the United States Supreme
Court declaring the right to abortion. Lennon, a very shrewd and
resourceful debater, made the most of the troublesome phrase, largely
in terms of the majority report, but spelling out why he contended that
the language was not revolutionary or extreme.

One delegate after another got into the fray; their questions being
really a form of argumentation. It was clear that almost everyone
wanted to say something on this highly controversial subject and on
which the convention was so noticeably taking sides. Women, blacks,
independents, and downstaters were sharply opposed to the proposed
language; Daley Democrats were strongly in favor. Lennon fielded the
questions with great skill, but he was persuading only the persuaded.

With the question concluded for the moment, Lewis Wilson
presented the minority views quite persuasively. He did not hedge. He
was blunt in stating his belief that the supporters of the majority report
were intent upon preventing legislation to permit abortions. His
argument for the minority report was supplemented by Bernard
Weisberg, as always shrewd in his analysis of the issues. It was easy to
understand why his coldly rational tone disconcerted those as
emotionally involved as Kelleghan. So the debate went on, some
almost trembling with emotion, others having at least the outer aspect
of calm and reasonableness.

Finally, Lewis Wilson was permitted to conclude for the minority.
Then the voting began, with Victor Arrigo and others explaining their
votes, as was permitted by the rules. Seldom did more delegates feel
more like explaining themselves, both for the record and their
consciences.

The motion to substitute the minority report for the committee
majority report was carried by 80 to 32. Despite all the debate, it was
not even close. The motion to approve the minority report, as

substituted, a technical necessity, was then carried 92 to 8. The convention had overcome what might have been one of the greatest obstacles to approval of a new constitution.

Final Preparations for Convention Presentation

On July 2, 1970, the Bill of Rights article came out of the Committee on Style, Drafting and Submission with very few changes. The Committee suggested that the old section on subordination of military power be moved to the militia article and that the section on elections be moved, as suggested by Peter Tomei, to the article on suffrage and elections. Nobody objected, and the removals were accomplished as a matter of course. Whether or not the changes in location had any effect constitutionally remains to be seen, but it is extremely doubtful.

For the rest, the proposed changes were truly stylistic, as contemplated when the role of the Style and Drafting Committee was delineated. Punctuation was added, subtracted or changed; words of greater clarity were substituted for those of lesser clarity; in all, the language was tightened up so that the meaning of each section became self-evident. Where the exigencies of convention realities required it, the sometimes archaic language of the older section, redolent with tradition, were retained.

In conformity with the floor vote on second reading, there were two separate submissions with respect to the Bill of Rights — whether to add the sentence, "No penalty shall prescribe death," in section 11 on limitation of penalties after conviction, and whether to add a new section with respect to nondiscrimination for the physically or mentally handicapped. It was already apparent that the latter proposed separate submission, forced by some who should have favored the inclusion of the section in the body of the constitution, was creating troubled spirits and rebellion. At third reading there was heated discussion of the matter which was resolved by inclusion of the provision in the Bill of Rights.

Third reading was the final stage in the proceedings; substantial amendments and substitutions were no longer freely permitted. For such changes the rules required, in the first instance, suspension of the rules by a constitutional majority, amounting to fifty-nine members, and then passage by at least the same vote. When Style, Drafting and Submission presented its report, with very little time left to complete the work, it was doubtful that the delegates would tolerate many suspensions of the rules.

The transition schedule declared that any rights, procedural or substantive, created for the first time by the Bill of Rights article, would be prospective and not retroactive. There could be no objection to this; and it was probably implicit anyway in due process.

The preamble and bill of rights were approved on final reading with only one nay vote but with fourteen passing. The Bill of Rights Committee had thus accomplished its objective more readily than the members had dared hope when the convention began months previously.

More than a year after adjournment of the convention, Jeffrey Ladd, who had cast the one negative vote, told Gertz the reasons for his opposition, since then somewhat softened. First and foremost, he was enraged by what he regarded as the cowardice of the assembly in voting for Arrigo's section on individual dignity and for the right to arms provision, known by both sides, he felt, to be meaningless if not mischievous. He was afraid of the self-implementing aspect of the section on nondiscrimination, and he thought the women's rights section and the provision on the handicapped were hypocritical. Ladd, a practical, unsentimental, and earnest young man, did not believe in pretense or the rhetorical.

Two sections proposed by the Bill of Rights Committee — on basic needs and the rights of public employees — were eliminated completely on first reading; basic needs because a constitutional majority was not obtained, the rights of public employees because the Cook County Democrats joined with certain downstaters against it. Two ancient sections, on free and equal elections and subordination of military power, were transferred to other articles by the Style and Drafting Committee; and two new sections — against discrimination on the basis of sex and the handicapped — were added, the first with virtually no struggle and the second after considerable maneuvering and pressure. In addition, there was considerable debates on some sections which were finally left largely as the committee had recommended them; other sections were expanded or contracted and considerably modified on the floor.

Despite the support of the Catholic bishops for the retention intact and unchanged of the religious freedom section, there was a group, largely Catholic in composition, that persistently sought to amend the section; the same was true of a similar section in the education article against the use of public funds for sectarian purposes, for which some wanted to substitute the general language of the First Amendment of the Federal Constitution or some other general language. Some professed to be constitutional purists; others were frankly in favor of giving assistance to parochial schools. The bishops thought this could be done through the present language; some delegates wanted to make this doubly certain. None of them reckoned sufficiently with the United States Supreme Court.

There was much less of a struggle than anticipated on the section against discrimination in employment and the sale or rental of property. In the end there were no more votes against the provision in the convention than in committee — a mere half dozen. This can be described as one of the miracles of the nine months of the convention.

As the convention progressed from the early, uneasy days of organization of the leadership and committees, through the three readings on the floor of the convention, with the ensuing excitement of debate, votes, and public discussion, it became increasingly clear that the early impression of the Bill of Rights Committee was changing. Where once there was hostility, amusement, bewilderment, and the feeling of impending disaster, there was now friendliness, admiration, and a sense of triumph. This was reflected in the media and even more in the conversation of delegates who constantly expressed their high regard for what the committee had done and how they had handled themselves in the convention. This came from both supporters and opponents of the proposed Bill of Rights.

This success, wrested from the anticipated depths of failure, was not wholly fortuitous. After the convention adjourned, the chairman reflected:

> I had made up my mind before our report was presented to the convention that I would studiously avoid affronting those upon whom we depended for votes. Despite my strong feelings on many issues, I determinedly restricted my participation in the debates — until our report was under consideration. Then I utilized all of the built-up goodwill. I tried to field the discussion. On the microphone and away from it, I put forth the most persuasive arguements I could muster. But I did not monopolize the time of the convention or, indeed, of the

committee. I pushed forward everyone who could help, whether it was
Foster, Lennon, Weisberg, Wilson, or anyone else. So a new reputation
was created, and we all basked in it.[5]

Not many days before the referendum on the new constitution,
Dorothy Clune of UPI wrote an article about the Bill of Rights that
was widely published in newspapers throughout the state. It gave a fair
and substantially accurate account of what had been done by the Bill of
Rights Committee and the convention and the atmosphere in which
they had worked. Dorothy Clune wrote:

> Born of some tough compromise, the bill of rights in Illinois'
> proposed constitution has won approval from liberals and conservatives
> alike.
>
> There is some irony in this ideological agreement because no section
> of the constitution deals with more fundamental political and philo-
> sophical concepts than the bill of rights.
>
> In it are contained statements relating to the place of the individual
> and the state in society, working definitions of freedom and provisions
> for all the "hardrock" rights such as due process of law, freedom to
> worship, speak and assemble.[6]

The Death Penalty Controversy

One of the matters that troubled Elmer Gertz most was the proposal to
abolish capital punishment, ultimately submitted to the voters as a
separate proposition and soundly defeated. Gertz had strong feelings
about the death penalty. He was intensely opposed to it as a matter of
conscience and on practical grounds. He had been involved in several
important capital cases, such as those of Jack Ruby, Paul O. Crump,
William Witherspoon, and Lyman Moore. He had filed *amici* briefs in
the Supreme Court of the United States for the American Civil
Liberties Union and various religious denominations. When he
became chairman of the Bill of Rights Committee at the convention, he
was concerned about how far he ought to go in the effort to place an
abolition provision in the new constitution. He had submitted a
member proposal on the matter. He consulted with Bernard Weisberg,
who shared his views on this as well as many other subjects. Much
eloquent and persuasive testimony was introduced before the
committee. But Weisberg and Gertz felt that an abolition provision

---

[5]Gertz, *For the First Hours of Tomorrow*, p. 148.
[6]Dorothy Clune, "Proposes Illinois Constitution — Liberals, Conservatives, Support the Bill
of Rights," *Chicago Daily Law Bulletin*, December 3, 1970.

would adversely affect the chances, already precarious, for the approval of the new constitution. The country, no less Illinois, was under the sway of the law and order syndrome, which called for getting tough with criminals. The electric chair and the hangman's rope were looked upon as the cure for crime in the streets. So, reluctantly and with sorrow, Gertz did not push the matter. He consoled himself with the conviction that the struggle for abolition would be won in the courts, particularly the Supreme Court, rather than in constitutional conventions, legislatures, or through a popular referendum.

When the Bill of Rights proposals came before the committee of the whole for consideration, Gertz learned that Wayne Whalen, Robert Canfield, and Philip Carey, an independent, a Republican, and a Democrat, were going to introduce an amendment to abolish the death penalty. The issue being raised, Gertz felt that, in good conscience, he had to support Whalen and his associates. Possibly it was not, after all, a lost cause if a former state's attorney like Canfield and a regular Daley Democrat like Carey could support it. There was much speechmaking for and against the proposal. On first reading, the abolition amendment was only narrowly defeated.

As Gertz was leaving the chamber after this defeat, a number of delegates, including a favorite, Lewis Wilson, came up to him and confided that while they had voted nay, if abolition were proposed as a separate submission they would be for it. Thereafter, although it was still nominally the Whalen-Canfield-Carey proposal, Gertz's role in lining up support for the separate submission was equally important. It won on second reading and did even better on third reading when Gertz persuaded some of the opponents to go along with him. Human nature being what it is, Gertz became cautiously optimistic that abolition might be approved by the voters. After all, his research in connection with the Witherspoon case, fortified by public opinion polls, had indicated that the people were increasingly opposed to taking the lives of convicted murderers. Then, as fate would have it, the fickle public changed its collective mind and demanded that the extreme penalty be on the books, if not in practice.

Wayne Whalen, who had introduced the abolition measure, was now preoccupied, to the exclusion of all else, with the campaign to secure approval of judicial merit selection. He could give neither time nor thought to the separate submission on abolition of the death penalty. Gertz and very few others were left to wage the fight. The Illinois Committee for the Abolition of Capital Punishment was formed. It was a good committee in the sense that the cause was good, the names of members and officers were good, and a decent effort was made. The distinguished lawyer, Albert E. Jenner, Jr., was honorary chairman, Hans Mattick, a well informed criminologist was the active chairman, and Willard Lassers and Gertz, who were co-counsel on many *amici* briefs, were vice-chairmen. Clement Stone and Dr. Preston Bradley were other prominent members of the committee. Ann Galloway and Pamela Scofield, two bright and committed young women, constituted the staff. A modest amount of money, about $10,000, was raised to wage a low-key campaign. It was felt that this was the best sort of campaign as it was the least likely to arouse strong opposition. Mattick, Lassers, and Gertz, the only really active members of the committee, planned activities, mostly with church groups and with black citizens. A very fine brochure was widely distributed. Some thought it the best single mailing piece of the entire campaign for the adoption of the constitution. There were radio programs and a few short appeals, but nothing of a sustained or continuous nature, just enough so that some were aware of the choice. On a Sunday before the referendum many churches had sermons in favor of abolition. Most of the effort was concentrated in Cook County, although Betty Ann Keegan and Robert Canfield did a little in the Rockford area.

There was very little in the way of organized opposition to abolition. Thomas Kelleghan did speak out on the matter, but he was almost alone. Neither political party took a stand, one way or the other. Labor took no stand. The Chicago Bar Association supported abolition, as did some church and civic groups. The law and order undercurrent in the end counted for more than any organized campaign, and abolition lost by about 2 to 1 — 673,302 yes and 1,218,791 no. Only the black wards of Chicago were overwhelmingly in favor of abolition, because the blacks were the principal victims of the racism implicit in the death penalty.

After it was all over, Gertz took stock of the situation. He was no longer sure that a low-key campaign had been as wise as he had originally thought. Perhaps more would have been accomplished through strenuous effort. It seemed clear, too, that if the support of the

Daley organization had been won, if it had been made a matter of party policy, abolition would have generated more votes.

Thus the battle for abolition still goes on. In the now eighteen years since the execution of James Dukes, a black, in 1962, no one has been executed in Illinois. But because of clamorous demand, the death penalty has repeatedly been enacted into law. It is a continuing battle of conscience, which, in the end, must be resolved on the side of life, rather than death.

After having been involved in such controversial and emotional issues, nothing gave Gertz more joy than the letter he received from President Witwer as the year 1970 neared its close. The convention was over, the new constitution had been approved by the people, and Witwer could appraise the results. He wrote to Gertz:

> I will always take the greatest pride in your appointment as Chairman of the Bill of Rights Committee. I could not have made a better choice and you measured up to the most severe and demanding challenges in leading the committee and the convention into an excellent result.
>
> I feel that of all the things accomplished by the new Constitution, no article thrills me more than the Bill of Rights.[7]

"All the bruises were cured, all the hurts vanished when I read and re-read these words," Gertz fondly recalls.

[7]Gertz, *For the First Hours of Tomorrow,* p. 159.

X

Suffrage, Elections, and Revision

While suffrage and constitutional revision are not necessarily related subjects, they were subsumed into one committee as a matter of expediency. The Chicago Bar Association had recommended that the convention have eight substantive committees, including a Committee on Bill of Rights and Suffrage, and a separate Committee on Constitutional Change. The third Constitution Study Commission, however, in its proposed rules, considered the Bill of Rights to be of such significance as to require a committee devoted to that subject alone. The commission also suggested, and the convention agreed, that neither suffrage nor amending would fully occupy a separate committee's full attention; thus, the two topics with their individual and lively issues were brought together in the Committee on Suffrage and Constitutional Amendment.

The story of how the committee effectively and efficiently dealt with the separate but equally important issues is excellently told in the fine volume *Ballots for Change: New Suffrage and Amending Articles For Illinois* by the committee's staff, Alan S. Gratch and Virginia Ubik. Both were totally involved in the committee actions as key staff members on whom the delegates relied fully as they deliberated and wrote the two articles. Similarly, we rely on their accurate analysis for what follows in this chapter.

HISTORY OF CONSTITUTIONAL CHANGE

Under Illinois' first constitution of 1818, constitutional revision could be effected by the convention method only. It took the vote of two-thirds of the members of the General Assembly to put the question of calling a constitutional convention to the voters. Once on the ballot, it took the affirmative vote of "a majority of all the citizens of the state, voting for representatives" to convene such a convention. Approval by voter referendum of proposals adopted by the convention was not a constitutional requirement. In 1824 and again in 1842, convention call questions were presented to the voters and defeated. In 1846 the proposition was submitted and carried, and a convention convened in 1847. Although not required under the amending procedure of the 1818 constitution, the product of this convention was submitted to and ratified by the voters on March 6, 1848, and on April 1 of that year became effective as the Illinois Constitution of 1848.

The 1848 constitution retained the convention process as a method of amendment with some procedural changes. More significantly, for the first time in Illinois an alternative procedure for effective constitutional revision was permitted, the so-called legislative method. Either house of the General Assembly could propose amendments. If two-thirds of the members elected to each of the two houses agreed, an amendment would be voted on a second time after an intervening general election. If a majority of the elected members of each house approved the proposed amendment the second time, the proposal, after being published in full at least three months preceding the election thereon, would be submitted to the electorate at the next election of members of the General Assembly. Upon approval by a majority of those voting at the election, the proposal would become law. Amendments could not be proposed to more than one article at any general election.

The 1870 constitution retained both the convention and legislative methods of amendment. It made procedural changes in the convention method and also made a substantive change in the legislative method by prohibiting the proposal of amendments to the same article more often than once in four years.

In 1950 the amending article of the 1870 constitution was modified by the passage of the Gateway amendment. Under the 1870 constitution, constitutional amendments proposed by the legislature had to be approved by a majority of the electors voting. This had proved to be too stringent. The Gateway amendment, designed to make constitutional revision easier, provided an alternative test for ratification: approval by two-thirds of the electors voting on the proposed amendment. In addition, Gateway allowed the General Assembly to propose amendments to three articles at the same session, and it required that all amendments proposed by the General Assembly be printed on a separate blue ballot or in a separate column on the general ballot.

The amending article of the Illinois Constitution of 1870 proved over the years to be particularly troublesome and unwieldy. Quality amendments had fallen by the wayside, primarily as a consequence of voter indifference. In 1970, many felt that if the convention did nothing more than revise this one article, the convention would be a success.

THE COMMITTEE

Although the Committee on Suffrage and Constitutional Amendments was the smallest of the convention committees — consisting of only nine members — it too had its contrasts in personality and philosophy. For instance, Chairman Peter A. Tomei and Vice-Chairman Charles W. Shuman could scarcely have been more different, in both background and personality.

Tomei was a Chicagoan, an independent Democrat, a Catholic, brilliant and scholarly, ambitious, driven, organized, while capable of forays into strange territories. He was a natural leader, charming at his best, sometimes abrasive, a good speaker, not always a good listener.

Shuman was a year younger than Tomei, a Republican, a Protestant, a farmer, the son of the long-time president of the conservative American Farm Bureau Federation. He was disappointed that the president of the convention had not given leadership positions to the Republican delegates, and he tried, unsuccessfully, to supply such leadership through a Republican caucus which Witwer sought to discourage.

Henry I. Green was elected to the convention from the same district as Shuman, and his appointment to the Suffrage and Constitutional Amendment Committee was a disappointment to him. In fact, with the exception of Tomei, no one appointed to it had mentioned that committee as a preference. Green was the grandson of Henry I. Green of central Illinois prominence, who had served with distinction in the 1920 Illinois Constitutional Convention. The younger Green, an investor involved in farming, educational administration, and banking, sought the delegate seat as a springboard to higher elected political office. Upon learning of his appointment to the smallest, and in his mind the least prestigious, of the convention's committees, and that Shuman was to serve as its vice-chairman, Green called Executive Director Pisciotte to inquire "if he had not been put out to the bone yard." Pisciotte assured him that the exact opposite was true; that Witwer considered the amending article of the constitution to be of paramount importance, and that he was gravely concerned about the impact that voting qualifications would have on any proposed document. While not fully convinced at that time, Green, like the other committee members, came to have a profound respect for the committee's subject. Ultimately they also realized the significance of their handling of issues on the overall success of the convention. As he did with other committees, Witwer appeased some of the disappointment on the assignment to this committee with additional assignments to procedural and ad hoc committees. Thus Green took an active part in the Public Information Committee and Thomas Miller was named chairman of the Committee on the Convention's Budget. Green also was to become deeply involved in the efforts to constitutionalize pension rights.

William A. Jaskula, a criminal lawyer who came to the convention with the backing of the Cook County Democratic organization, could be counted on to support the organization's leadership on all issues. Although a valuable member of the committee, who continually demonstrated his knowledge of the law and his ability to analyze issues, his loyalty to the regular organization at times caused him to go against what he otherwise believed.

Henry Carter Hendren, Jr., farmer and teacher, was a downstate conservative Republican, who took a strong law and order position on such issues as restoration of voting rights to former criminals. He was continually involved in efforts to bring "organization" to the downstate Republicans as a counter force to the Chicago Democrats.

The Reverend Joseph Sharpe, Sr. represented the same Chicago district as William Jaskula and also was supported by the Cook County Democratic organization. The only black member of the committee,

Reverend Sharpe advanced the cause of lifetime voter registration and computerized election procedures. He also joined the forces supporting the initiative method of amending constitutions and favored a lower voting age when his fellow committee members, with the exception of the chairman, did not.

The third member of the committee endorsed by the Cook County Democratic organization was William Lennon. He was a labor lawyer and possessed one of the sharpest minds on the committee. He knew he was part of a team and represented the interests of his political party. In the end, he did not support the new constitution, signing it only in dissent. In fact, he and Kemp were influential in getting the state AFL-CIO to come out against the proposed constitution.

Thomas H. Miller, the only Republican from the Chicago area on the committee, was a young man with political ambitions. He was a conservative in philosophy, and seemed to question the motives of other members. He did, however, respond to leadership, particularly where it might affect his future political career. When Witwer, a fellow Republican, was under a great deal of pressure to move the convention into substantive debate and was urging the committee to present the first convention proposal, resistance came from Miller, among others. It took a personal call from Witwer and a reminder of their common political bond for him to acquiesce and approve the committee's proposed amending article in time for the scheduled presentation to the full convention.

Stanley Klaus had a great sense of history. A retired teacher and full-time farmer, he continually posed the question of "What is fair?" He had not realized how significant the issues surrounding suffrage and amending were and came to be satisfied that the task he had been given was indeed substantial.

In summing up the characteristics of this seemingly neglected, but important committee, Alan Gratch and Virginia Ubik wrote:

> As disappointed as the members were with their assignments, the final composition of the committee did reflect the convention president's commitment to balance as equally as possible the membership of each committee in terms of geography, politics, age, and race. Four of the committee members were from Chicago. Three of these Chicagoans received the endorsement of the Cook County Democratic organization. The fourth was an Independent Democrat. The five remaining

members consisted of a Republican suburbanite, a central Illinois farmer, a central Illinois businessman, a retired teacher from south-western Illinois who was devoting full-time to farming, and a farmer-teacher from the far southeastern part of the state. With the exceptions of not including a female and being weighted with philosophical conservatives, the committee was a fair reflection of the views of the convention delegates.

When the committee first met then, there were eight men disgusted with their new-found responsibilities and, in some instances, as unaware of the suffrage and amending issues as the average Illinois citizen. The ninth member, who was pleased to be a committee chairman, was ready to rewrite the new articles and had his own ideas about easing the amendment process and expanding the franchise. Because of their initial lack of interest and position on the subjects at hand, the eight dissatisfied committee members were ready to be led. The situation was not one of nine divergent personalities trying to push through their individual ideas and plans for suffrage and amending. Instead, it followed the pattern of the chairman presenting his proposals and the committee reacting to them. Arguably, the members were successful as a group because they did not act, but reacted.[1]

Having resigned themselves to their appointments, the committee members gave brief thought to the manner of approaching their two distinct areas of responsibilities. They selected amending as their first subject, clearly recognizing that it would not be feasible to consider both suffrage and amending simultaneously. Amending would be the less controversial, and the body of literature, at least in relation to Illinois, was more substantial. Tomei had done considerable work on the subject, and would be more at home there as a starting point for his leadership. As they entered into this field, they rapidly realized that one of the primary reasons for the push toward a constitutional convention was the difficulty, if not impossibility, of modernizing the 1870 constitution.

The committee dealt with four amending-related issues without significant partisan polarization or individual emotion. No doubt the subject matter was less volatile than that handled by other committees,

---

[1] Alan S. Gratch, Virginia H. Ubik, *Ballots for Change: New Suffrage and Amending Articles for Illinois* (Urbana: Institute of Government and Public Affairs, University of Illinois, 1973), p. 9.

but the more logical, analytical approach was in large part due to the temperament of Tomei and Shuman; the committee members followed their guidance and leadership. The four issues were: (1) a more flexible amending process, (2) automatic submission of the convention call question, (3) a popular initiative method of amending, and (4) the establishment of standards for state action in the federal amendment process.

The absence of partisan differences was not to last throughout the deliberations of the committee. When committee members turned their attention to the suffrage topics, which involved not only political philosophies, but the potential for political loss or gain, careful reason and analytical discourse often took a secondary role. For example, the Democrats openly supported lowering the voting age to eighteen, a position endorsed by Mayor Daley. Tomei sought to open up the election process as much as possible and thus was less conservative than most of the other committee members. As with amending, the deliberations were guided by a Tomei-developed outline which divided the subject into four categories: (1) basic philosophy of suffrage, (2) voter eligibility requirements, (3) voter disenfranchisement, and (4) election administration.

The way the committee, and ultimately the full convention, dealt with the suffrage and amending issues is well documented by Gratch and Ubik and need not be repeated here in any detail. They conclude and summarize:

> The suffrage and amending articles developed and advanced by the committee, adopted by the convention with relatively few changes in substance, and now found in Articles III and XIV, respectively, of the Illinois Constitution of 1970, represent sound, balanced principles designed to promote quality government. The amending article continues the two traditional methods of amending a state constitution, by convention and legislative action, and adds two additional opportunities for the electorate to invoke its will, the automatic placement on the ballot of the convention call question and the initiative method for changing the legislative article (Article IV). The majority required to approve amendments has been modified with a view to applying an extraordinary majority standard which, based upon historical experience in Illinois, strikes a reasonable compromise between easing the way for future amendments and preserving the integrity and continuity of the basic law. The amending article will no longer be the cause for the failure

of sound changes to the constitution. The ills of the 1870 Constitution have been cured and new concepts designed to facilitate growth and adaption of the constitution to the needs of the future have been added.

The amending article, seems, however, to have two areas of potential weakness. Section I, pertaining to the convention procedure, does not expressly require election of delegates by nonpartisan ballot. Nor does it expressly require elected officials, principally members of the General Assembly, from being seated as delegates. The Illinois Constitutional Convention of 1922 failed largely because of its highly partisan atmosphere and the lack of diligence with which some delegates pursued their task. The Sixth Illinois Constitutional Convention of 1970 succeeded largely because it worked assiduously and did not become politically polarized. An antagonistic General Assembly might plant the seeds for a convention's failure by including in its enabling legislation items designed to accentuate partisanship in the delegate body. One such item might be the election of delegates by partisan ballot. Another destructive seed might be to load the convention body with members of the General Assembly, or other elected officials, who would divide their energy and attention (with the concomitant delays) between the convention and their other duties. Future generations will have to be on guard against such abuses.

The other area of possible weakness is in Section 4 of Article XIV pertaining to procedures in the federal amending process. The convention's amendment requiring the intervening election of at least a majority of the members of the General Assembly before the General Assembly may ratify a proposed federal constitutional amendment seems blatantly beyond the power of the states, and unconstitutional. [There may be question, too, about the extraordinary majority required for the approval of future federal constitutional amendments, as was later evidenced in the struggle over the adoption of E.R.A.] The Committee's proposal, which simply regulated the majority required for General Assembly action, seemed to approach the limit of constitutionality. This may be a situation where reaching for too much regulation may put Illinois back into the position of no regulation.

The changes made in the suffrage article may prove in time to be more significant than now appears. Section I of Article III makes clear that voting is a right, as distinguished from a privilege, and Section 2, concerning the restoration of the vote to convicted felons, illustrates the primacy of this right. The onus has been shifted from the citizen to the legislature to justify the reasonableness and necessity of any procedures or requirements that interfere with the citizen's ability to cast his ballot for candidates of his choice and have his ballot counted. The elimination of a county residence requirement and reduction of the local residence requirement to thirty days should significantly expand the body of eligible voters.

Section 3 of Article III establishes the dynamic character of this article's directives. Insuring the integrity of the election process and facilitating registration and voting by all qualified persons requires creative thought and action on the part of the General Assembly. If the anomalies, discriminatory classifications and practices, and archaic procedures of the existing election code are not corrected, one would expect, and hope, that this section 4 would be used as the basis for citizen outcry and attack through the courts.

The section 4 requirement that laws governing voter registration and conduct of elections be general and uniform could be used to rewrite those parts of the Illinois Election Code designed to perpetuate provincialism and preserve the status quo with respect to political party divisions throughout the state. If the General Assembly continues to fail to meet its responsibility, as it has in failing to adopt the recommendations of its own Election Laws Commission, one would hope that the public would rise to the occasion and force changes in the law by electing new legislators, demanding leadership by the governor, and requesting relief from the judiciary.

The state board of elections, mandated by section 5 of Article III, may prove to be the most significant idea for good government advanced by the suffrage article. Many of the shortcomings of the election system involve procedure. A forthright and aggressive state board of elections could do much to open the election process and establish consistent and uniform practices throughout the state. It could neutralize the election machinery so that it does not work to the advantage or disadvantage of any particular group or political party. The board of elections represents a threat to the established order. No one knows what it will do. Of course, the unknowns are not something that will go away or resolve themselves with time.

The authors conclude:

In our judgment the Sixth Illinois Constitutional Convention proved that the convention process can be an effective method for achieving sweeping constitutional review and change. In the amending and suffrage articles of the constitution they have been given a structure of government which, if used as designed, will meet the needs of today and tomorrow. Hopefully, the experience of the convention and its momentum towards efficient, responsible, and responsive government will not be lost.[2]

There may be missing from this account the drama and excitement of the narratives of some of the other committees. But this modestly conceived committee afforded a vehicle for its brilliant young chairman, Peter Tomei, to exert a large measure of leadership in the convention. Its deliberations did not exhaust all of his time or energies leaving room for study and activities in other areas. He was heard frequently and often with great effectiveness. His lapses were few. His accomplishments many, not least of all the work of his committee.

[2]Ibid., pp. 96-100.

XI

The Legislature: Something Old, Something New

From the perspective of twenty-twenty hindsight, President Witwer faced one of his most difficult challenges in making the appointments to the Legislative Committee. He had not expected this committee to be handling the most crucial issues; nor did most of the delegates judging by the fact that it placed fourth behind the committees on local government, revenue, and judiciary in their total number of preferences. It was, however, to receive the greatest workload and delegate attention, at least if member proposals assigned to it by the president are used as an index of activity.

The Legislative Committee, like the judiciary and revenue committees, would have the difficult task of attempting to champion constitutional reform, while keeping the forces of the status quo in check so the convention's work product would not be defeated at the polls. There would be widespread resistance among influential individuals and groups throughout the state, most visibly in the General Assembly, to any significant changes in the existing legislative article. Change would not be perceived as in the best interests of those whose livelihoods, clout, and ambitions were rooted in the institutional maintenance of the Illinois General Assembly. But while even the casual observer could expect that the Legislative Committee would be a volatile one, since it would be dealing with tough issues — backed by tough interests — no one, and certainly not Witwer when he was making the appointments, could anticipate the problems, conflict, and deadlock, or the crucial role this committee would play in the final drama of the convention.

THE COMMITTEE MEMBERS

Witwer faced several problems in finalizing the eleven appointments to the Legislative Committee, not the least of which was the selection of the chairman and vice-chairman. Two delegates — Robert Canfield and Paul Mathias — were thought by many to be naturals for the chairmanship. Mathias sought the Legislative Committee only as his third preference, and was not particularly disappointed when he was given the leadership of the Education Committee. But Canfield sought the Legislative Committee as his first preference, and openly and aggressively sought the chairmanship. He was bitterly disappointed, almost to the point of tears, when he learned he had been appointed vice-chairman of the General Government Committee. Canfield had served for a decade as a state legislator and was known to have rather fixed views on the operation of the General Assembly. Throughout the appointment process, Witwer tried to avoid giving committee leadership posts to anyone with predetermined notions on the issues to be faced by the committee in question. Added to that principle was Witwer's insistence that all Democrats in chairmanship positions should not come from Chicago. The search, then, for a downstate Democrat who could meet Witwer's other criteria for appointment, and who would also be acceptable to the Chicago Democrats, was not an easy one.

Witwer did not know, nor had he ever met, George Lewis prior to the convening of the convention. Lewis's credentials were formidable, and he brought to the convention a combined background of farming and law. Raised on an Illinois farm, he had demonstrated leadership capabilities when he sought and served as the national president of the Future Farmers of America. He held degrees with honors in both agriculture and law from the University of Illinois. While there were few Democrats elected to the convention from outside the city of Chicago, and even fewer who had a background that would suggest potential leadership among whom he could choose, President Witwer was optimistic about his appointment of George Lewis as chairman of the Legislative Committee. Like the chairmen of other substantive committees, he was a lawyer, and he had no known strong convictions on the issues with which the committee would be dealing. It only remained to be seen if those credentials would allow him to mold the diverse and strong personalities of the Legislative Committee into the consensus necessary for dealing with important legislative issues.

Legislative Committee Vice-Chairman Lucy Reum was one of several women appointed to responsible positions of leadership by the president. She had graduated cum laude from the University of Chicago, and had a long and distinguished record among the major volunteer groups in the state. She had also worked within the state Republican party and had held several party positions of prominence. Although an able individual in her own right, she often had to struggle for her own identity within the convention. Her husband was Walter Reum, who had served in the leadership of the Illinois House of Representatives and had sought, unsuccessfully, the Republican party's nomination for state treasurer in 1962. Walter Reum was frequently in attendance at the Legislative Committee meetings and at the convention proceedings. He was known to counsel Delegate Reum frequently on constitutional matters.

Three of the Legislative Committee members, Frank Stemberk, William Laurino, and Clifford Kelley, were elected to the convention with the support of the Chicago Democratic organization. Stemberk was born, reared, and educated in Chicago. At the time he was elected to the convention he was a Chicago police officer. He was one of the quieter members not only of the Legislative Committee, but of the convention as a whole. His demeanor, however, did not hide the fact that he did not intend to remain a policeman and that his activities at the convention were part of his efforts, later successful, to rise politically in the city of Chicago.

William Laurino had also spent his youth in Chicago and was educated in that city's schools and colleges. Prior to the convention, he was the field director for the Mayor's Citizen's Committee for A Cleaner Chicago.

Kelley was the only black delegate appointed to the Legislative Committee. Like Stemberk and Laurino, Kelley had spent his entire life in Chicago and had graduated from its educational system. Kelley attended John Marshall Law School; he had been extremely active in Chicago Democratic politics; and he had served as a hearing officer for the Illinois Secretary of State until his election to the constitutional convention. An extremely able, personable, and well-liked individual, Kelley was given the title as best dressed delegate during the festivities following the adjournment of the convention.

Kelley, Stemberk, and Laurino were all among the younger delegates of the convention, and all used the convention as a springboard to other political office. Stemberk and Kelley were elected and still serve as aldermen in the Chicago City Council; Laurino was elected and still serves in the Illinois General Assembly.

Perhaps the most colorful, and certainly the most controversial, member of the Legislative Committee was John Knuppel. While classified as a Democrat, he could be counted on to be unpredictable when it came to voting or supporting a particular issue, either in committee or in the full convention. He was easily excitable and his methods of expressing his position often were not confined to verbal communications. On at least one occasion, during the late night meetings held by the Legislative Committee, he and Delegate Peccarelli could be seen shedding their coats and ready to engage in fisticuffs to protect the honor of their temporarily forgotten principles. Knuppel was a lawyer and had served eight years as an assistant attorney general. He had openly sought the presidency of the convention, contacting the other delegates and distributing campaign materials on his own behalf. Knuppel, like several of his colleagues on the Legislative Committee, would not be an easy individual for chairman Lewis to deal with.

Like many of the women elected to the convention, Mary Pappas had established a distinguished career prior to election as a convention delegate. Educated in the Chicago public schools, she received her law degree from Loyola University and had been in the practice of law for some twenty years. She had also been active in education and in controlling juvenile crime. But like Delegate Reum, she would oftentimes have to exert her own personality to prevent the delegates from viewing her simply as an extension of her husband. She was the wife of Peter Pappas, who had for years served as chief lobbyist for the Illinois secretary of state. Like Walter Reum, Mr. Pappas was frequently present at convention activities, but unlike Reum, he had somewhat of a formal role. He handled several pieces of convention legislation that required funding by the Illinois General Assembly through the secretary of state's office.

Perhaps the delegate who brought the greatest stabilty to the Legislative Committee throughout its months of turbulence, was Louis James Perona. A lawyer from Spring Valley, he had been active in Republican party politics, had been a city attorney and a public defender. The role of informal leadership often fell to Perona, notable for the calm he maintained amidst furious circumstances.

Samuel Martin was the senior statesman of the committee, neither loud nor aggressive in his ways, and with a long background in business, banking, and the Illinois General Assembly. He was the only member of the committee to have been elected and to have served in the legislature. He served two terms in the Illinois State Senate and three terms as a state representative.

Anthony Peccarelli, a DuPage County lawyer with a background in public service work and activity in the Republican party, received his greatest notoriety for the introduction and advocacy of his member proposal calling for the parliamentary form of government for the state of Illinois. This proposal, the last member proposal submitted to the convention, received extensive attention by the wire services throughout the country. Serious or not, it had lively implications.

William Sommerschield, one of the younger members of the convention, sought appointment to the Legislative Committee largely as a result of interests developed as a Ford Foundation legislative intern in the Illinois General Assembly. Convention Vice-President John Alexander had served in a similar capacity, and Sommerschield, Alexander, and Legislative Committee counsel Charles Dunn often worked together to promote their mutual version of legislative reform.

In comparison with other substantive committees, the number of delegates who had indicated preferences for the Legislative Committee, and who were then assigned to that committee, was quite high. All but three of the delegates — Lewis, Stemberk, and Perona — had selected the Legislative Committee as their choice for committee assignment. Lewis, of course, was well compensated by his selection as committee chairman. Five of the eleven committee members had selected that committee as their first choice and three had indicated it as their second choice. The difficulties that the committee was to encounter later, then, certainly could not be traced to any widespread discontent over committee assignments. There was also a reasonably equitable balance of demographic interest among those appointed to the committee. Its political composition included five Democrats, three from Chicago and two from downstate; and six Republicans, one from Cook County and five from downstate. Several were from the so-called collar counties surrounding Cook County. Their ages covered the same spectrum that made up the convention as a whole; there were two women and one black as well as a variety of interests and professions among the eleven committee members.

PREPARING FOR CONVENTION PRESENTATION

The committee could not be accused of indolence. It carried out one of the more extensive schedules of hearing witnesses on the great number of proposals it received — indeed the largest number of any committee. When it was all over, 177 witnesses had appeared before the committee, many to present positions and to argue for constitution provisions sharply different from those held by committee members. The spectrum of testimony was for the maintenance of the status quo at one extreme to reform or revision of almost the entire legislative structure at the other. Many witnesses, including some incumbent legislators, advocated a reduction in the size of the legislative body. The Chicago Bar Association and the League of Women Voters supported single-member districts. The AFL-CIO, the Illinois Agricultural Association, and the Chamber of Commerce, groups not always necessarily on the same side of issues, testified before the committee in support of retaining cumulative voting for the House of Representatives. Considerable testimony was received on the structure and operation of the General Assembly; it was not too dissimilar from that which had previously been received by the Commission on the Organization of the General Assembly chaired by Representative Harold Katz. These included such items as annual sessions, the manner of filling legislative vacancies, and streamlining the rules to allow the General Assembly to cope with the increasing demands and pressures on its time.

As was true of other committees — for example, the Bill of Rights Committee — the diversity of background and variety of opinion in this committee made it extremely difficult to achieve compromise or consensus. After considerable heat, deadlock, abortive coalescence, and virtually no compromise, the committee presented what was possibly the lengthiest and most cumbersome of all the reports given to the full convention. It was not only voluminous in content, but it included numerous alternatives, as well as nine minority reports. In addition, two dissents were filed, one by Lucy Reum, the other by Anthony Peccarelli. Neither could obtain the necessary three votes for their respective views to be presented to the full convention as a minority report, although both did participate in other minority reports.

At the outset, however, things moved along fairly smoothly. During the month of January, the committee used its time to prepare for the long and difficult task ahead. Its hearings conducted at some length during February and March went quite well, largely due to the capable and neutral leadership of Chairman George Lewis. But as the committee hearings ended and the time came to make hard decisions and votes had to be taken to determine the majority report for the full convention, committee unity seemed to break down. Throughout April and May the conflicts and unsuccessful coalitions, and the inability of the committee to achieve a majority on several of the reform issues, became increasingly well known. The difficulties continued into June and had not been resolved by the time the report was submitted to the full convention on June 10. In fact, two informal factions had formed within the committee, neither of which included the chairman or vice-chairman. Democrats Kelley, Laurino, Knuppel, and Stemberk formed one bloc, and Republicans Martin, Pappas, Peccarelli, Perona, and Sommerschield formed the other. Neither could get the necessary six votes to form a majority under the rules of the convention. Chairman Lewis did join the Democratic coalition on the issue of legislative redistricting, but his one vote was not enough.

Divisive Issues

The method of redistricting after each decennial census was not the only substantive issue that polarized the Legislative Committee members. Other controversial issues included the size of the legislature, dual officeholding, single-member districts, and cumulative voting. Delegate Knuppel further complicated the deliberations by pushing for unicameralism. Informal leadership developed within each of the opposing groups. Clifford Kelley, Frank Stemberk, and Jim Perona emerged as informal leaders in various, but unsuccessful, attempts to bring about negotiations, compromise, coalitions, or consensus.

Consensus on the controversial issues was never achieved, and neither group could be recognized as the victor in the long struggle. The individual and often unyielding positions of the eleven committee members are revealed in the nine minority reports that were included in the committee's report to the full convention. The rules of the convention required that at least three committee members sign a minority report. There was no pattern to the signatures given to the minority reports, although each member signed at least one. Only three minority reports were signed by Democrats only; the Republicans came together on only two. The final legislative committee report, then, at least in terms of the more controversial issues, could not be regarded as a final work product. Much of the legislative report on the less controversial items, however, was accepted by the full convention. The recommendations made by the legislative committee in its majority report to the convention included:

Cumulative Voting — retain cumulative voting in the general election, but eliminate it in the primary election;

Numerical Size — reduce the numerical size of the General Assembly from 177 House members and 58 Senate members to 153 and 51, respectively;

Coterminous Districts — create coterminous House and Senate districts;

Residency Requirements — reduce state and district residency requirements for General Assembly membership from 5 to 2 years, respectively, to 2 years in the district;

Dual Officeholding — clarify and tighten the dual officeholding provision;

General Assembly Vacancies — streamline the filling of vacancies by providing for an appointment method rather than the special election method;

Bill Passage Requirement — eliminate the automatic "no" vote problem caused by death and resignation by changing the majority necessary for bill passage from a majority of members elected to a majority of members elected and serving;

Conflict of Interest — provide that a member shall abstain from voting on a bill if he has a personal or private conflict of interest in the measure, but that his vote shall not be counted as an automatic "no" vote;

Sessions — provide for annual sessions of the General Assembly and also for special sessions to be called not only by the governor but also by the legislative leadership;

Legislative Procedures — modernize several constitutionally imposed legislative rules of procedure such as journal entry, single subject, revival and amendment and reading at large;

Effective Date for Laws — require, with exceptions to be made at the discretion of the General Assembly, that laws passed at each session have a uniform effective date and that laws be published at least 30 days before they become effective; require that a three-fifths vote be obtained to make legislation immediately effective; require that laws passed after June 30 cannot become effective until the next calendar year unless passed by a three-fifths vote; exempt revenue and appropriation laws from the publication requirements;

Compensation and Allowances — modernize the compensation and allowance provision governing salaries and reimbursement for expenses;

Special Legislation — eliminate the obsolete "laundry list" prohibitions on special legislation;

Lieutenant Governor — remove the role of lieutenant governor as presiding officer in the Senate;

Legislative Investigations — clarify the legislative investigatory role;

Constitutional Initiative for Legislative Article — provide that the people of Illinois can propose amendments to the Legislative Article through constitutional initiative, but limit that right to specific subject matter in the article which would prevent the initiative from being used for other than amendments on the structure and procedures of the General Assembly.

The Legislative Committee was successful in recommending five appointment standards for legislative districts: compact, contiguous, substantial equality of population, municipal and county boundaries to be followed where possible, and a modified form of the existing tripartite. The latter meant that a good faith effort was to be required to divide legislative districts among (1) that part of Cook County within the present corporate limits of the city of Chicago, (2) that part of Cook County outside such corporate limits, and (3) the remaining counties of the state in a proportion which the population of the division bears to the total population of the state of Illinois.

However, when it came to the method of legislative apportionment, the committee chose to submit its report under convention Rule 24, and presented two alternatives, entitled Alternative A and Alternative B. Alternative A, supported by the five Democratic members of the committee, gave initial responsibility of reapportionment to the General Assembly, to be followed by a reapportionment commission appointed by the governor in the event that the General Assembly should fail to redistrict itself. Legislators were to be elected at large if the commission failed in its reapportionment efforts, to be followed then by the appointment of another commission.

Alternative B, supported by all of the committee's Republicans with the exception of Vice-Chairman Lucy Reum, bypassed the General Assembly as the initial agent of decennial reapportionment. Their plan called for a legislative apportionment commission appointed by the leadership of the General Assembly, and to include both legislative and public members. Alternative B contained an intricate method for a tie breaker in the event that the commission should deadlock and fail to submit an acceptable reapportionment plan.

Lucy Reum did not agree sufficiently with either Alternative A or Alternative B and chose to file a dissent to the Legislative Committee report. In her dissent, she stated that the alternative plans contained some concepts with which she agreed, but she felt that both plans failed to recognize the subtleties and harsh realities of the reapportionment problem in Illinois. She had the assistance of attorney Don H. Reuben, who had served as counsel to Republican State Treasurer, William J. Scott, a member of the state electoral board in *Germano v. Kerner*. She also had the assistance of attorney Richard R. Friedman, who had served as counsel to the Democratic members of the state electoral board in the *Germano v. Kerner* case. The Reum plan conformed to Alternative A in that the initial responsibility for reapportionment was placed in the General Assembly. Her plan also conformed to Alternative A in that a bipartisan commission would have the opportunity to reconcile differences which prevented the General Assembly from obtaining reapportionment. However, she eliminated the governor from the appointing process. She further differed with Alternative A by eliminating the provisions for an at-large election in the event of deadlock. Her substitute plan employed the bipartisan commission approach throughout all the phases, but she recommended a tie breaker to be presented by the presiding justices of the supreme court. In support of her substitute plan, Delegate Reum, in her dissent, stated that "it provides for a methodology in which the opportunity for compromise is present at every level. However, if the parties prove to be unyielding, a valid tie breaker concept is employed so that the remedy will be neither the chaos of an at-large election or a stalemate incapable of resolution."

The first reading debate on the Legislative Committee's report took place in the convention's Committee of the Whole from July 14 through July 22. That debate followed immediately the heated amending of the Judiciary Committee report, during which the controversial issue of appointed versus elected judges surfaced. With the exception of the controversial and pivotal issue of cumulative voting versus single-member districts of the House of Representatives, virtually all of the significant legislative article provisions were debated, amended, and adopted substantially as they would be incorporated into the final document and submitted to the voters for final approval. That is not to say that the convention accepted the Legislative Committee's report intact. Rather, the internal committee conflicts carried over onto the floor, and prevented the eleven committee members from coming together to support their report in a cohesive manner. The full convention upheld the Legislative Committee recommendations less often than it rejected them.

COMMITTEE ACCOMPLISHMENTS

The Legislative Article, as finally adopted by the full convention, contained a variety of alterations from the 1870 provisions, with varying degrees of significance. A major "cleaning up job" was undertaken in that the number of sections was reduced from 34 to 15. Outmoded provisions, such as those spelling out the government for the city of Chicago, lotteries, and the laundry list of prohibited specific legislation, were eliminated. The "tripartite" method of allocating legislative districts between Cook County, its suburbs, and downstate, was eliminated, as was the at-large election of legislators in the event of failure to redistrict by the General Assembly.

Other changes adopted in the new Legislative Article were:

Coterminous Senate and House districts;

Annual sessions, without limitation on subject matter;

A requirement that legislation passed after June 30 does not become effective until the next July 1 unless passed by a three-fifths majority;

A lowered, uniform age for election to the General Assembly (21) for both the House and Senate;

A mandate that vacancies in the General Assembly be filled within thirty days through an appointment method established by statute;

A reduction in the state residency requirement for legislative election from five years to two;

A provision that compensation and allowance be established by law;

A requirement that every bill need be read only by title on three different days;

A requirement that bills pertain to a single subject, but that the total subject matter need not be expressed in the title;

A modification of the amendment by reference prohibition of the 1870 constitution;

Establishment of four vetos for the governor: total veto, item veto, reduction veto, and amendatory veto.

The convention, then, in its legislative article, together with the executive article, was successful in incorporating virtually all of the provisions recommended by the Illinois Commission on the Organization of the General Assembly in its report to the 1967 session of the legislature.[1]

A basic conflict in the legislative article related to the election of state representatives. An historic debate went on with many ups and downs. It combined with the ongoing debate on the selection of the judiciary. In the end, the two struggles merged in an unexpected fashion, and a compromise was literally hammered out. This saved the convention and made possible the approval of the proffered constitution. This truly fascinating story will be told later in this narrative.

[1]Report of the Illinois Commission on the Organization of the General Assembly, *Improving the State Legislature* (Urbana: University of Illinois Press, 1967).

XII

The Executive Article:
Nothing Revolutionary

When President Witwer asked for and received delegate preferences for committee assignments, one member of the Executive Committee dubbed them "dream sheets," evidencing both a cynicism that personal preferences would take a secondary role to other considerations, and an awareness that Witwer obviously had to maintain a political, regional, and ideological balance on the committees.

There was some disappointment when the delegates who were to draft the executive article received their assignments. Only three of the eleven — Dwight Friedrich, Frank Orlando, and Charles Young — had given the Executive Committee as their first choice. Two delegates assigned to that committee — Chairman Joseph Tecson and James Parker — had asked for it as their second preference. The remainder, or a majority of the committee — Vice-Chairman Charles Coleman, James Gierach, John Leon, Louis Marolda, Harlan Rigney, and Ronald Smith[1] — had not listed it among their choices. The disappointment, at least for some, did not result so much from the matching of preference with selection, but from an awareness that the Executive Committee would not be involved with the "major" issues of the convention. In other words, their committee assignment was not viewed as one of the "plums," and they would not be dealing with issues that could determine the success or failure of the constitution at the polls. The Local Government Committee would be making

[1]The authors wish to thank Delegate Ronald Smith for the use of his extensive notes and partial drafts in the writing of this chapter, amounting virtually to collaboration.

206

recommendations on home rule, the Revenue and Finance Committee would have to tackle state debt and taxation, the Judiciary Committee had to resolve the question of the method of selection of judges, and the Legislative Committee had to determine the manner in which legislators were to be elected. The Bill of Rights Committee would be the battleground for numerous ideological issues, and would engender emotional responses from throughout the state. Those committees attracted the most attention; they were the glamour committees and held the potential for protecting or restructuring power.

The attraction to the "issue" committees was in large part also a carry-over from the campaigns the delegates had just waged. Voters and campaign workers had turned out over tax or judicial reform, maintaining or curtailing patronage, altering or maintaining the political structure, or even the general or vague concept of bringing up to date a "horse and buggy" constitution. But as Delegate Ronald Smith pointed out, "I found little more than enlightened curiosity about the nature of the executive branch of Illinois Government. Not once do I recall that a voter indicated to me that we had to do anything about the executive branch." Consequently, when the eleven men appointed to the Executive Committee convened they did not bring with them the feeling that the burden of the convention rested on the result of their deliberations.

COMMITTEE MEMBERS

Joseph Tecson was Witwer's choice for chairman of the Executive Committee. Tecson's stature as the Republican Committeeman of Riverside Township and as a leading lawyer in suburban Cook County made him a likely choice for a chairmanship. He had been active since 1959 when he had helped a Riverside neighbor in his unsuccessful quest for election to the United States Senate. That neighbor was Samuel Witwer; the victorious incumbent was the late Paul Douglas.

His appetite for politics whetted, Tecson remained active, and within a few years succeeded to the office of township committeeman, no small accomplishment, for the Republican party of suburban Cook County had traditionally been characterized as white, Anglo-Saxon, Protestant. Unlike the Democratic party of Chicago, it had not been a vehicle by which immigrants, their immediate descendants, blacks or other minorities, attained political, social, or economic status. Tecson's father, a member of the landed aristocracy of Luzon in the Philippines, as well as his family and forebears, were businessmen, governmental officials, and community leaders. The father had attended medical school in Chicago, winning skirmishes against the discriminatory politics of the 1920s, but lost the battle when the depression hit, forcing him to return to Luzon. During his stay in Chicago, he met and married a half-Polish, half-Irish girl. Joseph Tecson was born in 1928. The younger Tecson returned to Chicago in 1934, began to practice law in 1954, and focused on politics as a means of furthering his involvement in the community.

Although Tecson did not seek a chairmanship, it did not surprise him when Witwer tapped him to lead the Executive Committee. He was the only Republican township committeeman elected to the convention and had been involved in the movement for constitutional reform for a decade. He was close to Governor Ogilvie and to Attorney General William Scott and could easily serve as an informal liaison between the state Republican leadership and the convention.

The chairman had a reputation of being fair, diligent, and politically astute. As a soft-spoken man, his approach to the chairmanship was inevitably low-keyed. He was temperamentally suited to bringing men of divergent views together, and maintaining political dialogue at a reasonable decibel. On only one occasion during the several months of deliberation did any member of the committee raise his voice in spontaneous anger to another member. This contrasted sharply with the constant effervescence coming from the Bill of Rights Committee housed in the next room. If the Bill of Rights Committee attracted the attention of everyone, its neighboring committee was virtually ignored.

Tecson did not present himself as a leader of the suburban Republican faction at the convention. He never met with Scott or Ogilvie regarding the convention, but felt free to call upon their offices for information about state government. He saw his role as that of a good host. He deliberately forestalled any discussion of the major issues until the members of the committee had ample opportunity to get to know one another. He constantly encouraged committee members to interact as a social group, but he was ever-vigilant on the issues facing his committee.

Vice-Chairman Charles Coleman, a black, was the antithesis of Tecson. He was assertive, vocal, assured, while his chairman was deferential, modest and soft-spoken. Despite his outspokenness on the committee, he was not a leader among the black delegates. He was a member in good standing of the Daley organization. He rocked no boats, and if he ever rebelled, it had gone unnoticed. He was a Catholic in a racial group that tended to be Protestant and evangelical. He was a member of the Catholic Board of Education. He liked to fraternize with his colleagues, regardless of race, creed, or sex. He was sensitive to abridgements of black appointments, but was not sacrificial or truly crusading in spirit. He would always attract a hearing, although he might disappoint in the end.

Dwight Friedrich, an outspoken political veteran from Centralia in Marion County, was opposed to the calling of the convention, and in the end to the new charter itself. Indeed, he was opposed to change in general, and like Thomas Kelleghan of the Bill of Rights Committee, was a strong spokesman for the status quo. He had brought to the convention a combined business, banking, and farming background, but he was better known for his legislative experience and political savvy. He spoke bluntly, colorfully, and knowledgeably for his position, and could effectively "work the floor" for votes. He believed in patronage, the pork barrel, the two-party and free enterprise systems, and the American way of life. He also believed they were pretty much interrelated. When discussing patronage in committee, he pointedly stated, "What's the good of winning if you don't get the gravy that goes with it?" He was an advocate of electing as many state and local officials as possible, and felt strongly that the power of the executive needed to be decentralized, concluding that centralization was tantamount to a dictatorship. Thus, he shared the viewpoint of his Democratic counterparts from Cook County, and most of his colleagues from southern Illinois.

Beginning his lengthy legislative career in 1952, Friedrich was elected on "Ike's coattails." During the twelve years he served in the Senate, until his defeat in 1964 by the Johnson landslide, he chaired several powerful committees and was favored for President Pro Tempore of the Senate. Prior to the constitutional convention, he briefly returned to Springfield as a lobbyist for the Illinois Oil Council.

He did not take that position as part of a long-range plan to return to the Senate. Rather, Friedrich operated on the principle that "in politics, you take what comes." The convention, too, was an opportunity that "came along," thus he ran not out of a concern for constitutional reform, but because it was a public office to which he could get elected, and would possibly present opportunities for other offices after the convention. In that regard, Friedrich held a shared motivation with many other delegates, particularly those from Democratic Cook County.

Accustomed to the tougher forms of political advocacy, Friedrich never felt there were pressures from interests outside the convention, nor did he feel there was lobbying of any consequence in the Executive Committee. This was in sharp contrast to the viewpoint held by political novice Ronald Smith, who was concerned that Attorney General William Scott was bringing undue pressure on committee members. Friedrich's concern was that the convention suffered from a surplus of people who had no practical knowledge of state government. The convention was frequently a frustrating experience for Friedrich, who was used to deliberative politics in the legislative arena, where the battle lines were more clearly drawn. But he was protective of the Executive Committee, believing it to be one of the better committees in the convention. He was undoubtedly the most colorful member of that committee. He was easily the most familiar with the uses and abuses of raw power, and was equally aware of the ambivalent feelings his style created in many delegates. On one occasion he prefaced his remarks with the wry comment, "I want this to pass, and I don't know whether to speak for or against it."

Short and wiry, John Leon was a Daley loyalist. His voting record at the convention was remarkably similar to that of Richard Daley, the mayor's son. When this statistic became known, it seemed to some that Leon began voting contrary to young Daley on nonessential procedural matters. When chided about this, he insisted that he voted as he saw fit.

Leon was born and schooled in Chicago. In 1930 he considered himself a Republican and began his political career working for an independent candidate for Chicago City Council. In 1936 the incumbent Illinois governor, Democrat Henry Horner, broke from the political machine in Chicago. The regulars challenged Horner in the Democratic primary, but, after a heated campaign, Horner won the primary and easily regained the governor's office. John Leon worked his precinct for Horner. Leon recalled that "in those days the 'organization' had precinct workers five and six deep, and you had to fight your way in. The organization had jobs during the Depression. And if a fellow didn't have a job, he had plenty of free time to become active in politics and maybe get a job at some later time." Leon was an impressive precinct worker. He brought in large majorities for his party, and by 1939 became a regular precinct captain. He has worked the same precinct ever since.

Leon had the organization's endorsement to run for Illinois state representative in 1958. He was reelected in 1960, 1962, and in the 1964 at-large election. In 1966 he ran for the Illinois State Senate but lost by over 3,000 votes in the general election. In 1968 he ran for state representative and lost by four votes.

Out of office, John Leon ran for the next office available: delegate to the Sixth Illinois Constitutional Convention, without having any special viewpoint on the relevant issues. He led the ticket in the primary and in the general election. His running mate and eventual fellow delegate was the son of the committeeman of a neighboring ward in the district, William Laurino. Both ran as the candidates endorsed by the Cook County Democratic Organization.

Charles Young was the Attorney General's man on the committee, a seasoned politician, an experienced lawyer, a shrewd opponent. He did not have surface brilliance, but he often prevailed where the oratorical stars lost. A downstater, he could understand and sometimes affirm what the Cook County Democrats had in mind. He respected professionals and was skeptical of the unattached and independent rebels.

Frank Orlando did not seek the office of delegate; rather, the Democratic Senatorial District Committee (composed under Illinois law of the local ward committeemen in the district) sought him. Orlando was flattered by the "draft" and considered it an honor to be asked. He recognized that the time in Springfield would be disruptive on his family and law practice, but viewed it as an opportunity, difficult for a lawyer to ignore. His concern was more with serving than with getting elected. The other candidate to be endorsed was Harold Nudelman, a law partner of Chicago Alderman Thomas Keane. Keane was among the committeemen who sought Orlando's candidacy.

Orlando was the committee's optimist and cheerleader. He was without guile or cynicism and had a solid faith in the elective process. He expressed faith in the two-party system and the inevitable power of the voters to cleanse the system of rascals and incompetents. He said, "Somehow, the people always seem to correct the abuses of office-holders. They can sense the truth. In my twenty years in politics and in trying cases, I have found that the voters and juries have a way of figuring out the truth." He worked hard and asked penetrating questions of witnesses, but he never lost his confidence in the status quo.

When the enabling legislation for the constitutional convention was passed, James Parker did what most lawyers think about but never do — he decided to run for office. An attorney from Effingham with generations of family ties in the law and farming in that area, Parker came from the same district as Dwight Friedrich. This district was composed of all or parts of nine predominantly agricultural counties, and at one point was 135 miles long from end to end. It could be characterized as strongly opposed to any change in the Illinois Constitution. Effingham is at the crossroads of the Penn Central and Illinois Central railroads, and its economy is geared to the corn and soybeans harvested from the rich black soil of eastern Illinois. Parker was part of that farm ethic and considered himself a "Farm Bureau" candidate and delegate. Although the voters in his district were generally opposed to change, the Farm Bureau had reservations on that score and both Parker and Friedrich received its endorsement. Although Parker did not receive endorsement from the Republican Committee chairman in his district, he did serve as a spokesman not only for farm interests in the committee and convention, but for issues of interest to the Republican party generally.

Harlan Rigney, a roundish, ruddy, red-headed delegate from the north-western-most district in the state, was a skilled farmer and country politician with long and strong ties to the land in Stephenson County. Active in the F.F.A., he was elected national vice-president of that organization. Like several of the Rigney family before him, Harlan mixed his farming with elective politics, and at age twenty-five he was elected to the Stephenson County Board. He became its president and left the board eleven years later to serve as the district's delegate to the constitutional convention.

He sought the office of delegate as part of a continuing process in his interest in elective politics. His district, agricultural, conservative, and status quo oriented, was generally satisfied with the structure of government at the state and local level, with the exception of one issue — the hated personal property tax. Rigney made a promise to use the new constitution as the means of abolishing the tax. He diligently kept in touch with his constituency, sending back frequent tapes to local radio stations, beginning each with the greeting, "Hello, this is your Con Con Delegate, Harlan Rigney, reporting to you from Springfield." He also wrote a weekly news article for the district weeklies and went home every weekend to speak to various groups and organizations. He was not unique in his efforts at visibility on behalf of the convention. Numerous delegates did likewise; these efforts were undoubtedly useful in their later campaigns for election to other public offices.

Louis Marolda was one of the enigmas of the convention. He was one of the older persons to be elected as delegate and was the senior member of the Executive Committee. He was a retired fireman who had been elected largely on the coattails of Father Francis X. Lawlor, a dissident and controversial Roman Catholic priest who had an overwhelming following on the South Side of Chicago. The citizens of those Chicago neighborhoods regarded Lawlor as their champion of traditional church beliefs and rituals and of their battle to save their neighborhoods from the spreading black population. Marolda was sympathetic to Lawlor's views and tactics, and when Lawlor handily won the primary election, he set as his goal the winning of a victory for Marolda.

Marolda kept his opinions to himself. Even though he privately admitted to having been a Republican precinct captain at one time, he disliked the evils of job patronage because he had once lost a job after an election. He was quiet and gave common sense opinions when explaining his votes; towards the end of the convention he spoke vigorously on the need for the convention to conclude its business. He usually voted with Father Lawlor, but not at all times. At one point Lawlor presented a motion to the convention that failed for want of a second. Marolda sat in his seat, staring straight ahead; he did not volunteer the necessary second so that Lawlor could speak to his motion. At the same time, although he was somewhat of an independent, he did not meet nor generally relate to the nine delegates regarded as the independent group. He voted as he saw each issue, and it was not possible to determine any pattern, except that he was conservative on civil liberties issues. Everyone liked Marolda, but no one saw him as a leader or a spokesman. But then he never tried to be one.

James Gierach was the youngest member of the convention. Barely out of DePaul Law School, politically inexperienced, frail in appearance and demeanor, his interest in the convention was sparked by a newspaper article. Although a Democrat, he did not go before the "slatemakers." However, his candidacy took on a seriousness when one of the two candidates endorsed by the regular Democrats in his district dropped out of the race. His effectiveness on the committee was somewhat diminished by the controversy surrounding his election as discussed in Chapter VIII.

Ronald C. Smith was like no one else on the committee. He had not asked for assignment to the Executive Committee. Because of circumstances beyond his control, he did not achieve the distinction at the convention that might have been expected, considering the vigor and resourcefulness of his campaign for election as a delegate. He was bright with a quick Irish wit, independent, venturesome. He had been an aviator in the armed forces and only briefly in law practice with a railroad and as clerk of an Appellate Court justice. He was on the faculty of the John Marshall Law School. He and Elmer Gertz had won elections in their district as independents, despite strong Democratic opposition. They were the one team of that stripe to win in the state. Smith had not only thought about the issues, he had run and won on them. He had a following of bright young people like himself, several active in the Independent Voters of Illinois and in similar organizations. He was of the new breed in Chicago politics and bore watching. The convention would prove to be his testing time in government and in politics.

No doubt Chairman Tecson was aware of the political and ideological loyalties of the members of the Executive Committee. Dwight Friedrich was a tough politician who had served three terms in the Illinois Senate, not without controversy. John Leon was a member of the Illinois House of Representatives, only temporarily out of office, and a man doggedly loyal to the regular Democratic organization. Jim Gierach was younger, green, and because of his uncertain status as a delegate, potentially disruptive. Marolda was a retired fireman, pleasant and folksy, but no student of politics or government. Charles Young and Jim Parker were downstate lawyers, self-characterized as "conservative Republicans," from districts opposed to change. Frank Orlando, a lawyer and Daley loyalist, was assistant corporation counsel of the city of Chicago. Charles Coleman, also a lawyer and Daley loyalist, was black. Harlan Rigney, a young farmer, was likely to be conservative, but his district had displayed surprising voter independence by also electing Wayne Whalen, a liberal Democrat who had actively worked for the nomination of Eugene McCarthy for president in 1968. Ronald Smith, independent Democrat from Chicago, took both the legal and theoretical viewpoint, and was the committee's only member of the independent bloc. It would be enlightening to see how the chairman would weld this diverse collection of individuals into a cohesive committee. Would it produce any considerable changes in the executive article?

Staff counsel for the Executive Committee was Jack Isakoff, a professor in the Department of Government at Southern Illinois University. A veteran of the legislative process after many years as director of the Illinois Legislative Council, he clearly understood the issues, personalities, and political nuances of the Executive Committee's subject matter. He first appeared as a witness before the committee, and outlined what he believed the Executive Committee's deliberations should entail.

Isakoff, by virtue of his reputation and experience, was naturally a candidate for staff counsel to one of the substantive committees of the convention. He initially indicated to the executive director and the president of the convention that he was not interested. He had been with the "Little Hoover Commission" chaired by Walter V. Schaeffer (who was later to become a highly esteemed justice of the Illinois Supreme Court) and on the Commission on State Government — Illinois (COSGI). Both commissions had studied Illinois government with an eye to streamlining its executive branch. Both were composed of leading politicians, scholars, and bright young men.

In March 1970 Pisciotte, executive director of the convention, persuaded Isakoff to fill in as staff counsel for the Executive Committee. All other committees had been staffed and the committee members Isakoff would be working with were rapidly moving toward a vote on the issues before them and presenting their proposals to the full convention. The energies of the research staff needed direction, supporting arguments for the committee proposals needed to be drafted, and the committee report needed to be prepared. Professor Isakoff reluctantly procured a one-month leave of absence from the Department of Government at Southern Illinois University, but later his leave was extended to almost three months. With a Ph.D. in government, a law degree, and exposure to thousands of public figures and hundreds of public battles, he was well qualified to lend direction to the work of the committee. He was a man of strong opinions, but in spite of his experience and background, he correctly resisted the temptation to become a twelfth member of the committee. It was a temptation that some staff members could not overcome.

THE ISSUES

Numerous issues were raised in the course of the Executive Committee's long deliberations. Some were of critical importance. The committee wanted several changes in the executive article. For one thing, they wanted to reduce the number of elected offices. They wanted to undo the constitutionalizing of officials who might better be named by the governor, so that he could truly be responsible for them. Under the elective process, they often worked at cross purposes and were more interested in their own personal success than in the administration as a whole.

Tecson felt that two out of seven offices was a fair victory for the short ballot advocates. The two were the superintendent of public instruction and the combination of the governor and lieutenant governor into one package. Many felt that, with the treasurer's recommendation, it might also be possible to eliminate the election of the state treasurer. They knew that because of Paul Powell's power, they could not do anything with respect to the secretary of state.

One device the delegates employed to defuse the argument that they were favoring or exacting retribution from any particular individual currently serving in a constitutionally mandated elected executive office was to provide in the schedule of the constitution that the day of implementation for change not occur in the immediate future. Thus, the first "off-year" election was postponed until 1978. By delaying the implementation for eight years, no public official serving at the time of the convention could complain that this provision had been motivated by any hope of forcing him to run for an abbreviated term at the next election. They thus avoided the political issues involved to a great extent. Perhaps if the convention had chosen to delay other possible changes for several years, proposals that were theoretically desirable but politically unacceptable at the time of the convention would have been approved. Would the delegates have voted to abolish the death penalty if imposition were prohibited only after 1980? Would the appointment of judges, or election of state representatives from single-member districts, or the reduction of the number of legislators, or a variety of other proposals have faired better if such changes were not to have become effective for a decade?

Tecson felt the provision for delaying implementation of the new off-year election proposal to 1978 was good. There was no sense in injecting a constitutional issue with personalities, he thought, if such difficulty could be avoided. There was a net gain, he believed, in divorcing state government from the federal situation; otherwise, a presidential landslide could determine who would be elected to state office, rather that the qualifications of the state level candidate.

Tecson believed, too, that the committee was basically a reflection of the convention. Since Witwer had tried to achieve balance on all the committees, he no doubt felt that the Executive Committee had a balance of Chicago, suburban, and downstate delegates, Democrats, Republicans, and independents. In retrospect, Tecson reasoned that any other "balanced" committee would have reached about the same conclusions. He felt the committee was typical and qualified, although privately he would note that one or more of the committee members were quite weak. It was not a question about whether or not they went along with his views. They were simply not sufficiently disciplined and schooled in good government issues.

Needless to say, the Executive Committee had no dramatic displays, and no lines of witnesses formed at its doors. It did have some very fancy witnesses — two former governors, and all elected state executive officers. Rarely did the news media check the action, and it was something of a surprise when a Springfield paper carried a front page banner headline proclaiming the joint election of the governor and lieutenant governor. Certainly, the paper did not mean it as a slap at the highly respected incumbent Lt. Governor Paul Simon. Rather, it must have been a slow news day.

The Governor's Powers

On January 20, 1970, William Hanley, legislative counsel to Governor Ogilvie, addressed the committee on the veto power of the governor. Referring to Section 16 of the 1870 constitution, he noted that the veto is an "inherent" power of a strong executive, and that the governor of Illinois had such a power; he felt the power needed to be enhanced still further because of the growth in volume of enacted legislation.

Hanley's testimony was routine until he suggested the committee might consider recommending that the governor be given an amendatory veto power; that is, the power of the governor to "correct" a defect in a measure through partial amendment, rather than veto the entire bill. He further suggested that the legislative override of such a veto be limited to a simple majority. Hanley continued his "strong executive concept" testimony by suggesting that the committee also explore giving the governor a reduction veto on appropriation bills. James Parker asked whether the power of the reduction veto was of sufficient importance to include it in the constitution. Hanley preferred to defer to the Bureau of the Budget, but speculated that the reduction veto might take on a significance if new fiscal methods were to be employed at some future time in Illinois. No additional discussion was conducted on the amendatory or reduction veto.

Hanley also raised the issue of the need for a "veto session" in the legislature; that is, an automatic requirement that the legislature return for a period of time to consider all bills vetoed by the governor. He emphasized the need for such a session.

On April 30, the members of the Executive Committee met in the Coe Building in Springfield. All members were present, and before the afternoon came to a close, these eleven men would approve committee recommendations relating to the governor's power to convene and prorogue the General Assembly, the time limit within which the governor must sign a bill, and the governor's power to reduce an appropriation and to amend legislation. The latter two powers became a source of great dispute, but only after the people of Illinois approved the new constitution. Neither the reduction veto power nor the amendatory veto power were heatedly debated on the floor of the convention, nor was there substantial public concern over these new and considerable powers. But only a few months after the new constitution became effective, the legislature and the press were decrying the dictatorial powers conferred on the governor by the constitution.

The members of the Executive Committee were by and large skeptical of granting more power to the governor; with one exception, they were moderate to conservative in their political viewpoints. Moreover, there had been scant testimony brought before the committee during its four months of hearings and deliberations. Governor Ogilvie had not recommended or suggested that the chief executive of Illinois should have such power. Except for the proposal of Mrs. Netsch, the members of the convention were undoubtedly indifferent or hostile to the concept of investing the governor with either power. Nevertheless, in May the convention voted to approve the committee recommendation with minimal opposition.

State Treasurer's Office

When Professor Jack Isakoff first appeared before the Executive Committee, he had raised the question of whether or not the state's treasurer should be an elected official. In earlier times, the treasurer had been chosen by a joint vote of the two houses of the General Assembly. The 1848 constitution provided for the popular election of the office, and the 1870 constitution had stipulated that the treasurer be prohibited from succeeding himself in office. The defeated 1922 constitution called for a four-year single term, and it was not until 1958 that the office reverted from the two-year term to a four-year term.

Several prominent figures presented testimony at the convention calling for the elimination of the office of treasurer. Convention Vice-President Elbert Smith, who had been elected auditor of public accounts following the Hodge scandal, advised that Auditor Michael Howlett's suggestion that the treasurer's office be made a part of the auditor's office was not particularly sound. Smith recommended that the treasurer be appointed by the governor and, to insure political and functional balance, that the preaudit function be taken out of the Department of Finance, which was an executive department responsible to the governor. Smith further felt that the auditor should have only a preaudit function, and that the post audit responsibilities could be allocated to a variety of "fiscal watchdogs" responsible to the governor or to the legislature or to the public generally. He noted that the treasurer's function was to invest state funds and to sign checks, claiming that when the treasurer signs checks, this is largely a ministerial function in which he simply states that the money is in the treasury. He makes no judgment regarding the validity of the claim on the treasury. Smith did not feel that there were any particular economies to be achieved by making the treasurer's office a separately appointed office, and noted that the office was a traditional "proving ground" for other major offices in the state.

On January 21, incumbent state Treasurer Adlai Stevenson III addressed the convention. He called for numerous constitutional reforms, among them the startling plea for the elimination of the very office he held. The abolition delegates felt that it would be inconceivable that anyone would seek to retain the treasurer's office on the ballot following the remarks by an incumbent carrying the highly respected Stevenson name. On January 28, Stevenson and his assistant, Charles Woodford, appeared before the Executive Committee. He amplified his statement before the convention in plenary session. He pointed out that by eliminating the treasurer's office from the ballot the state could save virtually the entire appropriation for that office. While he agreed that someone had to be responsible for investing state money, most other functions of the office could be abolished because they were unnecessarily duplicative of functions performed elsewhere. He suggested that the convention recommend the continued election of the auditor and the attorney general.

The Ballot

The question of taking the treasurer's office out of elective politics was closely related to another, broader issue — that of shortening the ballot. The so-called "short ballot" advocates argued that there were too many elected officials in Illinois, citing the evils of voter cynicism, confusion, and ignorance; unresponsive government; and control of elective offices by political bosses.

The long ballot has resulted from two Jacksonian principles of democracy, both operative at the time of the adoption of the Illinois Constitution of 1870. First, the concept of "to the victor go the spoils," and the corresponding distaste for merit employment or civil service systems. But at the same time the general feeling was that no one official should have too much of the "gravy" at his disposal, thus preventing the development of a disproportionate share of patronage-based power. Nor should any official have unilateral power to deal with public funds.

Frank Orlando, for example, expressed his belief that the people in their wisdom had seen the excesses of power employed by the nineteenth century corporate executives, and did not want government power to be vested in any one official. The solution was simply to divide the major executive functions into several offices and to elect each office independently.

The fragmentation of the executive branch into several popularly elected offices was supported by the second Jacksonian principle that officeholders should be directly accountable to the voters. Thus, in Illinois in 1870, the executive branch was segmented into the office of the governor, the lieutenant governor, attorney general, secretary of state, treasurer, auditor of public accounts, and superintendent of public instruction. This was to provide needed checks and balances on both the functions and patronage within the executive branch. Moreover, each political party could normally be expected to retain at least one statewide elected office as a patronage and political base even in a landslide year for the opposite party.

The Governor. By 1970 there were many who felt that the governor's office could become the repository of too much patronage power. Those delegates who feared abuse of power by the chief executive were unwilling to accept the legislature as a sufficient check on the governor through the powers of appropriation veto, advice and consent, and impeachment. They were determined to limit the governor's access to patronage power by denying him the power to appoint major officeholders, the power to invest state money, the power to hire and fire public employees in the bureaucracy, and the power to interfere with the legislature. Some felt that the 1870 constitution provided for too strong a governor — he could veto legislation, he could serve for four years and succeed himself, he had thousands of jobholders at his disposal, the legislature could not easily override his vetoes, he was provided with a mansion and supposed generous budget, and, like all governors, he had considerable political influence. He could take his case to the public more readily than any other statewide elected official. When he appeared before the Executive Committee, Edward J. Barrett, long-time political power in Illinois, and one-time secretary of state, said that if the governor had too much power this was "fascism."

In Illinois there was an additional reason for some politicians to fear a powerful governor. They did not want a major figure in Springfield as a competitor for the political power held by the Democratic party in Cook County. As a practical matter, a Democratic governor was of more concern to the Cook County Democrats than a Republican governor. An ambitious or recalcitrant Democratic governor was an intra-institutional threat. A Republican governor could be dealt with as a major figure from the opposing party; publicly he could be labeled as the enemy, while privately he might be approachable on many issues. But to label a Democratic governor as the enemy, or vice versa, could lead to dissension in the well-organized ranks. A difficult Democratic governor could undermine the basic ethic of the Cook County Democratic party — loyalty.

Superintendent of Public Instruction. The office most frequently under consideration for elimination was the superintendent of public instruction. Ray Page, the incumbent, had come under attack from the Better Government Association during the summer and fall of 1969 when the convention candidates were campaigning for office. Page employees had publicly complained they were required to donate one percent of their salaries to a "flower fund" for Page's use. An announcement from Page's office confirmed the existence of the fund, stating that as of October 1, 1969, it would be renamed the "Ray Page Political Fund." Other investigations in 1970 indicated that Page had also weakened the state's Purchasing and Contracts Act by evading competitive bidding. The Democratic candidate for election to the office, Michael Bakalis, called on Page to use the "flower fund" to reimburse the state for funds Bakalis claimed were lost to the state by Page's failure to use competitive bidding. Page was defeated for reelection that November. The Illinois Congress of Parents and Teachers lobbied heavily to have this office taken off the ballot, declaring they wanted education in Illinois "taken out of politics." The only lobbying for the retention of this elective office was from the

Illinois Federation of Teachers. Their spokesman, Oscar Weil, in spite of unequivocal rebuffs, continued throughout the proceedings to lament the loss of influence in the state education offices. He saw it as an anti-labor move because it deprived the teacher's union of the power to endorse and support the election of a state official, and therefore the loss of power to influence the policies of the victorious candidate.

The short ballot and merit employee advocates found active and articulate support from the state's P.T.A. The combined lobbying power, and public sympathy for a proposal that seemed to be protecting the integrity of the classroom, supplied the needed push to overcome the natural resistance to the alteration of the status quo.

The Attorney General. An axiom of politics is that timing is everything. A diligent minority may win the day if it senses the right timing. But there are those issues for which the opportunity for action or change never materializes. Even a sovereign, deliberative, nonpartisan body, such as the Sixth Illinois Constitutional Convention, often responded more to the mood of the moment than to the theoretical merits of a proposal.

If ever there was an idea whose time had not come, it was that of removing the offices of attorney general and secretary of state from the ballot.

The Illinois attorney general, William J. Scott, was a young Republican who had carved out an image, real or imagined, as the "people's lawyer." He had brought some headline grabbing lawsuits against industrial polluters and had had the support of the *Chicago Tribune* since his earlier election as state treasurer. He was well regarded by political independents and popular with Republicans. After he appeared before the Executive Committee, Vice-Chairman Charles Coleman and the other Democrats praised his presentation. Scott, not unexpectedly, made a strong plea for retaining his as an elective office. Several days later the committee voted ten to one against changing the method of selecting the attorney general; Ronald Smith was the lone dissenter.

Scott's testimony and strong public opposition was not, of course, the sole factor leading to the committee vote. The Chicago Bar Association's Constitutional Revision Committee had voted to main-

tain the attorney general as an elected official, along with the governor
and lieutenant governor. Delegates Young and Tecson were closely
allied to Scott's office as special assistants to the attorney general. On
the day the full convention vote was taken on the question on first
reading, Scott personally lobbied the delegates. The vote was 74-6 for
retention of the attorney general as an elected office.

The Secretary of State. The statewide executive office which,
perhaps, was least justifiable as an elected office, but at the same time
the most difficult to dislodge from the ballot, was the office of secretary
of state. His sole constitutional duty was to be "keeper of the Great
Seal." Nevertheless, the legislature over the years had assigned an
array of largely ministerial functions to that office, and it became a
major stronghold of patronage, particularly in the downstate counties.
The convention delegates knew it would be suicidal to recommend
abolition of that office. To do so would virtually insure opposition to
any proposed new constitution, not only from the politically powerful
incumbent Paul Powell, but also from the thousands who were
attached to the office, directly or indirectly, for political influence and
employment. Powell, the downstate, folksy, master politician, had
been a member of the General Assembly for thirty years, and was
unique in the annals of Illinois politics for becoming speaker of the
House while a member of the minority party.

He was one of the first witnesses to testify before the Executive
Committee (on January 29), flatly opposing elimination of any
executive office from the ballot. He believed that all should remain
elective and "accountable to the people." In response to a question
about how he might suggest dealing with the length of the ballot — for
instance the famed three-foot ballot of 1964, Powell responded in his
drawl, "I've heard it said that the ballot in Illinois is so long that by the
time the voter finishes he is down on his knees." And he continued,
"Wouldn't we all be better off in this country if a lot more people were
down on their knees?" Powell spoke with the confidence of one who is
popular and entrenched; he simply was not going to be removed from
the ballot. His opposition could be fatal.

The delegates soon realized that the office of the secretary of state
was an "untouchable." Even when Netsch and Sommerschield rose on
May 28 to move deletion of the words "Secretary of State" from the

section listing the elected constitutional officers, every delegate knew it was for the record, with no chance of adoption.

A few delegates skirmished over the merits of this amendment, but the mood of the delegates was summed up when Mathias rose and stated: "I think the case for the elimination of the secretary of state as proposed in the amendment has been very adequately presented. I think also — as the advocates of the amendment have indicated — we know how the Convention is going to vote on this proposal; and I suggest, in the interest of saving time and getting on with the business of the Convention, that we proceed to vote."[2]

The members of the Executive Committee refrained from participating in extended debate on the issue, but Leon spoke briefly in defense of the office:

> The General Assembly has seen fit over the past many years to grant (the Secretary of State) extensive duties . . . to perform for the people of Illinois in a fashion that is in the best standards of honest, upright, efficient government. . . .
>
> . . . the Secretary of State licenses brokers, insurance agents, security salesmen — registration of securities, which I think is one of the great important tasks that he has — not once has he ever been accused of being owned by the brokers on LaSalle Street. He is working for the people, and I don't think much more has to be said on his behalf.[3]

The amendment failed by a vote of 20-74, with many delegates "taking a walk."

Some felt that Illinois would have abolished the elected secretary of state if the delegates have been confronted with Powell's wholesale abuse of his publicly elected office which became apparent after his death. Without doubt, Powell's political influence on the acceptance or rejection of a new document would not have played the profound role it did — political realities might have taken second seat to a public outcry for change.

Auditor of Public Accounts. The arguments for retaining the office of the auditor of public accounts as an elective office were in large part similar to those presented for retaining the office of the treasurer. The

[2]*Record of Proceedings, Sixth Illinois Constitutional Convention,* Vol. III, p. 1255.
[3]Ibid., p. 1256.

auditor's office, however, did present one additional concern for the delegates — that is, how to insure an independent auditor who would examine the books to ascertain the expenditure of public monies in accordance with appropriations, and at the same time prevent a recurrence of the scandals in the auditor's office in the 1950s.

Auditor Orville Hodge had used that office to invade the state's assets for his private use. His activities resulted in the Morey-Jenner-Rendleman report which stated: "The pattern of independent largely unintegrated autonomous constitutional offices, provided by the Constitution of 1870, served in substantial part to provide opportunities for the shocking malfeasance and irregularities, and to delay discovery and disclosure thereof."

Because of the Hodge scandal, it is conceivable that if the short ballot advocates had focused on the auditor's office, rather than on the treasurer's office, they might have eliminated at least one of the two fiscal officers from the ballot. They had seen the treasurer's office as being the most vulnerable, and once the convention had voted to retain that office on the ballot, maintenance of the status quo for the auditor was virtually assured. In the Executive Committee, the debate on the two offices was not premised on the assumption that the convention should select either the treasurer's office or the auditor for retention and the elimination of the other; rather, committee members attacked them individually and felt that each should rise or fall on its own merits. There was an abortive effort, led by Vice-Chairman Charles Coleman, to consolidate the two offices. Coleman's proposal (#457) provided for a comptroller and included the consolidation of the treasurer's office into the governor's office. This proposal, however, received little more than the minimum attention required by the rules of the convention.

Elections

The same individuals and organizations that supported taking the state treasurer off the short ballot also favored the election of statewide offices in nonpresidential years. Recent state constitutions (Alaska, Connecticut, Hawaii, Michigan) had so specified. Of the thirty-nine states that had gubernatorial terms of four years, twenty-nine held elections for the governor in nonpresidential years, and twenty-five of these were in even-numbered years. Thus the authority of example was often cited during the course of debate on virtually the entire document.

Among others, the League of Women Voters, the Model State Constitution, the 1967 report of the Commission on State Government — Illinois (the most recent official study of the state executive branch in Illinois), former Governor Kerner, the Illinois Agricultural Association, Adlai Stevenson III, Dean George Watson of Roosevelt University in Chicago, and the Joint Illinois-Chicago Bar Association Committee on Constitutional Revision all recommended that Illinois make the change. There were three delegate proposals on this point.

To our knowledge no one supported holding these off-year elections in odd-numbered years. The treasurer and superintendent of public instruction were already elected in even-numbered nonpresidential years, and it seemed natural to shift the election of other statewide officials to this time. State legislators were elected at this time, and of course many local elections were held in conjunction with these state elections. The expense of holding a new set of statewide elections in odd-numbered years acted as an instant deterrent.

The only significant, but nonetheless successful, resistance came from the regular Democratic organization of Cook County. Martin Tuchow spoke in opposition to the off-year elections. Tuchow stated privately that it would be bad for the party. The evidence available showed that off-year elections did not favor either party. The official argument was that fewer voters vote in the off-year elections, and therefore the state officials would be elected by fewer people. Dr. Jack Isakoff brought in a study to that effect. Perhaps the regular Democrats had some private knowledge that led them to believe that electing the state officers at the same time that the president was elected would enhance the power of the city to deal with Springfield and Washington.

COMMITTEE LEADERSHIP

Throughout all these weeks of debate Tecson maintained a good poker face and poker style. Few could ever quite figure out what he was thinking, although he always struck one as being absolutely honest and open in his dealings, at the table and in committee. Smith recalled that one night he joined a number of delegates and newsmen in a game of penny-ante poker. Through the evening a string of men came and went, a full sampling of the varying regions, orthodoxies, and allegiances of Illinois newswriters and delgates. It was not unlike the interminable chess matches carried on in the newspaper reporters' offices in the basement of the Old State Capitol, to which quiet Ed Gilbreth of the *Chicago Daily News*, Malcolm Kamin, and a handful of others would sometimes retreat from the compulsive oratory of certain delegates. The loudspeaker directly over the chess game made it possible to hear the speeches more clearly than if they were on the convention floor and many a chess game was interrupted by a call for a vote. Through the evening, Tecson kept up the chatter at the poker table, flicking his cigar, making the kind of bravado chatter and self-deprecating remarks that characterize the ritual of playing poker. And he kept winning — steadily, but never sensationally. Smith thought to himself, that's the way he ran the Executive Committee —unobtrusively, simply, with the right mixture of humor and seriousness, and never vulnerably.

The poker players who met on a regular basis were Tecson, Charles Young, Ed Gilbreth, John Camper, John Elmer, and David Connor. Camper objected to Tecson's exotic variations in which various cards would be wild, and certain combinations were required to play or to win. Camper was the youngest of the crowd, and retained a boyish charm, although his articles for the *Chicago Daily News* were mature and well reasoned. He would simply groan when Tecson, as dealer, would announce some incredible combination of high cards, wild cards, and losing cards. Once he declared he had come to play poker, not canasta.

COMMITTEE OUTCOME

This was the atmosphere in which the Executive Committee worked and in the end its product was largely a repetition of what had existed earlier. It certainly was not one of the revolutionary forces of the convention.

The executive article makes several significant changes in the direction of streamlining state government in Illinois. Although in one area, the short ballot, it falls short of reaching the theoretical ideal, the article is remarkable for two reasons.

First, the convention passed the proposed article with less debate than any other major article. This was in large part due to the resolve of the members of the committee to present the article as a package. Committee members who were seeking greater change felt that the revisions were substantially progressive, and concurred with other committee members that no member should file a dissent to the committee report. Given the temperament of the convention at that time, they believed that any changes made on the floor of the convention would be regressive. The Executive Committee members nonetheless agreed to let Smith note his disagreement with Section 1 of the new article. Smith took the position that the governor should appoint all executive officers in state government; in effect, Illinois should no longer have a "hydra-headed" executive article of government with six elected chief executives. Thus, the floor debate was considerably curtailed and the bulk of the challenges made were more for the purpose of making a record than changing the substance of the text as presented by the committee.

Secondly, virtually every change made was progressive. Perhaps this was because few regressive proposals were made to the Executive Committee. True, Delegate Peccarelli suggested that Illinois adopt the parliamentary system of government. Another recommended that the political party which lost the governor's race be empowered to appoint the attorney general so that the attorney general would indeed be a vigorous legal watchdog over the chief executive. Another witness, a member of the Executive Committee, seriously proposed that the constitution prohibit the adoption of any civil service in Illinois government. He strongly favored the patronage system because "if a man doesn't do a job he ought to be fired, and there is no way to get rid of someone who is on civil service." There were proposals that the governor be limited to one or two terms, and that there be an additional elected executive (such as an ombudsman, insurance commissioner, etc.).

Much of the testimony maintained there was no need to change anything in the executive branch. And, of course, there was much testimony that some modest changes would be helpful, if not essential, in making Illinois government more efficient.

During the first several years following the adoption of the constitution, there were frequent attempts, or at least calls, to alter a particular provision of the new document. For example, following Governor Walker's use of the amendatory veto power, the *Chicago Tribune*, in an editorial, called for the elimination of that executive power from the state's constitution. Ronald Smith, as he oftentimes did, countered by pointing out some of the thinking of the delegates when that particular provision was adopted.

He stated that he and the other delegates proposed and defended the new power of the governor, not on the basis of partisan politics, but rather from the feeling that a strong and flexible chief executive was needed and that the amendatory veto was an appropriate means to that end. Smith pointed out that the convention strengthened the hand of the legislature by giving it the power to override any veto by a three-fifths majority instead of by the previous insurmountable two-thirds majority. It seemed appropriate to strengthen the governor's hand in return, and the amendatory veto was one way the new constitution did that. "If we now revoke the governor's power, should we also restore the previous balance by returning to the two-thirds majority vote required to override the veto? Perhaps we should dismantle other parts of the new constitution, and return to the horse and buggy constitution which the voters previously wanted rewritten."

Smith states that he, too, was troubled by Governor Walker's use of the amendatory veto to force the General Assembly to readjust the state share of aid to the CTA. But he appropriately points out that the amendatory veto allowed the decision by the executive to be made in full view of the public rather than behind closed doors where the negotiations oftentimes put the public interest in second position. "We are replacing invisible government with visible government in Illinois," he said. He felt that the Field papers were more irritated by the merits of Walker's use of his new amendatory veto power rather than the fact that the governor, any Illinois governor, had such power. "Like all power, the amendatory veto can be used wisely or foolishly. Certainly if Walker had vetoed the CTA aid bill altogether, the Field papers would not recommend that the governor be stripped of his general veto power."[4]

Thus, an article which had appeared innocuous bred many difficulties and discussions as time went on.

[4]Interview with Ronald Smith.

XIII

Politics and the Judiciary

The judicial article and its evolution have been covered so well by Rubin G. Cohn in his book, *To Judge with Justice*, that there is little point in repeating the story here. As lawyers like to say, Professor Cohn's book is incorporated by reference. Since the present study purports to be a general overview of the constitutional convention, however, the authors feel that at least a summary of the Judiciary Committee's work should be included here. Later it is supplemented by President Witwer's memories. Much of the drama of the convention arose out of the struggle over the judicial article.

Prior to 1964, the Illinois state judicial system was complex, disorganized, undecipherable and badly in need of reform. The judiciary chaos was a reflection of the piecemeal way in which Illinois state government had been structured, changed, manipulated, and rearranged over the years since statehood had been achieved.

The Judicial Amendment of 1962 was the end product of a long and tumultuous period of political and professional conflict. For years legal leaders and educators had sought judicial reform in Illinois, with their principal concerns being:

—improvement in selection and tenure of judges;

—simplification of the chaotic structure of fragmented trial courts, including the abolition of the justice of the peace system;

—an independent appellate court to assume the bulk of appeals from trial courts with appellate jurisdiction in the supreme court reserved for the more important and novel issues of law;

232

—a centralized administration of the judicial system to eliminate the
inefficient utilization of judicial manpower and facilities;
—a more effective system of retirement and discipline of judges.

Previous attempts at judicial reform had been thwarted by the
difficult approval provisions regarding constitutional change. After
passage of the Gateway amendment, whereby constitutional amendments could be somewhat more easily approved, efforts to reform the
judiciary system were revived. The result was that the first fundamental
change in one hundred years of the constitutional judicial system in
Illinois was ratified by popular vote on November 6, 1962, and became
effective January 1, 1964. This 1962 judicial amendment was a
tremendous improvement, although from the perspective of the Bar
leadership and others, it fell far short of complete reform. It simplified
the judicial system by consolidating all trial courts into a single court of
unlimited original jurisdiction in each judicial circuit. An independent
appellate court was established, power was given to the supreme court
to administer the entire judicial system, and the removal or suspension
of judges for cause or disability was reformed. In spite of these and
other reforms, some viewed the Judicial Amendment of 1962 as a failure,
primarily because it perpetuated the adversary elective process for the
selection of judges; many regarded these elections as simply a
means for political organizations to determine who would be rewarded
with judgeships for performing political chores, often on the precinct
level. The debate between advocates of the elective process and those
who preferred merit appointment of judges continued with a good deal
of vigor. In fact, it was a most crucial issue in the Judiciary Committee
of the Sixth Illinois Constitutional Convention.

Although there were those who thought that many of the problems
of the judiciary had been solved by the 1962 Judicial Amendment, a
series of events preceding the convention forced the issue into popular
focus once again. A challenge to the integrity of a supreme court
decision, brought about by a self-proclaimed legal researcher named
Sherman Skolnick, and resulting in an investigation and the subsequent
resignation of two supreme court justices, caused a tremendous
uproar. Governor Ogilvie declared a "crisis in confidence" in the
judicial system and urged the adoption by the constitutional convention
of the merit selection of judges. The Illinois State Bar Association and
the Chicago Bar Association, both long-time advocates of the merit

plan, created a joint committee to make recommendations on the judiciary to the constitutional convention. Their major concerns were judicial selection and discipline of judges.

A complex mixture of influences on the delegates to the convention created conflict, tension, subgroup loyalties, manifested in the Judiciary Committee as well as throughout the entire convention. As we have already seen, the method of selecting committee chairmen and members may have exerted an influence on the Judiciary Committee and its decisions: In his capacity as president of the convention, Samuel Witwer wanted to appoint the committee members and chairmen, but was challenged by Dwight Friedrich, who supported the election of judges and felt that Witwer would load the Judiciary Committee with merit plan supporters. When the convention voted to grant the president the power to appoint the committees, Witwer proceeded to choose the members and chairman of the Judiciary Committee.

In the process of so doing, Witwer consulted with the leaders of the Cook County Democratic organization, Thomas Lyons and Paul Elward, since this organization viewed the judicial committee as one of the two or three most vital committees in the convention. He also conferred with Lyons in his capacity as vice-president along with the other vice-presidents, Elbert Smith and John Alexander. The Judiciary Committee makeup appeared on the surface to favor the Democratic organization's position supporting the election of judges, although the chairman was a downstate Republican who favored merit selection of judges, as did Witwer.

COMMITTEE MEMBERS

The membership of the eleven-person Judiciary Committee broke down as follows: four Cook County Democrats (Nudelman, vice-chairman — committed to elective judges, Linn — committed to elective judges, Hunter — committed to elective judges, and Nicholson — committed to elective judges); four downstate Republicans (Fay, chairman — favored merit selection, Kinney, — favored elective process, Yordy — favored elective process, and Ladd — favored elective process for circuit judges only); one Chicago Republican (Rachunas — favored elective process); two independent Democrats

(Willer — favored merit selection, Whalen — favored merit selection). In summary, at the time of appointment, seven favored elective process, one favored elective process for circuit judges and merit plan for supreme and appellate judges, and three favored merit selection for all judges.

The composition of the committee appeared to be a clear victory for the Cook County Democratic organization and the elective process for judges. However, Witwer felt that the balance was closer than appeared, since one member originally identified as pro-elective became pro-merit, the committee chairman was pro-merit, and Republican committee members favoring the elective process might switch, considering Governor Ogilvie's pro-merit announcement. As it turned out, neither Witwer nor the Democratic organization was completely correct in their assumptions.

William L. Fay, chairman of the Judiciary Committee, was a Harvard graduate and a lawyer who practices in Jacksonville. Some felt that he was too passive and quiet to be a good leader of his embattled committee. They felt that the resulting vacuum was only partially filled by the far more demanding Wayne Whalen and Jeffrey Ladd, two of the younger and more creative delegates. Fay was gentle and softspoken, with nothing Machiavellian in his makeup. But many, including Witwer, felt that these qualities helped, rather than hindered, Fay in his efforts to advocate merit selection in the face of determined, not to say raucous, opposition by the regular Democrats. Had he been more aggressive, there might have been even more polarization than there was.

A number of downstate delegates, observing the no-holds barred advocacy of the Cook County Democrats, were annoyed to the point of supporting the less strident Fay viewpoints. They were annoyed by what amounted to a bombardment of the Daley people — endless proposals for amendments, hard attacks, roughness of demeanor. They recoiled in sympathy for the more reasonable manner of Fay. Witwer felt that in some subtle way this led to the ultimate compromise at the convention that placed judicial selection as a separate submission.

Still, we must try to understand the viewpoint of the regular Democrats on the committee, led by the implacable Harold M. Nudelman. True, he was aggressive, temperamental, emotional and often discourteous, but he was unchallenged in his role as the zealous

supporter of the elective process. This Chicago lawyer, son of a
prominent lawyer in the Jewish community, was not merely a part of
the regular organization; he was strong in the once all-powerful inner
group of Alderman Thomas E. Keane, a man second only to Daley in
the ranks of leadership, and more ruthless and cunning. Nudelman
knew that the machinery could not move ahead without judicial
plums. This was one of the few remaining inducements for political
participation by shrewd and ambitious lawyers. Nudelman felt, too,
that his ethnic and religious group, like other minorities, was more
likely to get places on the bench through the politically oriented
electoral process than if some blue blood process was involved.

His fellow Jewish lawyer, David Linn, felt just as strongly, although
sometimes less stridently, than Nudelman. Born in Poland, not usually
a party activist, he had become a successful lawyer by his own efforts
and was sponsored by the party as candidate for delegate to the
convention in the same district that elected his wholly opposite
number, Mary Lee Leahy. In his desire to support the official
Democratic position, he could sometimes forget himself and jab
sharply at those he was usually more respectful of. His primary
interest, however, was in judicial ethics, rather than selection.

The other two Cook County Democrats on the committee were
blacks, both lawyers, both completely committed to elective judges,
not simply as a partisan matter but out of principle. Thomas E. Hunter
and Odas Nicholson, like people of their race generally, felt that the
only real opportunity that blacks had to rise to judicial office was
through the elective process, where their numbers and political
usefulness would be rewarded. They felt strongly that the Establishment, whether in the bar associations or in the white community,
would overlook them because they are not in the mainstream of
preferment.

Both Hunter and Ms. Nicholson had a good deal of ability and
intelligence. Both were articulate. Hunter was the quieter of the two,
less given to personal attack. Ms. Nicholson could offend by the very
ardor of the assault upon opponents, which at times seemed personal
and querulous in nature. As a young women, she had been the
secretary of Earl B. Dickerson, one of the elder statesmen of the black
community. She had learned through him of the difficulties
experienced by her community, and she felt them deeply. At the same

time, more than Dickerson, she had a large measure of personal ambition. She was a beautiful and striking figure on the floor and in the halls of the convention, well groomed but not permitting her femininity to get in the way of a determination to prevail. At the beginning of the convention, she had told Elmer Gertz that she admired him more than anyone at the convention. This did not prevent her from making a vehement attack upon Gertz when he opposed her in debate. Fortunately, the two reconciled personally, but never on the judicial issue, which, to her, did not permit a compromise.

The other members of the committee were a varied lot. Helen C. Kinney and Anne Willer, the remaining women, were studies in contrast. It was difficult to fathom Ms. Kinney, an enigma to many. She was a housewife turned attorney, who seemed to have her own views on everything, basic and minor. She ultimately filed her own separate statement on the selection of judges. Her views seemed to shift from time to time, because of influences not always understood. She was often effective as an advocate of her viewpoint, although some entertained doubts, at times, as to her motivations. President Witwer was puzzled as to why she found it necessary in the closing days of the convention to resort to technical and parliamentary devices and maneuvers. She seemed suddenly to be tied in with the Cook County Democrats, just as Arthur Lennon, a Republican like her, often served in the same capacity. Both very able and astute, they were not quite in the top echelons of leadership.

Anne Willer, too was a suburban Cook County housewife, and a highly independent Democrat with limited political involvement at the time she served as a delegate. She was, however, a League of Women Voters activist, liberal and idealistic, and with a strong interest in judicial reform. She was a staunch supporter of the merit plan. At first glance, one would not have thought she could be as strong-willed and determined as she turned out to be. She was not one of those who came up with many speeches, motions, constitutional proposals, but she was alert to all that was going on, as evinced by her later career.

Joseph Rachunas and Clarence Yordy had little in common, except that both were Republicans and started with a shared belief in the election of judges. They did, however, demonstrate open minds on the subject and other members of the committee, therefore, frequently tried to persuade them to alter their positions. Rachunas was young and relatively inexperienced in politics. His occupation was running a restaurant and catering service. He was Lithuanian in origin and a Catholic. The convention opened vistas for him, in contrast to the more mature seventy-year-old Yordy, one of the senior delegates. Yordy was a Mennonite, a small-time businessman and a farmer with an assortment of interests. He was a shrewd character and knew his way in a devious world, among calculating delegates.

Two young men left here for the last, Wayne Whalen and Jeffrey Ladd, were complicated and fascinating personalities. Whalen, almost instantly, and Ladd, by a gradual bootstrapping process, were recognized as among the truly dynamic delegates, not only on the Judiciary Committee but in everything that went on during the convention.

Whalen seemed older than his thirty years, certainly shrewder and, perhaps, wiser. He seemed born to backroom politics, although he devoted his talents largely to the liberal, independent cause. He could be both forthright and devious in turn. One had to reckon with him at all times even if one were the president of the convention to whom a debt of gratitude might be due by reason of an unexpected high appointment as chairman of a major procedural committee and a place on the strategic Judiciary Committee. He was possibly the most committed advocate of the merit selection on the committee. He lived in a small town, from which he was elected to the convention, but practiced law with a large and influential Chicago firm. Clearly he had a considerable future in his profession, but he liked playing with politics. It gave him pleasure to have been elected as an independent Democrat from a Republican area. He had been a supporter of Eugene McCarthy at the Democratic National Convention, but he was tougher and more determined than the senator.

Often working effectively with Whalen was Jeffrey Ladd, at twenty-nine, younger even than Whalen, and unlike him, a Republican and a budding businessman from a family that was well established in Crystal Lake. It surprised many to learn that he had been a seminarian at one time. Now he was married, contemplating a family and the study of law. The convention seems to have given him a taste for the calling shared by a substantial number of the delegates, certainly those in leadership roles. Initially, Ladd favored the election of circuit court judges and the appointment of reviewing court judges; but his views were not dogmatic. At that point he was susceptible to reasonable argument.

Here, then, was a committee of varied personalities. They were not pushovers for anyone.

THE ISSUES

In February 1970, the Judiciary Committee began formal hearings. The witnesses before it included every aspect of professional, public, political, business, labor, and civic concern, leaders of the bar associations, the deans of six law schools, supreme, appellate and circuit court judges, and many others distinguished in the field. If the quality of advice the committee received was to determine the results, the committee and the convention were, indeed, fortunate. But such things are often only a sort of facade. The decisions are reached by a different and far more complex process.

The committee considered two formal proposals to be submitted to the convention. One proposal included an assortment of noncontroversial changes dealing with:

- a) the appellate jurisdiction of the supreme court, giving the court virtually unlimited discretion, except in death cases, to determine by rule the cases it would hear;
- b) delegating to the supreme court the authority to adopt rules of conduct for all judges and magistrates;
- c) an affirmation of the authority of the General Assembly to impeach judges;
- d) the extension to magistrates of the constitutional designation of prohibited activities applicable to judges; and
- e) a grant of authority to the General Assembly to provide for the election of a single state's attorney for two or more counties.

A second more controversial proposal dealt with judicial disciplinary procedures. It was coauthored by Linn and Rachunas, accepted by both the committee and the convention, and comprised a two-step plan:

- a) the creation of a judicial inquiry board consisting of two circuit judges, three lawyers, and four nonlawyers to investigate charges and to determine if a reasonable basis existed to charge a judge with misconduct;

b) if the board so determined, it would file and prosecute a formal complaint with a court's commission, comprised of five members of the judiciary as provided in the existing judicial article.

Judicial Selection

The committee in late April turned its attention to the only significant and controversial issue, the election or appointment of judges.

An early straw vote on February 25 showed committee member support for the elective process, 6 to 5, and suggested at least a partial switch in the thinking of two members of the committee, Ladd and Rachunas. The vote was prematurely interpreted to mean that the merit plan was dead. It should have been understood that if two members could shift positions, others could as well.

On February 26, the Cook County Democratic proposal for the election of judges was introduced by Nudelman, vice-chairman of the committee and spokesman for the regular organization. On April 30, the Judiciary Committee took its first formal vote on the judicial selection issue, which showed greater support for the merit plan, especially at the supreme and appellate level, than previously assumed. This vote showed the shift of Rachunas from the elective to merit selection at the supreme and appellate court levels, the potential importance of Kinney who abstained on this vote because her goal of nonpartisan elections was not included, and the vulnerability of the Democratic organization's plan to secure elections of all judges. The committee decided to split into two subcommittees: (1) a pro-merit selection committee (consisting of Rachunas, Fay, Whalen, Ladd, Willer), and (2) a pro-election committee (consisting of Nudelman, Nicholson, Hunter, Linn, Yordy). Kinney announced, much to everyone's surprise, that she would be on both committees. At this point, Yordy, Rachunas, and Kinney were uncertain about their positions and their support was solicited by both sides.

On June 9, the pro-merit selection proposal drafted by Fay, was adopted 6 to 4 by the committee, with Kinney abstaining and Yordy providing the switch vote. Who would switch next, and in what direction?

The Fay draft provided for:

1) the merit plan for surpreme and appellate court judges;

2) the continued election of circuit judges; and
3) a separate submission which would allow the voters to approve or reject the merit plan for circuit judges.

The Fay draft seemed a perfect political compromise, portending majority support from the committee and the convention. It seemed to include a winning combination of ingredients. Whalen and Ladd were especially instrumental in getting delegate commitment to the Fay draft.

An attempt was made by the Chicago Democrats to reverse the positions of Yordy, Rachunas, and Kinney before the proposal was submitted to the convention, but without success. In fact, it turned out to be a brilliant victory for Whalen and Ladd and a defeat for the Chicago Democrats. Several factors went into this success:

a) Ladd expanded his support of the merit plan from supreme and appellate judges to all judges;
b) Rachunas changed from pro-elective to pro-merit;
c) Yordy changed from pro-elective to pro-merit; and
d) Kinney abstained.

What led Ladd, Rachunas, and Yordy to switch their positions was a complex set of reasons, including personal relationships, political pressures, intellectual independence, and psychological influences. In a real sense, this was a microcosm of the entire body of delegates. Very broadly speaking, Ladd's change was primarily the result of a personal intellectual decision; Rachunas's change the result of political and friendship pressures; Yordy's, the result of unhappiness with the Democratic organization's aggressive tactics; and Kinney's decision the result of a political deal and personal political aspirations, ultimately realized after the convention was over. The provision for popular decision on the issue of electing circuit court judges allowed delegates committed to the elective process "a way out"; for they could still campaign against the elective process in the separate referendum. This temptation to pass the decision to the people was ever-present. Indeed the delegates had to be reminded at times that they had been elected to make those decisions.

On June 25, the committee's third report was filed with the convention, including the majority recommendation (the Fay draft), a minority recommendation (supported by the four Cook County Democrats), and Kinney's separate statement of dissent. It was now up to all of the delegates, sitting as a committee of the whole, to decide. The debate was furious, the questioning prolonged. All knew that this was a make or break time.

On May 7, the convention had approved the noncontroversial aspects of the committee's report with little change. It was a respite before the main battles. On May 12, the majority and minority proposals dealing with judicial discipline had been introduced. They produced lively and sometimes acrimonious debate, but the majority proposal was eventually adopted. Now the convention was ready for the main bout.

On June 25, the majority proposal on judicial selection was introduced and on July 11, it was tentatively approved and sent to the Committee on Style, Drafting and Submission. This simple statement omits all reference to the classic struggle that was raging and in which many delegates participated. It was an issue on which virtually all held strong views.

A move on July 8 by Charles Young to delete the merit provisions and allow the appointment of supreme and appellate judges by the governor with the advice and consent of the senate failed by a small margin. The failure was primarily due to the fact that several pro-elective delegates were absent that day. The close vote indicated the perilous position of the merit plan and the necessity of holding together the coalition supporting the majority proposal. The Chicago Democrats, by being nine delegates short at roll call, had missed their best opportunity to kill the merit plan once and for all. It appeared that they were not well organized or disciplined. They should have sensed the dangers and provided against them.

The Karns amendment, submitted the same day as the Young amendment, referred to the majority proposal allowing for the nomination of judges "in primaries or by petition." It won by a vote of 74 to 8. This amendment embodied one of Kinney's objectives, and from this point on she actively opposed the merit plan and allied herself completely with the pro-elective forces. In return for recognizing this primary concern of hers — the nomination of judges by petition — she, a Republican, solidly joined the Chicago Democrats.

Kinney proposed on July 9 to delete the committee's majority separate submission merit plan proposal for circuit judges. This failed 50 to 56 with 7 abstentions, despite the fact that this time the Chicago

Democratic organization was present in full force. Whalen and Ladd, the prime strategists, managed to hold the pro-majority proposal together once again and kept the merit plan alive. It would not be the last time it would be the target of the Cook County Democrats and their allies.

On July 10, Nudelman moved to substitute the minority proposal (calling for the election of all judges) for the majority proposal. This was defeated on all three roll call votes. The Chicago Democrats produced their total block of 33 votes, but other pro-elective support was ending.

On July 11, majority proposals were approved 62 to 33 on first reading and sent to the Style and Drafting Committee. Second reading came on August 11. This time Kinney moved to amend the committee majority proposal by:

1) including in the main body of the article, provisions for the election of all judges, with nominations by petition for primary elections; and

2) providing for a vote on the merit plan for all judges in a separate submission.

Despite the previous votes, Kinney's proposal passed 58 to 49, with 7 abstentions. This was a victory for the Chicago Democrats and seemed to auger certain death for the merit plan. It was a surprising turn-about, but the explanation is fairly simple. By giving their votes to anti-branch banking downstate forces in return for votes on the Kinney amendment, the Chicago Democrats picked up the necessary extra votes. Barter and sale could take place in a constitutional convention as well as in a legislative body. Because of the generally high quality of the delegates, this maneuver was a surprise. The judicial article as amended was passed in second reading 103 to 3. It was then that the great drama of the convention unfolded, a story to be told later in this book.

XIV

Home Rule at Last

There can be no dispute that one of the most novel provisions in the new constitution is Article VII — Local Government, with its bold, even revolutionary grant of home rule powers to Cook County, Chicago, and all municipalities over 25,000 population, and others who "opted" for it. In fact, the Illinois Supreme Court said, in one of its first opinions on home rule, that

> the concept of home rule adopted under the provisions of the 1970 constitution was designed to drastically alter the relationship which previously existed between local and State government. Formerly, the actions of local governmental units were limited to those powers which were expressly authorized, implied or essential in carrying out the legislature's grant of authority. Under the home rule provisions of the 1970 constitution, however, the power of the General Assembly to limit the actions of home rule units has been circumscribed and home rule units have been constitutionally delegated greater autonomy in the determination of their government and affairs. To accomplish this independence the constitution conferred substantial powers upon home rule units subject only to those restrictions imposed or authorized therein.

This assessment certainly seems correct; whether the future of local government in Illinois will fulfill the delegates' great hopes for a modernized, efficient, responsive system of local governments is still an open question.

However things may turn out in the future, it was clear to many well before the convention got underway that some form of municipal home rule would be a major topic of discussion by those who would draft the new constitution. In fact, 70 percent of the delegates who finally gathered in Springfield signed proposals advocating such a move and over half of them told President Witwer that they wanted to be assigned to the Local Government Committee as their first, second, or third choice.

THE COMMITTEE MEMBERS

Given the level of popular interest in the subject of home rule, it is perhaps not surprising that the committee which gathered to discuss local government issues, comprised a number of individuals who had been, or were at that time still, active in local government affairs. Thus Madison L. Brown, Robert L. Butler, Edwin F. Peterson, David E. Stahl, John C. Woods, and Donald D. Zeglis had all served in local offices. Butler, Peterson and Woods had been mayors of their cities, and Stahl was deputy mayor of the state's largest municipality, Chicago. Brown and Zeglis held other positions of community authority. Daley was connected with big city government by birth, and otherwise, and it was natural for him to be concerned about such matters. Some felt that young Daley was a conduit for the strongly felt views of his father, particularly in the all-important area of home rule.

This was a committee of strong-willed and able men and women. The chairman and vice-chairman, Parkhurst and Carey, as well as Betty Ann Keegan, have already been described, and deservedly so, as being in the top leadership ranks of the entire convention. The inclusion of Mrs. Keegan has special significance, since she held no official rank. It was by strength of character, intelligence, perception, and determination that this lovely woman made her presence felt on the committee as well as in the convention. As a matter of fact, she was probably more effective in the convention as a whole than on the committee. Even though she ranked high among Democratic women of her county and in the state, she was virtually nonpolitical most of the time. She believed in good government, principles mattered more than all else. Her charm made her acceptable to those who might be affronted by the bright, more assertive Dawn Clark Netsch.

John Parkhurst, chairman of the committee, was a totally different sort of person. "Parky," as he was invariably called, was shrewd, calculating, even devious at times. He concealed his brains and strategy behind a veneer of conviviality. He was present and vocal whenever the delegates gathered to drink and gossip. One could not help but wonder now and then, how he found the time or inclination for his convention duties and such distractions. While he had been in the state legislature, he had been called the best freshman legislator. Almost instantly, he had become part of the leadership of the House of Representatives. In a similar way, the delegates thought of him as a natural leader of their convention, this more so in the early days than later. Many began to think, as the convention approached the closing months, that there was something wrong in Parky's leadership as the report of his committee was unduly delayed and, ultimately, released in language that was not clear. Parky's leadership was perhaps more scintillating than Witwer's, but Witwer, who was more dogged and decisive, generally accomplished what he sought rather effectively.

One reason the shine of Parkhurst's armor became less bright as the convention progressed was that the Democratic vice-chairman of the committee, Philip Carey, while not as convivial a character as Parky, was probably more firmly briefed by his party's stalwarts. Carey knew exactly what was expected of him. He could be friendly and often confiding and trustworthy, but he knew that there were tasks that he had to accomplish, tasks he would keep firmly in mind as he strove to complete them effectively and on time. If he wandered from the party line, it was only on a peripheral moral issue like capital punishment.

Among the three mayors on the committee, John C. Woods made a reputation for the brevity of his remarks on the floor of the convention. Edwin Peterson was even more brief; he said nothing. And Robert Butler was one of the best natural orators of the convention. Woods aroused expectations and was shrewd, but he made a principle out of aphoristic pronouncements that meant as much or as little as one chose to attribute to them. Peterson cultivated his bees at home, listened to his colleagues as they orated at length, and kept his own counsel. He had succeeded in life without clamor, and this was his style on the committee and in the convention. Humorous, unhurried, sometimes satirical, Butler made points when he was inclined to do so. He was a personality, rather than a leader.

David Stahl, the young, redhaired, bright Daley man, knew exactly what was expected of him and could perform well. Having worked closely with Chicago's fabulous mayor, he knew the problems of urban life and Mayor Daley's answers to them. He had married the daughter of James C. Downs, Jr., one of the movers and shakers of the city, who was content to let others grab the headlines. Stahl gave the appearance of independence and integrity. Months earlier, when Chicago had gone through the trauma of the peace demonstrations both preceding and during the Democratic National Convention, some said the troubles could have been avoided or lessened had Stahl been in town and in charge.

Joan Anderson, the second woman on the committee, was dynamic, intelligent, concerned. A committed Republican, she had a nonpartisan aura and was generally on the side of those who wanted good government results. She had defeated well-known persons in winning a place at the convention, and she was determined to be influential. It was difficult to define her exact role. Certainly, she was respected, consulted, reckoned with, but it was not always easy to put one's finger on exactly what she brought about.

Ted Borek, a successful businessman, a Republican stalwart, conservative by nature, distrusted the Democrats and feared that they might gain control of the convention for their ulterior purposes. He could always be counted upon to vote to thwart them. He took his work seriously and was liked even by those who disagreed with him.

Ralph Dunn, one of the mountaineers from Southern Illinois, was filled with local pride. He had come to the convention to advance a few favorite issues, but could compromise when necessary. Ray Johnsen was much more reserved and soft spoken than his abilities might have led one to expect. He was both an accountant and a publisher and was allied with the dynamic lieutenant governor, Paul Simon. The two had worked closely in their newspaper chain and in their campaigns. Johnsen was content to let Simon get public acclaim while he did as much as possible to advance Simon's career.

Donald Zeglis had unresolved, almost undefined ambition and a great wit. Now and then his influence was felt on the conservative side. The same could be said of the academic John Wenum, a gentle person, a scholar, but not a leader.

Madison Brown, a black, a Democrat, somewhat a scholar, towered physically above the other members of the committee. Sometimes he spoke very effectively. He was one of those upon whom the Democratic leadership depended. He was young enough to dream of taking over one day, but rebellion was not ingrained in him.

The committee was fortunate to have an excellent staff led by Professor David C. Baum, whose premature death soon after the close of the convention saddened all. Like so many of the other able committee counsel, arrangements had to be made for release time from his already busy schedule. Baum, a recognized legal scholar, was professor of law at the University of Illinois Law School. He had the difficult task of providing staff support to a committee that personified the geographic as well as the political divisions of the state. His research and staff work had to provide a scholarly framework, but also recognize the political realities with which he was dealing. He performed admirably, meeting the challenge of the substantive issues before the committee; he was, however, frequently frustrated and bewildered by the tactics engaged in by the committee leadership. Baum was ably assisted by Frank Renner, administrative assistant to the committee. A Parkhurst protege from Peoria, Renner distinguished himself as a new lawyer on the way up.

These men and women, so different in personality and political outlook, had to draft an article that would satisfy the widely recognized need among the larger cities for home rule, without surrendering to big city establishments. How did it work?

GETTING DOWN TO WORK[1]

At first committee deliberations went smoothly. The committee heard testimony on virtually every local government problem and from many local officials, including Mayor Daley. By April there was a consensus on the need to modernize county government, halt the proliferation of special districts, and grant some form of home rule to "larger cities." On the latter issue, the committee had proceeded quite slowly, since Chairman Parkhurst realized he "had a hot potato on his hands" every time the committee discussed home rule. Then in late April, Vice-Chairman Carey announced that he and most of the

[1] The authors are indebted to Ms. Ann Lousin who prepared much of what follows in this chapter. Ms. Lousin had the benefit of a close relationship with the convention as a member of its research staff, and has remained active and influential in implementation of the constitution.

Democrats wanted stronger home rule provisions. From that point on, the Democratic minority led by Carey took stronger positions on who should get home rule, how great the power should be, and how difficult legislative preemption of home rule power should be. By late May, the committee had divided into subcommittees, and the majority and minority on each proposal had begun drafting their own suggested provision. By July 16, 1970, both the majority and minority reports were filed, and floor deliberation could begin.

On first reading the full convention finally faced the problems with which the Local Government Committee had been wrestling for six months. Although there were changes in the article after first reading was finished, the truly momentous decisions had been made by this time. It is a tribute to the fairness and diligence of the committee that the essential positions taken by most of the committee were sustained by the full convention.

The Problem of the Counties

Although home rule problems held center stage, many delegates were also very concerned with a number of other issues that should be given some attention here. Among these was the great dispute over the structure of the offices of counties. It was generally agreed that Cook County needed home rule and that certain restrictions on county officers — such as the prohibition on treasurers and sheriffs succeeding themselves — should be removed. There was also a vague feeling that county government needed to be modernized, but there were few concrete proposals on how such modernization should be accomplished. In addition there was consensus on the need to halt the proliferation of special districts and to consolidate many municipal functions.

There was no consensus, however, on townships. In Cook County, townships formed the "indispensable" basic units of the Republican party and they performed a similar role, although perhaps not quite as vital, in many downstate counties. The GOP was understandably reluctant to surrender this base of power with its traditions and patronage, even though most township powers had been reduced, if not eliminated, by the passage of time.

Chairman Parkhurst wisely chose to present the article, even with its minority proposals and dissents, as a package. In his usual amiable way he briefly explained the "majority report," namely, the proposed article, section by section, highlighting the one or two main reasons for each provision and noting where the committee had failed to agree. Then Vice-Chairman Carey, equally amiably and intelligently, outlined the minority reports, most of which had been filed by the Chicago Democrats. As he finished, Carey said, "With that, we're ready to come to blows."[2] The convention applauded.

Within a few days, the delegates practically did come to blows. The first major issue of local government was the status of county boards and county officers. Although there were high feelings on the proper way to compose county boards, the delegates knew that the one man-one vote decisions had largely removed that matter from their consideration. In 1969 the General Assembly had passed a county board reapportionment act to reorganize the election of county board members in keeping with these decisions. The only really controversial county board organization was that of Cook County. Cook was unique in that its commissioners were elected from two districts — Chicago, which elected ten members from the city at large, and suburban Cook, which elected five members at large. The partisan composition of the county insured the election of ten Democrats and five Republicans, giving control to the Chicago Democrats. The only opportunity the Republicans had to control the board came in a "Republican year" when a Republican was elected chairman. This post, although it was always held by a regularly elected member of the board, was filled by a countywide election. During the 1950s and 1960s the suburban population of the county mushroomed, allowing an occasional Republican, such as Richard B. Ogilvie of suburban Northbrook, to be elected the chief executive. By 1970 it was clear that the statutory two-to-one ratio between city and suburban Cook no longer complied with one man-one vote standards and would become even more imbalanced in the next decade.

In order to prevent a sudden upset of the partisan and geographical government system of Cook County, the convention modified the majority and minority proposals of the Local Government Committee and produced a section which, in effect, kept the existing electoral system; it should be added, that the people of Cook County may change it in the future — for instance, to elections from single member

---

[2]*Record of Proceedings, Sixth Illinois Constitutional Convention,* Vol. IV, p. 3029.

districts. This solution seems the most practical for Cook County with its special problems. The 1970 Census showed that the suburbs had gained population at the expense of Chicago. Thereupon and as a result of a decision by U.S. District Court Judge Hubert L. Will, the Cook County board voted to increase the number of suburban members by one so that there were ten city members and six suburban members. This is very close to the one man-one vote standard although there will doubtless have to be another adjustment in 1980.

A much more complex problem was the election, appointment, or elimination of county officers. Under the 1870 constitution each county elected a county judge, county clerk, sheriff, treasurer, coroner, and clerk of the circuit court, and every county of at least 60,000 inhabitants also elected a recorder of deeds. A century later, many citizen groups wanted to abolish some county offices, or at least make them appointive; they naturally faced opposition from the incumbent county officers, often referred to as the "courthouse gang." The "short ballot" favored by citizens groups was the focal point of discussion, both in committee and on the floor. In the end, "pragmatic populism" won. Article 7, section 4c of the local government article allows the people of any county to eliminate any office by referendum. In effect, then, the convention sidestepped the issue of which county officers were most worthy of constitutionalizing. It rejected both a proposal to mandate the election of more than the sheriff, treasurer and clerk, and one to make the election of all officers permissive. It chose instead the middle ground of mandating election of three of the most powerful and traditional officers and allowing election or appointment of a coroner, recorder of deeds, assessor, auditor, and other officers as provided by the legislature or a county board. Taken together, it is clear that the convention decided there was some value in retaining the three major county officers, but that no officer should be forced upon a county whose people no longer wished to support that office.

The organizations of county officers were disappointed and feared that many counties would quickly eliminate county officers by referendum. In fact, the only office under serious attack was that of coroner. It was viewed as an outdated office that was largely an anachronism in a society with sophisticated forensic medical techniques. Experts in pathology could handle mysterious deaths and the police could handle routine ones. However, most rural Illinois counties are short of doctors, let alone forensic pathologists, and they would have found it difficult to spare a physician for the task. In the few counties that have used the new referendum procedure, people have voted to abolish the office of coroner. In those downstate counties, the county sheriff assumed the coroner's duties, while Cook County appointed a physician as its first "county medical examiner." Otherwise, the county officer's fears have been groundless — at least so far.

The Townships

After the convention had resolved the question of county officers' status, it turned to another traditional bastion of power — the township. In the 84 counties divided into townships and in Cook County, which has active townships only in the suburbs, the township is a basic unit of political party organization. Although some citizens' groups would have preferred to abolish all townships, the delegates knew that the entrenched interests in each township would fight abolition bitterly. Therefore, it chose the "populist" solution once more and merely made it easier for the people in an area with townships to abolish one or all the townships in a county. This solution met with general approval. If nobody's first choice, it was clearly the most acceptable compromise. To date, no township has been abolished.

THE CENTRAL ISSUE

Problems of county and township government paled alongside those of home rule. One of the most controversial issues of the convention, and certainly the most controversial issue of the local government article, home rule dominated the convention for over a week of "first reading." In retrospect, the story of the development of the home rule provisions seems almost a miracle and certainly one of the great stories of the convention.

The delegates themselves were intrigued by the possibilities of home rule powers for municipalities, as the support for the member proposals on home rule shows. After hearing testimony and holding long discussions on all facets of the issue, the Local Government Committee unanimously recommended home rule for at least some municipalities and at least Cook County. The only objections filed by committee members concerned the nature of home rule powers and the number of municipalities and counties which could have home rule. The Chicago Democrats, joined occasionally by some of their downstate allies, filed most of the minority reports, calling for the extension of home rule powers to all cities and counties. The majority wanted to grant automatic home rule status only to cities with a population of 20,000 or more and to counties with an elected chief executive officer. Then as now, only Cook County elected an executive. The minority also wanted to grant more revenue powers than did the majority. Committee unanimity on this broad recommendation was no small achievement. Few major issues of such proportions emerged from any other committee with such broad support. Undoubtedly, the consensus was a major factor in the convention's acceptance of home rule. Let us go back and see why the convention took such bold steps and had such high hopes.

When the delegates convened in 1969, local government in Illinois could hardly have been in worse condition. Illinois had more units of local government than any state, 6,454. Of these, about 1,500 were school districts designed to implement the system of "free common schools" mandated by Aritcle VIII of the old constitution and were, strictly speaking, creatures of the state. They were not truly local governments, although their governing boards were elected locally. The most striking characteristic of the remaining local governments was the large number of "special districts" — units which provide only a single service, such as police or fire protection, sanitation or street lights. The boards of most of these districts were appointed by circuit judges. In 1967 there were 2,313 special districts and the number was growing every year. Of the general purpose governments, 1,432 were townships and 1,256 were cities, towns, or villages. There were 102 counties, as there had been for a century.

The result of this proliferation was inefficient service — since few could take advantage of economies of scale — and unresponsive local government — since few citizens could determine which of the ten to fifteen local governments under which they lived provided which services.

Historical Reasons for Dilemma

The causes of this proliferation, especially among special districts, were rooted deeply in Illinois constitutional and political history. Article IX, sec. 12 of the 1870 constitution forbade any local government, even the largest county or city, to incur general obligation debt in excess of 5 percent of the assessed valuation of its property. Since the remaining provisions of the Revenue Article insured that local governments would be forced to depend almost entirely upon the general ad valorem tax upon real and personal property, the 5 percent debt limit severely hampered growing cities in their quest to provide needed municipal services.

The most common solution to the critical shortage of funds for capital improvements, such as public buildings, roads and street lights, was to create a special district; such districts existed solely for the purpose of issuing bonds to finance an improvement and administer its operation. Moreover, during the progressive, or reform, era at the turn of the century many people had thought that having these governments administered by judges would remove them from partisan politics. In practice, of course, the districts frequently turned out to be as "political" as if they had merely been departments of a county or city government.

Once a local government is created it develops its own constituency, users of its services will not tolerate its dissolution unless the service can easily be transferred elsewhere. By 1969, the general purpose districts bordering on each special district were usually at their own 5 percent debt limit and could not constitutionally assume more debt. Moreover, local officials realized that each district was a separate taxing unit, each with a "tax bite" deceptively small in comparison with the taxpayer's total bill. For political reasons, it seemed better to diversify the blame for an increase in taxes by keeping many taxing bodies.

The second reason for the dilemma of Illinois local governments was the heavy reliance upon the property tax. Like many midwestern states, Illinois was slow to adopt a state sales tax (1933) and did not adopt a state income tax until the very eve of the 1969 convention. As a result, the plethora of local governments forced to compete for the property tax dollar faced a growing taxpayer rebellion.

The third dilemma facing Illinois local government was the inability of the 1870 constitution and of the political forces throughout the state to meet the problems of rapid urbanization. Illinois had been a largely rural society with scattered small towns in 1870. By 1969, 80 percent of the population lived in the state's nine rapidly growing urban centers. Most of the remainder lived in scattered small towns; few still lived on farms.

The Special Chicago Dilemma

Chicago occupies a unique position in this demographic situation. At the time of the convention, the city housed fully one-third of the state's population, and Cook County about half the entire population of the state. In almost every respect, Chicago had the same constitutional powers as the tiniest hamlet in Southern Illinois, while Cook County had the same powers as a rural county with only a fraction of its population and growing pains. To be sure, the rural-dominated General Assembly had tried occasionally to grant Chicago extra powers, but to little avail. The 1904 "Chicago Little Charter" amendment (Art. IV sec. 34) tried to give the city a measure of home rule, but its procedure proved so cumbersome that it was eventually discarded.

Up to 1969, the legislature had no alternative but to circumvent the constitutional prohibition on special legislation by granting powers to a class composed of all municipalities "having a population of 500,000 or over" — the formula for Chicago alone. Since the burgeoning metropolitan area was equally hamstrung by restrictions on county powers, Cook County was designated in statutes as "any county having a population of one million or more."

These constitutional circumventions merely exacerbated the already existing polarization between the Chicago metropolitan area and the rest of Illinois. This "Chicago-Downstate" split had existed for some time and had enormous consequences for the Illinois economy, its society, and its politics. In fact, the natural antagonism between these two so completely disparate lifestyles had been a major fact of Illinois politics throughout the twentieth century and was often reflected at the convention. Downstaters, including most of the legislature and some at the convention, tended to equate Chicago with its mayor. They regarded Mayor Daley and his powerful political machine with a mixture of hatred and admiration.

The convention met at the end of a decade that had seen every state legislature in the nation turn to a "one man-one vote" system. In addition, Con Con delegates were elected from senatorial districts reapportioned in 1965. They reflected the shift in population from rural areas and small towns to large cities and suburbs. All of them knew that the 1970 census, to be taken as they were meeting in the Old State Capitol, would effect a further shift toward urban and metropolitan areas in the legislature. The emerging third force in Illinois politics — the one-third of the state's population in Chicago suburbs — were part of neither Chicago nor downstate, yet they were squeezed between both factions. No one could predict their influence either in the legislature or in politics generally.

Only one forecast could be made with certainty: Illinois would have to meet the local governmental problems and urban crises it faced in the last third of the twentieth century with new constitutional provisions which would not hinder the solution of these complex problems as did the 1870 constitution. Keeping this background information clearly in mind, it is now possible to turn to a consideration of how the convention dealt with the issue of home rule.

THE CONVENTION LOOKS AT HOME RULE

Chairman Parkhurst asked the ever-witty delegate John Woods to present the case for home rule. Woods opened with these memorable words: "I am supposed to talk to you about home rule. Home rule, many of you might know, is like sex — when it's good it is very, very good, and when it's bad, it's still pretty good."[3] Having thus put the issues dividing the committee into proper perspective, the convention turned to the first major issue: who should have automatic home rule powers. It should be noted that there was no real dispute over letting cities not having home rule obtain status by referendum. The dispute, which was clearly the threshold question, centered around the "trigger" for municipal home rule. Delegates argued at length for population thresholds ranging from 0 to 200,000 and finally adopted Delegate Daley's suggestion that no population threshold be required, in effect giving even the smallest municipality in Illinois automatic home rule status. This decision profoundly affected the rest of the first reading debate, for the question of which municipalities automatically

³Ibid., p. 3038.

obtained home rule status was inextricably intertwined with the question of how great those powers would be. Most delegates favored giving Chicago significant home rule powers, but few thought that a village of one hundred persons could use those powers effectively — or even needed those powers at all.

The most curious aspect of the home rule debate centers upon the willingness of the Chicago Democratic organization delegates to extend home rule powers to small municipalities whose interests were only remotely connected with Chicago's. The reason seems to be that the Chicago delegation had an informal alliance with a number of people representing downstate municipalities. If there was a strategy here, by and large it worked. The Chicagoans lent their support to the proposal to give every municipality home rule and the downstaters supported strong home rule powers, especially revenue powers for Chicago. Before the week of first reading ended, the convention had voted to grant home rule cities probably the most extensive and innovative constitutional grant of home rule in the country. By the end of first reading, the convention had established a "trigger" population of 10,000; after second reading it was put at 25,000 where it remained. Only about fifty cities thus obtained automatic home rule status. The delegates apparently looked at the magnitude of the powers it had designed and concluded that the 1,000 or so smaller cities simply did not need and probably could not handle such powers. By a clear majority the delegates wanted Cook County — burdened with half of the state's population, with its elected chief executive, and vast and myriad metropolitan problems — to have considerable leeway in solving its problems.

Revenue Provisions

The most controversial home rule powers were the revenue provisions. Almost every delegate knew that effective home rule depended to a great extent upon taxation and debt powers. As the Con Con saying went, "Control of the course follows control of the purse." There was little disagreement over granting home rule units "police power" —the power to pass laws regulating "public health, safety, morals and welfare," and to grant licenses to promote public welfare. Similarly, even strong home rule advocates conceded that criminal law was an area best left to the state legislature and judiciary. The real controversy arose over such powers as granting licenses for the purpose of raising revenue, imposing an income tax or occupation tax, and incurring local debt.

Licensing for revenue purposes differs from licensing mainly to regulate for the public welfare in that the fee charged for the revenue license exceeds the cost of administering the license. In short, the person seeking to hold the license must not only pay the administrative cost of the license, but pay a "tax" into the city treasury as well. The potential for abusing one or a few occupations is obvious. By imposing a requirement of a license with a heavy fee on door-to-door salesmen or restaurants serving liquor, a government may require a few businesses to pay a disproportionate share of the tax burden as a "penalty" for doing that particular business. The majority of Local Government Committee members had rejected the minority proposal to include licensing for revenue in the grant for home rule powers. On first reading the committee minority, four Chicago Democrats and two downstate Democrats, were initially successful in persuading the convention to include licensing for revenue as a home rule power on the grounds that it was a valuable way to raise local revenue and was no more subject to abuse than other business taxes. However, after a weekend recess in which members of the committee majority and other opponents personally lobbied several delegates, the convention reconsidered the question and, except for Delegate Keegan's brief futile attempt to reinstate it on second reading, the issue was dead.

The majority of the Local Government Committee had also recommended that the power to tax incomes, earnings, or occupations was excluded from the home rule power grant. The Illinois income tax, which in large part is derived from earnings, was less than a year old when the convention met. As expected, the new flat rate was unpopular, although most observers considered it fairer than the sales tax or real property tax and it was certainly not as hated as the personal property tax. The "occupation tax" was the technical name for the 5 percent Illinois state and local sales tax. To most delegates, therefore, "occupation tax" simply meant the sales tax so suspiciously regarded by many Illinoisans.

The seven Democrats on the Local Government Committee submitted a minority proposal to allow home rule units the power to impose income and occupation taxes. The first reading debates show that the delegates discussed whether home rule units really needed new sources of revenue and whether these two taxes were suitable sources. The delegates were aware that their decision a month earlier to abolish the personal property tax would deprive local governments of revenue; that occupation taxes, income taxes, and revenue licensing were functionally equivalent to each other; and that each could be abused by a local government. Delegates argued the full spectrum of opinion. Some advocated prohibiting the legislature from ever authorizing a local income or sales tax in the future, while some argued that home rule units should be allowed plenary power to impose all taxes.

In the end, and as usual, the convention took the middle road. By the end of first reading everyone knew that neither revenue licensing, non-graduated income taxes nor occupation taxes would be in the grant of home rule powers. It was also clear that the legislature would be able to authorize these revenue sources in the future. Since the convention met at a time when public animosity to taxes was reaching a peak, the delegates decided not to risk total rejection of their constitution by an electorate unconvinced that future city dwellers might need these sources of revenue. The onus of authorizing these taxes now rests with the General Assembly and city councils.

The debt powers of home rule units was the last of the controversial revenue powers to be considered. Section 6j of article 7 allows the General Assembly to limit the amount of debt which a home rule county may incur, whether or not payable from *ad valorem* property tax receipts. It also allows the legislature, by a three-fifths vote in each house, to limit any home rule municipal debt except debt payable from *ad valorem* property tax receipts. Section 6k supplements section 6j by establishing those debt limits based upon the population of the municipality. Although many delegates had strong feelings about debt in general, the only truly disputed debt provision was that on municipal debt guaranteed by *ad valorem* property tax receipts.

The Local Government Committee report indicated that its proposal — greater debt limits for cities with larger populations — was a compromise between those who wished to leave the entire matter to local governments, the legislature, or the economic constraints of municipal bond markets, and those who favored a tight constitutional debt limit, such as the 5 percent debt limit under the 1870 constitution.

In this instance, the minority were not Chicago Democrats, but four downstate Republicans who thought the "free debt" provisions for municipalities were much too generous.

Although the convention debates are not clear, apparently the wary delegates wanted to leave the technical subject of debt to future generations. Ultimately, they adopted to a large extent the committee solution of granting greater debt powers to larger cities. Chicago, the only city with a population of 500,000 or more, is in a class by itself and, in recognition of its unique problems, has a debt limit equal to 3 percent of the assessed valuation of its property; other cities over 25,000, the automatic home rule threshold, have a limit of 1 percent; and smaller cities — which may obtain home rule by referendum only — have a limit of one-half of one percent. Certainly, this seems a more reasonable limit than the old 5 percent across-the-board limit for all cities.

It remains to be seen whether home rule cities will ever seize the opportunity to incur larger debts. Since adoption of the constitution, most municipal bond houses have become increasingly skeptical of the security of municipal bonds and the 1975 crisis in New York City's finances only enhanced an already troubled market for bonds. Free market forces will probably prevent a similar crisis in Illinois municipal finance for the foreseeable future.

The Legislature and Home Rule Units

The last controversial issue of home rule was legislative preemption. This technical and highly political issue involved the manner by which the General Assembly can remove — partially or completely — home rule power from home rule units. The Local Government Committee tried to fashion the structure of legislative preemption around Illinois political realities of the 1970s. The majority proposed requiring a three-fifths vote of each house of the legislature only when a taxing power or a power the state did not exercise was being preempted. It suggested allowing the legislature, by a constitutional majority of one-half of each house, to declare a matter to be exercised exclusively by the state or to be exercised concurrently with the state. The most controversial part of the majority proposal was to allow the legislature to establish "standards and procedures" for the exercise of home rule powers.

The minority proposed both requiring a three-fifths majority "across-the-board" and deleting the "standards and procedures" provision. The political reality was that since Chicago, the suburbs, and downstate would each elect about a third of each house of the legislature in 1972, a three-fifths majority requirement could be achieved only with the consent of virtually all of the legislators from home rule cities, including Chicago. This is nearly impossible to achieve. A simple majority, however, allowed more leeway and might be possible to obtain without Chicago's consent. Over the six-day debate on preemption, the delegates wrestled with the problem of allowing the local diversity and innovation experimentation which truly meaningful home rule promised while preserving the need for statewide standards on matters of such importance that no local nonuniformity could be tolerated. For example, John Parkhurst, as chairman, said that a state air pollution control act might establish a statewide standard to be enforced by local officers. Unless the state could effectively compel home rule units to obey the law, dirty air from a home rule unit could pollute the air of neighboring communities.

THE FINAL ARTICLE

Eventually the convention substantially adopted the majority proposal but deleted the "standards and procedures" section as the minority had suggested. It decided, in effect, that home rule units needed extraordinary protection against limitations on their taxing powers to protect their revenue base and against "dog in the manger" preemption by which the legislature removed the power from home rule units but failed to exercise that power itself. It also decided that the legislature could easily abuse the standards and procedures provision by using it to cut away at the substance of a home rule power. However, it declined to hamstring future legislatures in attempts to achieve statewide regulation by requiring three-fifths majority for *all kinds* of preemption.

There were other provisions in the local government article that were of more than passing interest, even if not discussed here. The long and short of it was that local government in Illinois had clearly entered a new age.

XV

Finance and Revenue: The Expedient Course

Dawn Clark Netsch, vice-chairman of the Revenue and Finance Committee, once said that, ideally, a state constitution should simply state that in the area of fund-raising the General Assembly shall have power to levy taxes. As a matter of fact, not even that need be said, because that fundamental power is inherent in sovereignty. But if such a simplistic statement were adopted, no new constitution would ever be ratified by the voters, so great is the suspicion concerning all unspecified and unlimited taxing powers. The increasingly burdened taxpayer wants to make certain that his government will not bankrupt him or itself in the irresistible itch to raise and spend money. So the revenue article, whatever its details, has always been the object of special attention. A constitution will stand or fall depending on the electorate's reaction to it. Write an acceptable revenue article and all else can be absorbed, as it were, in the rest of the document. Provisions that standing alone might be controversial and unacceptable, such as compulsory open housing, will be ignored if the government's fund-raising process is relatively painless. Thus it has been from the beginning of constitution-making in Illinois, and thus it was during the drafting of the 1970 constitution.

THE HISTORICAL PERSPECTIVE

The revenue provisions were basically established by the constitution of 1848 and were carried over into the constitution of 1870. Only one of the many attempts to amend the revenue article succeeded in the century that followed.

Sections 1 and 2 of the revenue article of that constitution were especially controversial; they called for "levying a tax, by valuation, so that every person and corporation shall pay a tax in proportion to the value of his, her, or its property . . ." Obviously, this egalitarian principle was not as simple as it sounds, and, from the beginning, it occasioned problems and perplexities. Some of these were severe indeed, especially with respect to personal property assessment and intangibles. Real property could be understood and it had relatively few complications, but personal property was increasingly complex, as the financial world multiplied the available instrumentalities and sought means for avoiding the net of the tax assessment.

Increasingly, in Illinois as elsewhere in the Union, there was a dilemma. People wanted government to satisfy more needs, in a variety of areas, including transportation, health, and education to name but a few. These things cost money, much money, more than was readily available. At the same time, the people revolted against the necessarily rising cost of their new and augmented services. If new services were costly, then inflation was sometimes even more costly, complicating what was already excessively complex. Legislators, under the guidance of economists, tax experts and financial nostrum-peddlers, sought for new and painless means of acquiring the necessary wherewithal, and taxpayers sought new loopholes through which to escape the unwelcome burdens.

When the stock market crash of 1929 brought about a desperate depression that went on well into the 1940s, Illinois tried to adopt a graduated income tax as the way out. It was fair and it was readily productive of revenue. But the Illinois Supreme Court struck it down, limiting the state and local taxing bodies to property, occupation and franchise taxes. A retail sales tax was passed. It had various ups and downs in the General Assembly and in the courts; but, as modified from time to time, it has been with us as a seemingly permanent part of the taxing system.

During World War II, there was a respite in the ceaseless revenue struggle; indeed, there was a state surplus. But the general revenue fund dwindled throughout the 1950s, while taxes rose steadily. In 1961, Governor Otto Kerner, a Democrat, called for measures to avoid state bankruptcy. In the political maneuvering that ensued, two opposing groups emerged: the one, consisting largely of business interests, wanted to maintain the existing tax structure, since it was less costly to them; the other, a heterogeneous group, consisting of the less affluent, wanted to change the tax structure to make it more fair and less painful to them. A revenue study commission, which was appointed by the governor and which began meeting in 1961, came to the rather trite and obvious conclusion that expenditures had to be decreased and revenue increased in order to avoid a more severe crisis. It did not suggest any bold or basic changes in the taxing structure. This was a victory for the business interests and the status quo. Thereafter, the level of concern increased even further. Moreover, the sales tax, already a great burden for the poor, could no longer provide adequate revenue. Desperation finally led to an attempt in 1966 to revise the revenue article. The General Assembly proposed an amendment that would finally accept the need for an income tax and, as a sugar coating for this bitter pill, would abolish the personal property tax. But the voters did not buy it. The amendment was rejected.

Still, the problem persisted. In 1969 Governor Richard Ogilvie, a Republican, courageously proposed a 4 percent flat rate income tax on individuals and corporations. This was modified down to 2.5 percent tax on individual incomes and enacted by the legislature and signed by the governor. Much to the surprise of some, the Supreme Court, which had once rejected it, now found the income tax to be constitutional. This led to the hope that further tax reform was now possible. It was at this juncture that the constitutional convention convened.

THE COMMITTEE

The Revenue and Finance Committee appointed by President Witwer was a political microcosm of the state, as was the entire body of delegates. Thus there was a tug of war within the committee between the monolithic Cook County Democratic delegation at one end, dominated by Mayor Daley who seemed to know precisely what he wanted, and the Republicans at the other end, who were by no means a cohesive group. At the same time, it was the most popular committee, judging by the fact that almost everyone seemed to want to be on it. While it was the largest committee at the convention, it was not large enough to accommodate all and only eighteen were chosen. One was reminded that the task of choosing it was difficult indeed. One drastic solution might have been the one taken by the finance committee of the City Council of Chicago which sometimes included the entire membership of fifty persons. Instead, President Witwer strove, almost desperately, to balance the committee by choosing representatives from almost every major interest group in the state. That the committee did not collapse under the demands placed on it, that it actually completed its task in a reasonable manner, is a tribute to it and to the convention. The committee heard 158 witnesses and considered dozens of proposals. No one who sought easy answers could find the atmosphere congenial. It was necessary to resolve differences, to conciliate, to accept much less than perfection. There would not be the one sentence revenue article that Dawn Netsch had pronounced as the unattainable ideal.

John Karns was chairman of the committee. He did not profess to be an expert in the field. The experts had their pet projects and commitments, and President Witwer did not want them to be in control. He wanted a person of Jack Karns' charm and lack of abrasiveness, who, while being a regular Democrat, would be courteous and fair and provide an opportunity to speak to anyone who had anything to say. Perhaps there would be a consensus; certainly nothing would be imposed from above. Karns was a prominent attorney in St. Clair County and came from a leading family. His father had been a prominent judge, who sometimes served in Cook County on special assignment. Karns himself had been state's attorney in his county. He was generally liked. He created no rancor.

In some respects, Dawn Clark Netsch, vice-chairman of the committee, differed considerably from the chairman. She regarded herself as a professional and some thought she looked down her nose at them as a result of this. She tried to be one of the boys, but she would not surrender principle which made things difficult at times. She was an independent Democrat, who never hesitated to differ with her colleagues, sometimes with pain-inflicting language and occasionally affronting the regular Democrats. She was a professor at the Law School of Northwestern University, had been an assistant to Governor

Kerner, and had served on the constitution study commission. Besides her duties on the committee, she achieved a leadership role on the floor of the convention and was heard on most, if not all, issues.

There were a number of financial experts on the committee — Maurice Scott, Jeannette Mullen, Ray Garrison, Stanley Johnson, James Brannen, Joseph T. Meek, and possibly Paul Elward. Elward was certainly one of the most vocal delegates, with a compulsion to influence everything that was going on publicly or that he feared might be going on behind his back. In addition, there were David Kenney and Frank Cicero, Jr., a bright and vocal young lawyer. There were others from various parts of the state and various occupations and political affiliation. Six were from Chicago, four more from Cook County, and six from outside the Chicago area. Nine were Democrats and nine, Republicans. One of the convention vice-presidents, Thomas Lyons, was assigned to the committee and played a major role in its deliberations and decisions. It would be easy to fill pages with portraits and profiles of the variegated committee members, and there is the temptation to do so in the cases of several, especially Elward, Meek, and Scott. For the most part, they were sophisticated, strong-willed, and imbued with the knowledge that they were working in an important, perhaps the most important, field, one that might readily determine the fate of the total product of the convention.

The committee secured in Glenn W. Fisher, professor of Government and Public Affairs at the University of Illinois, a true expert in taxation matters and one who was easy to work with. An authority on tax matters and a prolific author on the subject, he organized the work of the committee superbly and eased the individual burden. Fisher was ably assisted in the staff work by Ann Lousin and at various times by Joyce Fishbane. With Fishbane, he wrote *Politics of the Purse*, a full and superb account of the revenue committee, and on which we rely in this chapter.

GETTING DOWN TO WORK

The committee heard first from experts and then turned to special interest groups to hear their recommendations. No one had easy solutions. No one could absolve the committee from making its own hard decisions.

A Finance Article

Wholly new to Illinois constitution-making was the decision to create a separate finance article. It would deal with budgeting, appropriations, and accounting for public funds. With the vast increase in, and complexity in, state functions and the monumental fiscal demands, it was indispensable that order and control be attained to prevent waste, duplication, corruption, inefficiency, and the other evils of bureaucracy. The committee went about this task with great care, studying background papers, hearing the testimony of experts, and drafting no less than eighteen member proposals in this area alone. It also conferred with the Local Government Committee, for while the constitution might be divided into discrete articles, in actuality there were no such tidy packages. Committee concerns and the articles being drafted were interrelated. Confusion and contradiction had to be avoided.

Most decisions in the finance area were easily reached with little controversy. Thus it was generally agreed that there had to be a balanced budget. Achieving it, however, was another matter. The matter of earmarking highway use funds also created disagreement. Some proposals passed that called for detailed procedural requirements, rather than leaving great flexibility. Paul Elward favored such detailed procedures, while Dawn Netsch, the advocate of a one-sentence revenue article, wanted constitutional flexibility. By mid-March the article was basically agreed upon and a subcommittee, chaired by Stanley Johnson, was named to draft it. The committee decided to list all state agencies to be included in the executive budget, to avoid misunderstanding or ambiguity. Due to disagreement on the debt limitation provision, it was eventually excluded from the article. After it had been smoothed out and reworded for style and uniformity, the committee on April 28 unanimously agreed upon its first report. The article was clearly the result of rational decision making, efficient and harmonious.

On first reading before the committee of the whole, the provision of the finance article creating most concern was that giving the governor a reduction veto. It was decided that it should be possible for such a veto to be overridden by a simple majority, thus weakening the governor's power to reduce items. On second reading, the article was further amended with regard to the appointment and tenure of the auditor general. Thus amended, it passed. After some technical details were worked out with the Committee on Style and Drafting, the finance article was adopted on third reading, 104 to 1, and became a part of the new constitution. Euphoria reigned at this juncture. Even the sometimes acrimonious Paul Elward beamed in approval.

The Revenue Article

Easy as it was to get a finance article, it set no precedent for the revenue article. This article was extremely difficult to draft and hard to pass because of the monumental differences between members. At times, in fact, the differences seemed unabridgeable. At other times unexpected alliances were formed. Thus at various stages, the regular Democrats were glad to enlist the aid of irregular independents such as Elmer Gertz. Occasionally, when the views of Gertz and Lyons coincided, Gertz even spoke out for the regular viewpoint on the floor of the convention. He was told at one juncture by Elward that he should join the Democratic caucus. At another time, when there was no longer agreement, he was told that he was personally insulting. This added to the gaiety of the proceedings, rather than causing any particular illumination.

There were three main areas of disagreement on the revenue article — real estate classification (a must for Cook County Democrats), income tax limitation (a special concern for corporations and, to some degree, for all), and personal property exemption (people generally disliked the personal property tax but corporations and farmers were vehemently opposed to it). The process of decision making in these and other areas was complicated by lack of information, misinformation, political and interest group pressures, regional jealousy, fears about the effect of certain decisions on public acceptance of the proposed new constitution, and other less well defined fears. As Hamlet well knew, the unknown is generally an area of great concern, not only to a constitutional convention. The committee's deliberations and decisions were a reflection of the overall political landscape of Illinois, aggravated only at moments by personality clashes.

The constitution of 1870 implied that all property within a taxing unit should be assessed uniformly. Thus legal questions inevitably arose as to whether property, whether real or personal, could be classified and then assessed uniformly within the classification. For many years, Cook County classified in an extra-legal, if not illegal, fashion. It was one of the principal ingredients of its assessment system. If it fell, chaos might well result. The convention felt that it would be best to put the existing classification system of Cook County on a constitutional basis, rather than to rely upon the fortuitous circumstance of any on-going court challenge. It voted not to retain the uniformity clause. It was decided to authorize classification in downstate counties, and to ensure that the assessment level of the highest class would be no more than three times the assessment of the lowest class.

The Republican version of the income tax had been approved, as already mentioned, by the Supreme Court. It required a flat rate, rather than a graduated tax, as under the federal income tax. It differentiated between individuals and corporations, with the corporate rate set at 4 percent and the individual rate at 2.5 percent, a politically welcome classification. The Democrats knew they could make political capital out of the imposition of an income tax by their rivals. Later they defeated Governor Ogilvie's attempt at reelection largely on this ground. At the same time, they knew an income tax was necessary. The question was how to retain it without losing their appeal at the polling places. Tentatively, the committee decided that the rate for individuals could not be more than 4 percent through the year 1979 ("postpone a decision" was often a safe rule). It was also decided, by way of compromise, that the maximum differential between individuals and corporations on the tax would be 8 to 5. The temptation always exists to tax corporations, for they are often in a better position to pay a tax than individuals, and they do not have a vote. However, if private enterprise is penalized too savagely, it will do business elsewhere. So a balance must be struck.

In the past there had been much difficulty in trying to tax personal property, whether tangible or intangible. For example, the taxable situs of certain kinds of intangible property could be moved out of the state just before assessment date and returned just after assessment date, thereby escaping the personal property tax completely without being in violation of any law. Opinions differed widely on the tax. Local governments, dependent upon it for public school financing, were reluctant to have it abolished without knowing what would replace it. Some replacement taxes also created problems. If real property taxes were simply increased there could be strikes by home owners, with resulting political damage. Some charged that the Chicago Democratic organization used personal property taxes to its political advantage, lowering or raising the taxes in special cases where party or candidate contributions or fees might result. All in all it was an elaborate system that was basically unfair and unequal if not downright corrupt. The terms "clout" or "fix" were frequently bandied about to describe it.

While the delegates were deliberating this issue, an amendment to abolish the personal property tax was scheduled to be voted on. This amendment further complicated the situation. What would be the effect of a vote either way? It could not be controlling, since the public had the final word. But psychologically it could have a definite effect. If the constitution were approved, it would override anything decided on at the election. The delegates had to resolve the issue in the light of what was likely to happen at the polls. Moreover, there was the difficult question of the income tax, an issue that further exacerbated an already difficult situation. Neither could be resolved without consideration of the other.

Downstaters wanted to abolish all personal property taxes, while Cook County Democrats wanted to abolish only those relating to individuals. Which would be in the new constitution? This was a question involving both economics and politics, with geography being a decisive force.

The committee majority barely agreed — 10 to 8 — on a package dealing with income tax, real property tax, and personal property tax. All of the Democrats voted for it. After much discussion — some of it quite heated — among committee members and the staff, a final report was prepared and signed by all eighteen members. These signatures were given not so much as a sign of approval as an attestation to the genuineness of the report, which was accompanied by minority proposals and dissents concerning income and property taxes.

The committee's proposal included provisions that:

(a) any county with over 2,000,000 population (that is, Cook County) could classify real property for taxation purposes;

(b) the General Assembly may classify real property for purposes of taxation in other counties;

(c) the level of assessment for taxation of the highest class shall not be

more than 2½ times the level of the lowest class;
(d) the General Assembly may classify personal property for the purposes of taxation, may abolish such taxes, and may authorize the levy of taxes in lieu of personal property tax; and
(e) the General Assembly may enact a flat rate income tax, with the rate imposed on corporations not to exceed the rate imposed on individuals by more than a ratio of 8 to 5 until January 1, 1979 (again the solution of postponement).

In arriving at its programs, the committee seemed to disregard the experts and to be swayed, instead, by interest group pressures. The people were the paymasters in this area, as they are in others. There was no spirit of certainty about the results. There was concern over the saleability of the article, rather than its inherent virtues. Committee members were concerned about their own personal interests and preferences, and interested in gaining points that might later be traded for other issues. They seemed to be asking the ancient question: "If I am not for myself, for whom shall I be?" Thus, the revenue article involved a different sort of decision making process than had the finance article, which was looked upon as noncontroversial. The finance article was new and had not accumulated any foes. Everyone was its friend, primarily because such friendship cost nothing politically. On the revenue article the committee reached a compromise and was satisfied. At least, they had confounded those who thought they would never reach an agreement. Now it was up to the convention as a whole to dispose of the revenue matters. One could be sure that the process of disposition would be a stormy one.

The majority recommendation with respect to the income tax was countered by minority proposals and ideas expressed for the first time on the floor. They included (a) permitting a graduated tax, (b) constitutionalizing the then existing 8-5 ratio on the flat rate income tax, (c) placing a percentage limitation on the rate of the tax, (d) eliminating all constitutional restraints on legislative power in this area (again, the Netsch thinking as to the article as a whole), and (e) tying the state tax to the federal income tax laws.

After much debate on the first reading, some of it excessively confusing, the income tax 8 to 5 ratio was eliminated, the flat rate tax was maintained, a 5 percent limit on individuals was agreed on, and a permissive tie to the federal tax laws was approved. The income tax matter was then sent to the Committee on Style and Drafting. That committee was not supposed to make substantive changes, but what passed for stylistic revision sometimes took on substantive proportions. Many would be on guard to prevent such changes.

With respect to the classification of real estate, Chairman Karns presented a compromise to the delegates which was accepted better than two to one — 65-25. According to it counties were allowed to classify for the purposes of taxation, provided that assessments within each class were kept uniform and agricultural property was assessed at the same level as single family residential property. This was the ideal package politically, with something in it for Chicago Democrats, downstaters and the agricultural interests. While not a model, it could also be defended on substantive grounds.

As mentioned earlier, downstaters were generally in favor of abolishing all personal property taxes. This would be a boon to farmers, who had to buy and maintain all sorts of costly equipment to carry on their precarious occupation. With equal fervor, Cook County Democrats wanted the tax retained on corporations, but not for individuals. The final first reading showed a narrow victory — 58 to 46 — for those who would abolish all personal property taxes.

Thus, after first reading, the situation was roughly as follows:

(1) in the area of income tax, the principal source of state revenue, there would be a flat rate, with a 5 percent limit on individuals, and a permissive tie to federal income tax laws;

(2) as to real property tax, all counties were allowed to classify property, the rate for the highest class to be no more than $2\frac{1}{2}$ times the lowest class, and agriculture property to be assessed at no higher than single family residential property; and

(3) all personal property taxes would be abolished by 1979, and the General Assembly could authorize replacement revenue to local governments.

This was a practical, not a scientific, solution. It was not based upon principle, but upon interest, to subject a serious situation to a pun. It took a pro-Cook County position on real estate classification, and an anti-Cook County position on personal property taxes. The defeated Chicago Democrats would be on the alert to regain what they had lost.

In this spirit, the second reading process began. When it was over, a maximum 8 to 5 ratio of corporate and individual income tax had been reinstated through Republican support. The 5 percent income tax limit was removed, despite support for such a limit. The income tax has never been popular, however necessary, and ways were always being sought to make it comparatively painless. On the floor, a compromise was worked out on the personal property tax. The convention voted to abolish the tax by January 1, 1979 (again, the *Manana* principle), replacing the revenue lost by local governments through the imposition of statewide taxes solely on those relieved of the personal property tax. If such replacement was by a tax on income, then the 8 to 5 ratio was to be followed, and in no event was the replacement tax to be on real estate. Classification of real estate for assessment purposes was to be allowed, but only in counties with more than 200,000 population.

No substantive changes were made on third reading, the enactment stage, and the article was adopted basically as it was after the second reading. The only item not settled until the final debate was the proposal to submit separately a 5 percent income tax limit. This was the pet project of Rachunas, who had theretofore displayed no great skill on the floor of the convention. He fought strenuously for this limitation, knowing that it would have a good popular reception, no matter how the delegates looked upon it. Voters are always ready to vote for anything calculated to decrease their taxes. They don't always recognize that this may mean decreased services. Their goal is more service and less payment. Some solid Republicans who had previously opposed a limitation now voted for it, perhaps because they thought it could not get a majority of the votes at the convention. This prompted the Democrats, who had previously proposed a limitation, to reverse their votes. Ultimately, the Rachunas proposal lost, and the revenue article was approved by substantial majority, 80 to 24.

Joyce D. Fishbane and Glenn W. Fisher, authors of the monograph in this series on the revenue and finance articles, summed up the situation astutely:

> Illinois now had a revenue article substantially changed in format and content from that in the 1870 Constitution. It grew out of a process which involved many participants using all the techniques and strategies available to them to achieve their goals. With great effort, the continual conflicts between organized groups were slowly resolved. The result was an article reflecting the defined and also not-so-well defined goals of the

organizations involved, the personal values of the delegates, the pressures from the press and the public, and the desire to ensure acceptance of the document. It was to last possibly another one hundred years, but the article this convention produced was a representation of the political makeup of the state of Illinois in 1970.[1]

THE AFTERMATH

When the convention was over, and the ratification battle was on, the new constitution was opposed because of its revenue article by such diverse groups as SOS (Save Our State) on the right, and the AFL-CIO and NAACP on the left, each for its own reasons. Mayor Daley, the friend of both labor and management, found the new constitution acceptable and was largely responsible for its approval in the December 15, 1970 referendum; but he, too, felt that the revenue article favored capital rather than labor. He announced that he would work toward revision.

One aspect of the document that did indeed cause lingering concern was the compromise worked out on second reading for it contained what may well be called a time bomb destined to explode on January 1, 1979. Section 5(c) provides:

> On or before January 1, 1979, the General Assembly by law shall abolish all ad valorem personal property taxes and concurrently therewith and thereafter shall replace all revenue lost by units of local government and school districts as a result of the abolition of ad valorem personal property taxes subsequent to January 2, 1971. Such revenue shall be replaced by imposing statewide taxes, other than ad valorem taxes on real estate, solely on those classes relieved of the burden by paying ad valorem personal property taxes because of the abolition of such taxes subsequent to January 2, 1971. If any taxes imposed for such replacement purposes are taxes on or measured by income, such replacement taxes shall not be considered for purposes of the limitations of one tax and the ratio of 8 to 5 set forth in Section 3(a) of this Article.

Put more simply, *ad valorem* property taxes would be abolished by a regularly enacted law, and not automatically. Furthermore, this would be done on or before January 1, 1979, but only if replacement taxes

---

[1] Joyce D. Fishbane and Glenn W. Fisher, *Politics of the Purse: Revenue and Finance in the Sixth Illinois Constitutional Convention* (Urbana: Institute of Government and Public Affairs, University of Illinois, 1974), pp. 161-162.

were concurrently enacted. It is an ambiguous, poorly drafted section which has created much uncertainty and confusion. The replacement provision does not specify how the replacement revenue is to be distributed. Must each unit of government be protected against any loss of revenue or is it sufficient that the total amount returned to local governments and school districts equal the amount of revenue lost? Must the amount lost be recalculated each year or does the amount lost in the first year become the replacement floor? Another difficulty created by the provision arises from the lack of a definition of "classes relieved on the burden."

It was felt that by postponing the effective date of this section until January 1979, the General Assembly would have time to work out the difficulties. However, it soon became evident that the General Assembly did not find this task any easier than did the convention. In the fall of 1978 the voters of the state were given the chance to adopt an amendment to Section 5 of Article XIV. This amendment would have eliminated the January 1, 1979 date for the abolition and replacement of the tax. The proposed amendment also made permissive rather than mandatory the requirement that the legislature abolish the tax. This amendment was defeated.

As the 1979 date approached, Illinois courts gave indications that this section would be interpreted as a mandate to the state legislature to abolish the personal property tax and to provide replacement revenue. This meant that the property tax would not be automatically abolished and that the courts would not intervene to force the legislature to comply with the mandate. This expectation proved to be false when early in 1979 the Illinois Supreme Court ruled that Section 5(c) of Article XIV prohibits the levy extension or collection of *ad valorem* property taxes for calendar year 1979 and thereafter. The court further stated that the General Assembly remains under a continuing mandate to comply with the requirements of the section. (*Client Follow-up Company et al. v. Hynes*) This decision precipitated a fierce struggle in the General Assembly over the question of what taxes should be used for replacement of the personal property tax levies. As of this writing (June 1979) no decision has been reached.

XVI

New Goals for Education

Prior to the convention, education for Illinois citizens was viewed by many as having the potential to prohibit a successful convention, or adoption of any proposed amendment. That, however, was not to be the case as Jane Buresh accurately relates in her volume, *A Fundamental Goal: Education for the People of Illinois*. As a key staff member and participant observer of the convention's Education Committee, Ms. Buresh has fully analyzed the issues, conflicts, strategies, and resolutions, and we rely heavily on her volume for what follows in this chapter.

The committee structure of the convention, which grew largely out of a set of proposed rules drafted by the second Constitutional Study Commission and approved by the convention's temporary rules committee, included an education committee among its nine substantive committees. The inclusion of such a committee was not without controversy. Although most state constitutions include an education article, opinion has been divided on whether such a provision is necessary or even desirable. Since education is reserved for state government by the federal constitution, any reference to it in a state constitution may be unnecessary. In the study commission there was a short-lived attempt to eliminate an education committee from the convention and thus an education article from the constitution. A basic tenet of any constitutional convention is that "to have a committee is to have an article in the constitution." No committee is going to labor only to recommend that no article result from its efforts. The move to eliminate the committee in the study commission was led by commission member Samuel K. Gove of the University of Illinois, who had researched the politics of higher education and who for years had been an informal behind-the-scenes lobbyist around the Springfield scene for the University of Illinois and for higher education generally. He did not consider an education provision a necessary part of a constitution. Gove was adamantly and successfully opposed by Samuel Witwer, also a commission member. Witwer took both a broader and more pragmatic view and felt strongly that a committee should be established to deal with various educational issues. Witwer was especially concerned with the controversial ban on aid to nonpublic schools, one of the most emotional and potentially destructive issues that the convention delegates would face. Witwer felt it was essential that there be an outlet within the structure of the convention for pent-up emotions in such issues, so that they would not spill over dysfunctionally onto the other substantive committees. Gove's proposal was defeated and an education committee was proposed and established.

Under the rules of the convention, Witwer was required to appoint eleven delegates to the Education Committee, and, as in the case of all the substantive committees, he sought for balance in its makeup. He appointed two blacks and nine whites; eight men and three women; five downstate, three suburban Cook County, and three Chicago delegates; three Chicago Democrats, two downstate Democrats, five downstate or suburban Republicans, and one who called herself an independent but voted with the Republicans; five educators, three lawyers and two city employees; nine Protestants, a Jew, and a Catholic. All were college graduates, and the median age was forty-nine.

As was the case with the other committees, Witwer had difficulty in matching his desired balance with the delegates expressed preferences for committee appointments. Only five delegates listed the Education Committee as their first choice, seven sought it as their second preference, and nine indicated the committee as their third choice; thus only twenty-one delegates expressed any interest at all for the Education Committee. Of the five who had it as their first choice, four — Buford, Clyde Parker, Patch and Pughsley — were actually appointed. Only two of the second choice preferences — Bottino and Howard — were appointed, and the remaining five — Fogal, Dove,

Kamin, Mathias, and Evans — had not listed the Education Committee among their choices at all. Fogal, Dove and Kamin had all listed the Legislative Committee as their first preference, Mathias sought the Revenue and Finance Committee, and Evans indicated a first preference for the Executive Committee. Mathias and Evans were appointed chairman and vice-chairman, respectively.

Because of ideological differences and a complex of other factors, the committee was soon split into two factions, each with strong ideas on the amount of reform that should be included in the final education article. This division was recognized not only by members of the committee, but also by the press, which dubbed the two groups the "Young Turks" and the "Old Guard," a term apparently first used by Tony Abel of WCIA-TV in Champaign, Illinois. The Young Turks comprised a social group as well as a committee faction; in fact, the camaraderie among them made voting against one another very difficult. Malcolm Kamin was recognized as their leader. In addition to being the leader of the committee, Chairman Mathias, at least internally, was known as the leader of the Old Guard. Most of the Young Turks were Democrats and all of the Old Guard were Republicans. But there were other differences which played at least as great, if not a greater, role in the chasm between the two groups. The average age of the Young Turks was thirty-eight, while that of the Old Guard was sixty-two. Furthermore, the Young Turks may have subconsciously resented the much greater educational experience of the older group and the smugness this may have engendered. Meanwhile, the Old Guard was apparently incensed at the frequent failure of several of the Young Turks to arrive on time for committee meetings.

THE COMMITTEE

Malcolm Kamin was a bright, ambitious, and vociferous lawyer from Chicago, thirty years old, a Democrat, and a Jew. Much to the distress of President Witwer and the official parliamentarian, he was the convention's self-appointed amateur parliamentarian. Kamin was a member of the Chicago Democratic organization and had political ambitions which caused him at times to support positions he actually opposed — though not on educational issues.

Kamin was frequently seen with another Young Turk, Franklin Dove of Shelbyville. Dove was the grandson of a delegate to the ill-fated 1920-22 Illinois Constitutional Convention and was following the family tradition of liberal political activities. He was thirty-four years old, a Democrat, and a Protestant. Because his interests lay elsewhere, he was initially disappointed about being named to the Education Committee; but once he became enthusiastic about his task, he was one of the committee's most influential members. It is to him and to Kamin that most of the credit is due for the careful wording of the new sections of the education article. Dove had an air of gravity which helped the Young Turks to be taken more seriously by the older members of the committee and by the convention itself.

If Kamin and Dove were responsible for the exact wording of the new sections of the proposed education article, Samuel Patch was responsible for its spirit. Patch was a colorful, articulate black, a former teacher and city employee of Chicago, age thirty-seven, a Democrat, and a Protestant. Totally pledged to education as a means of providing increased opportunities for black children, Patch, unlike other members of the Young Turks, was optimistic about the chances of writing an excellent education article. It was his enthusiasm that eventually helped the other younger members take a greater interest in writing a new article.

The member of the committee closest to Patch was William Fogal, a young political science professor from Pekin, thirty-six years old, a Democrat, and a Protestant. His cordial manner endeared him not only to the younger committee members, but also to the Old Guard, and it is likely that without his intermediary efforts the rift which developed between the two factions would never have healed.

Of the three women on the committee, Betty Howard of St. Charles was certainly the most articulate. She was thirty-nine years old and a Protestant. An advertising and public relations executive, Howard was accustomed to having her opinions heeded by both males and females, and was one of the convention's most ardent sponsors of the women's rights section of the proposed Bill of Rights. Although a Republican from a largely Republican district, she held views in committee that placed her with the Young Turks, all of the rest of whom were Democrats. Her presence, in addition to adding zest, prevented the two sides from being seen as simply Republican vs. Democratic factions.

The last delegate who might be considered a member of the Young Turk faction was Gloria Pughsley, an employee of the city of Chicago, and the committee's other black member. She was fifty-four years old, a Protestant, and a Democrat. None of the committee members came to know Pughsley well, as she was ill during most of the committee hearings. When she did speak, she spoke emotionally; her significant impact at committee meetings was swelling the voting strength of the Young Turk faction. At the full convention, she voted strictly with the Chicago Democratic organization.

The chairman of the committee, Paul Mathias, was an able lawyer from Bloomington, age sixty-seven, a Protestant, and a Republican. Because of his experience in not only educational matters but also in state government, President Witwer tapped him for leadership of the committee. Mathias was a member of the Citizen's Advisory Committee to the Board of Education and had been legal counsel to the Illinois Board of Regents. He was seen as tied to higher education. In other areas of education, however, his lead was followed by the Old Guard. Mathias was greatly respected at the convention and was often consulted by President Witwer.

Perhaps the most beloved member of the committee was J. Lester Buford, at seventy-two the convention's oldest delegate. A former superintendent of schools from Mt. Vernon, Buford had long been a highly regarded leader in education in Southern Illinois. He was a Protestant and a Republican. While well liked by all members of the committee, Buford was seen by the Young Turks as a member of the educational establishment, a term used to refer to the traditional organized groups concerned with educational policymaking, such as the state PTA, boards of education, and the Illinois School Problems Commission, as well as individuals who had made their careers in the administration of educational facilities. Buford's inexhaustible supply of anecdotes and joviality often helped to ease tension, and his efforts to reach compromise brought him closer to the Young Turks.

Louis Bottino from Wilmington was one of the quieter delegates; in the committee that discussed aid to nonpublic schools, few delegates realized he was a Catholic. His reserve was constant except in discussions on financing public schools, when he berated the committee for not giving close enough attention to the subject. Bottino, a Republican, age fifty-three, was a college professor and a former legislator and county superintendent of schools. He was originally a member of the Young Turks faction, but switched sides when the controversy began.

Anne Evans, a housewife from Des Plaines, was the committee's vice-chairman. Age forty-five, a Protestant, and an independent Republican, she became a mother to all of the members. She sincerely worried about them, their health, and their problems. Her sensitive soul was appalled by the breakdown in committee relations, but she was not successful as a peacemaker. Although she had been regarded as a liberal Republican, she voted with the Old Guard faction because she had more faith in their opinions on educational matters. Evans was the most conscientious member of the committee and could often be found in the committee office doing research on issues with which she was unfamiliar.

Clyde Parker, age sixty-six, a Protestant, and a Republican from Lincolnwood, was perhaps the most inflexible member of the committee. He had a doctoral degree in education and preferred to be called "doctor." He had long been associated with education as a professor and as a superintendent of schools. By his own admission, the views he had developed over the years were not changed by anything he heard in committee or at the convention.

While not properly a member of the committee, Dr. Richard G. Browne, the committee counsel, was himself an unsuccessful candidate for delegate and took a great interest in the content of the article. Although his sense of humor and wealth of knowledge endeared him to the members, he was a former executive director of the Illinois Board of Higher Education and his experience in the educational establishment tended to cast him with the Old Guard in the minds of the younger faction. When asked, Browne was not reticent in expressing his opinions, which generally placed him with the Old Guard.

Browne's tendency to lean toward the attitudes of the Old Guard were "balanced" by the presence of the other professional on the staff of the committee. Jane Galloway Buresh, the bright young doctoral candidate from the University of Chicago, who served as administrative assistant to the committee, tended to be identified more closely with the Young Turks. She provided research and administrative assistance to the entire committee, and was objective in doing so, but because of her youth and her attitudes toward educational policy, she tended to sympathize more with the younger members of the committee, and probably would have been a member of that group had she been a delegate. Not only because of her extensive experience in educational politics in Illinois, but also because of her doctoral training at the University of Chicago as well as her energy and enthusiasm, she lent significantly to the drafting and development of the Education Article. Both she and Dr. Browne were very much an integral part of the committee operation, and their thoughts and positions were well known; at the same time they were successful in maintaining the necessary distance between delegates and staff.

Committee Operation

During the course of its activities, the Education Committee followed the general guidelines of the delegates for "openness" and conducted forty-four meetings in Springfield, sometimes jointly with the Bill of Rights Committee or the Executive Committee. It also held numerous meetings throughout the state, during which a great deal of time was devoted to hearing testimony from expert witnesses, citizens, and interest groups. The committee sought as much involvement from the public as possible, and tried to make the public feel it had a say in the formulation of educational policy in the new constitution. Members of the Education Committee, perhaps more than those of other committees, were very much aware of the need for public exposure in order to insure a favorable attitude at a later referendum. They were keenly aware that recent failure in other states had resulted largely from the issue of state aid to private and parochial schools.

In addition to expert testimony from individual citizens and lobbyists representing educationally related interest groups, the committee also relied on other sources for input of information. They resolved themselves into several subcommittees, obtained research from sources outside the convention, had the committee staff and convention staff generate information for them, and heard testimony from other delegates on member proposals they had submitted. It is conceivable that the delegates of the Education Committee were swayed by the pressure of interest groups such as the Illinois Education Association, the Illinois Congress of Parents and Teachers, or the Illinois Catholic Conference. There was, however, very little visible pressure from either these or any other groups. The issue of financing public schools provoked the only obvious incidence of lobbying in the committee. Representatives of the Illinois State Chamber of Commerce attempted to get delegates to vote against total state financing, while representatives of the Welfare Council of Metropolitan Chicago attempted to gain votes for such financing. Most educational organizations seemed content to present their positions and then to let the committee handle the situation. The only lobby that, while applying no obvious pressure, seemed to be a significant factor in determining delegate positions was that of higher education; the education lobbyists were very much involved in attempting to protect higher education interests from elementary and secondary education as those interests might come into conflict in a proposed State Board of Education.

The delegates seemed to be little influenced by expert testimony, by research, by member proposals, or by the work of their subcommittees. There was a desire, at least in the area of aid to nonpublic schools, not to alarm the voters through recommendations for drastic change, but most of the older committee members had their minds made up on educational matters prior to any committee meetings. They felt that their many years of experience in the field of education had molded their views, and these were not to be altered by pressures from the uninformed. Apparently the Young Turks formed their opinions during early discussions among all members of the committee, and were not swayed to any greater degree by research, witnesses, constituents, lobbyists, or member proposals than were the Old Guard. Conflict developed because the older delegates would have been content merely to remove anachronisms and to provide for a State Board of Education, while the younger members wanted to force innovation and to create an article that would "make a difference." They sought provisions that would emphasize education as a statewide priority. Like the Old Guard, the younger members remained convinced of their correctness and logic, and refused, for a time, to change or to compromise. The factions of the committee developed out of fundamentally different viewpoints and conflicting feelings about the significance and potential of education. Once they had coalesced, those factions took on an exaggerated importance in the minds of the members. Defeating "the other team" became a goal in itself. Eventually most of the members realized they were playing games and subordinated the importance of the factions to the larger goal of compromise in order to draft an education article.

The article the committee finally submitted was written in such a way that it would not arouse the opposition of the voters despite its innovative features. As with the Bill of Rights Committee, what initially appeared as some irreconcilable differences between the committee members turned out to be one of the definite advantages of the committee. This ultimately resulted in a superior work product that was presented to the full convention and ultimately to the voters. The balance and openness with which the committee operated are significant factors in its success.

THE ISSUES

In addition to deleting portions of the 1870 article, the committee handled five general topics: the structure of the educational system; the objectives of education; higher education; aid to nonpublic schools; and the financing of the public school system.

Article 8 of the 1870 Illinois Constitution contained three provisions on education — sections 2, 4, and 5 — which were inappropriate for constitutional stature and which would be recommended for deletion. Section 4, which prohibited school officers from making a profit from sale of school property, and section 5, which provided for a county superintendent of schools, were deleted with little fanfare or objection; section 2, which related to public school property acquired by gift before 1870, faced some controvery before it, too, was deleted.

A STATE BOARD

Education groups and interests throughout the state hoped that one of the accomplishments of the constitutional convention would be the creation of a State Board of Education. At the time of the 1970 convention, Illinois and Wisconsin were the only states without a statewide educational policymaking body.

Prior to the convening of the convention, both throughout the state and in the General Assembly, there was a good deal of interest in the possibility of creating a statewide Board of Education. But there were several obstacles to the creation of such a board. First, there was the question of selecting a superintendent of public instruction; second, there was the manner in which the board members themselves would be selected; and third, there was the scope of jurisdiction of any possible board.

The office of Superintendent of Education had been created in 1854 by statute; it decreed that the superintendent was to be appointed by the governor for a two-year term. The constitution of 1870 changed the name of the office to Superintendent of Public Instruction and made it an elective four-year position. The main goal of those seeking either an appointed superintendent of public instruction or appointed board members was that education, unlike other aspects of state government, must be kept out of partisan politics. Those who favored the appointment process felt that qualified individuals have neither the political skill to run for election, nor wish to risk their careers or spend the money needed for a political campaign. They also felt that especially in the case of the state's chief education officer a person should be chosen for his professional qualifications rather than for his vote-getting ability and, while in office, should be concerned with the job before him, rather than with reelection. Those who favored electing officers argued primarily from the point of view of leaving such power to the people. It was thought that officers chosen in popular elections would be more responsive to the popular will. The Illinois Federation of Teachers was the only significant organization opposed to the creation of a State Board of Education. Dwight Friedrich, a member of the Executive Committee, led the effort to keep the office elective, and was partially responsible for a joint meeting between the Education and Executive committees on this issue. When the committee finally began to consider the best possible structure for education throughout the state, general agreement developed on the need for a State Board of Education, but committee members continued to be seriously split on the question of how the board would be selected.

The committee was also undecided at the outset of its deliberations on the extent of the board's jurisdiction. A preliminary vote showed six members favoring a single board for all public education (kindergarten through the university) while four opted for a state board to cover only kindergarten through the twelfth grade. At this early point in the deliberations, none of the members favored leaving the question to the discretion of the legislature. On the question of the selection of the board, four of the delegates wanted an elected board, five favored leaving it up to the General Assembly, and no one desired an appointed board.

There were no clear-cut positions on the question of jurisdiction prior to the convention. Most witnesses before the committee were in favor of two boards, one for education through grade twelve and one for higher education. This was the stand taken by the various representatives of higher education, as well as the Illinois Education Association, the Illinois State Chamber of Commerce, and the Conference on a State Board of Education and an Appointed Superintendent — a group made up of educators and laymen. Their most frequently cited reason was that higher and lower education have different problems and different responsibilities. Professor Samuel Gove, mentioned at the outset of this chapter, was one of their chief spokesmen; he was also chairman of the Ad Hoc Advisory Committee on the convention of the Board of Higher Education. Arguing for the other side were Cook County Superintendent of Schools Robert Hanrahan and Superintendent of Public Instruction Ray Page, both of whom favored an overall board. They argued that to have two separate boards would simply continue the fragmentation of educational policy in the state and would not serve to bring about a cohesive policy.

As the committee continued its deliberations, a slight erosion in the support for a super board began to take place. At the same time a trend began to set in for those who favored leaving the question of jurisdiction to be provided by law. On February 18, none of the committee members had favored leaving the jurisdiction question to the legislature; by March 12, the committee was unanimously in favor of letting the General Assembly decide the question. The transition that took place during this three-week period may not have been so much the result of outside pressures, information, or opinions, as it was a realization that compromise was needed to allow the provision to get through the convention and to win approval by the voters.

On the issue of selecting board members, the preliminary vote in the committee showed four in favor of an elected board and five choosing to leave the manner of selection to the General Assembly. No one at this time voted for a board appointed by the governor, although Bottino, Mathias, and Evans favored an appointed board established by the legislature. As was the case with the issue of jurisdiction, the committee arrived at a compromise and a virtually unanimous agreement over language submitted initially by Frank Dove. He proposed that "there shall be a State Board of Education selected on a regional basis. The number of members, their qualifications, terms of office, and manner of selection shall be provided by law." The term "selected," Dove made clear, was intended to mean either elected or appointed. Parker still voted in favor of an elected board, and Patch was not particularly happy but seemed to prefer voting with the other Young Turks as opposed to siding with Parker. Buford was placated by inclusion of the phrase "on a regional basis," for his greatest fear had been a lack of representation for southern Illinois. But the need for compromise and the concern over the pending debate on educational goals, practically forced the committee to accept unanimously the final working submitted to the full convention:

> There shall be a State Board of Education selected on a regional basis. The number of members, their qualifications, terms of office, and manner of selection shall be provided by law. The board shall establish goals, determine policies, provide for planning and evaluating educational programs, recommend financing and have such jurisdiction powers and duties as provided by law.
>
> There shall be a chief state educational officer appointed by the State Board of Education.

Educational Objectives

It was the general feeling among education experts, witnesses, and committee members that section 1 of the 1870 education article, providing only for a common school education, was inadequate to express the importance of education in the modern world, and that there needed to be a new emphasis on education. The general intent of those who took this position was that the state should provide a high quality education for all, regardless of race or religion, and that such education should include higher educational institutions as well as other institutions and services which might be desirable. The suggestion was also made that free education be provided to those with physical and mental handicaps.

The subject of educational objectives was very much on the mind of many of the witnesses who appeared before the committee. Many simply affirmed the need for high quality education and others made specific proposals. There was little agreement on how strong a provision there ought to be, length of schooling, or the ages to be included.

If educational objectives was the topic most on the public's mind, it was also the one that caused the most dissension among members of the committee. It was, in fact, the subject that divided the committee into the Young Turks and the Old Guard; it was also the committee's action on this issue that caused the most public outcry. Elements of controversy were inherent in the group and could reasonably have been anticipated because of the background of the committee members. The two black delegates, Patch and Pughsley, were obviously unhappy with the extremely inadequate education being offered to minority groups in the city of Chicago. The lawyers on the committee, Kamin, Dove, and Mathias, were aware of the hortatory nature of the section on objectives, and their professional training might logically have led them to seek a statement of goals which was as concise and simple as possible. The educators, Parker, Buford and Bottino, and to some extent Fogal, might have been expected to be more concerned with implementing specific educational goals. Evans and Howard, who had had a great deal of experience with the League of Women Voters, might have opted to go along with the lawyers for a simple statement and with the educators for an implementation of certain specific goals.

Thus, the lineup of forces for this discussion could have been Patch and Pughsley against the rest of the committee; this would have resulted in no controversy, since two delegates would not have constituted enough of a minority report (three being required for that purpose). For whatever reasons, the array of forces became one black, two lawyers, one professor, and one League of Women Voters member against one lawyer, three educators, and one member of the League of Women Voters. The basis of division was obviously not background or exclusively professional training. Instead, the criteria were age, friendship, and, most importantly, ideas as to how much reform should be introduced into the section.

Educational objectives did not appear to be unduly controversial at the outset. However, after several attempts at language and several compromises that failed, the committee on March 11 was deadlocked in a five-to-five stalemate which prevented either majority or minority reports from being written. Throughout this time, Delegate Pughsley was away from the convention due to illness. Both sides realized that the problem of educational objectives could not be passed on to the General Assembly for resolution as had been done with the question of a state board of education. This board policy decision had to be resolved by the convention and, before it could be taken up by the full body, there had to be compromise and resolution in the committee itself. The committee remained deadlocked through March 20 and began receiving sharp criticism from the public. At the base of the deadlock was the attempt on the part of the younger group to rewrite the committee's proposal so that it would bind the state to public education as a "paramount" obligation. Controversy had also arisen over the elimination of the word "free" from the Education Article. Tony Abel from WCIA television in Champaign-Urbana and a frequent observer at the scene of the convention, reported to his viewers that "no other committee at con-con is factionalized in such an apparent manner as the Education Committee. While the battle lines may be drawn on philosophical grounds, the borderlines of the two camps are surprisingly coincidental with age groups — lending some credence to observations that the skirmishes within the committee are in reality a kind of mature generation gap."[1]

Public reaction to the omission of the word "free" was strong, and was instrumental in leading the committee members to reach a consensus. They also began to realize that a unanimous committee report would make the position of the group stronger when the report was presented to the full convention. Then too, like so many of the other committees, they began to take pride in their work and sought to reconcile their differences so that their proposal would be the one that ultimately went into the new constitution and become policy for the state, rather than some alternatives, possibly ill considered, and hastily put together on the floor of the convention.

It was Fogal who on April 8 addressed his colleagues on the committee. Citing the importance of education to the people of the

---

[1]Tony Abel, WCIA Television Station, Champaign-Urbana, telecast March 13, 1970.

state, he called for an end to the divisiveness and presented a new proposal which met with immediate acceptance. After some minor revisions, it was approved by the full committee and read as follows:

> The paramount goal of the people of the state shall be the educational development of all persons to the limits of their capacities.
>
> To achieve this goal it shall be the duty of the state to provide for an efficient system of high quality public educational institutions and services.
>
> Education in the public schools to the secondary levels shall be free. There may be such other free education as the general assembly provides.[2]

The final compromise resulted from the factions of the committee, the need to appease the public, the desire to create a unanimous committee proposal, and Fogal's intermediary efforts. Development of the section had been incremental — a gradual compromise between little change and radical innovation.

Higher Education

The Illinois Constitution of 1870 referred to higher education only in passing and contained no specific provisions for education beyond the secondary level. In 1870 the delegates had opposed providing higher education at public expense, but by 1970 the need for longer educational preparation in order to live and work effectively was apparent. While higher education was no longer considered a luxury by the general public, however, a somewhat different attitude was found among members of the committee on education. Although they recognized the place and need for higher education, the majority of the committee, especially the educators, felt this aspect of education had received undue attention and support at the expense of elementary and secondary education. In fact, the attitude toward higher education on the part of several Education Committee members, bordered on hostility. It was this attitude which explained the array of forces for and against the concept of a super board to govern all education. In its initial committee vote on February 18, Buford, Dove, Fogal, Kamin, Howard, and Patch favored a super board. Bottino, although somewhat

[2]Jane Galloway Buresh, *A Fundamental Goal: Education for the People of Illinois* (Urbana: Institute of Government and Public Affairs, University of Illinois, 1975), p. 46.

antagonistic toward higher education, apparently thought the levels of education were sufficiently different to warrant two boards, as did Delegate Parker. The Young Turks especially were concerned that education be treated as a whole and supported one board to govern over all educational levels. Chairman Mathias introduced a member proposal which declared: "The general assembly shall establish and support such public institutions of higher learning as may be desirable." He generated a good deal of interest and lobbying on behalf of his proposal and sought support from the Ad Hoc Advisory Committee of the Board of Higher Education. The advisory committee, led by Professor Gove of the University of Illinois, and composed of representatives of various higher educational systems in Illinois, was very active in insuring that a super board was not created and would not have jurisdiction over higher educational interests. The presence of so many people from higher education circles, including even President David Dodds Henry from the University of Illinois, was initially irritating to many of the committee members. They were apparently persuasive enough, however, to change slightly the positions of some of the committee members. They were at least successful in persuading Kamin that the inclusion of a super board in the committee's recommendations might well result in the opposition of higher education to the entire education article.

AFTERMATH

The actions of the full convention at first, second, and third reading were not dissimilar to the deliberations of the Education Committee. In both there was conflict over the degree of change to be incorporated into the education article. Due to the special nature of the subject, the full convention allowed the Education Committee to take the lead on its article. Convention delegates looked to committee members as the experts in this area. Furthermore, no one wished to appear to vote against education. While the full convention was unwilling to accept any provision that it believed to be too radical in nature, the final article was permitted to retain much of its original and innovative strength.

The education article was not a significant factor in the final adoption of the new Illinois Constitution; in fact, relatively little attention was given to education by the press or by individuals or groups working for or against passage of the proposed constitution. But it is possible that the article may promote some of the most far-reaching changes in the new state charter — changes in the methods of financing education, in the scope of education, and in the very nature of the educational process in Illinois.

Section 1 of the article provides almost limitless possibilities for increasing the scope of education by calling for the education of all people to "limits of their capacities." This goal, when taken with the sentence "Education in public schools through the secondary level shall be free," can be interpreted to mean that adults as well as those under twenty-one must receive education through the high school level at no charge — a concept of educational responsibility unique in this country. If this reasoning holds true, the article apparently requires that the physically and mentally handicapped be guaranteed an education to the limits of their capacities. It was predicted at the convention that the sentence, "The state has the primary responsibility for financing the system of public education," would be a subject for legal challenge. By September of 1973, the Illinois Supreme Court had already handed down its first interpretation of that sentence. In *Blase v. State* (55 Ill. 2d 94, 302 NE 2d 46, 1973), the plaintiffs had sued to force the state to provide at least 50 percent of the funds for Illinois public school systems, basing their suit on the word "primary" of section 1 of the education article. Relying on the transcripts of the 1970 convention, the court held that the sentence on financing was merely hortatory — "that the sentence was intended only to express a goal or objective, and not to state a specific command."

The action (or nonaction) taken by the convention, which perhaps proved most significant in assisting the adoption of a constitution by the voters, may have been its decision to leave section 3 on aid to nonpublic schools unchanged. By doing so the delegates proved that they were not trying to change everything about the old constitution. What was good and acceptable to the people was left intact to continue to serve the people of Illinois.

XVII

General Government: Banking and Saving

The General Government Committee was a sort of catch-all for the convention. Issues and areas of concern that could not be fit in elsewhere, were taken care of here. It was one of the middle-size committees, with only eleven members and was headed by one of the strong men of the convention, Thomas J. McCracken, a conservative, suburban, Democrat affiliated with the regular Democratic organization. McCracken was a banker, a lawyer, and an accountant, highly competent in whatever he undertook. Until aroused, he seemed to be in repose, almost sleepy in bearing. Aroused, he could roar, snarl, insult, attack and destroy. He may have been partisan, but he was trusted, even by his opponents. When he spoke, those listening believed him since all knew he would not knowingly lie. He had an ability to express himself clearly on complicated issues, and few at the convention knew more about finances and accounting. McCracken steered the committee in an almost low-keyed fashion, often without appearing to do so. He was also able to delegate responsibility to others on the committee without surrendering his overall authority.

The vice-chairman of the committee, Robert R. Canfield, a Republican from Rockford, was a low-keyed man who had achieved considerable success as a lawyer and public figure, despite a certain lack of charisma. Notwithstanding his scruples of conscience against capital punishment, he had been an excellent state's attorney of his county, the president of the Illinois State's Attorney Association, and active in the reform of the Illinois Criminal Code. He had been named

293

"Mr. State's Attorney of Illinois" and honored by the bar associations and his church. He had been a state representative and a state senator, and while in the senate had been the co-chairman of the Illinois Crime Investigating Commission. He aspired to a position of leadership at the convention, but did not achieve the influence and stature of others.

There were others on the committee who had existing or potential stature, especially David Davis, Michael J. Madigan, David E. Connor, and Mary Lee Leahy. The rest were persons who held the interests of their colleagues, even when they lacked influence — Edward H. Jenison, Edward J. Rosewell, James S. Thompson, Maxine Wymore, and William R. Armstrong. It was not at all a dull group, even though it did not deal with earthshaking matters, with the possible exception of environment and banking.

COMMITTEE MEMBERS

David Davis was a big man, a towering figure, and his abilities matched his physical proportions. He was a direct descendant of the David Davis who had loomed so large in Lincoln's life on the legal circuit, as political confidant and campaign mentor and as a Supreme Court appointee. His descendant, too, had excelled in the state senate from 1953 to 1967. Like McCracken he was a conservative, although of the opposing party; some thought him a reactionary. He held strong views on the rules of the convention (he was vice-chairman of the Rules Committee), on the work of his own substantive committee, and on the convention as a whole. His influence was often felt, and he spoke with conviction, almost with a sense of certainty. Despite these strong qualities, he had a warm and human personality as well as a certain flair. If one wanted to dine well in the Springfield area, one asked Davis.

David Connor, a Peorian, was part of the establishment in his community and at the convention. He had once been named the "Outstanding Man of the Year" by the Junior Chamber of Commerce; in an unclamorous manner, he was a distinguished person. He belonged to all the proper business, civic, religious, and political groups, had been a Phi Beta Kappa at Yale, and had served in the Navy during the war. No one would have been surprised to see him rise to the top of the convention, even though he had a certain restraint and aloofness.

One of two women, but the only independent appointed to the General Government Committee, was Mary Lee Leahy. She was young, bright, forward, extremely articulate. She knew what she wanted and why, and did not hesitate to advance her causes, sometimes to the discomfort of the regular Democrats. Mary Lee was an exigent personality, by any test. If she did not understand an issue, she would study it until it was clear to her. She had a unique partnership with her husband, Andrew. If she had not decided to become a delegate, he would have done so. They conferred, collaborated, and triumphed together. It was a more transparent relationship than that between Lucy Reum, vice-chairman of the Legislative Committee, and her distinguished husband, Walter.

Michael Madigan, one of the younger delegates, was already committeeman of his southside Chicago ward. It was apparent that he had a bright future in politics. He was the buddy of the mayor's son, Richard, and it was already clear that they influenced each other considerably. When Gertz declared on the floor of the convention that he had been a registered Democrat for more than forty years, Madigan, half-seriously, asked Gertz not to register with that party any longer. At the same time, he asked Gertz if he would address the members of the ward organization. This sort of ambivalence was characteristic of the sometimes brash, but generally assured, young man. He seemed to school himself as he observed others.

Edward Jenison was everyone's friend, but he exercised little direct influence. He had been in Congress and in the General Assembly, and he was a publisher of a newspaper. He had many endearing personal characteristics, best brought out in the Sazarac Caucus, the drinking and talking group of the neighboring tavern which many delegates patronized. In as serious a body as the constitutional convention, there is much need for the kind of indirect, general persuasion provided by a nonactivist like Jenison.

Of a somewhat similar low key was Edward Rosewell. Strongly committed to the Democratic party and the Daley organization, he was liked even by those who, unjustly, downgraded his abilities. He would gather the wayward brethren when a vote was about to be taken on a matter of concern to the organization. Although a bachelor, he had none of the abandon of some of the other unattached delegates. Indeed, he seemed a highly moral, highly principled person, polite and unselfish. He had a love for art and all things beautiful, if they were not too far out.

James S. Thompson was big, handsome and self-assured. He had the air of an unworried person. A farmer, he seemed like a modern-day Sybarite. William Armstrong, too, was big and congenial. A school teacher, he thought first of educating himself. The convention was his first great opportunity.

And there was Maxine Wymore, whom Elbert Smith called "holy Max," because she headed the chaplaincy committee. She looked upon all that occurred with avid interest. If she was not a leader, she was a good learner.

Mrs. Leahy used to characterize the General Government Committee as the "garbage bag" of the convention: it was given all the proposals that did not go to any of the other eight substantive committees. So it got a considerable variety of subject matters. Mrs. Leahy wanted to learn about several subjects, and she did not wish to compete with any of her other eight independent colleagues. In one of the early meetings, as she recalled, the nine independents agreed to seek different committee assignments so they would have broad knowledge to bring to their private meetings. The General Government Committee was her first choice when President Witwer asked the delegates for their preference. Later she was to discover that she was the only delegate to list that committee as "first" choice. As a result, she found herself in strange company on the banking issue.

Several delegates with banking interests found their way onto the General Government Committee. Thomas J. McCracken, chairman of the committee, was chairman of two banks in Cook County. David Davis was chairman of a national bank in Normal and held stock in another bank. David Connor was vice-president of a bank in Peoria, the second largest bank outside of Cook County. Edward Rosewell was employed by the Continental Bank in Chicago. All of these bankers favored the removal of all constitutional provisions relating to banking. Floor debate was later to make clear that at least delegates Davis and Connor favored branch banking.

THE ISSUES

The committee heard no less than twenty-six witnesses. McCracken admitted during floor debate that the complete list of witnesses as well as tapes "went south at the time of separation of service of our secretary." This lent an air of mystery to the deliberations.

Several witnesses appeared during the "road show" hearings rather than journeying to the General Government Committee hearings in Springfield. Strange as it may seem in the light of what occurred at the convention, no member of the general public discussed the banking issue at either the regional hearings or the committee hearings in Springfield. With the exception of witnesses for the Chicago Bar Association and the Illinois State Chamber of Commerce, all witnesses had a direct interest in banking.

Banking

It soon became apparent to the committee members that the ultimate issue was branch banking. Those who favored branch banking wanted all banking provisions deleted from the constitution; those who opposed branch banking wanted to retain the referendum or impose a greater than majority vote to permit branch banking by legislation. Roland Blaka, state commissioner of banks and trust companies, urged the committee to require two-third legislative approval in order to establish branch banking. Committee members, as well as witnesses, were divided on the question as to whether an extraordinary legislative majority was more restrictive than a referendum.

On May 12, 1970 the committee, by an 8 to 3 vote, recommended the deletion of all sections dealing with banking from the proposed constitution.

The majority report of the committee stressed the fact that the banking provisions of the 1870 constitution had been adopted to protect the public from unscrupulous banking practices. In that day, it said, banks were organized with insufficient capital, the officers did not need to have financial skill, and loans were granted with inadequate security. Banks floated their own currency; there was no uniform rate of exchange. Long after banks had folded, their currency would continue to change hands. But conditions had changed since then. Banking, the report went on to say, was intensely regulated both by federal and state governments. Federal regulation included the Federal Reserve System and the Federal Deposit Insurance Corporation. Thus, the public no longer needed the protection afforded by the 1870 constitution. Indeed, sections 6, 7, and 8 of Article XI were outmoded.

The referendum requirement of section 5 was viewed by the majority as restrictive, since the Illinois Supreme Court had ruled that every change in the banking law must be approved by referendum.

Other financial institutions had developed during the century, including savings and loan associations, credit unions, currency exchanges, small loan companies, trust companies, and insurance companies. None of these were subject to the restrictions of the 1870 constitution. To treat banking differently could put banking at a significant disadvantage in competing with these institutions, for the latter could adjust to changing practice without approval by the voters at referendum.

The majority report also noted the growth of national banks regulated, not by the state, but by the federal government. A state bank could turn in its state charter and seek a national charter — if the rules governing national banks were more advantageous. At the time of making the committee recommendation, federal law permitted branch banking by national banks only in states permitting state banks to branch. However, that could be changed by act of Congress.

As a final note, the majority report indicated that no other state required a referendum to adopt changes in banking laws.

The majority shied away from debating the merits of branch banking but, instead, insisted that regulation of the banking industry, as well as all other industries, should be done by legislation, not by constitutional provision. This was a constant refrain during the convention. Delegates were reminded that they were writing a basic charter, a constitution, not a series of statutes.

A minority group within the committee took the position that such a controversial issue as branch banking ought to be decided by the voters. Their report characterized the dispute as one of "big" banks vs. "little" banks and asked that the constitution protect the "hometown" banks of downstate Illinois. The minority clearly feared the possibility of undue influence by the large banks, declaring that the referendum process had not really slowed the growth of the banking industry.

The matter came before the committee of the whole on first reading on May 20.

During early meetings of the General Government Committee, Chairman McCracken had named individual committee members as floor managers for particular issues. The floor manager was responsible for seeing that member proposals on the particular subject were scheduled for hearing, that witnesses were notified, that the committee pursued action on the issue, that all of the necessary details were attended to. If a proposal on the particular issue passed out of committee, the floor manager would present the issue to the convention sitting as a committee of the whole, assuming, of course, the floor manager could support the committee proposal. During this presentation, it will be remembered, delegates were free to ask questions for an unlimited time.

David Connor was the committee's floor manager for banking. A few days before the committee proposal was scheduled for presentation to the floor, Chairman McCracken and Connor approached Mrs. Leahy outside the committee hearing room to ask her to present the committee proposal to the floor of the convention. They indicated that Connor's connection with the banking industry and outspoken position in favor of branch banking might prejudice the committee's recommendations. Mrs. Leahy agreed to make the floor presentation. After all, she felt that the constitution ought not to be burdened with cumbersome legislative details.

Presentation of the committee proposal was the first order to substantive business at 9 a.m. on May 29, 1970. This was the first controversial committee issue to reach the floor of the convention. Mrs. Leahy spent a grueling two-and-one-half hours responding to delegate questions only to find out when she resumed her seat that her husband had pulled a muscle in his back and had been hospitalized in traction. Members of the convention were often beset with such personal problems. They learned that "the show" had to go on. Mrs. Leahy tried to stress that there was no need to regulate one industry by constitutional provision, that the General Assembly could regulate the banking industry as it did all other industries, including other financial institutions. She reiterated, in essence, the stand of the majority report.

But the questions on the pros and cons of branch banking persisted. She insisted, almost righteously, that the merits of branch banking were not before the convention, that those issues were policy determinations that should be made by the General Assembly, that the General Assembly could protect the public interest in its decisions.

It was clear during the question period that many delegates, particularly downstate delegates, had been repeatedly contacted by banking interests.

Active, too, in opposing deletion of the referendum requirement were the currency exchanges. And no small wonder! Sixty percent of the nation's currency exchanges were in Chicago. Branch banking might offer them serious competition, particularly in the inner city. Father Lawlor, a delegate from the southwest side of Chicago, said he had received sixteen telegrams from currency exchanges in his district urging him to oppose deletion of the referendum requirement. Elmer Gertz was contacted by a currency exchange lobbyist on the basis of friendship. He was, by no means, alone.

The first order of business after the majority and minority recommendations had been explained was perfection of the minority report.

Ralph Dunn, the chief delegate proponent of so-called unit banking, moved to amend the proposal by substituting a two-thirds General Assembly vote in order to amend banking statutes. During his presentation he revealed that there were fifty banks in his southern Illinois district, and that he had campaigned to protect the unit banks. At least, he was frank in his professions.

The emotional appeal of the unit bank side of the issue was best presented by Joseph Meek:

> I can do no other, ladies and gentlemen, than oppose a change in our banking laws which would surely threaten the very existence of neighborhood and small-town banks. Historically, over the years, I have fought for Main Street merchants and their bankers. I have fought for the commercial interests around our so called squares, simply because I believe the real strength of America is in its cross-road towns and once-busy downtown business areas. The fight may be in vain. Even after forty years of effort, the mortality of the little store is only matched by the mortality of the little town. The symptoms of death, or the crippling unto death of County Seat towns and their small subsidiaries, can easily be forecast. The doctor leaves, the school interests are transferred elsewhere, and then the bank folds, and the town is dead. . . .

And even in these communities where the death knell is indeed heard, the advent of impersonalized branch banking must be of concern to those who must have the deep participation of an entire community in the solution of its problems. The manager of a branch bank, like a branch store, is of necessity almost always a temporary citizen. He does well here; he is then moved there. He has no deep home roots. He has no broad concern in the welfare of his town; he cannot afford the time to take such interest. He is incessantly prodded by those who understandably must make the profit — skim the cream — and look to the overall big production for the profit. There is an absentee ownership about banks and stores and all such enterprises which worries me individually very much.

There are now too few rugged individuals who live in the towns where they run their banks, know the folks of the town, contribute mightily to the objective of that town, and rise swiftly to the task of defending their beloved communities. Their selfishness is born of a desperate desire to live. These little people cannot lock up and go elsewhere. . . .

Even as the one man-one vote principle has turned the political power of this nation away from the farm and the little towns, and into the big city and its suburbs, so has it become necessary in these less populous areas for those who would retain the balance in our country to utilize all the available political strength to defend its philosophy. The defense of this way of life is weakened in direct ratio to the loss of the hometown bank — of the home-town ownership. . . .

I hope for compromise — the kind of compromise that Mr. Dunn has just suggested. I hope for elimination of the current referendum, but I also hope for a three-fifths or two-thirds vote on any branch banking proposal. Without it, I must stand proudly with my heritage, even under the deaths of even myself or of the little towns. Thank you very much.[1]

In interesting contrast to Meek's comments were those of Leonard Foster, a frequent gadfly of the gathering:

Mr. President and fellow members, my position on this issue is determined by my knowledge of my community, and that community right now is dying faster than my political future. And I think we need a bank to bring it back to life.

Back around 1960 we had a very good community out in Garfield Park, around the Madison-Pulaski shopping area. I think, out of the first fifty shopping areas in the metropolitan Chicago area, we were something like number 8 or 10. We used to turn about $44 million a

[1]*Record of Proceedings, Sixth Illinois Constitutional Convention,* Vol. II, p. 1130.

year, I think in retail trade. And between '60 and '65, just about all the
people that were living there went somewhere else to live, and a lot of
new people came in, and they didn't have the same income or job
opportunities, and a lot of them were on welfare, and things began to
change.

And six or eight years ago, the National Bank of Commerce left and
went downtown and merged with another bank and took $50 million,
and then Apollo Savings and Loan went down to Michigan to play
games and go broke with $60 million, so that means that in the course of
one year $110 million in deposits were outside of our community and we
were the only area that did not have a bank. We tried to form a bank, and
we couldn't.

And now that community is dying. As far as I know, the Madison-
Pulaski shopping area last year turned less than $28 million in retail and
this year they will be doing good if they can turn $20 million. We are just
about down to four big chain stores, and everybody else is out of
business, because — among other things — the merchants won't come
in to replace people that move out because there is no place for them to
put their money at night. They have to take it home in their cars and
drop it off in the morning downtown.

Now, I don't know if Dave Connor or Jim Brannen or somebody else
is just huffing and puffing, waiting to open a branch at Madison-Pulaski
and provide us with full banking services; but I know that under the
present setup, we aren't going to get it. And we need it. And, therefore, if
there is any way that we can free up these crazy — I don't understand
banking laws. I don't try to. But it certainly seems to me that it's awfully
hard to get a bank going somewhere once they have failed. And if some
existing bank could be given a chance of seeing if our community can
support at least a branch operation, I think we ought to free things up so
that we get a chance.

And for that reason, I am in favor of anything that makes it possible
for the banking business, at least in the city of Chicago, to be operated
like any other business and not subject to all these — to me — arbitrary
and unreasonable restrictions. Thank you.[2]

At this point Dunn withdrew his amendment in favor of Ronald
Smith's amendment to require a referendum only upon legislation
establishing non-unit, or branch banking. This was an attempt to
remove all other statutory changes in banking law from any restrictions
beyond the normal legislative process.

[2]Ibid., p. 1134

Smith accepted George Lewis' motion to substitute the word "branch" for non-unit banking. Finally, the branch banking issue was clearly isolated. It could not be avoided.

And for the first time the threat that had been rumored was articulated on the floor; Lewis said, ". . . I feel it is now that we are at the crossroads of success or failure with respect to our product."[3] From that moment on it was clear to some that the unit banking interests would seek to defeat the entire document if they did not receive some protection. It angered Mrs. Leahy that banking interests — on both sides of the question — could dare to equate branch banking with serious constitutional issues — for example, the Bill of Rights, selection of the judiciary, makeup of legislative districts. But they did and they lobbied delegates right through the end of the convention. It was one of the less seemly aspects of the convention.

The Smith amendment carried 59 to 48 (with 3 pass, 1 present). But, after further debate, the Smith amendment failed to substitute for the majority proposal 46 to 59 (with 5 pass, 1 present).

Chairman McCracken then moved that the majority proposal be sent to the Committee on Style, Drafting and Submission.

George Lewis moved to amend the majority proposal by requiring three-fifths approval of the General Assembly for the establishment of branch banking. At that point, the only statement on the integrity of the convention was leveled by Lewis. In the afternoon of May 20 he made one of his long and forceful speeches, in the course of which he said:

> I think the reasons are appalling to me as a delegate to this convention. I have examined the records of the votes on branch banking in the State Legislature; and I have found a group of delegates who in the past have never voted for anything smelling of branch banking, and then here today I find a complete reversal of that vote. And I ask why, and I think I know the reason, and I am not going to state it. Only those persons who have — for the first time in the history of this state for 100 years — have changed their vote and changed their position, for what? Only they really know. But I think I also know.
>
> And I think this is a power struggle that these delegates here are not aware of. And it is my contention and my feeling and I feel it very sincerely that the struggle has not commenced. And I intend to go all the

[3]Ibid., p. 1137.

way — I do not intend to stop here — because I know the struggle is not for dollars and cents, but it is for millions.[4]

Lewis was pleading for support for his amendment that required that no law providing for any branch or branches for a state bank or trust company created under the laws of Illinois could be enacted, amended, or repealed by the General Assembly except by a vote of three-fifths of the members elected to and serving in each house. He succeeded in implying that there had somehow been venality involved on the part of some of the delegates and some of the individuals and groups outside the convention, who were pushing for branch banking.

David Davis immediately asked for the floor as a matter of personal privilege. This he was able to obtain only after President Witwer had continually overruled John Knuppel's demand for a recess. Davis declared:

> Mr. President some remarks have just been made on the floor of this convention, which seem to imply an evil conspiracy or an impugning of the integrity of members of this body. I think that if Mr. Lewis had any information in this regard, it is his obligation to fully disclose whatever it is he has. Otherwise, I would say that he has done a fine job of obfuscation, that he has impugned the integrity of members of the committee on General Government — all of them, without being specific in any regard — and I would ask at this time Mr. Lewis that in all fairness if you have specific charges that you want to direct at me or at any other member of this convention, that you do so at this time.[5]

President Witwer immediately challenged Lewis to come forward with any charges that he might have to direct at any member of the convention. Lewis again gave a somewhat rambling response, but offered no specific proof of his charges.

After adjournment, Witwer summoned Lewis to his office in the Old State Capitol to discuss the veiled threats and charges that he had brought before the convention. The president asked Lewis point blank if in fact he was aware of any venality that had taken place or was about to take place between any delegates and any individuals or groups who were attempting to have their wishes carried out in the convention. Lewis responded in the negative and stated that he had not intended to

[4]Ibid., p. 1151.
[5]Ibid., p. 1152.

bring any such charges before the convention and that his remarks had been misunderstood. Witwer directed Executive Director Pisciotte to obtain the transcript of the afternoon's proceedings, so that the precise intent of Lewis's remarks could be delineated. Kurt Sivertsen, the court reporter for the convention's proceedings on the afternoon of May 20, made the transcript immediately available to the president. On the basis of the transcript Lewis argued that it was not his intention to point out any behavior on the part of the delegates, but, rather, that he was talking about legislators in the Illinois General Assembly. Lewis was then virtually directed by the president to make a statement of clarification before the convention.

The delegates reconvened the next morning, Thursday, May 21, at 9:00 A.M., and after the usual roll call and announcements, President Witwer immediately recognized Lewis, who made a clarifying statement.

> If yesterday, as a delegate to this convention, I in anyway and to any extent misused this assembly, then I can only ask for your individual and collective forgiveness.
>
> I have checked the transcript of what was said yesterday and tried to examine what I might have said yesterday that would have caused the distinguished Delegate Davis to have arisen from his chair.
>
> After it was over I still wondered exactly what I could have said that would have caused that, and I did find a sentence that apparently did. That sentence was when I said, "I have examined the records of the votes on branch banking in the State Legislature; and I found a group of delegates. . . ."
>
> Obviously I was mistaken when I said the word "delegates." I meant "state legislators" in the past who had not voted for branch banking.
>
> This, I think, probably will justify Delegate Davis in wondering what I was saying. I think it and the remainder of the verbal comment without looking at the record certainly justified his comment.
>
> In my remarks yesterday I did not intend to impugn the honesty or personal integrity of any delegate sitting in these chambers. I have no evidence of any payoffs or promises of payoffs and I am confident that none have been suggested. I recognize that the product of a realized system of branch banking may be the increased investment by large banks and projects that are good and essential for this state. That kind of argument is certainly legitimate for delegates to have considered among many other factors in casting their vote. I intended to infer no venality. I

only intended to bring out in the open what others apparently realized but had not said. I did not intend to impair the product of this convention for which we all are working so hard to successfully present to the people.

Lewis put the issue to bed, at least on the surface, with his attempt at lighthearted comment:

> Now as soon as possible let us get back to the issues of yesterday and continue on the Ladd's purification of Connor's Branch in which lies Knuppel's Slippery Rock upon which I seem to have slipped while innocently strolling down a gardener's path.[6]

But the Lewis Amendment was defeated (48-48-1-1).

James Thompson then made a last stab at stemming the tide by moving to allow the General Assembly to provide for county-wide branch banking but imposing a statewide referendum on any statutory change providing for statewide branch banking. He noted, "I think the I.B.A. (Illinois Bankers Association) may be ready to compromise at this point."[7] Many delegates were becoming convinced that such compromise was necessary to save the entire document, a conviction that was only to grow over the summer.

The Thompson amendment failed miserably (14-83-7).

The majority proposal was sent to style and drafting by a relatively slim vote (60-38-2-6); several delegates voting yes indicated they were open to further review of the issue on second reading, that they just wanted to get on to other issues.

But, somehow, getting on to the other issues never really got the convention over the bitterness engendered by this debate on the first controversial issue to come before the delegates in their role as a committee of the whole.

Second reading on the banking issue came on August 6. Delegates Parker, Yordy, Howard, and Martin moved to amend by requiring a three-fifths majority of both houses of the General Assembly to establish branch banking. By this time the idea of the three-fifths vote dominated the convention. Much of the debate centered upon whether that was more restrictive than a referendum. Who really knew?

The amendment lost by a tie vote (52-52-5).

[6]Ibid., pp. 1155-1156.
[7]Ibid., p. 1164.

After a ruling by the president that the proposal would be tabled if it did not receive 59 votes, the proposal favoring complete deletion was sent to style and drafting by a vote of 85-17-1.

On August 31, the time for third, or passage reading had arrived.

Many delegates were convinced that the unit banking interests would work to defeat the entire document. Some were frightened that the branch banking issue would jeopardize other issues, particularly judicial selection and selection of members of the House of Representatives. Throughout the convention delegates constantly discussed possible vote trades — and branch banking was usually on the agenda of any such discussion. Finally the delegates suspended the rules in order to consider a banking amendment (74-14-18).

Ralph Dunn then submitted his amendment to require that branch banking be established by either a constitutional majority of the General Assembly or three-fifths of those voting on the question — whichever was greater. Dunn readily, but sadly, admitted that this was "a watered-down version."

After perfecting the language, the amendment carried 86-19-20.

By now thoroughly disgusted, Mrs. Leahy explained her "No" vote:

> My vote in no. I can remember on first reading the deletion of the banking sections went off by one vote, and perhaps that was the greatest mistake this Convention has made, because it seemed to me the banking issue lurked in these halls after that with incredible proportions. But, I don't want to berate the industry because, to be perfectly honest, I don't have the words fit for the record to do it. I do think, though, that we ought to thank all the thousands of industries and professions in this state who did not bother us with their intra industry disputes.[8]

Mrs. Leahy was surprised at the large number of delegates who voted "pass" at various stages of the deliberations. She realized not many independents from Chicago voted — perhaps in response to lobbying from neighborhood banks, but also in deference to constitutional "purity." Innocence was easily lost by the conflict of issues. Mrs. Leahy was not bothered by lobbyists after her handling of the matter on first reading. They must have assumed she was a hopeless case.

[8]Ibid., V, p. 4526.

At least two procedural decisions were made in the course of all this that would substantially affect other issues in later debate:

1. After explaining the majority and minority reports, David Davis moved to divide the question, that is, to make sections 6, 7, and 8 one question and keeping section 5 as a separate section. There was no opposition to deletion of sections 6, 7, and 8. President Witwer granted the request for separation and then entertained motions relating only to section 5.

2. After Ronald Smith's amendment had replaced the minority proposal, the chair was asked what would happen if the final proposal did not achieve the required votes. President Witwer indicated it would need 59 votes to go to Style, Drafting and Submission, but it was not precisely clear if the proposal would remain tabled or if the 1870 section would be resurrected.

President Witwer was to rule definitively on this question when the banking issue was heard on second reading. After an amendment to require a three-fifths vote failed by a 52-52-2 vote, it appeared likely the majority proposal might not muster the 59 votes. At this point, this colloquy took place:

> Mr. McCracken: I have a motion, but in all fairness Mr. President, I think that everyone ought to be informed of the consequences of a failure to get fifty-nine votes to my motion to pass it back to Style and Drafting. I don't know exactly what I am suggesting we send back to Style and Drafting. I guess it's our recommendation that the old provisions be deleted. What if my motion fails? What would be the consequences?
>
> President Witwer: Well, I think that it would — if it takes more than the majority of the vote, but less than fifty-nine, it would be on the secretary's table again and would have to be raised; because there will be no deletion until it has been voted through the first, second, and third reading.[9]

There were more important issues than branch banking before the convention, but none led to more heat and dismay. A few more such issues and the convention could easily have been wrecked.

Environment

Mary Leahy was the main proponent of yet another proposal of the

[9]Ibid., p. 3718.

General Government Committee. This one, however, did not meet the opposition faced by the banking report. In fact, her proposal concerning the right to a healthful environment became analogous to motherhood and apple pie. The environment was a popular issue in the summer of 1970, and the fact that many of the delegates' children were lobbying their parents for a "yes" vote did much to help speed the passage of the proposal. The final provision submitted by Style, Drafting and Submission was adopted by the delegates 97-5, earned a separate article status. Article XI basically specified that the legislature provide for the conservation and protection of the scenic beauty and resources of the state. It also established the right of individuals to a healthful environment. Although this article may not seem as important as some others, Leahy felt it was worth the effort if for no other reason than because of what it said to future generations about the delegates.

Protection of the environment is an article of faith for many people. The hard decisions in this area come when this faith is confronted with economic costs. Should environmental purity stand in the way of jobs and prosperity? Undoubtedly, the issue will be fought out in the courts and in halls of academe as well as elsewhere! It may be difficult to circumvent the clear intent of the new article, but courts are capable of performing great acrobatic feats.

The General Government Committee attempted to constitutionalize sportsmen's dreams of conservation, but their efforts here were defeated on the floor of the convention. They were more successful in proclaiming further policy in the form of assistance to transportation, protection of pension funds, and a few other provisions. The omnibus committee engendered more excitement than had been anticipated.

XVIII

The Culmination

From the very beginning many, if not most, delegates realized that a so-called "single package" submission of the final document would result in a rejection of the proposed constitution. This had been the case with the product of the Illinois Constitutional Convention of 1920-22 and subsequently in numerous other states. It became clear that the only way to make any headway was to submit highly controversial issues separately. Those provisions generally regarded as more acceptable could then be submitted safely in one package. This had been done, to a certain extent, with the 1870 constitution. The delegates to the 1969-70 convention seemed to accept this tacitly although no practical steps were taken on the matter. It was thought to require more careful consideration on the part of the Committee on Style, Drafting and Submission, the leadership of the convention, and, indeed, by all concerned delegates. This was how the situation stood upon completion of second reading on August 14, 1970; with adjournment scheduled for August 27, 1970, this left only a short time for either consideration or final action if the convention was to fulfill the almost frantic need for early completion of the assigned tasks.

Several issues were possible candidates for separate submissions. In addition to the selection of judges — whether of all courts or the circuit court judges alone — there were also the matters of the franchise for eighteen year olds, capital punishment, and the handicapped. There were other possibilities, too, but they were limited in number. No one seriously thought of submitting everything as separate propositions so that, in effect, the people themselves would make the ultimate decision on each provision and the ultimate conformation of the "package." Such an approach might be described as democracy pursued to its ultimate absurdity.

Witwer was troubled, as well he might be, by the manifold problems of separate submission. He consulted with Wayne Whalen, chairman, and George Braden, special advisor, of the committee charged with guidance on the submission. If the document were fragmentized how would it be determined what constituted a "majority of those voting at the election" as required by the 1870 constitution? In an effort to get answers to these vexing questions, Witwer talked with newspaper editors, the supreme arbiters some thought of public opinion. He heard from many people, including members of the lower house in the General Assembly, who threatened to vote against the proposed constitution if single-member districts were included in the package rather than as a separate proposition. There were those who felt the same way about judicial selection. Clearly, some items were too hot to be contained in any package. But there could not be too many of them without creating confusion.

These things were tied in with the writing of the required Address to the People, and with the explanation of the different provisions, particularly those that made basic changes. And there was the problem of choosing a date for the referendum on the document, including its separate submissions. Should it be at the time of the general election in November 1970? Should it be at some later or earlier date in November or December of that year or even in January of the following year? Witwer knew that his noncooperating vice-president, John Alexander, abetted by Sommerschield and others, favored a date in January 1971.

Witwer held a series of significant meetings. On August 19, he met with Lloyd Wendt and other members of the editorial staff of *Chicago Today* to discuss these and other related problems. The next day, *Chicago Today* published what Witwer regarded as an excellent editorial on the subject. That same day he met with Roy Fisher and several other writers of the *Chicago Daily News*, as well as Carl Wiegman, chief editorial writer of the *Chicago Tribune*. This time Wiegman agreed with him on the danger of placing highly controversial items within the main document. It would be much better if they were submitted separately. Witwer researched almost feverishly the 1848 and 1870 constitutions in order to find guidance. He talked with Wayne Whalen again and felt discouraged by what he regarded as Whalen's noncommital attitude.

The next day he talked with Lyons, with whom he knew he had to reckon if the all-important support of Mayor Daley was to be obtained. Lyons thought his people would be adamant about both cumulative voting and the election of judges; they would have to be kept within the main document. But he would think over the matter, Lyons assured him. Witwer talked with a Chicago banker whom he knew to be close to Mayor Daley. This man was a lawyer and was intrigued by the problems raised by Witwer. He said that he would talk with Lyons, if not Daley himself. Witwer now phoned Whalen again, who once more seemed unresponsive, although he admitted that there would be no unsurmountable drafting problem if Witwer's ideas of separately submitting the alternatives of the controversial issues to the voters were accepted by the convention.

On August 23, Witwer spent most of the day telephoning leading delegates in order to explain the situation as he saw it. Many of them seemed concerned. The next day he talked with one of Governor Ogilvie's top administrative aides and seemed to win him over. He said he would converse with the governor and report back. On the same day, he briefed the convention reporters for three Chicago newspapers — John Camper of the *Daily News*, Charles Wheeler of the *Sun-Times*, and Edith Herman of the *Tribune*. He told them that he would appear before the Committee on Style, Drafting and Submission the next day to make his suggestions. Word got out that the Daley Democrats thought he was trying to put across merit selection of judges in some tricky fashion. He spent time with McCracken, a Daley leader, in order to persuade him of his good faith and the necessity of an alternate method of procedure. McCracken was cordial enough, but clearly concerned about the possible defeat of the system of elective judges. Witwer telephoned others, such as Ralph Dunn and Joan Anderson. All seemed to have some quarrel with any plan that appeared to downgrade their beliefs with respect to judicial selection or repre-sentative districts. They could not see that in the best interest of their own ideas, as well as the basic document itself, they had to agree upon a strategy that would ease the path to approval for the constitution while giving voters the opportunity to express a preference on the more controversial features.

On August 26, Witwer attended the meeting of the Committee on Style, Drafting and Submission at the Bismark Hotel in Chicago. The atmosphere was tense and Witwer was apprehensive. Chairman Whalen and most members of the committee seemed cool, if not downright hostile. The downstate Republicans were opposed to any plan of submission that would remove the issue of single-member districts from the main document. Organization Democrats remained suspicious that Witwer was trying to maneuver in favor of merit selection of judges. Witwer left the meeting feeling, as he said, "thoroughly discouraged, irate, and with little hope." Did he have no friends? Did everyone fail to see that what he was proposing was in the best interests of all, and was not in the least, partisan? Witwer decided that he could not press the matter any further lest he create rancor, bitter and protracted debate, and disaster.

He remained convinced that adoption of the constitution depended upon placing cumulative voting in the package and submitting single-member districts as a separate proposition. So he worked with Lucy Reum, a Republican but the principal proponent of cumulative voting, in order to obtain the necessary votes. He canvassed delegates. He was open and above board in this effort, recognizing he might offend those who did not share his concern.

Support began to grow for Witwer's strategy. Governor Ogilvie announced his approval of Witwer's plan. This prompted a number of downstate Republicans to rally to his viewpoint; even Wayne Whalen began to soften. Weisberg, too, suggested during the convention debate that some acceptable compromise might be worked out.

Witwer met with concerned persons until late during the night of August 27. Delegates Ladd, Whalen, and Tecson, and Witwer's counselor, Richard Lockhart, were among the participants. They recognized that they had to resolve the problem of the form of the ballot if there were to be a main document along with separate submissions. What would be the requisite electoral majority — those voting generally at the election, those voting on the main document, or those voting on the separate propositions? It was too serious an issue to resort to any form of gimmickry. George Braden, then in the East, was called and the respected Rubin Cohn was consulted also. Finally, all agreed upon the verbal form and substance. Would the majority of the delegates go along with them? That remained to be seen. The delegates were often unpredictable and certainly not infallible. They could err, just as legislators could be misled. Not as often, perhaps, but enough to worry so conscientious a presiding officer as Witwer.

In Witwer's judgment, the turning point of the entire convention occurred on August 28, when Lucy Reum's amendment prevailed. It brought about a reversal of the vote on single-member districts. Now genuine compromise was possible; and a true coalition was in process, although not at first observed. The delegates began to speak publicly, as well as privately, on the new turn of events. The single-member district advocates had been unwilling to compromise, but now the Reum victory made it apparent to all, except the most rabid, that there had to be some sort of arrangement between those concerned about judicial selection and themselves. Perhaps the solution was to have both matters submitted as separate propositions. Thus, both would have the possibility of success if they could rally voters to their causes, without placing the rest of the constitution in peril. Because the delegates were anxious to get to a reception being hosted by President and Mrs. Witwer, the single-member resolution was not finalized and was, therefore, open to parliamentary action on the 29th. This was a fateful blunder on the part of the Democrats. It affected the outcome of the convention and might well have jeopardized adoption of the constitution itself.

Early the next morning, Witwer was greeted on arrival at his office by a good government group consisting of Republicans and independents — Ladd, Tomei, Weisberg, Elbert Smith, Parkhurst, Shuman, Dawn Clark Netsch, and Mary Lee Leahy among others. Young Jeffrey Ladd, increasingly respected by more and more delegates, seemed to be the principal spokesman for the group. They told Witwer that almost miraculously they had lined up sixty-three delegates, perhaps more, who were prepared to agree to separate submissions of judicial selection and representation in the House. Was the president interested in this, and would he help? Witwer could not help reminding them of their earlier hostility when he had brought up the same sort of plan at the Chicago meeting. He wanted to know if their vote count was accurate, and if the coalition would survive any assault from the Daley Democrats who wanted judicial election to be a part of the package, rather than a separate submission. The organization Democrats were tough combatants, who knew how to fight. They would not hesitate to resort to anything, fair or foul. Men like Lyons, McCracken, and Elward were masters of invective and abuse. They knew every parliamentary angle. They specialized in the kind of maneuvering that could win without numbers. Witwer said he would not stand in the way of those who had come to him that morning; he would treat them fairly, but inwardly he was skeptical. Ladd thereupon said, quite bluntly, that Witwer would have to be with them all the way if they were going to prevail. Would he throw his full weight with them? Witwer said, simply, "We'll take it as it comes." And the meeting adjourned. Witwer felt that he was about to preside at the most momentous session of the convention.

Witwer was still uncertain that the coalition could hold together. He felt, as the debate went on, that he was fair to all sides and especially helpful to Whalen. As debate progressed throughout the day he began to feel that he was becoming more openly a supporter of the coalition. If his rulings at this point had been different the coalition might have collapsed and he did not want this to happen.

A roll call on a motion to approve the final reading failed 53 for (less than the requirement as set forth in the rules), 24 opposed, 23 abstaining, thus keeping the matter on the secretary's table. The loss on this roll call issue was partly attributable to the fact that seven Chicago Democrats, including Lyons, were absent, reportedly recovering from the previous evening's festivities.

Later a motion to take the legislative article from the secretary's desk passed and then a motion was made to approve it on final reading. At this critical point, Whalen moved to suspend the rules to consider amending the legislative and judicial articles and presented the coalition's plan to remove multi-member districts and elective judges from the main document. Confusion and turmoil prevailed at this juncture, but eventually Whalen's motion to suspend the rules passed. Following a recess, the Keegan, Wilson, and Whalen (KWW) amendment was offered and passed 70 to 39. This provided, through separate submissions, for popular choice of legislative districts and the method of selecting judges. Neither side got what they wanted, but they prevented the Chicago Democrats from having their way in the main package. The coalition behind the KWW amendment was more an emotional response to the relentless and cold tactics of the Chicago Democrats rather than a joinder of common ideology or interests. It was basically a coalition of Republicans and independent Democrats who no longer wanted to be bullied by any machine.

Witwer has long felt that the seeds for the convention's ultimate success were sown on August 26, 27 and 28, when he had been almost alone in advocating the kind of compromise that now seemed on the way. He believes that the press support he engendered, the support of Governor Ogilvie, the lobbying he did among some delegates, were essential ingredients. Out of these things grew a strategy that was developed during the sessions of August 29 and 30 and September 1. As a result, Whalen became a remarkably effective leader of the coalition. He held on doggedly with the able assistance from Mrs. Keegan, Wilson, Shuman, Weisberg, Mrs. Leahy, Cicero, and, indeed, all of the independents and their allies. Disappointed single-member district advocates like Stanley Johnson became steadfast supporters of the new plan. As often happens, luck played an important part in the final result. The absence of some Democratic stalwarts at one decisive morning session was, perhaps, an indispensable ingredient. The puritanical Elward glowered in rage at this turn of events, but he was powerless. The voices and votes were not there at the moment when it counted. The coalition prevailed.

On August 30, Fay moved the judicial article be approved, the terms of debate followed. Then Young again offered an amendment, to allow the appointment of judges by the governor, with the consent of the Senate. It failed by only one vote. The Fay motion to approve the judicial article passed 71 to 35, with 4 voting pass. Thus, the delegates sought to complete their work. It should be noted the Convention was running out of time and money, and the delegates were willing to work well into the evening. Their dedication to the constitution is best exemplified by their willingness to stay in session for eighteen hours in order to complete their task.

Now only a few technical difficulties were left to complete the constitution. As we shall see, these presented some unforeseen obstacles that threatened the success of the convention.

OTHER LAST—MINUTE PROBLEMS

Delegate Sommerschield brought up the first item of controversy when he made an inquiry of Kelley, who headed the Committee on Closing Day Ceremonies, about the meaning of a delegate's signature on the document. He asked whether delegate signature on the constitution would be an endorsement of the document or simply an attestation of their position as delegates. Kelley appropriately responded that that topic was not within the purview of his committee. President Witwer, however, declared that when the convention completed third reading and had approved the schedule and the form of the ballot, delegates would legally have completed the new constitution if that was the intent of the body, and that the signature was simply a ceremonial step that was customary and traditional.

Peter Tomei added to the uncertainty of the winding up of the convention when he asked permission to sign the document after the official closing ceremonies because he would have to be out of the state on September 3. President Witwer began to respond that he saw no objection to this request, but as might have been expected, Paul Elward objected, pointing out that to allow one delegate to sign in absentia could possibly lead to many of the delegates doing likewise. Vice-President Alexander got into the discussion by asking the chair whether or not there would be a wrap-up vote on the proposed constitution as a total package or whether or not the vote on each provision following third reading would be the final vote on the document. His concern was not so much a legal question, but more a question of constituent visibility. In other words, he wanted to be certain that his constituents would know precisely how he stood on the document because at that time it was not clear that he would support the proposed document. Witwer responded: "I think if it is the will of the body, we can have a wrap-up vote; but I do believe that as we approve at third reading for final passage specific articles, they have, unless they are withdrawn before adjournment sine die, become articles that we will be submitting. And I don't believe that their validity will then depend upon the final wrap-up vote, Mr. Alexander; but I think that a wrap-up vote will be complementary and highly acceptable."[1]

---

[1]*Record of Proceedings, Sixth Illinois Constitutional Convention,* Vol. V, p. 4459.

Witwer's concern, of course, as president, was not only moving the business of the convention; he also wanted to prevent the possibility of an article or a vote being overturned at a later time after it had been "put to bed" with a final third reading vote. He was concerned that a ruling requiring a final wrap-up vote to give the proposed document legal effect could leave the door open for last minute maneuverings and possible changes that could be detrimental to the ultimate product and adjournment of the convention.

Several delegates, such as Elward and Friedrich, would have preferred postponement of any wrap-up or finality of the document until the last possible moment. This would enable them to work their will to the final moment of the convention. Knuppel wanted to put off any finality of the delegates' position on the document until after December 15 when the election was to take place, and the issues submitted as separate questions would be determined by the voters. His point was that he would not know until that time whether he would support the document, depending upon which of the separately submitted provisions would prevail. Witwer assured Vice-President Lyons that no changes were to be made by the Style and Drafting Committee after the delegates finished with an item on third reading; the item would be sent directly to the printer and would appear intact in the total document. This document would then be returned to the convention for ceremonial signing on September 3. The president also assured Delegate Coleman that it was not the intent of the chair or of the convention to circumvent Rule 10, which spelled out the role of the secretary in not only closing the convention but also in delivering the actual document to the secretary of state. He assured Coleman that he had no intention of holding the document himself. Friedrich, not unexpectedly, objected to any concern about a closing ceremony and stated: "This business of trying to rig this convention so it will accommodate the pomp and ceremony doesn't impress me at all."[2] Delegate William Lennon expressed agreement with Friedrich and indicated he did not understand the concern for speed, and why it was that everyone was hastily attempting to move toward adjournment on Thursday, September 3:

> I say to you, sir — and I want it for the record — that I object to this

[2]Ibid., p. 4462.

procedure. All of a sudden we are in a hurry. We haven't been in a hurry for nine months; but now at the most vital stage of our proceedings, the thing that we will send forth to the electorate and say, "This is what we agreed upon after nine months of deliberation" — all of a sudden we are going to get it on Thursday, hastily read it, and allegedly sign it. I protest very seriously, sir, to this procedure and I say to you that it is wrong.[3]

Lennon's concerns, of course, were simply the same as those who were looking for delaying tactics even at this late date. The objections over the signing procedures also emanated from those who were not certain at this point whether they would be approving the document and, of course, did not want their signature on the new constitution if, in fact, they were to oppose its adoption in the projected referendum.

The controversy over the manner and significance of the signing or nonsigning of the document was carried over to the next day (September 1) when Ladd gave a further progress report of the Committee on the Closing Day Ceremonies. He reviewed once more the many details involved, adding that Buford, because he was the oldest delegate, would be asked to make the motion to adjourn sine die, and that the delegates would not be allowed to explain their vote if, in fact, a wrap-up vote was taken on the total document. He had hardly finished his report when Elward picked up the theme from the day before and again brought up his objection to delegates being allowed to sign the document after the closing day ceremonies. Lyons was concerned about not being able to explain the delegates' votes, and Vice-President Alexander continued to be concerned about "establishing a public record" regarding his support or nonsupport for the proposed new constitution. Kemp asked that a place be provided on the document for signators who would be dissenting from the document. Elbert Smith responded to Kemp, and in so doing supported President Witwer, that the signature constituted simply an attestation that the signer was, in fact, a delegate and that the document was, in fact, the offered document without any implication that the signor favored or dissented from the total document or any particular part of it. Smith stated that if, in fact, the signing was an endorsement and not simply an attestation, that he would support Delegate Kemp by providing a means for expressing a dissent. The issue was ultimately

[3]Ibid., p. 4462.

resolved and a determination made that the signing was an attestation and did not, in fact, constitute support of the document. As it turned out, Kelleghan would not sign the final document. He stated, solemnly: "Mr. President, I respectfully decline to sign this document for the reason that I fear that the people who sent me to this convention from my district in DuPage County will interpret the act of signing as approval of this constitution. I do not approve of it, and I do not think it is in the best interests of the people of this state."[4]

Paul Elward was the only other delegate who did not sign the final document stating as his reason: "Because I have not had the time to check this document, I decline, sir, to sign it at this time."[5] Kemp and William Lennon signed the document but noted their dissents. With regard to the matter of signing at some time other than at the closing ceremonies, the delegates adopted a resolution directed to the secretary of state which provided for any delegate not able to attend the closing day ceremonies to have an opportunity within thirty days of the adjournment sine die to sign the document which would be in the possession of the secretary of state. Four delegates — Cicero, Linn, Raby, and Tomei — were not able to attend the final ceremonies and took advantage of the resolution to sign the document at a later date, or as in the case of Delegate Linn, he gave power of attorney to Delegate Nudelman to sign on his behalf at the closing ceremony.

The question of the manner and significance of signing the final document was by no means the most heated controversy to reach the convention in its closing hours. James Kemp was to raise a question which was to delay the conclusion of the convention and to serve as one of the final tests of the delegates.

During the course of the convention, the staff had to enter into numerous contracts for hundreds of thousands of dollars for the printing of various convention materials. The need was oftentimes for rapid printing of large amounts of material in numerous copies. Consequently, it was necessary to use not only virtually every printer in Springfield but other printers throughout the central Illinois area. While the criterion of speed was certainly of paramount significance, the underlying, or first principle, for letting a contract followed by the executive director of the convention was that, where possible, the

[4]Ibid., p. 4674.
[5]Ibid., p. 4673.

printer was to be a union firm. This procedure was discussed with the union-related delegates, particularly James Kemp, and the policy met with Kemp's general approval.

However, when it came to the printing of the final document, other factors had to be taken into consideration, such as the ability to print the document under severe time pressures and to do it in a manner that would be befitting the importance of the document in a type style and on paper that would stand up over a long period of time. Obviously, delegates would want to preserve a document to which they had contributed so much. The convention staff, in anticipation of these needs, researched those printers that could carry out the job and found that R.R. Donnelley and Company in Chicago was one of the few in the country that both could take on the job and was willing to do so. Frequent meetings were held with R.R. Donnelley representatives weeks in advance of the closing ceremonies in anticipation of the final needs of the convention. Unfortunately, R.R. Donnelley was not a union shop. When this came to Kemp's attention, it was to lead to the major final controversy of the convention. He began the debate with the statement:

> I must vigorously protest the use of nonunion labor in a state that has almost two million union employees. To me, this is extremely distasteful and for those persons who say they are anxious to make friends and influence people with reference to the support of this end product, I would respectfully suggest that this is a poor start.
>
> If this convention insists upon taking this position then I shall be compelled to do all I believe necessary in calling the organized labor movement's attention to what appears, to me at least, to be an obvious slap in the face.[6]

Ladd responded by pointing out that it was not a case of union or non-union, but simply that R.R. Donnelley was the one printer found to have the skill to carry out the job in the limited time available. He also pointed out that R.R. Donnelley, a nonunion shop, had been frozen out of the printing of some eleven million copies of the newspaper insert explaining the document that was to be distributed throughout the state. This was by far the more lucrative contract, and Ladd emphasized that the union shops would be benefiting economically

[6]Ibid., p. 4541.

from that job, and that there was very little money to be gained from the printing of the actual document used at the signing and delivered to the delegates.

William Lennon and Richard Daley immediately joined Kemp in the objection to the use of a nonunion printer for the final document. Daley stated: "I object to the use of a non-union printer. During my campaign I received the full endorsement of the AFL-CIO. Also the Joint Teamsters Council #25. I had the privilege of attending during my campaign the plumbers' union meetings and also the labor union meetings in Chicago and the County of Cook. I strongly object to the use of any non-union workers."[7]

Lennon, in joining the cry of protest, stated that he saw nothing sacred about adjournment on September 3 and suggested that any adjournment be put off until the question of printing could be straightened out. Kemp, through some considerable parliamentary maneuvering, forced the delegates to take a position by introducing a resolution that directed the convention's officers and staff to "take whatever measures are necessary to terminate the work now being done by nonunion printers for this convention and are necessary to ensure that any printed material promulgated by this convention be printed by union workers and bear the printer's union label." After debate and parliamentary maneuvering first to suspend the rules and then to lay the motion on the table, Kemp finally had his resolution presented to the delegates and asked that a roll call vote be taken for the record.

Although the delegates were under severe time constraints and were trying desperately to complete their task before closing day ceremonies, some three dozen delegates took the opportunity to speak for or against Kemp's resolution. Kemp's resolution ultimately passed by a vote of 60 yeas, 39 nays, 2 passes, and what presiding officer Elbert Smith referred to as one cackle. The cackle vote stemmed from David Connor's statement that he thought there might be several delegates taking the position they did because they were too "chicken" to stand on their own principles. They feared the detrimental impact it might have on later campaigns and elections in which they might be involved. Connor may have been correct, for a sizeable number of delegates felt

[7]Ibid., p. 4541.

moved to take the floor to explain their position, either for or against the resolution, and to relate their support of unions and their own or their family's involvement with unions over the years.

The final vote on the resolution generally followed party lines; virtually all those opposed to the Kemp resolution were Republicans, with the exception of Betty Keegan, a Democrat, and Wayne Whalen, an independent. There were, however, several Republicans who joined the Democrat-led resolution and voted in the affirmative with Kemp. Their motivations were not clearly known, but one could suspect that they had future political ambitions and felt that a vote against the Kemp resolution may well have engendered some needless union opposition. Betty Howard, for example, was chairing the subcommittee on printing the material for the closing day ceremonies and, though she was quite tearful in having to reject all of the Donnelley printed material at the last moment, she did, in fact, vote with Kemp on the resolution.

The specter of union strength in Illinois elections was certainly present during the debate that day. Because of the lateness of the hour that they chose to present the resolution, Kemp and his group were accused by some of the delegates of using the opportunity to "grand stand" or to generate publicity either for themselves or for the unions. They had known of the staff policy on unions throughout the convention and had allowed other nonunion materials to be used, such as the delegate handbook and delegate nameplates.

The result of the adoption of the Kemp resolution was that the plates and proofs that had already been put together by R.R. Donnelley had to be literally scrapped and a last-minute union printer had to be found to put together the necessary materials. As a compromise, Pisciotte had obtained permission from the R.R. Donnelley executives to turn over the plates to a union printer to be used by the union shop and on which then could be placed the union bug. That compromise was emphatically rejected by Kemp, who had the upper hand and was not about to yield on this excellent opportunity to generate publicity, not only for himself but for the union interests.

The final special committee appointed by Witwer was the committee on the president's closing address to be presented to the convention and to the state immediately prior to the adjournment of the convention sine die. Witwer appointed David Kenney as chairman of that committee, largely by virtue of Kenney's position as vice-chairman of the permanent procedural committee on public information. He also appointed to that committee delegates Canfield, Cooper, Daley, Davis, Keegan, Netsch, and Nicholson. Due to various delays, Kenney did not make his report to the delegates until September 2, the day before adjournment sine die. The delay stemmed largely from the fact that an initial draft prepared by Kenney went through considerable reworking, discussion, modification, and debate. It was only after it had gone through four drafts that Kenney felt comfortable bringing the committees recommendations to the full body of delegates. As might be expected, the report and suggested address were received not without considerable further debate, amendment, and controversy. Virtually the entire day's business on September 2 was taken up with perfecting the president's address. It was not taken lightly, because it would be the first official communication the convention as a body would have with the public and the press on its newly proposed document. All of the individual delegate's concerns would have to be satisfied by the address and consequently all of the different interests and the diversification of the individual delegates and of the entire state would somehow have to be embodied in that address. It would have to stand as the official record of the convention on the question of whether or not the new document was perceived by the delegates as a step backward or as a progressive move forward and whether or not it was to be viewed as outstanding, superior, or just average. The address also had to tell the press and public, in shorthand form, precisely what the new constitution contained and at the same time what it did not contain.

There was an amusing byplay at the last regular session of the convention before the ceremonial closing. The organization Democrats would not give up, so there was still the possibility of delay and further mischief. Without consulting anyone, Gertz, who sensed danger in the situation, moved for adjournment, a nondebatable motion. Everything was tried to thwart the motion, including an unprecedented roll call, but the motion passed, and the whole thing was tied up neatly. Now that he had the right package and the right separate submissions, Witwer could rest more easily; all who had put so much into the effort could rejoice.

A day of glory for Witwer

By Edward S. Gilbreth
Of Our Springfield Bureau

SPRINGFIELD, Ill. — It was Samuel W. Witwer's day of glory, the high point in a lifetime devoted to state constitutional reform.

The silver-haired president of the Illinois constitutional convention was showered with accolades in formal and informal ceremonies Thursday marking con con's final adjournment.

The glow of warm feeling for Witwer enabled delegates who have been at each other's throats for months to embrace, exchange words of affection, and depart Springfield in a state of euphoria.

THE EMOTIONAL binge began in the House chamber of the Old State Capitol.

Delegates and hundreds of spectators grew hushed as Witwer descended from the rostrum and sat at the desk Abraham Lincoln used when the Great Emancipator was a legislator in the same chamber.

Enclustered by a score of television cameras and newspaper photographers, Witwer signed the proposed new constitution. As he arose, the assembly burst into applause.

Applause greeted each of the other delegates called upon to sign the historic document. Many were accompanied by wives or children as they strode down the aisle to Lincoln's desk.

WHEN IT WAS his turn to sign, Ted A. Borek of Chicago

pushed aside the ceremonial pen used by the others, and plucked up the desk's feather quill pen to affix his signature.

Discord was sounded by only two delegates, Paul F. Elward of Chicago and Thomas C. Kelleghan of West Chicago, both of whom declined to sign the document. Elward said he wanted more time to study the constitution, and Kelleghan said he did not approve of con con's product.

Harmony, however, prevailed through most of the proceedings.

Thunderous applause followed a rendition of the Lord's Prayer by gospel singer Mahalia Jackson. Several in the chamber wept as she concluded singing the majestic prose.

SHORTLY BEFORE adjourning, the convention presented Witwer with a bronze plaque engraved with the words of the new constitution's preamble.

Witwer, his voice husky and low, responded:

"For each of you over these months, I have developed the most affectionate regard . . . farewell, and Godspeed."

Later, at a champagne reception in the St. Nicholas Hotel, delegates hugged and some wept as they bid each other farewell, their last farewell after nine months of virtually living together through con con's labors.

THE CONVENTION staff bestowed awards on favorite delegates.

Miss Odas Nicholson of Chi-

cago received the best-dressed lady delegate award, and Joseph T. Meek of Western Springs was given the secretaries' sweetheart award.

There were two best-dressed male delegate awards. The "Kenilworth division award" went to Witwer, and the "soul division award" to Clifford Kelley of Chicago, a black delegate known for snazzy outfits.

A special award went to Mamie Gertz, wife of Elmer Gertz of Chicago, chairman of con con's bill of rights committee. Mrs. Gertz, who daily supplied delegates with candy and watched over their general health, was given the "Jewish mother-of-the-year" award.

LATER Thursday night, delegates entertained the con-con staff at a farewell party in the Warehouse, a Springfield night club, where there was more hugging and tears.

"After all the griping we did about ending the convention, now we're all sad about going home," said one delegate.

By consensus, Mrs. Betty Howard of St. Charles was named chairman of a committee to set a con-con reunion in Chicago on Dec. 15, the night returns will be coming in from the referendum on the new constitution.

"It's just too bad we won't be seeing each other before then," she said.

Victor A. Arrigo of Chicago agreed.

"You know," he said, "There is an old Italian saying, 'Every time you say goodby, you die a little.' That's how most of us feel tonight."

So ended the convention's regular work. Next followed the ceremonial closing day proceedings. Edward S. Gilbreth, correspondent for the *Chicago Daily News*, accurately captured the mood of the delegates in his report on September 4, 1970.

XIX

Approval by the People and the Courts

During the period following the adjournment sine die and up to about ten days before the election when Mayor Daley announced his support for the constitution, Witwer had many telephone conversations with Louis Ancel. They discussed ways and means of trying to acquaint the mayor with the important changes in the new constitution, particularly in the field of home rule, and why he should support it. Ancel had known the mayor quite well and was close to his attorney, corporation counsel Raymond Simon. He talked with the latter on several occasions, and it is likely that Simon in turn talked with the mayor about the importance of many aspects of the constitution in assisting Chicago with its problems. Now that the mayor is gone, one cannot say to what extent these conversations influenced his ultimate decision to support it, but it is reasonable to suppose that they were of considerable importance. During this period there was much uncertainty on the part of some of the stronger business interests. In addition, Witwer was not really sure about how to interpret a series of articles written by George Tagge for the *Chicago Tribune*, which purported to be objective treatments of the new constitution, but seemed strongly negative. This was particularly true of those dealing with the Revenue Article and matters of taxation. Some of the headlines were particularly worrisome. Kingman Douglass, who was then chairman of the committee leading the referendum campaign, had close connections with the *Chicago Tribune* and did his best to counteract these adverse developments. Witwer was immensely pleased and relieved when on the Sunday before the election there appeared on the front page of the *Chicago Tribune* a strong editorial by its publisher Harold Grumhaus, urging all-out-support for the new constitution and pointing out what would happen in the state if the people failed to seize the change to bring the basic law up to date.

If there was any one aspect of the new constitution that might explain Mayor Daley's support it was, of course, home rule. There was such a great need in the city of Chicago for the kind of broadened authority it afforded, that he could not turn it down, despite his apparent dislike for the 8 to 5 flat rate tax ratio as well as other sections which union labor had also condemned. This was the grant of power that made Daley willing to gamble on adopting the new constitution while defeating the merit selection of judges and single-member districts.

On the night of December 15, many of the convention delegates and staff, as well as supporters and well-wishers, gathered at the Sherman House in Chicago to receive the election returns and to anticipate adoption of the convention's work-product by the Illinois voters. Understandably, the jovial atmosphere — it was the first reunion of the delegates and staff — was filled with nervous excitement. For many, the gathering represented the end of an intense effort that had begun several years earlier. For convention President Samuel Witwer, it was the capstone of an effort he had helped initiate almost a quarter of a century earlier.

Regardless of their involvement, the delegates were cautiously optimistic. They had a right to be, for they had done their homework, and everything possible had been done to insure success. They had picked what appeared to be the correct date and type of election, the more controversial items had been separately submitted, widespread endorsements had been received, the delegates had conducted mini-campaigns on behalf of the document, and the opposition failed to crystalize in time. Equally significant, the delegates had conducted a convention which allowed the voters to go to the polls with a positive attitude toward the proposed constitution. By developing the reputation of hardworking individuals, they were able to overcome obstacles that many thought would lead to the convention's failure. But most important, the delegates were confident they had produced the best possible document that would be acceptable to the voters within the practical political realities of the state. The optimism of the delegates proved to be well founded for on December 15, 1970, the new constitution of the state of Illinois was approved by its citizens by a vote of 1,122,425 to 838,168. As with previous constitutional elections, voter turnout was light, with the Cook County majority being the decisive factor in obtaining a favorable vote for the constitution. Twice as many Cook County voters turned out as did downstate voters. Although the voter turnout was light, the thirty counties that supported the constitution represented over 75 percent of the state's population.

The new constitution had now been approved by the people and would provide the basic foundation for government in Illinois. Despite the confidence of the delegates in the constitution, some persons have complained that the Illinois Constitution of 1970 had led to an excessive amount of litigation; there have indeed been numerous suits involving home rule, the revenue article, the electoral board, the legislative initiative, and the amendatory veto. On balance, however, these have been only what one might call a normal amount of judicial interpretation of sometimes novel provisions. Two hundred years after the birth of this republic, there are still landmark rulings by the Supreme Court on the consequences of the various sections of the federal constitution, particularly the thirteenth and fourteenth amendments. There can be no doubt that, after a relatively short time, the meanings and implications of most portions of the new constitution of Illinois will be settled.

LEGISLATIVE INITIATIVE

One case is worth special attention which arose out of an interpretation and use of the legislative initiative section. Since it was believed that the General Assembly might be unwilling to submit proposed amendments to the electorate to restructure the legislature, the new constitution provided that, in very limited circumstances, proposals might be put on the ballot through petitions signed by a designated substantial number of voters. This popular initiative was expressly "limited to structural and procedural subjects contained in Article IV," the legislative article.

During the reform administration of Governor Dan Walker, there was considerable public and media outcry against "double dipping" by legislators, advance drawing of salaries, and conflicts of interest. These were matters that could readily be cured legislatively, and, in fact, the legislature did seek to correct the evils, at least in part. Although they scarcely pertained to legislative structure and procedures in any collective and realistic sense, a group calling itself the Coalition for Honest Government, led by vigorous, young Patrick Quinn, circulated petitions to correct the deplorable situation through constitutional amendments. They received much support from the public and media. Many could not understand, or professed not to believe, that a constitution could be amended only in the circumstances set forth in the amending article, even if there existed popular clamor for change.

In January 1976, Witwer, as the former president of the convention was first asked his views concerning the three prepared amendments and their constitutionality. As was his wont, he first studied the matter, having known very little about it up to that time. At this point the press and public had not yet become excited by the issue. After studying the proposals, Witwer became convinced that they were not only poorly drafted, consisting principally of legislative detail, but that they also were of doubtful constitutionality. His initial reaction was to discuss their essential weakness as a matter of policy. It was not until the circulation of the petition began to threaten the integrity of the constitution that Witwer publicly did more than attack the petition's substance.

When Edward Gilbreth, political editor of the *Chicago Daily News*, telephoned Witwer and asked how he stood on the matter, Witwer responded with a condemnation of the proposals. Articles appeared in the *Daily News* and *Sun-Times*, quoting Witwer at length. Soon the television and radio stations, which had endorsed the proposals, called upon Witwer for rebuttals and asked him to appear on interview shows. Until well into April, Witwer had no notion that the proposals could possibly secure the requisite number of signatures. It had always been difficult to get the required number of voters to express themselves through petitions.

Witwer began to receive calls from former delegates to the convention, who were disturbed. It was then that Witwer and Louis Ancel met to discuss the situation. They agreed that something had to be done to protect the Constitution. Ancel said that he would be willing to join Witwer in a law suit based upon the theory that the taxpayers' rights were being infringed by the wrongful expenditure of money for unconstitutional balloting in a constitutional referendum.

Witwer then communicated with most of the people who subsequently became the plaintiffs in the case. A conversation with Louis J. Perona turned out to have particular significance, since he was the sponsor of the popular Initiative Section; and being a plaintiff in the case his opposition to the petition became very significant in the eyes of the Supreme Court of Illinois. Perona himself indicated a desire to be plaintiff as did the others who subsequently signed the complaint. Witwer does not recall any delegate who expressly rejected the idea of a court challenge. Dawn Netsch, a constitution purist, who had been very active in opposition to the petition throughout the year, felt there was a real danger if any litigants went to court and lost; it would almost certainly trigger the successful outcome of the referendum on the petition. Witwer and his associates felt they had an excellent chance of winning the law suit and scarely considered the possibility of a defeat.

Thomas Lyons, a vice-president of the convention, who Witwer had originally hoped would become a plaintiff in the case, indicated that his position as a ward committeeman would be seized upon by the opposition. But he was willing to join Louis Ancel and Witwer as co-counsel. Ancel's office had the principal burden of work in the case. He was ably assisted by his partner, Stuart Diamond and a young associate, Gordon Levine. Witwer worked on the theory of the case, was the major public relations spokesman, and did the bulk of the oral argument before the courts. Lyons was extremely helpful as was Ann Lousin, a professor at the John Marshall Law School who had been on the research staff at the convention. She had a substantial part in the preparation of the briefs.

The plaintiffs represented all shades of political orientation and all parts of the state. The lead plaintiff was Elmer Gertz, an independent with leanings towards the Democratic party. At that time he, like Ms. Lousin, was on the faculty of the John Marshall Law School and as the *Chicago Tribune*, once his foe, now proclaimed he, like Dawn Netsch, was a constitutional authority. Thomas McCracken, a suburbanite and an organization Democrat with conservative leanings, had been chairman of the General Government Committee at the convention. Elbert Smith, a downstate Republican of considerable reputation, had been a vice-president of the convention. Another Republican, Lucy Reum, a Cook County suburbanite, had been vice-chairman of the legislative committee and was an office holder, as a Republican, in the Walker administration. Maurice Scott of Springfield had much standing as an expert on taxation. And there was the aforementioned Louis James Perona, a downstate Republican. The plaintiffs all had knowledge, standing, and the proper credentials.

Witwer believed that the significance of the case could not be overstated. Had the matters gone on the ballot, it is likely they would have been adopted and the amount of mischief done to the new constitution would have been substantial. It might have resulted in unwise and emotionally-presented amendments which in time could have largely defeated the successful outcome achieved by the Convention. Witwer felt that a significant aspect of the case was that it demonstrated that the leading delegates were prepared to stand behind their document and to protect it against improper attack. At the same time, it demonstrated a rather callous response on the part of some media. Editorial directors of television stations Channel 2 and Channel 5 in Chicago, for example proposed that the people had the right to change their constitution anytime they wished if they got enough signatures, regardless of what the amending article required. With the exception of the *Chicago Tribune*, especially the support given by Clayton Kirkpatrick, there was very little support on the part of the metropolitan newspapers for the position assumed by the plaintiffs in the case.

The case seemed to come and go as if it were not a matter of great significance, yet in the history of Illinois constitutionalism, it was a landmark case and a turning point in the implementation and interpretation of the new constitution.

Surprisingly, the only delegate who gave the plaintiffs any argument was David Kenney of Carbondale. Kenney was motivated by a concern that the case would preclude any further attempts to deal with the problem of cumulative voting vs. single-member districts. He wrote to the *Chicago Tribune* after the initial decision by Judge Nathan Cohen, assailing both the Judge and Witwer. Jeffrey Ladd, who early indicated an interest in the case and regretted that he could not be of counsel, responded to the Kenney letter and appeared in response to several television editorials. Elmer Gertz and Ann Lousin and a few others wrote in defense of the suit.

Ultimately, the Illinois Supreme Court resolved the issue in favor of the plaintiffs, but the bitterness did not subside.

There have been many other cases interpreting the new constitution. There will be many more. There will always be those who stand guard so that the intent and integrity of the document is not impaired.

XX

History for the Future

The test of any new constitution is not necessarily how its provisions sound nor what they seem to portend, but how it serves the people of a state and their government. A new constitution can be abused by a devious chief executive or a mischievous legislature. It can be misinterpreted ignorantly or deliberately by the courts. Permissive and even mandatory provisions can become inoperative by non-use or for want of judicial enforcement. One should not judge the effectiveness of a basic charter too quickly. Considerable time must elapse. It took almost a century for the Fourteenth Amendment of the United States Constitution to take on its current coloration. It is only a few years since the Illinois Constitution for 1970 went into effect. Its trial period is still going on and will continue to for some time. Still, some tentative conclusions may be reached.

GOVERNOR OGILVIE AND THE 1970 CONSTITUTION

Upon passage of the new charter, Governor Richard Ogilvie immediately appointed a special task force to draft legislation to implement the new state constitution.[1] In praising the new constitution, Governor Ogilvie listed two advantages that would be available to the ordinary taxpayer: a partial homestead exemption; and the elimination of the sales tax on food and medicine. The governor felt that the new revenue

[1] For a detailed account of the Citizens Task Force on Constitutional Implementation see Samuel K. Gove and Thomas R. Kitsos, *Revision Success: The Sixth Illinois Constitutional Convention* (New York: National Municipal League, 1974), pp. 138-145.

334

article was a great incentive not to increase income taxes or allow income taxes to be passed by local governments. He noted that the judicial article included several improvements among which was the section barring judges from accepting salaries or fees from any other jobs or positions. He felt that the primary reason for the passage of the Illinois Constitution was that it was less idealistic and more pragmatic. Ogilvie stated that of primary importance was the establishment of a new relationship between state and local governments, based on powers now available through the new constitution.

His administration witnessed the passage of the enabling legislation, the constituting of two official study commissions, the election of delegates, the drafting of the new constitution and its approval by the voters, the selection and functioning of an implementation commission, and the arrival of the effective dates for various provisions. During this period, the state also experienced the initial use of some sections by the governor and by the General Assembly, as well as by municipalities and other units of government. It saw the first interpretations by the courts, and treatises and articles by legal scholars. For another thing, Chicago, in particular, began to utilize the home rule provisions. But Governor Ogilvie's administration ended abruptly with his defeat in 1972 by the exigent and strong-willed Dan Walker.

The Walker administration had four years to observe how it worked and to get an impression of how it might affect the future of Illinois. Governor Walker could at least attempt to determine the direction in which the document was going. He worked closely with a number of persons, like Mary Lee Leahy, who had helped draft the new constitution. He had ideas of his own and forceful persons at his side to help carry them out. How well or ill Governor Walker functioned in the constitutional field is possibly too controversial or unclear at the moment for definitive judgment. Opinions will vary in accordance with the political and personal predilections of the observer. We have felt that much would be gained by having the governor give us his opinion on the new constitution.

GOVERNOR WALKER ON THE 1970 CONSTITUTION

Naturally, we asked the governor, first of all, about his reactions to the executive article, how he felt about governing under it.[2] He replied: "I think the executive article of the new constitution is very very good. It does make for a strong executive. I think that, particularly at the state government level, there is a need for a strong executive. We've read and heard a lot in recent years about the so-called imperial presidency in Washington and how the president of the United States has taken powers away from the legislative branch of government, has become all-powerful, that the legislature needs, in Washington, to reassert itself. I think that's an accurate observation with respect to the federal government. I think, however, that it's not accurate with respect to the state level. Indeed, I think I could make a pretty good argument that one of the problems we have at the state level is that legislatures are increasingly encroaching on the executive branch of government and not the other way around. Specific examples — we find abuses, that's too strong a word, you find extensions of the so-called oversight responsibility of the legislature to the point where legislative committees are actually trying to make or force administrative decisions in the departments and agencies of state government.

"The broad panoply of veto powers the governor has in Illinois I think is very very good. I don't think I'd really change that. I think in retrospect, and most everyone would agree, that perhaps there should have been more guidelines written into the constitution with respect to the amendatory veto power, because my predecessor and I were in a quandary as to how far you could go. As a lawyer I recognize the principle that that's for the Supreme Court to spell out in a case-by-case way, but it does lead to some problems."

Walker added: "Another area that I think needs some clearing up. . . is the matter of inclusion of substantive language in an appropriation bill. That was a constant source of difficulty in our administration."

We asked about the reorganization power given to the governor. He thought, "the power may be somewhat illusory, if I understand it correctly. You could submit a reorganization plan and let's say the legislature does not reject it within the 60-day period, it becomes effective under the constitution. But that doesn't do the job. . . . Suppose you wanted to put together the department of public aid and the department of children and family services. You submit a plan, it's

<hr>

[2]Interview with Governor Dan Walker, May 1977.

not rejected, it goes into effect. But what about those literally hundreds of statutes on the books that contain specific powers and references to each of those two deparments? Does the adoption of a reorganization plan automatically amend all of those statutes? Don't you have to go back and submit legislation to make the body of law correspond with your reorganization? If you do have to do that, then what is the point of the reorganization, to begin with, and I would raise a serious question as to whether reorganization can even become effective until you have amended all the laws. So what is the benefit of this so-called shortened procedure?"

We suggested that it was the constitutional intent that if the reorganization plan contravenes the statutes, it must be submitted to the legislature specifically for that purpose. Walker quickly responded: "The question is what does contravene mean? Obviously, even if you come to the conclusion that it does not contravene, what about the amendments that have to be taken care of? If a statute says that in the case of a child abuse the Department of Children and Family Services shall do thus and so. And let's suppose that you submitted a reorganization plan that combines children and family services and public aid and it has become effective. Does this mean that a court would automatically interpret that to mean that the new department carries on the functions of the Department of Children and Family Services without amending that statute? That sounds logical, except, if you think about it there may be horrible confusion because of the conflicting language in the various statutes."

We interpreted Walker's words to mean that the reorganization provision will not really be used for large-scale reorganization.

"It will be used for cosmetic purposes, for political purposes," he added.

"It is like the sunset laws. It sounds very nice until you start thinking it through as to what it really means, and, when you find out, it doesn't mean a whole lot."

We then asked about the coupling of the governor and lieutenant governor. "This was a serious mistake by the drafters of the constitution," Walker thought, "and I can only guess it just was not thought through. They should have had a requirement that any candidate for governor running in the primary can select his own lieutenant governor candidate and then they run as a team in the primary, so you would not have the situation that affected me where, as a result of the primary, I was nominated for governor in 1972 and Neil Hartigan was nominated for lieutenant governor. We could not live together. It has been suggested by some that I should have worked with him, although I don't think that is realistic. I had a lieutenant governor who owed his loyalty totally to Mayor Richard J. Daley. How in the world could you include someone in top policy, if you knew that as soon as the meeting was over he would go out and call Dick Daley, who was out to get me and create a problem for me. So it just isn't realistic and should not be done that way. And that is one of the things that ought to be changed at the earliest possible opportunity."

What about taking away the old provision about the lieutenant governor presiding over sessions of the Senate?

Walker responded: "I like the way the new constitution is set up where the incumbent governor only convenes the Senate to vote for its presiding officer. He does not have to remain while the vote is taken. He certainly has the option to delegate it to the lieutenant governor if he wants to. It was good that there was a recognition by the convention of the necessity for separation of power in this respect. The legislature should stay out of the executive branch of government, and the executive branch should stay out of the legislature's domain. We should not have commissions, for example, in state government where you have a combination of appointees by the governor and by the legislature. That ought to be stopped. The responsible members of the legislature think that it is not a good idea. And I think we ought to move further in that direction. And I think it would have been helpful if the drafters of the constitution had spelled it out in more detail."

We reminded Walker about the appropriations and budgetary process that were intended to streamline the process and make it more rational. How did he view the process from start to finish; was it a rational process, or did it have many pitfalls that really cause problems?

"I think overall it is rational," Walker responded; "there certainly are some changes though that ought to be made, but I am not at all sure that they ought to be made in a constitutional context. I think the budgetary process is something that by and large should be spelled out by law with only the broadest kind of provisions in the constitution relating to it. For example, we ought to abolish this crazy concept of budgetary balance that we have in the state of Illinois. But that should be done by statute. . . ." We interrupted to ask: "What would be your feeling if they would have gone one step further and said that there shall be a balanced budget and had stipulated precisely who was to determine the amounts of revenues that were to be coming in against which the appropriation should be balanced? As it exists now, there are any number of people who can and do give their estimates."

Walker agreed that this is one of the major problems that has arisen. "The constitution provides, for example, that the legislature shall make an estimate of revenues and shall not appropriate beyond the amount of the revenues. But you and I know that they did it every year while I was governor. That is, they appropriated far beyond the amount that the state could afford to spend under any estimate. And that provision was, therefore, unrealistic."

The discussion then turned to primaries. Walker expressed the wish that the constitution would have provided for an open primary. "The only way we are going to get it in this state is through a constitutional provision. I understand an effort is going to be made to put it on as an initiative, what do they call it, an advisory initiative? But that isn't going to get the job done, unfortunately."

Did he think cumulative voting has worked in giving us more independence?

"It gives us more independence and that is good. Sometimes it works badly, as we all know, but given our present tight control of the old line regulars in both parties, we had better stick with cumulative voting for a while."

And this brought us to the twenty-year provision which mandates the voters to consider a convention.

"You should have made it ten to fifteen years in view of how the times are changing." Walker thought this was a sampling of the thinking of the first governor to live through his entire administration under the Illinois Constitution of 1970.

EX-DELEGATES IN LATER YEARS

There is another way of looking at the constitution and the convention which produced it. How have the participants in its processes — the delegates and staff — fared since the adjournment date? This is another way of asking how the public has looked upon those persons responsible for the new basic charter of the state. Have they been rewarded or punished, praised or castigated?

It is no exaggeration to claim that a new elite was created in 1969-1970. In all parts of the state and even in distant areas of the nation, delegates and staff members have been sought out for preferment, and their counsel has been sought. Since the men and women involved were relatively young at the time of the convention, it must be said that, much as they may have accomplished thus far, their most fruitful days lie ahead. Their activities have touched all three branches of state government — the legislature, executive, and judicial areas. They have achievements, too, at the county, municipal and local government level in general, in academic and professional services, and as writers, consultants, and publicists. It has not been simply a matter of partisan preferment. Their work and its qualities have sometimes transcended party lines. They have been lauded often; and candor compels one to admit that sometimes, they have been criticized.

The biographies of persons connected with the Sixth Illinois Constitutional Convention are impressive indeed. As a group, they continue to advance the cause of good government. Their experiences in Springfield in 1969-1970, helped equip them for their substantial achievement elsewhere.

To cite only two examples from the legislative area: Michael Madigan has been elected majority leader in the House of Representatives of the General Assembly and has been praised even by a journal of the intellectuals, the prestigious *Chicago* magazine; and Dawn Clark Netsch has been called by the same oracular publication, a leader of the state Senate.

Just as he was a leader in the public agitation leading to a constitutional convention, as well as during the course of the convention itself and in the campaign to secure the adoption of the new constitution, President Witwer has had a distinguished record of public service in the years since then. He has served continuously as a consultant to the Illinois attorney general on constitutional matters, which have come up frequently and in every form and guise. He has argued, or been on the briefs, in a number of important cases in the Supreme Courts of both Illinois and the United States involving interpretation of the constitution of 1970. He was especially persuasive in his arguments before the Supreme Court of Illinois in the case involving the legislative initiative provisions. He served as consultant to the constitutional conventions of Montana and Texas. He has written and spoken extensively on the new constitution in various journals and conferences. Many of the delegates, such as Robert Butler, Philip Carey, David Davis, Stanley Johnson, Betty Ann Keegan, Clifford Kelley, Jeff Ladd, Odas Nicholson, John Parkhurst, Al Raby, Maurice Scott, Charles Shuman, Wayne Whalen, John Wenum, and John Woods continued to be involved with the constitution by serving on the Constitutional Implementation Committee appointed by Governor Ogilvie. Several of the delegates used the exposure and training they received at the convention as a stepping stone into a political career. In addition to Madigan and Netsch, Richard M. Daley, Ralph Dunn, Dwight Friedrich, Edward Jenison, John Knuppel, William Laurino, John Leon, Tom Lyons, Virginia Macdonald, Thomas Miller, Harold Nudelman, Harlan Rigney, and Anne Willer have served in the Illinois General Assembly while many others have continued to serve the state through various elective or appointive offices.

Philip Carey, John Karns, Harold Nudelman, Paul Elward, Helen Kinney, David Linn, Frank Orlando, Anthony Peccarelli, James Strunck, Gerald Sbarboro and William Lennon have been successful judges in the legal arena. Delegates were also able to use the experience as a background and training tool for others. Several have acted as consultants to such states as North and South Dakota, Montana, Texas and Louisiana in the matter of constitutional reform. Others have used the experience as resource for various articles and books on state constitutions and constitutional reforms.

Many of the delegates and staff, such as Ann Lousin, Elmer Gertz, Joe Pisciotte, and Dallin Oaks have taken academic and administrative posts in universities across the country and thus continue their influence on state government.

It may safely be concluded that the Sixth Illinois Constitutional Convention was a training school for many talented men and women. Its effects will long be felt not only in this state, but throughout the nation. It indeed created a democratic elite.

We think there are several conclusions that can be drawn. A constitutional convention cannot succeed unless it is really needed and wanted, as was the Sixth Illinois Constitutional Convention. If one is not sure that new deliberations will lead to a better charter, there is little point in starting this long, involved, and frequently frustrating process.

LESSONS FOR THE FUTURE

It was not, however, only the governors of the state and former delegates to the convention who were affected by the events of 1969-70. What of the effect on the state as a whole and what lessons were learned that might be useful to those who may one day again face the reality of a constitutional convention? And even if the times demand a new attempt at constitution making, the right people must be assembled at the right place, with proper advance preparation and guidance. A partisan group will have difficulty writing a non-partisan document. A convention lacking leadership may not be able to produce a sound charter. A convention must be open, democratic in its deliberations, and fair to the delegates, the media, and the public. It must give opportunities for participation. Respectful attention must be paid to dissenters, without permitting obstruction. There must be adherence to schedules and rules without enslavement by rigidity. There must be a willingness, in the end, to compromise. There must be acceptance of the certainty that no perfect constitution can be produced or ratified; that one must aim at the very best that is attainable. There must be an understanding that even a non-political, non-partisan convention does not operate in a vacuum. It is part of a social process, involving political and social issues; demography is part of democracy. It is not enough that the delegates be convinced of their own good faith and the work that they have done. They must be able to sell themselves and the proposed charter to the electorate.

Judged by these standards and others of a like nature, the Sixth Illinois Constitutional Convention succeeded admirably. The delegates took the Illinois Constitution out of its one hundred-year-old straitjacket and gave future generations of citizens the opportunity for reasoned and careful change in the fundamental law governing their everyday lives. It produced a charter for a new day.

But this day, like all days, will end. Attrition by the courts and legislators and special forces will wear away some of the fine points. The people should not hesitate at that time to embark once more upon a constitutional voyage of exploration which may chart new territories and new concepts.

Appendix I

CHRONOLOGY OF EVENTS

Aug. 17, 1965 Governor signs HB 1911, 74th General Assembly, creating the first Illinois Constitution Study Commission.

July 24, 1967 Governor signs SB 1376, 75th General Assembly, creating the second Illinois Constitution Study Commission.

Nov. 5, 1968 Voters approve the call of the Sixth Illinois Constitutional Convention.

Jan. 29, 1969 First report of the second Constitution Study Commission.

Feb. 4 HB 200, 76th General Assembly, the enabling act for the convention, submitted to the House by the Constitution Study Commission.

Feb. 5 SB 193, 76th General Assembly, the enabling act for the convention, submitted to the Senate by the Constitution Study Commission.

Apr. 10 SB 834, 76th General Assembly, recreating the second Constitution Study Commission, submitted to the Senate.

Apr. 21 HB 1957, 76th General Assembly, recreating the second Constitution Study Commission, submitted to the House.

May 7 Governor signs SB 193, the enabling act, to which appropriations for salaries and for convention expenses rejoined. (Appropriation for election expenses goes through as amended SB 194, passed June 19, 1969.)

343

June 17	76th General Assembly pass HB 1957, recreating Constitutional Study Commission.
July 10	Illinois Supreme Court upholds constitutionality of enabling act in *Livingston v. Ogilvie.*
Sept. 23	Primary election of delegates.
Nov. 18	General election of delegates.
Dec. 1-3	Press orientation: "Orientation Seminar for Newsmen." Illinois Beach State Park.
Dec. 5-7	Orientation of delegates in Springfield.
Dec. 8	Convention convened, Hall of House of Representatives, Capital Building, Springfield. Witwer elected temporary and permanent President.
Dec. 9, 1969	Witwer Address.
Dec. 9-10	Temporary Rules Committee meets.
Dec. 16-17	Temporary Rules Committee Report filed, debated, and most rules approved.
Dec. 17	Election of Smith, Lyons, Alexander, Nicholson as Constitutional Convention officers.
Dec. 18, 1969- Jan. 5, 1970	Christmas recess.
Jan. 6, 1970	Delegates to work four days a week. Announcement of membership, chairmen and vice chairmen of the committees. Appointment of committee to examine the credentials of delegate James Gierach. Witwer assigned vice presidents to Procedural and Substantive Committee. Witwer appointed subcommittee on meetings out of Springfield. Member proposals 1-32 introduced.
Jan. 8	Formal report on the Constitution Study Commission. Member proposals 33-40 introduced.
Jan. 13	Proposed rule on personal economic interest disclosure. Report of Public Hearing Subcommittee. Member proposals 41-53.
Jan. 14	Addresses to the convention by Lt. Gov. Paul Simon and Auditor of Public Accounts Michael J. Howlett. Member proposals 54-79.

Jan. 20   Addresses to the convention by Chief Justice Robert C. Underwood of the Illinois Supreme Court and Secretary of State Paul Powell.
Member proposals 80-98.

Jan. 21   Address to the convention by Adlai E. Stevenson III, state treasurer.
Member proposals 99-129.

Jan. 22   Rule 62A, personal disclosures adopted.

Jan. 27   Address to the convention by Ray Page, superintendent of public instruction.
Member proposals 130-156.
Witwer appoints ad hoc committee to examine daily journals.

Jan. 28   Member proposals 157-183.
Witwer resolution on submission of Constitution to voters.

Feb. 3   Witwer presents Constitutional Convention financial report.
Member proposals 184-209.
Brannen resolution to submit constitution to public in major package with controversial portions to be considered separately.

Feb. 4   Proposed schedule of work of the convention submitted and approved.
Committee on Public Information presents report.
Member proposals 210-248.
Consideration of constitution submission.

Feb. 5-16   Recess for public hearings throughout state.

Feb. 9   Local hearings in Rockford, Peoria, and Marion.

Feb. 11   Local hearings in Waukegan, Arlington Heights, Wheaton, Joliet, Homewood-Flossmoor.

Feb. 17   Report of Committee on Rules and Credentials.
Financial Report of Constitutional Convention.
Member proposals 249-267.
Consideration of budget for Constitutional Convention.

Feb. 19   Member proposals 268-297.

Feb. 24   Report on public hearings.
Member proposals 298-318.

Feb. 26   Member proposals 319-339.
Easter recess, March 26 - April 7 approved.

Mar. 3   Address to the convention by U.S. Senator Ralph T. Smith.
Report of Committee on Style, Drafting and Submission.
Witwer names Scott, chairman and Carey, cochairman to ad
hoc committee on move to Old State Capitol.

Mar. 5   Member proposals 429-512.
Work progress reports given by committee chairmen —
McCracken (General Government), Parkhurst (Local Govern-
ment), Mathias (Education).

Mar. 6   Local hearings in Champaign-Urbana, East St. Louis,
Alton, Rock Island-Moline, Quincy, and (some southern
Illinois city).

Mar. 10   Member proposals 513-523.
Committee reports given by Gertz (Bill of Rights), Fay
(Judiciary), Tomei (Suffrage and Amendment).
Deadline for filing member proposals.

Mar. 12   Report of the Constitution Study Commission.
Report on hearings held outside of Springfield.
Committee Proposals No. 1, Suffrage and Amendment.
Member proposals 524-582.

Mar. 20   Convention moved into permanent quarters in the Old State
Capitol building.

Mar. 25   Address to the convention by State Senator W. Russell
Arrington.

Mar. 26   General Government Committee Proposal No. 1 introduced.
General Government Committee Proposal No. 2 introduced.

Mar. 27-Apr. 6 Easter recess.

Apr. 7   Address to the convention by U.S. Senator Charles W. Percy.

Apr. 8   Submission and approval of Gierach report.
General Government Committee Proposal No. 3 introduced.
General Government Committee Proposal No. 4 introduced.

Apr. 9   General Government Committee Proposal No. 5 introduced.

Apr. 10   Committee on the Judiciary Proposal No. 1 introduced.

Apr. 14   Affirmative vote on post-November 3 submission date.
Committee on Education Proposal No. 1 introduced.

Apr. 16   General Government Committee Proposal No. 6 introduced.

Apr. 17   General Government Committee Proposal No. 7 introduced.

Apr. 28   Committee on Revenue & Finance Proposal No. 1 introduced.

May 6	Suffrage and Constitutional Amending Committee Proposal No. 2 introduced.
May 12	General Government Committee Proposal No. 8 introduced. Committee on the Judiciary Proposal No. 2 introduced.
May 13	John Gardner does not speak.
May 14	Text of Gardner's proposed speech placed in record.
May 15	Report of the Committee on Rules and Credentials. Committee on the Executive Proposal No. 1 introduced.
May 22	General Government Committee Proposal No. 11 introduced. General Government Committee Proposal No. 12 introduced. Committee on Bill of Rights Proposal No. 1 introduced.
May 28	General Government Committee Proposal No. 13 introduced. General Government Committee Proposal No. 14 introduced.
June 9	General Government Committee Proposal No. 15 introduced.
June 16	Committee on Revenue and Finance Proposal No. 2 introduced.
June 25	Committee on the Judiciary Proposal No. 3 introduced.
June 30	Committee on the Legislature, Majority & Minority Proposals introduced.
July 1	General Government Committee Proposal No. 16 introduced.
July 10	Committee on Local Government Proposal No. 1 introduced.
July 22	General Government Committee Proposal No. 17 introduced. General Government Committee Proposal No. 18 introduced. Committee on Education Proposal No. 1 introduced. Resolution No. 65 approved.
Aug. 15-26	Drafting recess.
Sept. 2	Address to the people filed and corrected.
Sept. 3	Closing ceremonies: signing of final draft, speeches by Ogilvie and Witwer; resolution of delegates commending President Witwer.

Dec. 15   Referendum on proposed constitution passes 1,122,425 to
               838,168.

July 1, 1971   New Constitution in effect.

Appendix II

CHRONOLOGY OF COMMITTEE REPORTS

During the Sixth Illinois Constitutional Convention, delegates were permitted to introduce any kind of proposal that would revise, alter, or amend the 1870 Illinois Constitution. A total of 582 such member proposals was introduced. Each was assigned by President Witwer to one of the nine substantive committees for careful consideration. After months of research and debate on these and others that had originated in the various committees, the number of proposals was reduced to thirty-one, and each formed the basis of a committee report. These reports were then filed by the relevant committee chairman in accordance with the regulations for consideration by the entire body. The following list is a chronology of the committee reports introduced to the convention by a specific committee.

Suffrage and Constitutional Amendment Committee Proposal No. 1 — Proposed a revised Article on Constitutional Revision.

March 12	Introduced
March 20	First Reading
April 7	First Reading completed; sent to Committee on Style, Drafting and Submission

Style, Drafting and Submission Proposal No. 2

June 17	Introduced
August 5	Second Reading
August 5	Second Reading completed; sent to Committee on Style, Drafting and Submission

Style, Drafting and Submission Proposal No. 15 — Article XV changed to
Article XIV

August 27	Introduced
Sept. 1	Third Reading
Sept. 1	Third Reading completed. Enrolled.

General Government Committee Proposal No. 1 — Eliminated Section 13 of
Article IX, Columbian Exposition.

March 26	Introduced
April 9	First Reading
April 9	First Reading completed; sent to Committee on Style, Drafting and Submission

Style, Drafting and Submission Proposal No. 5

July 2	Introduced
August 6	Second Reading
August 6	Second Reading completed; sent to Committee on Style, Drafting and Submission

Style, Drafting and Submission Proposal No. 15

Deleted from proposed constitution

General Government Committee Proposal No. 3 — Proposed elimination of
the section separately submitted entitled "Convict
Labor".

April 8	Introduced
April 10	First Reading
April 10	First Reading completed; sent to Committee on Style, Drafting and Submission

Style, Drafting and Submission Proposal No. 5

July 2	Introduced
August 6	Second Reading
August 6	Second Reading completed; sent to Committee on Style, Drafting and Submission

Deleted from proposed constitution

General Government Committee Proposal No. 4 — Proposed elimination of
the section separately submitted entitled "Canal".

April 8	Introduced
April 10	First Reading
April 10	First Reading completed; sent to Committee on Style, Drafting and Submission

Style, Drafting and Submission Proposal No. 4

July 2	Introduced
August 6	Second Reading
August 6	Second Reading completed; sent to Committee on Style, Drafting and Submission

Deleted from proposed constitution

General Government Committee Proposal No. 5 — Proposed elimination of constitutional prohibition of lotteries and gift enterprises.

April 9	Introduced
April 10	First Reading
April 15	First Reading completed; sent to Committee on Style, Drafting and Submission

Style, Drafting and Submission Proposal No. 5

July 2	Introduced
August 6	Second Reading
August 6	Second Reading completed; sent to Committee on Style, Drafting and Submission

Deleted from proposed constitution

Committee on the Judiciary Proposal No. 1 — Proposed a revision of a number of Sections of Article VI, Judicial Article, and adoption without revision of several other Sections of that Article.

April 10	Introduced
April 15	First Reading
April 22	First Reading completed; except for Sec. 16; sent to Committee on Style, Drafting and Submission
May 7	Sec. 16 approved and sent to Committee on Style, Drafting and Submission

Style, Drafting and Submission Proposal No. 7

August 4	Introduced
August 11	Second Reading
August 11	Second Reading completed; sent to Committee on Style, Drafting and Submission

Style, Drafting and Submission Proposal No. 15 — Article VI

August 27	Introduced
August 29	Third Reading
August 30	Third Reading completed. Enrolled.

Committee on Education Proposal No. 1 — Proposed a revision of Article VIII of the Constitution. Restated the goal of public education, and provided for free public schools. Provided for a State Board of Education and appointment of the chief state education officer. Retained Section 3 of Article VIII which forbids public funds for sectarian purposes. Deleted the Superintendent of Public Instruction from the state officers who are elected and eliminated Sections 2, 4 and 5 of Article VIII.

April 14   Introduced
April 22   First Reading
May 6   First Reading completed; sent to Committee on Style, Drafting and Submission

Style, Drafting and Submission Proposal No. 11

August 9   Introduced
August 13   Second Reading
August 13   Second Reading completed; sent to Committee on Style, Drafting and Submission

Style, Drafting and Submission Proposal No. 15 — Article X

August 27   Introduced
August 31   Third Reading
August 31   Third Reading completed. Enrolled.

General Government Committee Proposal No. 6 — Proposed elimination of Section 33, Article IV of the present Constitution entitled "State House Expenditures."

April 16   Introduced
April 28   First Reading
April 28   First Reading completed; sent to Committee on Style, Drafting and Submission

Style, Drafting and Submission Proposal No. 5

July 2   Introduced
August 6   Second Reading
August 6   Second Reading completed; sent to Committee on Style, Drafting and Submission

Deleted from proposed constitution

General Government Committee Proposal No. 7 — Proposed elimination of Article XIII of the present Constitution entitled "Warehouses."

April 17	Introduced
April 28	First Reading
April 28	First Reading completed; sent to Committee on Style, Drafting and Submission

Style, Drafting and Submission Proposal No. 5

July 2	Introduced
August 6	Second Reading
August 6	Second reading completed; sent to Committee on Style, Drafting and Submission

Deleted from proposed constitution

Committee on Revenue and Finance Proposal No. 1 — Proposed a separate Finance Article to establish the responsibility for financial decision-making and fiscal control.

April 28	Introduced
May 5	First Reading
May 5	First Reading completed; sent to Committee on Style, Drafting and Submission

Style, Drafting and Submission Proposal No. 12

August 10	Introduced
August 11	Second Reading
August 14	Second Reading completed; sent to Committee on Style, Drafting and Submission

Style, Drafting and Submission Proposl No. 15 — Article VIII

August 27	Introduced
August 31	Third Reading
August 31	Third Reading completed. Enrolled.

Suffrage and Constitution Amending Committee Proposal No. 2 — Proposed a revised Article on Suffrage and Elections and separate submission of an 18-year-old voting proposal.

May 6	Introduced
May 12	First Reading
May 19	First Reading completed; sent to Committee on Style, Drafting and Submission

Style, Drafting and Submission Proposal No. 3

June 17	Introduced
August 5	Second Reading
August 5	Second Reading completed; sent to Committee on Style, Drafting and Submission

Style, Drafting and Submission Proposal No. 15 — Article III also Separate Submission

August 27	Introduced
August 28	Third Reading
August 28	Third Reading completed. Enrolled.

General Government Committee Proposal 8 — Proposed elimination of Sections 5, 6, 7 and 8 of Article XI, commonly known as the "banking" provisions.

May 12	Introduced
May 20	First Reading
May 21	First Reading completed; sent to Committee on Style, Drafting and Submission

Style, Drafting and Submission Proposal No. 5

July 2	Introduced
August 6	Second Reading
August 6	Second Reading completed; sent to Committee on Style, Drafting and Submission

Committee on the Judiciary Proposal No. 2 — Proposed a method for discipline and retirement of judges and magistrates.

May 12	Introduced
May 19	First Reading
May 22	First Reading completed; sent to Committee on Style, Drafting and Submission

Style, Drafting and Submission Proposal No. 7

August 4	Introduced
August 11	Second Reading
August 11	Second Reading completed; sent to Committee on Style, Drafting and Submission

Style, Drafting and Submission Proposal No. 15 — Article VI

August 27	Introduced
August 29	Third Reading
August 30	Third Reading completed. Enrolled.

General Government Committee Proposal No. 9 — Proposed a revised
Separation of Powers Article.

May 14	Introduced
May 15	First Reading
May 15	First Reading completed; sent to Committee on Style, Drafting and Submission

Style, Drafting and Submission Proposal No. 9

August 6	Introduced
August 10	Second Reading
August 10	Second Reading completed; sent to Committee on Style, Drafting and Submission

Style, Drafting and Submission Proposal No. 15 — Article II

August 27	Introduced
August 28	Third Reading
August 28	Third Reading completed. Enrolled.

General Government Committee Proposal No. 10 — Proposed elimination of
Article I of the present Constitution entitled "Boundaries".

May 14	Introduced
May 15	First Reading
May 15	First Reading completed; sent to Committee on Style, Drafting and Submission

Style, Drafting and Submission Proposal No. 5

July 2	Introduced
August 6	Second Reading
August 6	Second Reading completed; sent to Committee on Style, Drafting and Submission
	Deleted from proposed constitution

Committee on the Executive Proposal No. 1 — Presented a complete revision of
the Executive Article.

May 14	Introduced
May 26	First Reading
May 28	First Reading completed; sent to Committee on Style, Drafting and Submission

Style, Drafting and Submission Proposal No. 6

July 31	Introduced
August 6	Second Reading
August 7	Second Reading completed; sent to Committee on Style, Drafting and Submission

Style, Drafting and Submission Proposal No. 15 — Article V

August 27	Introduced
August 29	Third Reading
August 29	Third Reading completed. Enrolled.

General Government Committee Proposal No. 11 — Proposed elimination of separately submitted Section of the present Constitution entitled "Illinois Central Railroad".

May 22	Introduced
June 11	First Reading
June 11	First Reading completed; sent to Committee on Style, Drafting and Submission

Style, Drafting and Submission Proposal No. 5

July 2	Introduced
August 6	Second Reading
August 6	Second Reading completed; sent to Committee on Style, Drafting and Submission
	Deleted from proposed constitution

General Government Committee Proposal No. 12 — Proposed elimination of Sections 4, 9, 10, 11, 12, 13, 14, 15 of Article XI, commonly known as the "railroad" sections.

May 22	Introduced
June 11	First Reading
June 11	First Reading completed; sent to Committee on Style, Drafting and Submission

Style, Drafting and Submission Proposal No. 5

July 2	Introduced
August 6	Second Reading
August 6	Second reading completed; sent to Committee on Style, Drafting and Submission
	Deleted from proposed constitution

Committee on Bill of Rights Proposal No. 1 — Presented a revision of the Preamble, the confirmation without change of a number of sections of the present Bill of Rights, change in other sections of the present Bill of Rights, and several addition sections to the Bill of Rights.

May 22	Introduced

May 29   First Reading
June 11   First Reading completed; sent to Committee on Style, Drafting and Submission

Style, Drafting and Submission Proposal No. 4

July 2   Introduced
August 5   Second Reading
August 6   Second reading completed; sent to Committee on Style, Drafting and Submission

Style, Drafting and Submission Proposal No. 15 — Article I

August 27   Introduced
August 27   Third Reading
August 28   Third Reading completed. Enrolled.

General Government Committee Proposal No. 2 — Proposed a revised Militia Article.

May 26   Introduced
April 9   First Reading
April 9   First Reading completed; sent to Committee on Style, Drafting and Submission

Style, Drafting and Submission Proposal No. 1

June 21   Introduced
June 30   Second Reading
June 30   Second Reading completed; sent to Committee on Style, Drafting and Submission

Style, Drafting and Submission Proposal No. 15 — Article XII

August 27   Introduced
August 31   Third Reading
August 31   Third Reading completed. Enrolled.

General Government Committee Proposal No. 13 — Proposed an Article consisting of prerequisites to seeking and conditions for holding office.

May 28   Introduced
June 12   First Reading
June 12   First Reading Section 1 completed; sent to Committee on Style, Drafting and Submission
June 16   First Reading Sections 2, 3 and 4 completed; sent to Committee on Style, Drafting and Submission

Style, Drafting and Submission Proposal No. 9

August 6	Introduced
August 10	Second Reading
August 10	Second Reading completed; sent to Committee on Style, Drafting and Submission

Style, Drafting and Submission Proposal No. 15 — Article XIV
  Renumbered Article XIII

August 27	Introduced
Sept. 1	Third Reading
Sept. 1	Third Reading completed. Enrolled.

General Government Committee Proposal No. 14 — Proposed revised
  Corporations Article.

May 28	Introduced
June 17	First Reading
June 17	First Reading completed; sent to Committee on Style, Drafting and Submission

Style, Drafting and Submission Proposal No. 14

August 12	Introduced
August 14	Second Reading
August 14	Second Reading completed; sent to Committee on Style, Drafting and Submission

Style, Drafting and Submission Proposal No. 15 — Article XIV
  Renumbered Article XIII

August 27	Introduced
Sept. 1	Third Reading
Sept. 1	Third Reading completed. Enrolled.

General Government Committee Proposal No. 15. — Proposed a revised
  Sovereign Immunity Section.

June 9	Introduced
June 11	First Reading
June 17	First Reading completed; sent to Committee on Style, Drafting and Submission

Style, Drafting and Submission Proposal No. 9

August 6	Introduced
August 10	Second Reading
August 10	Second Reading completed; sent to Committee on Style, Drafting and Submission

Style, Drafting and Submission Proposal No. 15 — Article XIV
                Renumbered Article XIII

August 27	Introduced
Sept. 1	Third Reading
Sept. 1	Third Reading completed. Enrolled.

Committee on Revenue and Finance Proposal No. 2 — Proposed a revised Revenue Article.

June 16	Introduced
June 23	First Reading
June 30	First Reading completed; sent to Committee on Style, Drafting and Submission

Style, Drafting and Submission Proposal No. 8

August 5	Introduced
August 7	Second Reading
August 10	Second Reading completed; sent to Committee on Style, Drafting and Submission

Style, Drafting and Submission Proposal No. 15 — Article IX

August 27	Introduced
August 31	Third Reading
August 31	Third Reading completed. Enrolled.

Committee on the Judiciary Proposal No. 3 — Proposed amendments of Sections of Judicial Article relating to election or selection of judges and their tenure, amendments to the structure and organization of courts, the judiciary, clerks, other matters relating thereto, and a Separate Submission Proposal.

June 25	Introduced
July 1	First Reading
July 14	First Reading completed; sent to Committee on Style, Drafting and Submission

Style, Drafting and Submission Proposal No. 7

August 4	Introduced
August 11	Second Reading
August 11	Second Reading completed; sent to Committee on Style, Drafting and Submission

Style, Drafting and Submission Proposal No. 15 — Article VI
                Separate Submission

August 27	Introduced

August 29   Third Reading
August 30   Third Reading completed. Enrolled.

Committee on the Legislature Majority and Minority Proposals — Proposed
         Article on the Legislature.

June 30   Introduced
July 14   First Reading
July 22   First Reading completed; sent to Committee on Style,
              Drafting and Submission

Style, Drafting and Submission Proposal No. 10

August 7   Introduced
August 12   Second Reading
August 13   Second Reading completed; sent to Committee on Style,
              Drafting and Submission

Style, Drafting and Submission Proposal No. 15 — Article IV
              Separate Submission

August 27   Introduced
August 28   Third Reading
August 31   Third Reading completed. Enrolled.

General Government Committee Proposal No. 16 — Proposed an Environment
         Article.

July 1   Introduced
July 22   First Reading
July 22   First Reading completed; sent to Committee on Style,
              Drafting and Submission

Style, Drafting and Submission Proposal No. 9

August 6   Introduced
August 10   Second Reading
August 10   Second Reading completed; sent to Committee on Style,
              Drafting and Submission

Style, Drafting and Submission Proposal No. 15 — Article XI

August 27   Introduced
August 31   Third Reading
August 31   Third Reading completed. Enrolled.

Committee on Local Government Proposal No. 1 — Proposed Article on Local
         Government.

July 10   Introduced

July 22   First Reading
July 31   First Reading completed; sent to Committee on Style, Drafting and Submission

Style, Drafting and Submission Proposal No. 13

August 12   Introduced
August 13   Second Reading
August 14   Second Reading completed; sent to Committee on Style, Drafting and Submission

Style, Drafting and Submission Proposal No. 15 — Article VII

August 27   Introduced
August 30   Third Reading
August 30   Third Reading completed. Enrolled.

Committee on Education Proposal No. 2 — Provided that the State shall provide major support for pubic education through the secondary level.

July 22   Introduced
August 4   Rejected

General Government Committee Proposal No. 17 — Proposed a Conservation Article.

July 22   Introduced
July 31   First Reading
August 1   First Reading completed.

Style, Drafting and Submission Proposal No. 9

August 6   Introduced
August 10   Second Reading
August 10   Second reading completed; sent to Committee on Style, Drafting and Submission

Style, Drafting and Submission Proposal No. 15 — Article XIII

August 27   Introduced
August 31   Third Reading
August 31   Laid upon Clerk's desk for lack of majority vote

General Government Committee Proposal No. 18 — Proposed a Transportation Article.

July 22   Introduced
August 1   First Reading

August 1	First Reading completed; sent to Committee on Style, Drafting and Submission

Style, Drafting and Submission Proposal No. 14

August 12	Introduced
August 14	Second Reading
August 14	Second Reading completed; sent to Committee on Style, Drafting and Submission

Style, Drafting and Submission Proposal No. 15 — Article XIV
Renumbered Article XIII

August 27	Introduced
Sept. 1	Third Reading
Sept. 1	Third Reading completed. Enrolled.

Appendix III

SOME CON CON FACTS AND FIGURES*

*From "Calling and Holding Illinois' Sixth Constitutional Convention," unpublished paper by Dorothy Nadasdy, administrative assistant to Con Con President Witwer.

Table 1

INTERNAL BUDGET OF THE SIXTH ILLINOIS
CONSTITUTIONAL CONVENTION

Salary and expenses of members of the Convention

Item	Amount budgeted	Amount expended
President's salary	$13,500	$13,500
($1,500 x 9 months)		
Vice Presidents' salary	32,400	32,400
($1,200 x 3 x 9 months)		
Monthly salary for members	550,000	545,489
($625 x 8 months x 110 members[a])		
Per diem expenses	855,000	854,850
($75 x 100 days x 114 members[b])		
Meals, lodging, incidental		
expenses of 116 members[c]	426,880	431,541
Postage	13,920	13,920
($120 x 116 members)		
Mileage	192,149	190,818
Subtotal	2,083,849	2,082,518

Other expenses incident to conducting the business of the Convention

Personal services	500,626	473,052
Clergy for invocations	1,000	620
Staff travel	5,000	4,944
Consultants (honorariums and travel)	10,000	6,091
Rental and maintenance of real property	29,065	41,661
Purchase and lease/purchase of equipment	54,500	65,400[d]
Relocation of furniture and equipment	2,500	3,055
Operation and use of microphones and		
recording equipment	15,000	31,666[e]
Verbatim transcripts	10,000	61,815
Telecommunications	35,000	32,912
Computer usage	5,000	146
Books and pamphlets	3,500	2,663
Postage; printing of member proposals, committee		
reports, journals, letterhead, etc.	200,000	153,673[f]
Office supplies	5,000	12,974
Cleaning, painting & restoring		
Old State Capitol	--	4,406
Contingency	17,740	179
Subtotal, other expenses	893,931	895,257
Grand total	$2,977,780	$2,977,775

[a]Excludes president and three vice presidents and two legislators who served as members.
[b]Excludes two members who received a salary as State legislator.

Table 1 (cont'd)

cInterim legislative commissions and committees received $10 for meals, $10 for incidentals, and $12 for lodging in the Springfield area. (See Sec. 8 of the enabling act quoted above.)

d$14,426 was later redeposited in the State's General Revenue Fund when members purchased, at the original purchase price, their desks and chairs used in Convention. Following the Convention all other furniture was turned over to existing State agencies.

eIn addition to recording the debates, a verbatim transcript was kept as directed by Sec. 11 of PA 76-40.

fPostage, $11,597; printing, $142,076. Approximately 1,000 copies of the Journals and Committee reports were printed for the immediate use of the Convention. $200,000 has been appropriated to the Secretary of State's office for the final printing of the verbatim Debates, Journals, Committee reports, and other supporting materials.

Source: Convention Journal, Tuesday, February 3, 1970; letter to members from the president and executive director dated March 22, 1971; and vouchers of the Convention.

Table 2

MONTHLY SALARIES FOR EMPLOYEES OF THE SIXTH ILLINOIS CONSTITUTIONAL CONVENTION

Position	*Monthly rate*
Executive Director	$2,000
Executive Assistant	2,000
Chief Committee Counsels (median salary)	1,500
Chief Clerk	1,350
Public Information Officer	1,350
Administrative Assistants	650-950
Research Coordinator	850
Assistant Chief Clerk	750
Research Assistants	700
Executive Secretaries	700
Information Representatives	575-750
Clerk Stenographers	435-575
Account Clerks	435-575
Minute Clerk	575
Clerk-Typists	350-435
Duplicating Clerk	350
Switchboard Operator	395
Sergeant-at-Arms and Doorkeeper	800
Doorkeepers	395
Pages	350
* * *	
Special Counsel to the Convention	$35 (hourly rate)
Consultant to the President	$75 (daily rate)
Parliamentarian	Expenses onlya

aThe Parliamentarian continued to receive his salary from the University of Illinois in Urbana; therefore, he accepted remuneration for expenses only.

Source: Convention Journal, Tuesday, February 17, 1970.

Table 3

CONSTITUTIONAL CONVENTION APPROPRIATIONS 1965-1971

	Amount appropriated	Amount expended
Vote on proposition on whether to hold a Convention[a]	(see note)	(see note)
Constitution Study Commission I (1965-67; 1965 H.B. 1911)	$20,000	$18,142
Constitution Study Commission II (1967-69; 1967 S.B. 1376)	75,000	71,903
Constitution Study Commission III (1969; 1969 H.B. 1957)	100,000	69,201
Reimbursement to local election officials for expenses incurred at the primary election of delegates (1969 S.B. 194)	2,500,000	2,499,573[b]
Reimbursement to local election officials for expenses incurred at the general election of delegates (1969 S.B. 194)	2,500,000	2,498,281
Deficiency appropriation for the primary and general elections mentioned above (1969 S.B. 1276)	1,550,000	1,192,258
Salaries and expenses of members of Convention (1969 S.B. 193)	1,750,000[c]	1,750,000
Supplemental appropriation for salaries and expenses of members (1970 S.B. 1514)	127,780	127,780
General expenses of the Convention; mileage and postage allotment for members (1969 S.B. 193)	1,100,000	1,099,995
Administrative expenses of the Auditor of Public Accounts (1969 S.B. 193)	30,000	11,935
Legislative Reference Bureau — to assist Convention (1969 S.B. 371)	50,000	33,002
(1970 S.B. 1218)	16,998	16,834
Illinois Legislative Council — to assist Convention (1969 S.B. 371)	50,000	31,131
(1970 H.B. 3537)	30,000	13,277

Table 3 (Cont'd)

	Amount appropriated	*Amount expended*
To Secretary of State for publication and dissemination of proposed constitution together with explanatory information — tabloid form	1,225,000	873,821
Printing and distribution by printer to 102 county clerks		(340,833)
Postage and handling charges from county clerk to electorate		(351,219)
Paid to newspapers for inclusion as supplement to newspaper		(178,223)
Tape recording of constitution for the blind		(3,414)
Miscellaneous expenses incurred by Secretary of State		(132)
Reimbursement to county clerks for conduct of special December 15, 1970 election on the adoption or rejection of the proposed Constitution (1970 H.B. 299)	3,300,000	3,298,292
Deficiency appropriation for the December 15, 1970 election (1971 S.B. 616)	140,000	118,638
Appropriation to Secretary of State for printing and publication of Convention's verbatim Debate, Journals, Committee reports, etc. (1971 S.B. 795)	200,000	200,000 (est.)
Grand Totals	$14,764,778	$13,924,063

[a]Since this referendum was held in conjunction with the November 1968 general election, no cost information is available.

[b]The primary election actually cost $2,955,296 while the general election cost $3,234,814. A deficiency appropriation was necessary and is shown in the table.

[c]Detail provided in Table 2.

Source: Department of Finance, 52nd and 53rd Annual Reports; conversations with officials of the Index Division, Office of the Secretary of State; and members of the staff of the Illinois Legislative Council and Legislative Reference Bureau.

Index